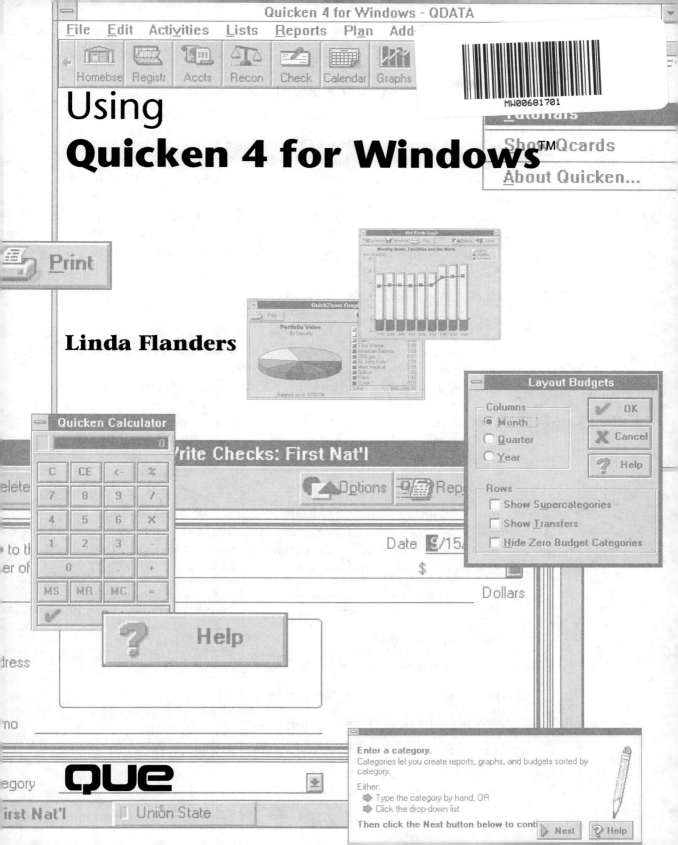

Using
Quicken 4 for Windows™

Linda Flanders

que

Using Quicken 4 for Windows

Copyright© 1994 by Que® Corporation.

Library of Congress Catalog No.: 94-68831

ISBN: 1-56529-933-7

97   96   95   4   3

Interpretation of the printing code: the rightmost double-digit number is the year of the book's printing; the rightmost single-digit number, the number of the book's printing. For example, a printing code of 94-1 shows that the first printing of the book occurred in 1994.

Screen reproductions in this book were created with Collage Complete from Inner Media, Inc., Hollis, NH.

Publisher: David P. Ewing

Associate Publisher: Don Roche, Jr.

Managing Editor: Michael Cunningham

Product Marketing Manager: Greg Wiegand

Associate Product Marketing Manager: Stacy Collins

Credits

Publishing Manager
Nancy Stevenson

Acquisitions Editor
Jenny L. Watson

Product Director
Joyce J. Nielsen

Developmental Editor
Kezia E. Endsley

Technical Editor
Brad Manning

Technical Specialist
Cari Ohm

Acquisitions Coordinator
Deborah Abshier

Editorial Assistant
Jill Stanley

Book Designer
Paula Carroll

Cover Designer
Dan Armstrong

Production Team
Angela Bannan
Stephen Carlin
DiMonique Ford
Karen Gregor
Aren Howell
Debra A. Kincaid
Bob LaRoche
Pete Lippincott
Malinda Lowder
Angel Perez
Victor Peterson
Kris Simmons
Michael Thomas
Jody York

Indexer
Chris Cleveland

Composed in *Stone Serif* and *MCPdigital* by Que Corporation

About the Author

Linda A. Flanders is a Certified Public Accountant and holds a Bachelor of Science degree in Accounting from Indiana University. She has worked in public accounting for Arthur Andersen & Co., and private accounting for Mayflower Group, Inc., where she specialized in taxation. She currently operates a small individual tax practice. She is the author of Que's *Using Quicken Version 3 for Windows, Using Quicken Version 7 for DOS, Using QuickBooks for Windows*, and *Using Microsoft Money 2.0*.

Trademark Acknowledgments

Contents at a Glance

Contents

3 Defining Your Accounts   53

4 Organizing Your Finances   67

III Planning for the Future with Quicken for Windows 281

14 Scheduling Future Transactions 283

15 Preparing Financial Forecasts 309

16 Monitoring Your Investments 317

Introduction

If you're like most people, your personal bookkeeping takes you hours and hours each month. You probably sit down three to four times a month to pay bills, each time gathering paperwork, writing checks, entering checks and deposits into your checkbook register, calculating your bank account balance, and addressing envelopes. Then, when your monthly bank statement arrives, you must sit down again to perform the tedious task of balancing your checkbook by checking off cleared transactions, adding outstanding deposits and checks, and performing the reconciling calculations.

After you endure all these ordeals, heaven forbid if your bank account balance doesn't agree with the bank's! That crisis means spending even more time trying to find the error(s). All these tasks, just to keep your financial records in some semblance of order. But keeping your financial records in order is a task that you *can't* overlook or trust to an outdated or ineffective financial system.

If you invest your money in any type of securities, you absolutely must keep track of your investments or you won't know whether your investment strategies are paying off. If your focus is on income-producing investments, you need to monitor those investments to make sure that the income yields are maximized. If your focus is on growth investments, you need to monitor those investments to make sure that they are growing at a satisfactory level. No matter what your focus, you need to monitor your investments to make sure that they don't dwindle away. Of course, you can entrust this process to your investment advisor or broker, but you will want to be on top of things to make sure that the experts are doing their job with *your* money.

And everyone is trying to get ahead and save for the future. But how do you know how much you will need to send your kids to college or to retire in the lifestyle that you've always dreamed of? Or what about that new car or home that you've been saving for? You need some way to keep track of your savings progress to make sure that you reach your financial goal. Certainly, many financial consultants or planners are more than willing to work with you and devise a savings scheme to take care of all your future concerns—but not without a price.

And let's not forget Uncle Sam's share of your hard-earned money. Because income taxes are as certain as death, you need to make sure that you've either withheld enough or saved enough to cover your tax liability each year. With confusing and convoluted tax calculations, this task alone can be overwhelming.

Quicken 4 for Windows is your solution to most, if not all, of your financial needs. In the last year, Quicken has become a household word. You've probably seen articles in *Newsweek* and *USA Today* about the thousands of "Quicken addicts" who can't tear themselves away from their Quicken programs. You may have even overheard people talking about Quicken in the subway, at the office, at the grocery store, or your neighborhood park. Today, more and more people are using Quicken to help with the boring and long process of bookkeeping and financial management and the necessary—but sometimes complex—task of monitoring their investments. Quicken significantly cuts down on the time they spend performing financial tasks such as paying bills, reconciling bank statements, and creating financial reports. Quicken helps them devise saving strategies for retirement *and* college for the kids *and* the new home. And now Quicken can even help them estimate their tax liability at any time during the year.

With Quicken, you can speed up your record-keeping activities and have a little fun, too. By using windows that resemble what you're used to seeing on the desktop (checks, check registers, bank statements, and so forth), you quickly and easily can enter your financial transactions, print checks, reconcile your bank account, create budgets, and generate reports and graphs so that you can analyze your finances.

Quicken for Windows' investment features help you track each of your investments so that you easily can manage your portfolio. Quicken's financial planners can be of great help in determining your future financial needs. Quicken's savings goal accounts can help you track the money that you set aside for some future expenditure. And Quicken's new Tax Planner can help you estimate the amount of income tax you'll owe next April 15th.

To truly have a handle on your finances, you must keep track of your income and expenses so that you know how much money is coming in and how much is going out. Quicken helps you do that. To make informed decisions about spending, you must know exactly where you are (financially) at any given time. If you want to take a vacation to Europe or buy a new car, for example, you immediately know what you can afford. Quicken helps you make these decisions by presenting the financial data that you need in a format that is meaningful to you. That's what this book is really about: Making better financial decisions by using financial information—financial information that Quicken can help you collect, store, and use.

In this age of supertechnology, you can accomplish on a computer almost anything you do behind a desk. Bookkeeping and financial management are no exception. With a well-designed software package, you can perform all your financial activities, including tracking your investments, in far less time and with far less frustration.

If you are considering the installation of a personal or small-business accounting package like Quicken, if you have decided to install Quicken and want a little extra help, or if you already are using Quicken and want a reference source that goes beyond the information provided in the user's manual, *Using Quicken 4 for Windows* will help. This text includes a wealth of information about Quicken for Windows Version 4 and about managing your personal or small-business finances.

After you read this introduction, you will know what Quicken for Windows Version 4 is and whether the program suits your needs. This introduction also identifies the contents of each chapter.

CPA Tip: Author's Testimonial

You may think that most computer-book authors learn many programs but use only a few. Well, you're right. And the programs that we authors end up using are the programs that have proven to work the best. Because we do learn numerous programs so that we can write about them and tell users, like yourself, the ins and outs of the program, we have a better-than-average feel for which programs work the way they're supposed to and save us the most time.

As a CPA, I'm particularly interested in financial programs like Quicken for Windows. The last thing that I want to do is spend more time than I have to with financial tasks, such as writing checks, balancing the checking account, preparing a budget, updating investment accounts, and so forth. But as a CPA, I'm extremely critical of software publishers that promote their products as the "only financial software" that I need and then fall short of the mark. Many do.

(continues)

(continued)

Quicken, however, meets all my expectations for a financial software package, and then some. I've been using Quicken for six years (beginning with Quicken for DOS, of course). And with each new version of the program, Quicken keeps getting better and better. (As a matter of preference for the Windows environment, I switched from Quicken for DOS to Quicken for Windows, but for those of you who continue to use DOS software, Quicken for DOS offers the same activities that you find in Quicken for Windows.)

I use Quicken for all my financial needs. I probably save the most time by using preprinted checks to write checks. At any given time, I may have 25 checks to write and print. With Quicken, I can perform this task almost effortlessly and in little time. I also appreciate the tasks I can perform with Quicken that used to take hours, such as reconciling my bank account at the end of the month, preparing a budget and then comparing actual to budget data, gathering tax information in April, putting together financial statements, and updating my investment account values. With Quicken, I can do all these things while the sun is still shining—no more late nights spent with calculators and spreadsheets!

I welcome you to the world of Quicken and encourage you to learn everything you can about the program. In time, you'll be using Quicken for all your financial needs, too, and probably will become another one of those "Quicken addicts."

What Is Quicken for Windows?

Quicken for Windows is a computer-based bookkeeping system you can use to manage your personal or business finances. Quicken for Windows is developed for use with Microsoft Windows. Windows is an environment surrounding DOS, the disk operating system. With Windows, you can accomplish the same tasks that you can with DOS but through the use of a graphical user interface (GUI), which provides visual choices and options for performing tasks. With Windows programs, all your choices can be visible, which provides easier access to program features.

When working in a Windows program, you can load other programs and quickly switch from one to another. Within the same application (like Quicken for Windows), you can display multiple windows so that you can work faster and easier.

Used in the simplest way, Quicken maintains your check register for you by deducting payments and adding deposits to your checking account balance.

Quicken eliminates the possibility of overdrawing your account because of an arithmetic error.

The real value of Quicken, however, stems from several other features the program provides:

- Quicken enables you to use your computer and printer to generate checks, which is a real time-saver if you find yourself writing many checks at home every month.

- Quicken enables you to use the information stored in your check register to report on your income and expenses, track tax deductions, estimate your tax liability, and compare your actual income and expenses to what you originally budgeted.

- You can use Quicken to perform bookkeeping for most personal and business assets and liabilities, including personal investments, business receivables, personal credit lines and mortgages, and business payables.

With these extra features, individuals can track and manage their finances closely, and many small businesses can use Quicken as a full-fledged accounting package. (Quicken enables you to generate personal and business income statements, balance sheets, and cash-flow statements.)

New Features in Quicken 4 for Windows

If you have used earlier versions of Quicken for Windows (or Quicken for DOS), you will want to know what Quicken 4 for Windows has in store for you. Quicken for Windows features new to Version 4 are indicated throughout this book by a special icon, just like the one next to this paragraph in the margin. The following is a list of the new features in Quicken 4 for Windows:

- *Quicken Homebase system.* Quicken's new Homebase system provides an alternative means for accessing the most commonly used commands in Quicken, like creating accounts, writing checks, using the Register, and so forth. To learn about Quicken Homebase, refer to Chapter 2, "Learning Your Way Around Quicken for Windows."

- *Estimating income taxes with the new Tax Planner.* A great new feature in Quicken 4 for Windows is the Tax Planner that estimates your income tax liability at any time during the year. The Tax Planner uses your

Quicken data and/or any other data that you want to enter to calculate your tax liability and determine whether your withholding is adequate or whether you need to pay quarterly estimated taxes. Refer to Chapter 12, "Estimating and Preparing for Income Taxes," to learn how to use Quicken's new Tax Planner.

■ *Financial forecasting.* Quicken includes a new financial forecasting feature that allows you to project your cash flows for the future, based on scheduled transactions and estimated amounts that you enter. To learn how to create a financial forecast, refer to Chapter 15, "Preparing Financial Forecasts."

■ *Savings goals.* In Quicken 3 for Windows, the savings goal account was introduced so that you could set up a special account to track your savings. In Version 4, you set up a savings goal based on the item that you want to save for. You can then contribute or withdraw from this special savings goal account and monitor your progress through the use of an on-screen Progress Bar. See Chapter 18, "Saving for the Future with Quicken," to learn how to use this helpful feature to monitor your savings.

■ *Snapshot reports.* Quicken snapshot reports summarize your data and provide an instant overview of your finances. Creating snapshot reports is covered in Chapter 19, "Creating and Printing Reports."

■ *Supercategories for budgeting.* Quicken 4 for Windows lets you group categories together into *supercategories* so that you can use them in your budgets. Using supercategories is explained in Chapter 17, "Budgeting with Quicken."

■ *New account types.* Quicken 4 for Windows includes two new account types; *Savings* and *Money Market.* Refer to Chapter 3, "Defining Your Accounts," to learn about these new accounts.

■ *Searching and replacing data.* With Quicken's new Find/Replace command, you can search transactions for specific criteria and then change the items Quicken finds. In Chapter 7, "Using Quicken Shortcuts," you learn how to search and replace data.

■ *Updating portfolio prices online.* Quicken 4 for Windows provides the capability of updating your investment portfolio prices using Portfolio Price Update, an online financial service. To learn how to update stock prices online, refer to Chapter 16, "Monitoring Your Investments."

■ *Displaying calendar notes as Quicken Reminders.* Quicken 4 for Windows displays calendar notes from the Financial Calendar in the Quicken Reminders window each time you start Quicken. To learn about displaying calendar notes, refer to Chapter 14, "Scheduling Future Transactions."

■ *Memorizing graphs.* Now, when you customize a graph to include the transactions that you want, you can memorize the graph so that you can recall it easily later. Memorizing graphs is explained in Chapter 20, "Using Graphs to Analyze Your Finances."

■ *Locking memorized transactions.* You can lock a memorized transaction so that it doesn't change when you memorize another transaction with the same payee. Refer to Chapter 7, "Using Quicken Shortcuts," to learn how to lock a memorized transaction.

■ *Selecting accounts with the new Account Selector Bar.* The Write Checks window and all registers include an Account Selector Bar that you can use to select another account quickly to work in. Chapter 3, "Defining Your Accounts," shows you how to use the Account Selector Bar.

■ *Write Checks button bar.* The Write Checks window in Quicken 4 for Windows includes a button bar for common commands, such as deleting and finding checks. See Chapter 5, "Writing and Printing Checks," to learn how to use the button bar.

■ *Transfer button in the button bar.* The new Transfer button in the Register and Write Checks button bars simplifies the process of entering transfer transactions. Refer to Chapter 6, "Using the Register," and Chapter 11, "Managing Your Assets and Other Liabilities," to learn how to transfer transactions among accounts.

■ *Recategorizing transactions.* With Quicken 4 for Windows you can replace the category assigned to selected transactions with another category. Chapter 4, "Organizing Your Finances," explains how to recategorize transactions.

■ *Easier account set up.* The new Guide Me option acts as your very own "hand holder" to help you set up new accounts in Quicken. Refer to Chapter 3, "Defining Your Accounts," to learn about this new option.

■ *New on-screen check artwork.* For your viewing pleasure, Quicken 4 for Windows provides several options for displaying artwork on the check face in the Write Checks window. Refer to Chapter 5, "Writing and Printing Checks," to learn how to display check artwork on-screen.

■ *Fiscal year option.* You can set up Quicken to group your transactions by fiscal year, instead of by a calendar year. You choose the month that starts your fiscal year. To learn about setting the fiscal year option, refer to Chapter 1, "Preparing to Use Quicken for Windows."

■ *Setting up accounts with deferred tax status.* In Version 3, you could establish investment accounts as deferred. Now, you can establish any account as tax-deferred so that you can track IRAs, 401(k), Series EE Savings Bonds, and so forth. See Chapter 3, "Defining Your Accounts," to learn how to set up an account with deferred tax status.

■ *New P&L Comparison Report.* Quicken 4 for Windows includes this new report that compares income and expenses for two periods. Refer to Chapter 19, "Creating and Printing Reports," to learn about this new report.

■ *Reindexing Quicken files.* If necessary, you can instruct Quicken to reindex a file, or reconstruct the data's index file. Chapter 21, "Managing Your Quicken Files," describes the reindexing process.

What This Book Contains

Using Quicken 4 for Windows consists of 22 chapters (divided into 5 parts) and one appendix. The following sections provide an overview of what each chapter discusses.

> **Note**
>
> If you read the book from cover to cover, you may notice a little repetition in some places; repetition is inevitable because the book also serves as a reference.

Part I: Learning Quicken for Windows

Part I, "Learning Quicken for Windows," includes eight chapters that, as the part title implies, help you learn the basics of Quicken so that you can perform most tasks.

Chapter 1, "Preparing to Use Quicken for Windows," guides you through the steps you need to take before you start using Quicken for Windows, including ordering any preprinted forms you need, learning to use the system, choosing a starting date, and setting up Quicken to print (if you haven't printed in other Windows applications).

Chapter 2, "Learning Your Way Around Quicken for Windows," gives you a quick introduction to the mechanics of actually working with the program. You learn how to start the program, use the menu bar and the Iconbar to choose commands and options, tap into Quicken's online help feature, and exit the program when your work is finished. If you've been using a previous version of Quicken for Windows, you may want to skim this material.

Chapter 3, "Defining Your Accounts," walks you through the steps to set up the accounts that you use in Quicken, such as your bank or checking account, credit card accounts, and so forth. The chapter also describes a few basic concepts you need to know from the start if you use Quicken for more than just a single bank account.

Chapter 4, "Organizing Your Finances," discusses one of Quicken's optional and most powerful features—the capability to categorize and classify your income and expenses. The categories make it easy to determine tax deductions, the amounts spent for various items, and the types of income that go into your bank accounts. The classes also enable you to look at specific groups of categories, such as expenses relating to specific clients, jobs, or properties. Chapter 4 defines Quicken's categories and classes, describes why and when you should use them, shows the predefined categories provided within Quicken, and explains how to use these categories. The chapter also outlines the steps for adding, deleting, and modifying your own categories and classes.

Chapter 5, "Writing and Printing Checks," describes one of Quicken's core features—the capability to print checks. The chapter includes instructions for completing the Write Checks window, where you provide the information Quicken needs to print a check. You also learn how to record, review, edit, and print checks. Not everyone wants or needs to use Quicken to print checks, but if you do, Chapter 5 is the place to start.

Chapter 6, "Using the Register," explains the steps for using Quicken's fundamental feature—its Register. This chapter gives a complete explanation of what the Register is, what information it contains, and how to use it. If you're not going to use Quicken to print checks, you need to understand how to use the Register so that you can enter your manual transactions in the program.

Chapter 7, "Using Quicken Shortcuts," describes how to use the special Quicken features to speed up your work in Quicken. This chapter describes some of the special Quicken features that, although not essential, can make check-writing faster and the Quicken Register easier to use.

Chapter 8, "Reconciling Your Bank Account," discusses one of the important steps you can take to protect your cash and the accuracy and reliability of your financial records. This chapter first reviews the reconciliation process in general terms and then describes the steps for reconciling your accounts in Quicken, correcting and catching errors, and printing and using the reconciliation reports that Quicken creates.

Part II: Getting the Most from Quicken for Windows

Part II, "Getting the Most from Quicken for Windows," consists of Chapters 9 through 13. In these chapters, you learn how to use Quicken for Windows to its maximum potential.

Chapter 9, "Managing Your Credit Cards," explains how to use Quicken's Credit Card Register to record credit card purchases and payments, and reconcile your account against your credit card statements. And if you have a Quicken for Windows VISA card, Chapter 9 shows you how to set up an IntelliCharge account so that you can receive your credit card statements on disk or by modem.

Chapter 10, "Tracking Loans," explains how to use Quicken to keep track of amortized loans. You learn how to set up loans (such as mortgages, home equity loans, car loans, and so forth), make loan payments, refinance a loan, and delete a loan when it's paid in full. Quicken handles variable interest rate loans and alternative loan calculation methods, including Canadian amortization. In Chapter 10, you also learn how to use Quicken's Loan Planner to compute loan variables (payment, principal, interest rate, and term).

Chapter 11, "Managing Your Assets and Other Liabilities," describes some of the special features that Quicken 4 for Windows provides for personal use. You can track cash and other assets (such as real estate), as well as liabilities (such as a non-amortized loan to a friend). Recording all your assets and liabilities in Quicken completes your financial picture so that you can assess your net worth at any given time.

Chapter 12, "Estimating and Preparing for Income Taxes," is an important chapter. This chapter tells you how to make sure that the financial records you create with Quicken for Windows provide the information you need to prepare your federal and state income tax returns. The chapter also briefly discusses the general mechanics of passing data between Quicken and an income tax preparation package, such as TurboTax. In this chapter, you also learn how to use Quicken's new Tax Planner to estimate your tax liability at any time during the year.

Chapter 13, "Paying Your Bills Electronically," describes how you can use Quicken to pay your bills electronically by using the CheckFree service. Electronic payment isn't for everybody, but if you're a Quicken user, you should at least know what's involved and whether it makes sense for you.

Part III: Planning for the Future with Quicken

Part III, "Planning for the Future with Quicken," consists of Chapters 14 through 18. These chapters show you how to use Quicken beyond the basics to plan for your future financial needs.

Chapter 14, "Scheduling Future Transactions," shows you how to use Quicken's financial calendar to schedule bills to be paid in the future. Using the financial calendar helps you avoid paying bills late and also helps you schedule your cash flows for future needs. In this chapter, you also learn how to use the reminder features in Quicken, such as Billminder, Quicken Reminders, and calendar notes so that you don't forget to pay a bill, make a deposit, or attend that important meeting.

Chapter 15, "Preparing Financial Forecasts," explains how to use Quicken's new forecasting feature to help you project your future cash flows. This chapter shows you how to create a forecasting graph and how to analyze the data provided by this helpful tool.

Chapter 16, "Monitoring Your Investments," describes the Investment Register that Quicken provides for investors. This chapter shows you how to enter investment transactions easily using on-screen forms for buying and selling securities, recording investment income, selling short, buying and redeeming U.S. savings bonds, and numerous other activities. If you want to monitor your investments and stay on top of their performance, read through Chapter 16 to see the tools and options that Quicken provides specifically for managing investments.

Chapter 17, "Budgeting with Quicken," discusses one of Quicken's most significant benefits—budgeting and monitoring your success in following a budget. This chapter reviews the steps for budgeting, describes how Quicken helps with budgeting, and provides some tips on how to budget more successfully. If you aren't comfortable with the budgeting process, Chapter 17 should give you enough information to get started. If you find budgeting an unpleasant exercise, the chapter also provides some tips on making budgeting a more positive experience.

Chapter 18, "Saving for the Future with Quicken," explains how to use Quicken's savings goal account to earmark funds to save toward specific goals and how to monitor your progress with the new Progress Bar. This chapter also shows you how to use three of Quicken's financial planners: the Investment Savings Planner, the Retirement Planner, and the College Planner. Quicken's financial planners help you play out "what-if" scenarios to see results quickly.

Part IV: Analyzing Your Finances with Quicken

Part IV, "Analyzing Your Finances with Quicken," shows you how to use Quicken to analyze your finances through the use of reports and graphs. Part IV consists of Chapters 19 and 20.

Chapter 19, "Creating and Printing Reports," shows you how to sort, extract, and summarize the information contained in the Quicken Registers by using the Reports options. Quicken's reports enable you to gain better control over and insight into your income, expenses, and cash flow.

Chapter 20, "Using Graphs to Analyze Your Finances," describes the Quicken graph feature. If you want to see relationships between your income and expenses, assets and liabilities, actual and budget amounts, and investment portfolios, read Chapter 20 to learn about the various graphs that you can create on-screen and print.

Part V: Managing Quicken for Windows

Part V, "Managing Quicken for Windows," shows you how to manage your Quicken files and customize the Quicken program. Part V consists of Chapters 21 and 22.

Chapter 21, "Managing Your Quicken Files," describes how to take care of the files that Quicken uses to store your financial records. This chapter describes how to back up and restore your Quicken files, make copies of the files, and purge from the files information you no longer need.

Chapter 22, "Customizing Quicken," describes how to change program options to customize, or fine-tune, Quicken's operation.

Appendix

Using Quicken 4 for Windows also provides one appendix. Appendix A, "Installing Quicken 4 for Windows," discusses the hardware and software requirements to use Quicken for Windows and shows you how to install the Quicken 4 for Windows program.

Conventions Used in This Book

A number of conventions are used in *Using Quicken 4 for Windows* to help you learn the program. The following examples for these conventions can help you distinguish the different elements in *Using Quicken 4 for Windows*.

CPA Tips: Helpful Financial Advice

This book includes CPA tips, formatted the way this paragraph is formatted, to provide advice that will help you better manage your finances.

Note

This paragraph format indicates additional information that may help you avoid problems or that should be considered in using the described features.

Caution

This paragraph format warns you of problems you may encounter when you are learning how to use Quicken.

Tip
A paragraph in the margin (like this one) suggests an easier or alternative way to execute a procedure in Quicken.

The following special typefaces are used in this book:

Type	Meaning
italics	New terms or phrases when initially defined
boldface	Information you are asked to type, and letters that appear underlined on-screen in Quicken menu and dialog box options
`monospaced type`	Direct quotations of words that appear on-screen or in a figure

Names of menus and dialog boxes are shown with the initial letter capitalized. Commands and options also appear with initial capital letters (such as **O**pen and **P**rint).

Ctrl+Enter indicates that you press and hold the Ctrl key while you press the Enter key. Other key combinations, such as Shift+Tab and Alt+H, are performed in the same manner.

Homebse   Registr   Accts   Recon   Check   Calendar   Graphs   Reports   Sm

Quicken Help   F
How To Use Help
Tutorials
Show Qcards
About Quicken...

Part I

Learning Quicken for Windows

Print

Layout Budgets

	OK
Month	Cancel
Quarter	Help
Year	

Show Supercategories
Show Transfers
Hide Zero Budget Categories

Enter a category.
Categories let you create reports, graphs, and budgets sorted by category.
Either:
➡ Type the category by hand, OR
➡ Click the drop-down list
Then click the Next button below to conti   ▶ Next   ? Help

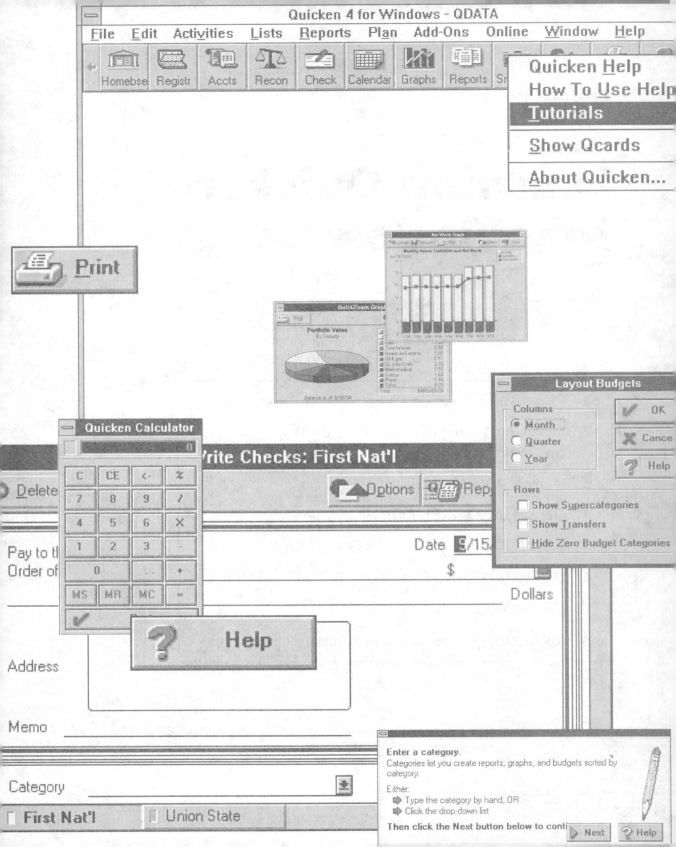

Chapter 1

Preparing to Use Quicken for Windows

Preparing to use Quicken for Windows isn't difficult. If you are new to computers, however, a little hand-holding and emotional support never hurts. Chapter 1 walks you through the steps for preparing to use Quicken for Windows. Don't worry that you may not know enough about computers, Quicken for Windows, or computer-based accounting systems. Simply follow the instructions and steps described in this chapter.

In this chapter, you learn how to do the following:

- Choose a *conversion date* (the best date to start using Quicken to automate your finances)

- Start Quicken 4 for Windows for the first time and set up your Quicken system

- Register your Quicken 4 for Windows software

- Select your financial year

- Order checks and other supplies from Intuit

- Prepare to print in Windows

Choosing a Conversion Date

Choosing a conversion date is a critical decision you must make before you can enjoy the advantages of an automated accounting system. The *conversion date* is the day on which you stop using your old manual system and begin using your new Quicken system. The more frequently you expect to use Quicken, the more important is the conversion date.

Perhaps you don't intend to use Quicken to summarize income and expense transactions or to monitor how closely you are sticking to a budget; all you really want is a tool to help you maintain your checkbook and produce checks. If so, the conversion date isn't so important.

If you intend to use Quicken to organize your income tax deductions, estimate taxes, calculate business profits, or plan budgets, however, you should designate a clean accounting cutoff point for the date you begin keeping records with Quicken. From the conversion date forward, Quicken handles all your accounting information. Before the conversion date, your old accounting system still provides your accounting information.

Pick a natural cutoff date that makes switching from one system to another easy. Often the best time to begin a new accounting system is at the beginning of the calendar year or your fiscal year. All income and expense transactions for the new year are then recorded in the same place. Picking a good cutoff date may seem trivial, but having all your tax deductions for one year recorded and summarized in one place saves you valuable time and effort.

> ### Note
>
> No matter which date you decide will begin your Quicken system, at any time you can enter transactions dated before your start date. Quicken automatically places previous transactions in the proper date order in the Register. Refer to Chapter 6, "Using the Register," to learn how to enter transactions in the Register.

Tip
To start using Quicken at the beginning of the month, first take time to summarize your accounting information from the old system. Make sure that you don't record the same transaction twice or forget any.

If you can't start using Quicken at the beginning of the year, the next best time is at the beginning of a month. If you do start at the beginning of a month, you must combine your old accounting or record-keeping information with Quicken's information to get totals for the year. When calculating tax deductions, for example, you must add the amounts Quicken shows to whatever your old system shows.

The worst time to begin using Quicken is in the middle of a month. With no natural cutoff point, you are even more likely than at the beginning of a month to count some transactions on both systems and to forget to record others in either system.

> **Caution**
>
> Two common errors are possible after you choose an accounting cutoff date: you may record the same income or expense transaction in both systems and therefore count the transaction twice when you combine the two systems to get your annual totals, or you may neglect to record a transaction in one system because you think you recorded it in the other system. Your records will be wrong if you make either error. To ensure that you have entered the appropriate transactions in Quicken, be sure to review the transactions in the Register against those in your manual system.

> **CPA Tip: Document Your Deductions**
>
> If you use data from your manual system and your Quicken system to complete your income tax return, make sure that you keep adequate worksheets and documentation for any items you deduct. If audited, you want your documentation to show clearly that you added amounts from your manual system to your Quicken system to arrive at your deductions.

Starting Quicken 4 for Windows

Once you've installed Quicken, starting the program is easy. After you start Windows, just double-click the Quicken 4 icon from the Quicken program group window. You also can start Quicken by highlighting the Quicken 4 icon and pressing Enter.

If you're a new Quicken user, when you start Quicken the first time, the Quicken New User Setup window (see fig. 1.1) is displayed. Refer to the section, "Setup for New Quicken Users," later in this chapter to learn where to go from here.

If you have used Quicken for DOS or previous versions of Quicken for Windows, you simply open the Quicken file that you want to start working in and go from there. Read the section "Setup for Current Quicken Users" later in this chapter to learn how to open a Quicken file.

Fig. 1.1
When a new user starts Quicken for the first time, the Quicken New User Setup window is displayed.

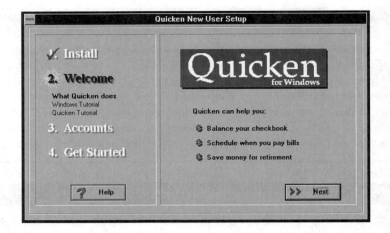

Setting Up Your Quicken System

If you're new to Quicken, you start out a little differently than users who used Quicken and already established at least one Quicken data file from a previous version of the program. For new users, Quicken guides you through the start up; helping you create your first accounts (checking and savings accounts and a credit card account) and selecting a predefined category list (the list of categories that you want to use to classify your income and expenses). If you have used Quicken before (Windows or DOS), setting up your Quicken system is simple; just show Quicken where your previous version data file is and open the file. Quicken automatically updates files from previous versions of Quicken for use in the new version.

Note

As you begin to use Quicken, notice the message boxes that appear on-screen. These boxes, called *Qcards*, are brief help messages that appear at places you are likely to need help entering information. You learn more about Qcards in Chapter 2, "Learning Your Way Around Quicken for Windows."

Setup for New Quicken Users

For new users, the first time you start Quicken, the Quicken New User Setup window (see fig. 1.1) is displayed. This window lists the topics to address to get your Quicken system set up; Install, Welcome, Accounts, and Get Started.

Because you've already installed Quicken (see Appendix A, "Installing Quicken 4 for Windows"), the next step that you may want to take is to view the tutorials provided with the program. Note that tutorials are not available unless you are running Windows 3.1 or using a VGA monitor.

If you want to view the Windows and/or Quicken Tutorials, click the **N**ext button in the Quicken New User Setup window. Quicken moves to the next window and asks whether you want to see a tutorial on Windows. If you are a new Windows user, choose **Y**es to view the Tutorial. Otherwise, choose **N**o.

After you view the Windows Tutorial or choose **N**o, Quicken asks whether you want to see the tutorial that provides an introduction to the program. If you are a new Quicken user, choose **Y**es to view the Quicken Tutorial. Otherwise, choose **N**o.

Quicken returns to the Quicken New User Setup window (see fig. 1.1). You're ready for the third topic—Accounts. Because you're new to Quicken and are just now establishing a data file, you need to create at least one account in your file. *Accounts* in Quicken are similar to the accounts you use to keep track of your transactions—such as checking, savings, and credit card accounts. Quicken lets you create one checking account, one savings account, and one credit card account at this time. Choose **N**ext to create your first account.

> ### Note
>
> After you start using Quicken, you can create as many accounts as you need to keep track of your finances. Refer to Chapter 3, "Defining Your Accounts," to learn how to create other accounts in Quicken.

The next windows tell you what you need to create accounts (like your checkbook, bank statement, savings statement, and so forth). Choose **N**ext at each window. Quicken next asks whether you have a checking account that you want to create. If so, choose **Y**es, otherwise choose **N**o to move to the next window to create a savings account.

If you choose to create a checking account, Quicken displays the appropriate windows so that you can enter the account name, balance, and the date the balance relates to.

Follow these steps to create your first checking account:

1. In the **A**ccount Name text box, type the checking account name, using up to 15 characters (including spaces). You can't use the following characters in an account name:

   :] [/ | ^

   For example, type your bank's name, such as **First National**, or just use the name **Checking**.

2. Choose **N**ext. Quicken then asks whether you have your last bank statement for the account. If so, choose **Y**es and proceed to the next step. If you don't have your last bank statement, choose **N**o. Quicken creates your checking account with a $0 balance as of the date that you are creating the account. Choose **N**ext to create a savings account and/or a credit card account.

3. If you have your bank statement, enter the date of the statement in the **S**tatement Date text box.

4. Choose **N**ext. In the **E**nding Balance text box, enter the ending statement balance shown on your bank statement by typing the dollar amount (no dollar sign is necessary). For example, to enter $1,345.89, type **1345.89**. Although you are entering the ending balance from your statement, this balance becomes the starting balance for your checking account in your Quicken system.

> **Caution**
>
> When you enter the ending balance from your last bank statement as the starting balance in your checking account, you must enter all uncleared transactions in the Register after you begin using Quicken. In other words, you must include all transactions that haven't cleared through your checking account by the date of your bank statement. If you overlook these transactions, you will have difficulty reconciling your account. Chapter 6, "Using the Register," explains how to use the Register.

5. Choose **N**ext. Quicken tells you that your checking account has been created with the balance that you entered as of the date that you entered as your statement date.

6. Quicken next displays the appropriate windows so that you can create a savings account and/or a credit card account. The steps for creating

these two account types are similar to creating the checking account in the previous steps 1 through 5. Set up the appropriate accounts and choose **N**ext.

7. When you return to the Quicken New User Setup window (see fig. 1.1), you're ready to get started using Quicken. But first, you need to select the categories that you want to use in Quicken. A *category* describes and summarizes common income and expenses, such as salary, insurance, utilities, and so on. Categories group your income and expenses so that Quicken can classify your transactions for reporting, graphing, budgeting, and income tax purposes. In simple terms, categories describe where your money comes from and where it goes. (Chapter 4, "Organizing Your Finances," describes Quicken's categories in more detail.) Quicken includes two predefined sets of categories, for home/personal use and for business use. Choose **N**ext to select the categories that you want to use.

8. Quicken asks whether you want to use business categories. If you want to set up Quicken for home and business use, choose **Y**es. Quicken includes business categories as well as home categories in your file.

If you want to set up Quicken for your home finances only, choose **N**o. When you choose **N**o, Quicken automatically includes the home categories in your file.

> **Note**
>
> Be sure to choose the category list that works best for you. If you plan to use Quicken in your business, make certain that you choose to include business categories. You can, however, modify your category list at any time to add, edit, or delete categories so that the list contains just the categories that you need. Refer to Chapter 4, "Organizing Your Finances," to learn more about using categories.

9. Quicken returns to the Quicken New User Setup window (see fig. 1.1) and provides a few instructions for using Quicken. Choose **D**one and you're on your way.

What you see next is the Register for the checking account (or savings or credit card account if you didn't create a checking account) that you just created. Figure 1.2 shows the Register for the checking account named *First Nat'l.*

Fig. 1.2
The Register for the first account that you create appears after you complete the Quicken New User Setup window.

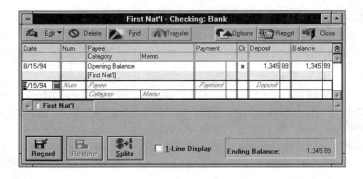

Tip
Now that you've created your first account(s) and selected your predefined categories, be sure to review Chapter 2 for a complete explanation of Quicken fundamentals.

Note

All transactions relating to your checking account are entered in a Register, such as checks, deposits, and ATM withdrawals.

Setup for Current Quicken Users

If you were using Quicken for Windows Version 1, 2, or 3, you can upgrade the current version of your program to Version 4 quickly. When you install Quicken 4 for Windows (see Appendix A), the program converts previous version files to Quicken 4. Your Quicken 1, 2, or 3 files, however, aren't changed in any way. You still may use Quicken 1, 2, or 3 files after installing Quicken 4 for Windows.

If you were using Quicken for DOS Version 5, 6, or 7, your existing files are updated automatically when you install Quicken 4 for Windows. Quicken reads your existing Quicken 5, 6, or 7 files directly and converts your data, but doesn't change your data. You still can use Quicken for DOS files after installing Quicken 4 for Windows.

If you were using Versions 3 or 4 of Quicken for DOS, Quicken updates your files when you open them; however, you can't reopen updated files with Quicken 3 or 4 for DOS after you use them with Quicken 4 for Windows.

Before you can begin using Quicken 4 for Windows after it's installed, you must show Quicken where your data files are located and open the data file that you want to use. After you open your data file in Quicken, your system is set up and you're ready to begin using the new version of Quicken.

To set up your Quicken system with previous Quicken for Windows version data files or to set up your Quicken system with Quicken for DOS (Version 3, 4, 5, 6, or 7) files, follow these steps:

1. Choose **F**ile from the menu bar at the top of the Quicken screen. Quicken displays the **F**ile menu, shown in figure 1.3.

Fig. 1.3
The **F**ile menu includes the **O**pen command so that you can open other Quicken files.

2. From the **F**ile menu, choose **O**pen. You also can choose the **F**ile **O**pen command by pressing Ctrl+O. Quicken displays the Open Quicken File dialog box (see fig. 1.4).

Fig. 1.4
The Open Quicken File dialog box lists all other Quicken files. You can change the directory and/or the drive where Quicken looks for data files.

3. In the File **N**ame list box, choose the Quicken for Windows Version 1, 2, or 3 file, or the Quicken for DOS previous version file that you want to use. If necessary, change the directory in the **D**irectories list box by double-clicking the directory name. Also, if necessary, change the drive where Quicken looks for data files in the Dri**v**es drop-down list box. Note that Quicken automatically selects Quicken Files (*.QDT) as the type of files to locate in the List Files of **T**ype drop-down box.

Quicken opens the file that you selected. You're now ready to use Version 4 of Quicken for Windows.

Registering Quicken 4 for Windows

To take advantage of technical support from Intuit, to receive notification of upgrades, and to learn about subsequent special offerings to Quicken customers, you must register your Quicken 4 for Windows software.

If you purchased Quicken 4 for Windows directly from Intuit, you don't need to register your software; it's already registered. If you purchased your Quicken 4 for Windows program from another source, there are two methods for registering your software:

■ Complete the registration form included in your Quicken 4 for Windows software package and mail it to Intuit.

■ If you have a modem connected to your computer, select Software **R**egistration from the Online menu. Quicken displays the Quicken 4 for Windows Software Registration dialog box. Fill in the two dialog boxes that Quicken displays with the appropriate information. Then select the **R**egister command and Quicken initializes your modem and transmits the registration information to Intuit.

Selecting Your Financial Year

For most of you, you'll use a calendar year (January 1 to December 31) to summarize your transactions in Quicken. But if you're using Quicken in your small business or if you just prefer to use a fiscal year, you can now change the working calendar in Quicken to reflect a 12-month period other than the standard calendar period. Quicken reflects your financial year in budgets, reports, and graphs.

To select the financial year that Quicken uses, follow these steps:

1. Choose **O**ptions from the **E**dit menu or click the Options button in the Iconbar at the top of your Quicken screen. Quicken displays the Options dialog box shown in figure 1.5.

Fig. 1.5
Click the Options button in the Iconbar to display the Options dialog box.

2. From the Options dialog box, click the **G**eneral button. Quicken next displays the General Options dialog box that you see in figure 1.6.

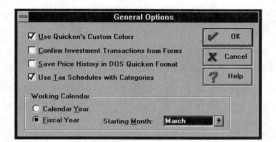

I

Learning Quicken

Fig. 1.6
The General Options dialog box includes options that you can change in your Quicken program.

3. In the Working Calendar box, click the **F**iscal Year button. Quicken blackens the button to show that it has been selected. Note that, by default, the Calendar **Y**ear button is already selected.

4. At the Starting **M**onth drop-down list box, click the arrow button to display the months in the year. Move down the list to display the month that you want to select and click to select it.

5. Click the OK button to save the changes that you made in the General Options dialog box. Quicken returns to the Options dialog box.

6. Click the Close button.

Note

Quicken automatically saves the account(s) that you have created in your Quicken file. Be sure to exit the program, however, before quitting your Quicken work session or your work may not be saved. Refer to Chapter 2, "Learning Your Way Around Quicken for Windows," to learn how to exit Quicken.

Ordering Check Forms and Other Supplies

You don't need to use Quicken for Windows to print your checks to benefit from the program, but Quicken's check-writing feature is a time-saver. The time saved, however, doesn't come cheaply. Expect to pay between $45 and $85 for 250 computer check forms. Usually, you spend more for check forms in the course of a year than you originally spent for the Quicken software.

Obviously, you want to make sure that you make the right decision about ordering checks. Two situations merit the expense of check forms: you write many checks at home or at work (more than two dozen each month), or you plan to use Quicken for Windows for a business and want the professional appearance of computer-printed checks.

> **Note**
>
> You still will use manual checks (those you write by hand) even if you choose to use Quicken check forms. Home users, for example, need manual checks for trips to the grocery or the department store. And business owners need manual checks for unexpected deliveries that require immediate cash payments (when access to a computer isn't available).

If you decide to use Quicken to print checks, you must order preprinted check forms for every checking account for which you want computer-printed checks. The least expensive and easiest source of preprinted check forms is Intuit, the manufacturer of Quicken. Intuit offers laser and continuous-feed checks. You also can order from Intuit other supplies, such as deposit slips, double-window envelopes, and stationery.

Quicken 4 for Windows provides a few different ways to order from Intuit. One way is to use the Intuit Check Catalog enclosed in your Quicken 4 for Windows software package and mail the order form to Intuit. You can mail your order form to:

> Intuit, Inc.
> Supplies Department
> P.O. Box 51470
> Palo Alto, CA 94303

Be sure to enclose your check or money order if you are paying by either method.

You can also fax your order for checks and supplies to Intuit at (415) 852-9146.

 New to Version 4 of Quicken for Windows is the Intuit Marketplace feature that allows you to order checks and supplies by filling out an on-screen order form. You can then print the order form and mail or fax it to Intuit or send your order to Intuit by modem. If you're already working in Quicken, just choose Intuit **M**arketplace from the Online menu. If you're not currently

using Quicken, double-click the Intuit Marketplace icon in the Quicken program group (see figure 1.7). (Quicken adds the Intuit Marketplace icon to the
Quicken program group when you install Quicken 4 for Windows). Quicken
displays the Intuit Marketplace screen shown in figure 1.8. Just click anywhere in the Intuit Marketplace screen to access the Intuit Order from that
you can complete by following the on-screen instructions.

Fig. 1.7
Double-click the
Intuit Marketplace
icon in the
Quicken program
group to access
Quicken's ordering
system.

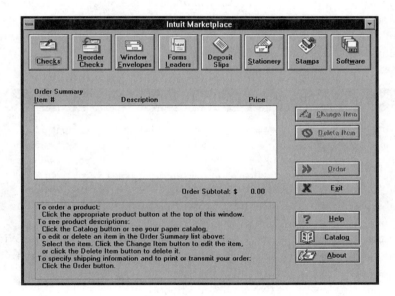

Fig. 1.8
Click anywhere in
the Intuit Market-
place screen to
access the Intuit
Order form.

Note

If you send your Intuit Order Form to Intuit via fax or modem, provide a valid credit
card number and expiration date to pay for your order.

Tip
You can also access
Intuit Marketplace
by selecting Order
Checks from the
Activities menu.

CPA Tip: Choosing a Starting Number for Preprinted Checks

When choosing a starting number for your computer checks, consider two points. First, start the computer-printed check form numbers far enough away from your manual check numbers so that the numbers don't overlap or duplicate (duplications can cause confusion in your record-keeping and reconciliations). Second, start your computer-printed checks with a number that quickly shows you whether you wrote a check manually or with Quicken. For example, if your manual checks start with the number 1 (like 14356), you might start your computer checks with the number 5 (like 55000).

Deciding Which Checks to Use

When you order preprinted checks, you make choices about size, style, or color, and you decide whether the check is multipart or has voucher stubs. Intuit offers continuous-feed check forms and laser check forms. Refer to the Intuit Check Catalog to see a description and illustration of each type of check.

CPA Tip: Using Quicken to Print Checks

Printing checks with Quicken assures that you don't fall behind in entering your financial transactions. When you write manual checks, putting off entering transactions for those checks in Quicken for Windows is easy. As a result, you may find that you have several transactions to enter in Quicken at one time if you let yourself fall behind.

The number of parts in a check refers to the number of printed copies. With a one-part check, only the actual check form that you sign is printed. With a two-part check, a copy is printed at the same time as the original. With a three-part check, you get two copies plus the original.

Multipart forms probably aren't necessary for most home uses. In a business, however, you can attach the second parts to paid invoices as a fast and convenient way of keeping track of which checks paid which invoices. You can place the third copy of a check in a numerical sequence file to help you identify the payee more quickly than you can by using the check number alone.

> **Note**
>
> If you use multipart checks, keep in mind that the check forms may wear out your dot-matrix printer's head (the points that strike the printer ribbon and cause characters to be printed) or may cause your laser or inkjet printer to run out of ink more quickly. Check your printer's multipart form rating by referring to your printer manual. Verify that your printer is rated for at least the number of parts you want to print.

The voucher stub, also called the *remittance advice*, is the blank piece of paper attached to the check form. The voucher stub, which is approximately the same size as the check form, provides extra space for you to describe, or document, the reason for writing the check. You also can use this area to show any calculations involved in arriving at the total check amount. You can use the voucher stub space to describe how an employee's payroll amount was calculated, for example, or to define the invoices for which that check was issued. As with multipart checks, voucher stubs probably make more sense for business use rather than home use.

If you are unsure about which check forms to choose, review the sample checks that Intuit includes in your Quicken 4 for Windows software package. Try out the checks in your printer to experiment with preprinted check forms.

Preparing to Print

If you have been printing reports or documents using other Windows applications, you're ready to print checks, reports, lists, and graphs with Quicken. See Chapter 5, "Writing and Printing Checks"; Chapter 19, "Creating and Printing Reports"; and Chapter 20, "Using Graphs to Analyze Your Finances," to learn how to customize printer settings, use other printers, or choose a different paper size and orientation.

> **Note**
>
> If you haven't printed from a Windows application, you must set up Windows to use your printer or printers before you can print from Quicken.

To set up Windows to use your printer(s), follow these steps:

1. Type **win** at the DOS prompt and press Enter to start the Windows program.

2. Make sure that the Program Manager window is active. If it isn't, double-click the Program Manager icon or press Ctrl+Esc to display the Windows Task List. From the Windows Task List, choose Program Manager, or use the arrow keys to highlight Program Manager and press Enter.

3. From the Program Manager, locate the Control Panel icon (usually in the Main group). Double-click the Control Panel icon to display the Control Panel window.

4. From the Control Panel window, double-click the Printers icon to display the Printers dialog box.

5. Examine the printer shown in the Default Printer box to see whether the correct default printer and printer port (such as LPT1) appears. If it doesn't, select a printer from the Installed **P**rinters list box and choose the S**e**t As Default Printer button.

6. If you want to install other printers to use with Quicken for Windows, choose the **A**dd button and select a printer name from the **L**ist of Printers. Choose **I**nstall and follow the on-screen instructions.

From Here...

You've learned how to start Quicken and set up your system. Before jumping right in, you may want to review the following chapters:

■ Chapter 2, "Learning Your Way Around Quicken for Windows," covers the basics of using Quicken and makes getting the most from Quicken that much easier. You learn your way around the Quicken application window, how to choose menu commands and options using the mouse and keyboard, how to switch among Quicken windows, and how to get help when you need it. If you've used previous versions of Quicken for Windows, you can probably skip this chapter. If you're switching from a previous DOS version of Quicken, you'll want to review this chapter to familiarize yourself with the differences in the Windows version.

- Chapter 3, "Defining Your Accounts," shows you how to create accounts in Quicken. In this chapter, you learn how to create your first accounts. If you need to create other accounts such as an asset account to track the value of your home, or an investment account to track the securities in your portfolio, Chapter 3 shows you how.

- Chapter 4, "Organizing Your Finances," contains important information about setting up categories in Quicken. All of the transactions that you enter in Quicken should be assigned to a category so that you can track your income, expenses, and tax items, create budgets, estimate your tax liability, and generate financial reports. Chapter 4 is a chapter you shouldn't miss.

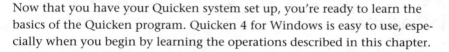
Chapter 2

Learning Your Way Around Quicken for Windows

Now that you have your Quicken system set up, you're ready to learn the basics of the Quicken program. Quicken 4 for Windows is easy to use, especially when you begin by learning the operations described in this chapter.

In this chapter, you learn how to do the following:

- Start the program

- Use Quicken menus

- Use the Iconbar to choose menu commands and options

- Arrange the desktop

- Get help from Quicken when you need it

- Exit from the program when your work is finished

Starting Quicken

In Chapter 1, you learned how to start Quicken for the first time. You start your second session almost the same way; however, you don't have to bother with creating an account, selecting categories, or opening your Quicken file this time.

> **Note**
>
> When you exit Quicken, the file that you were using is saved and reopened the next time that you start the program.

To start Quicken, follow these steps:

1. At the DOS prompt, type **win** and press Enter.

2. From the Windows opening screen, move the mouse pointer to the Quicken icon in the Quicken group window.

3. Double-click the Quicken icon to start the program. (Mouse operations are explained in more detail later in this chapter.)

Quicken starts and opens the last file that you used.

Reviewing the Quicken Application Window

When you start Quicken, the Quicken application window and the Quicken file that you used last opens automatically. (Refer to Chapter 21, "Managing Your Quicken Files," to learn how to open other Quicken files.) The Quicken application window appears, as you see in figure 2.1. (Note that other windows may appear on-screen, depending on which windows were open when you last used Quicken.) Before you begin to learn your way around Quicken for Windows, review the Quicken application window.

Fig. 2.1
This Quicken application window appears when you start the program.

At the top of the window is the *title bar*. Title bars are a common element in all Windows programs. The title bar indicates which program you are using and the filename of the open file. In figure 2.1, *Quicken 4 for Windows - QDATA* appears in the title bar. This means that you're working in Quicken 4 for Windows and using the QDATA file.

Under the title bar, the Quicken *menu bar* appears. The menu bar includes ten menus with commands and options for performing activities in Quicken. Using the menu bar is explained in the section "Using Quicken Menus" later in this chapter.

The next row of icons is called the *Iconbar*. The Iconbar contains icons (or pictures) that represent Quicken commands or options. Selecting commands or options from the Iconbar is much easier than selecting the same commands or options from the menu bar. Using the Iconbar is discussed later in the section "Using the Quicken Iconbar."

In the following sections of this chapter, you learn how to move around the Quicken application window and how to choose the commands and options that you use to perform activities in Quicken.

Working with the Mouse and Keyboard

Quicken, as with most Windows programs, works equally well with a mouse or the keyboard to move around the screen or choose commands. The mouse probably makes learning and searching through the program menus easier. Sometimes, however, using a combination of the mouse and keyboard is the most efficient way to work within Quicken.

Quick keys can save you steps in choosing menus, commands, or options when using the keyboard. Quick keys usually combine the Ctrl, Alt, or Shift key with a letter key or a function key but also may be a single function key. Quick keys are listed to the right of the command or option name in the menu, as shown in figure 2.2.

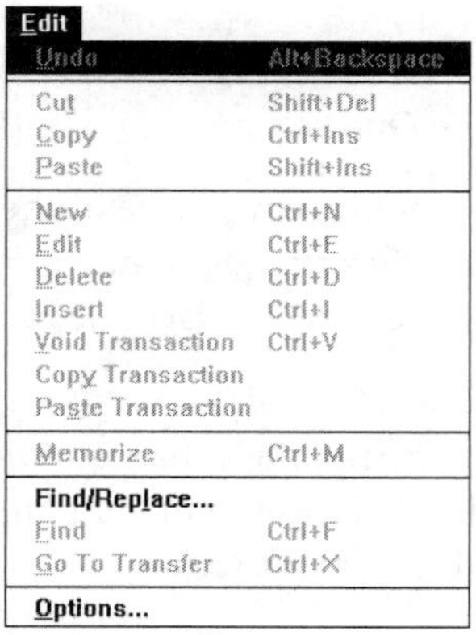

Fig. 2.2
The Edit menu shows several quick keys next to the menu names.

> **Note**
>
> Throughout this book, instructions for using the Ctrl, Alt, or Shift key with another key appear as Ctrl+*letter* (as in Ctrl+F, for example). This notation indicates that you press and hold the first key while you then press the second key. If the second key is a letter key, the key you press can be in upper- or lowercase.

Quick keys are listed next to the menu command or option. Use quick keys to select menu commands and options from the keyboard.

Refer to the table on the back inside cover from a complete listing of quick keys that you can use in Quicken to access menus, select commands and options, and move more quickly within the program.

Using Quicken Menus

Quicken operates through commands and options. You access Quicken commands from separate menus contained in the menu bar at the top of the Quicken application window. Quicken commands are used to initiate an operation or procedure within the program, to display another menu of commands, or to display dialog boxes to select options. Options define how certain Quicken operations and procedures are performed and enable you to make selections.

Figure 2.1 shows the Quicken menu bar, which contains 10 different menus: **F**ile, **E**dit, **A**ctivities, **L**ists, **R**eports, Pl**a**n, Add-Ons, Online, **W**indow, and **H**elp. These menus contain various Quicken commands. When you select a menu name from the menu bar, the menu is pulled down and displayed below the menu bar.

Accessing Menus from the Menu Bar

To access menus from the Quicken menu bar, follow one of these procedures:

- Place the mouse pointer on the name of the menu that you want to pull down and then click the menu name. To choose the **F**ile command on the menu bar, for example, place the mouse pointer on the word **F**ile and click.

- Press Alt to display the highlight bar, use the right- and left-arrow keys to move the highlight bar to the menu name on the menu bar that you want to select, and then press Enter.

or

Press the Alt in combination with the underlined letter in the menu name (bold in this book) within the menu bar. For example, press Alt+F to access the **F**ile menu.

When you access a menu from the menu bar, Quicken displays the pull-down menu.

Choosing Menu Commands and Options

You can use the mouse or the keyboard to choose commands from a menu. To choose commands from a menu by using the *mouse*, place the mouse pointer on the command that you want to choose and click.

To choose commands by using the *keyboard*, use one of the following procedures:

> **Note**
>
> Before you can select a menu command using a mouse or the keyboard, you must first access the menu from the Quicken menu bar as explained in the previous section.

■ Use the up- and down-arrow keys to highlight the command you want to choose, and then press Enter.

■ Press the underlined letter within the command name. To choose the **D**elete command from the **E**dit menu, for example, press D.

> **Note**
>
> Throughout the remainder of this book, the term *choose* relates to using the keyboard or mouse to choose a menu, command, or option. "Choose **F**ile," therefore, indicates that you should press Alt+F or click the word **F**ile on the menu bar.

When a command from a pull-down menu is followed by ... (an ellipsis), Quicken displays another window or dialog box when you choose this command. When you choose the **O**ption... command from the **E**dit menu, for example, Quicken displays the Options dialog box (see fig. 2.3).

Tip
A quick way to view all the Quicken pull-down menus, or lists of commands, is to use the right- and left-arrow keys to move the highlight bar from one menu name to another when one pull-down menu is displayed.

Tip
You can choose some commands by using quick keys. Quick keys are listed to the right of the command in the menu. (A quick keys table appears on the inside back cover of this book.)

Learning Quicken

Fig. 2.3
The Options dialog box appears when you choose the **O**ptions... Command from the Edit menu.

Removing Menus from the Screen

If you don't want to select a command or option from a pull-down menu on-screen, follow one of these procedures:

- Click the menu name in the menu bar.

- Press Esc to remove the menu; however, the highlight bar remains in the menu bar until you press Esc again. At this point, you can use the right- and left-arrows to move to another menu command.

Using the Quicken Iconbar

Quicken displays an Iconbar beneath the menu bar at the top of the screen. The Iconbar contains icons (or pictures) along with text (or labels) so that you can select a Quicken window, list, or activity quickly.

> **Note**
>
> You can select icons from the Iconbar only by using the mouse. You can't use the keyboard to select an icon.

By default, the Iconbar contains the icons listed in table 2.1.

Table 2.1	**The Default Icons on the Iconbar**
Icon	**Function**
Homebse	Accesses Quicken's Homebase feature
Registr	Displays the Register for the current account
Accts	Displays the Account list
Recon	Displays the opening window to reconcile an account
Check	Displays the Write Checks window

Icon	Function
Calendar	Displays the Financial Calendar
Graphs	Displays the Create Graphs dialog box
Reports	Displays the Create Reports dialog box
SnpShts	Displays the new Snapshot report
Options	Displays the Quicken for Windows Options dialog box
Print	Prints the current Register or checks
Help	Displays the Help window for the current Quicken window or menu

To select a function from the Iconbar, simply point to the icon with the mouse pointer and click.

Scrolling the Iconbar

If all the icons in the Iconbar aren't visible, you can scroll the Iconbar left or right by clicking the left- and right-arrow buttons at each end of the Iconbar (review fig. 2.1).

Changing the Iconbar Display

If you want to continue to display the Iconbar but want to change its size so that more of the application window is visible, you can choose to show only icons, only text, or icons and text.

To change the Iconbar display, follow these steps:

1. Choose **E**dit on the menu bar. Quicken displays the **E**dit menu.

2. From the menu, choose **O**ptions or press **O**.

    Quicken displays the Options dialog box, shown earlier in figure 2.3.

3. Choose the **I**conbar option button. Quicken displays the Customize Iconbar dialog box, shown in figure 2.4.

4. Select the Show **I**cons check box if you want icons displayed on the Iconbar. Quicken enters a check mark in the check box (or removes an existing check mark). Quicken displays the change on the Iconbar.

Fig. 2.4
Use the Customize
Iconbar dialog box
to change the
display of the
Iconbar. Select to
show icons only,
text only, or icons
and text.

Select the Show **T**ext check box if you want text displayed on the
Iconbar. Quicken enters a check mark in the check box (or removes an
existing check mark). Quicken displays the change on the Iconbar.

If you want icons *and* text shown in the Iconbar, select the Show **I**cons
and Show **T**ext check boxes. (By default, Quicken shows icons and text
in the Iconbar.) Quicken displays the change on the Iconbar.

5. Choose OK.

6. Choose Done in the Options dialog box.

> **Note**
>
> You can customize the Iconbar by adding icons, editing and deleting existing icons,
> setting up an icon to open a specific account, or setting up an icon to enter a specific
> transaction. Refer to Chapter 22, "Customizing Quicken," to learn how to customize
> the Iconbar.

Arranging the Desktop

The *desktop* refers to the way your screen is arranged with respect to open
windows and their position within the screen. You can arrange open windows in a cascading (or overlapping) format. If you have windows that have
been reduced to icons, you also can arrange the icons within the Quicken
screen. You also can clear your screen by closing all windows. Options from
the **W**indow menu are used to arrange your desktop.

After you have the desktop the way you want it, with certain windows open and in the position you want them, you can save the desktop so that each time you open your Quicken file, windows and their position are exactly the same as the previous work session.

Arranging Windows and Icons

You can arrange windows in a cascade. If you're working in the Write Checks window, for example, you can open the Bank Account Register for your checking account and have it displayed behind (cascade) it. When you cascade windows, the window that appears on top is the active window.

To cascade windows, choose **C**ascade from the **W**indow menu.

You also can arrange icons (windows that you have reduced to a small picture by clicking the down arrow in the upper-right corner of the window) horizontally at the bottom of the screen. To arrange icons, choose Arrange **I**cons from the **W**indow menu.

Closing Windows

If you want to clear your screen, you can close all open windows and all windows that were reduced to icons. To do so, choose Close **A**ll Windows from the **W**indow menu.

Saving the Desktop when Exiting

As you work in Quicken, you may prefer to have the same windows open each time you start the program. You can instruct Quicken to save the open windows and their positions so that each time you start Quicken, the same windows are opened and in the saved position. You also can instruct Quicken to save the desktop automatically as it is displayed when you exit.

To save the current desktop to be displayed each time your Quicken file is opened, follow these steps:

1. Choose Save **D**esktop from the **F**ile menu to display the Save Desktop dialog box, shown in figure 2.5.

Fig. 2.5
With the Save Desktop dialog box, you can save the current desktop or save the desktop automatically as it appears when you exit Quicken.

2. Choose the Save **C**urrent Desktop button.

3. Choose OK to save the current desktop.

To have Quicken automatically save the desktop as it appears when you exit the program, follow these steps:

1. Choose Save **D**esktop from the **F**ile menu to display the Save Desktop dialog box (refer to fig. 2.5).

2. Select the Save Desktop on **E**xit button.

3. Choose OK.

> **Note**
>
> When you save the desktop, Quicken saves the desktop only in the current file. To save the desktop in other Quicken files, open each file and then select the appropriate desktop setting, as explained earlier.

Getting Help

Quicken provides a significant amount of on-screen help for users. Almost anytime you get stuck, you can turn to Quicken for help.

As an alternative way to access commonly used commands and features, Quicken 4 for Windows includes a new Homebase system. Quicken Homebase lists the commands required in the following areas: Setup, Day to Day, Reports, Planning, Investments, and Tools. You learn how to use Quicken Homebase later in this section.

If you want a brief tutorial on Quicken, you can take the Quick Tour. In the Quick Tour, you can select from eight topics that each gives a general overview of the program. If you're uncomfortable with Windows, you also can take the Windows tutorial. You learn how to take the Quicken tutorial in the section, "Taking a Quick Tour of Quicken," later in this chapter.

For beginning users, Quicken provides Qcards that serve as on-screen "cues" to help you with each item in a window or dialog box. The Qcard appears within a window or next to a dialog box and explains each part of the window or dialog box as you go. Qcards are explained later in this chapter in the section, "Using Qcards."

On-screen information provides step-by-step help with Quicken windows so that you know the exact procedure for performing an activity. You can access the Quicken Help system at any time from almost any window.

These help options are described in the following sections.

Using Quicken's Homebase System

Previously in this chapter, you learned how to select commands from Quicken menus and use the Iconbar to perform tasks. With its new Quicken Homebase system, Quicken 4 for Windows offers a new and easy way to access its most commonly used features, like creating accounts, using the Register, writing checks, reconciling your bank account, and so forth. Quicken Homebase includes six different areas from which you can choose to get a listing of activities that you can perform.

To use Quicken Homebase, follow these steps:

1. Choose **H**omebase from the Acti**v**ities menu or click the HomeBse icon from the Iconbar. Quicken displays the Quicken Homebase window shown in figure 2.6.

2. Six different areas are listed in the left side of the Quicken Homebase window. As an area on the left is selected, Quicken displays, as buttons, the features or activities that can be performed within that area. Select an area by clicking it or pressing the Alt key in combination with the underlined letter. Notice in figure 2.6, Quicken displays the activities for **S**etup as Create Accounts, Category List, Intuit Marketplace, Printer Setup, and Quicken Tutorial.

3. To select an activity, click the button that represents the activity that you want to perform. When you select an activity, Quicken displays the appropriate window or dialog box for you to perform the activity.

Fig. 2.6
Quicken
Homebase is a new
and easy way to
access Quicken's
most commonly
used features.

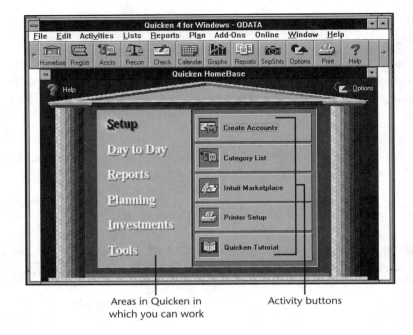

Areas in Quicken in
which you can work

Activity buttons

4. When you complete an activity that you selected, Quicken returns to the Quicken Homebase window. You may now select another area or another activity or double-click the Close button to exit Homebase.

Changing the Way Quicken Homebase Works

If you want to change the way the Quicken Homebase system works, you can change any of three of the Homebase options. To change an option, follow these steps:

1. Select the **O**ptions button in the Quicken Homebase window. Quicken displays the HomeBase Options dialog box shown in figure 2.7.

Fig. 2.7
Change the
way Quicken
Homebase works
by changing
options in the
HomeBase
Options dialog
box.

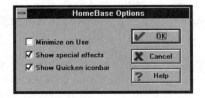

2. To minimize the Quicken Homebase window to an icon when you select an activity, select the Minimize on Use check box.

3. To show special graphics when switching areas in the Quicken Homebase window, select the Show Special Effects check box.

4. To display the Quicken Iconbar at the top of the screen while displaying the Quicken Homebase window, select the Show Quicken Iconbar check box.

5. When you have selected the Homebase options that you want, select OK.

Exiting Homebase

You can leave the Quicken Homebase system at any time. To exit Homebase, click the Close button or press Esc.

Taking a QuickTour of Quicken

Quicken includes a tutorial that you can use to get a general overview of the Quicken program.

To view the Quicken Tutorial, follow these steps:

1. Choose **T**utorials from the **H**elp menu. Quicken displays the **T**utorials submenu, shown in figure 2.8.

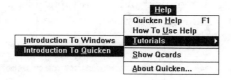

Fig. 2.8
You can choose to view the Quicken Tutorial from the **T**utorials submenu.

2. Choose Introduction To **Q**uicken. Quicken displays the Quick Tour screen (see fig. 2.9).

3. Choose the topic button that you want to view. Quicken displays information on the topic that you selected.

4. When you're finished with Quick Tour, return to the Quick Tour screen (by choosing the **T**opics button) and choose E**x**it.

Fig 2.9
The Quick Tour
screen includes
eight topics from
which you can
choose to get
an overview of
the activities
performed in
Quicken.

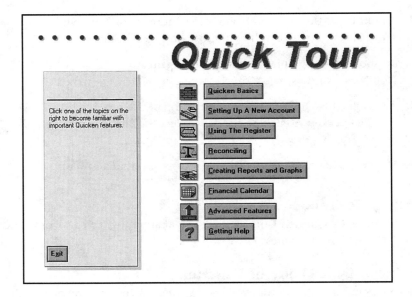

Using Qcards

Quicken provides help and tips on various fields in a window or dialog box in rectangular boxes called *Qcards*. Qcards are on-screen cues to help you fill out each item in a window or dialog box. As you move from item to item, Quicken displays the appropriate Qcard for the current field. Each Qcard presents Help for the current field and, when applicable, includes a Next button to display a second Qcard. Figure 2.10 shows the Qcard for the Category field in the Register.

Fig. 2.10
The Qcard for the
Category field in
the Register
window.

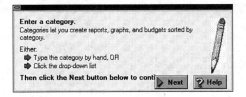

The display of Qcards doesn't interfere with entering information or data in windows or dialog boxes. Qcards always are displayed within the current window or next to the current dialog box and don't prevent you from seeing the current field.

From a Qcard, you can access the Help system for additional help with the current window by clicking the Help icon (refer to fig. 2.10). Quicken displays the Help window when you click the Help icon.

After you become comfortable with Quicken, you may want to turn off the Qcard feature. You can remove Qcards from the current window or turn off the Qcard feature completely so that Qcards are never displayed as you work in Quicken. These options are discussed in the following sections.

Removing Qcards in the Current Window

You can turn off or remove Qcards from the current window without turning off Qcards for other windows or dialog boxes by double-clicking the Close button at the top left corner of the Qcard.

Turning Off Qcards throughout the Program

If you're feeling comfortable with Quicken and don't need the added help from the Qcards for any window or dialog box, you can turn the Qcards feature off (disable it) so that Qcards no longer appear.

To turn off Qcards throughout the program, follow these steps:

1. Display the **H**elp menu by selecting **H**elp from the Main menu.

2. Click the **S**how Qcards command to remove the check mark. Note that by default, this command is selected so that Qcards are displayed.

If you need to turn Qcards back on, perform the same steps above to select the **S**how Qcards command.

Using Quicken's Online Help System

Quicken's online Help system assists with menu commands and options, provides definitions of financial and Quicken terms, explains Quicken procedures (like writing checks or reconciling a bank account), and gives tips for using the program.

To get help information from the Help system, choose Quicken **H**elp from the **H**elp menu. Quicken displays the Quicken 4 for Windows Help window for the selected menu command or the Quicken window that you are currently working in (see fig. 2.11).

Tip
Rather than choose Quicken **H**elp from the **H**elp menu, you can press F1 to access the **H**elp system or click the Help icon in the Iconbar to display directions for the current window or dialog box.

Fig. 2.11

When you select
Quicken Help
from the Help
menu, Quicken
displays the
Quicken 4 for
Windows Help
window.

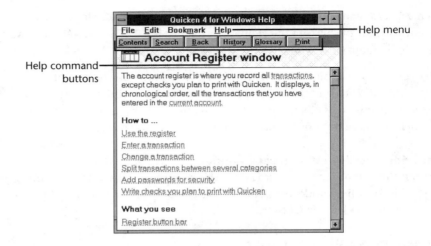

Help menu

Help command
buttons

Exiting the Program

After you finish working in Quicken, you need to exit the program so that
you don't risk losing or damaging any of your financial data. To exit Quicken
and to save your file, choose E**x**it from the **F**ile menu. Your Quicken file is
saved automatically.

Caution
Don't exit Quicken by turning off your computer—otherwise, data from your current work session may not be saved!

CPA TIP: Back Up Your Files Before Exiting
No matter what level of computer experience you have, keeping backup copies of your company or home files is *always* advisable. You can back up your Quicken files each time you exit the program by choosing **B**ackup from the **F**ile menu. Back up time varies depending on the number of transactions in your Quicken file, however, it shouldn't take more than one to two minutes. Refer to Chapter 21, "Managing Your Quicken Files," for more information on backing up your files before exiting Quicken.

From Here...

Now that you know how to get around in Quicken, you'll want to review the following chapters to learn how to get your accounts and categories set up so that you can start entering your financial transactions:

- Chapter 3, "Defining Your Accounts," shows you how to create accounts in Quicken. In Chapter 1, you learned how to create your first accounts. If you need to create other accounts, like an asset account to track the value of your home, or an investment account to track the securities in your portfolio, Chapter 3 shows you how.

- Chapter 4, "Organizing Your Finances," contains important information about setting up categories in Quicken. All of the transactions that you enter in Quicken should be assigned to a category so that you can track your income, expenses, and tax items, create budgets, estimate your tax liability, and generate financial reports. Chapter 4 is a chapter you shouldn't miss.

Chapter 3

Defining Your Accounts

If you followed the steps outlined in Chapter 1, "Preparing to Use Quicken for Windows," you already have defined one account (probably a checking account) as part of setting up your Quicken system. But you may have more than one checking account, one or two savings accounts, and even certificates of deposit for which you want to keep records with Quicken. If you want to use Quicken to track more than one account, you need to define these accounts in Quicken. You then can use Quicken to record transactions in the accounts and track transfers between accounts.

You can add other Quicken account types (Credit Card, Money Market, Asset, Savings, Cash, Investment, and Liability Accounts) to your Quicken file so that you can record and track all your financial activity—not just transactions that occur in a bank account. These account types are explained in general later in this chapter, and more specifically in later chapters. This chapter also gives you some tips on creating accounts—information that should make working with multiple accounts easy.

Quicken stores accounts in the Account List, which includes the account name, account type, account description, number of transactions entered in the account, account balance, and number of checks to print (for checking accounts only). From the Account List, you can open an account, add a new account, edit an existing account, or delete an account.

In this chapter, you learn about the following:

- Quicken account types

- How to decide which accounts to add to your Quicken file

- How to add another account—specifically, bank accounts—and add extra detail about an account

- How to access the Account List
- How to edit and delete accounts
- How to sort the Account List
- How to select an account to use

Defining Account Types

Before you go any further, you should learn a little more about accounts and the types of accounts that you can use in Quicken. A Quicken account is similar to the accounts you use to keep track of your transactions—such as checking, savings, and credit card accounts. You use other types of accounts to track the value of your assets and investments or the principal balance of your liabilities or debts. The types of accounts you can add and use in Quicken are as follows:

- *Checking account.* This account type is the most commonly used. Use checking accounts to set up accounts from which you write checks. You learn how to create a checking account in this chapter.

- *Credit Card account.* This type of account keeps track of your credit card activity, including purchases, payments, other credits, finance charges, and credit card fees. With Quicken for Windows, you can set up an IntelliCharge account to track your Quicken VISA card activity electronically. Chapter 9, "Managing Your Credit Cards," has more information about credit card accounts.

- *Money Market account.* Quicken 4 for Windows provides a separate account type to set up a money market account. You may write checks from a money market account in Quicken. You learn how to create a money market account in this chapter.

- *Asset account.* Use this account type to record and track the value of the things you own, such as your home or auto, or your business's accounts receivable and fixed assets. You learn more about other asset accounts in Chapter 11, "Managing Your Assets and Other Liabilities."

- *Savings account.* The savings account type is new in Quicken 4 for Windows. Create a savings account for savings-type accounts that earn interest. This chapter shows you how to create a savings account.

■ *Cash account.* A cash account keeps track of your cash expenditures, such as the cash you spend on vacations or dining out, or your business's petty cash fund. Chapter 11, "Managing Your Assets and Other Liabilities," has more information on how to use cash accounts.

■ *Investment account.* Use Investment accounts to track your investments, such as stocks, bonds, and mutual funds. The investment account is an advanced feature in Quicken, so be sure to read Chapter 16, "Monitoring Your Investments," to learn about this account type.

■ *Liability account.* Use this account type to record and track the debts you owe, such as the mortgage on your home or other outstanding loan balances. For a business, you can use the other liability account type to track accounts payable or a credit line with the bank. Chapter 10, "Tracking Loans," explains liability accounts used to track amortized loans in Quicken. Chapter 11, "Managing Your Assets and Other Liabilities," has more information on liability accounts for other types of loans.

You need only one account to start using Quicken: your checking account, the account from which you write checks and make deposits. If you're just learning Quicken, don't worry about setting up additional accounts. Chapters 4 through 8 explain how to enter transactions and write and print checks from your checking account. As you get up to speed with Quicken, start adding other accounts to your Quicken system to complete your financial picture.

Deciding Which Accounts to Add

When you first set up accounts for Quicken, adding accounts can get out of hand. You can define Quicken accounts for every checking account you have, regardless of whether the account is active. You also can define Quicken accounts for each of your savings accounts, credit union accounts, money market accounts, and perhaps even accounts for certificates of deposit (CDs). Rather than indiscriminately define accounts for every bank account you have, consider a few ideas and rules for determining which of your accounts should be Quicken accounts:

■ If you want to write checks on the account by using Quicken, you must define a Quicken account.

- If you want to use Quicken's reconciliation feature to explain differences between your records and the bank's, credit union's, or brokerage house's statement, you must define an account.

- If you have transactions in an account that you want to include in Quicken's tax reports or profit-and-loss statements, you must define a Quicken account. You can have, for example, charitable contributions or mortgage interest transactions in separate bank accounts.

The following factors indicate that you probably *don't* need to define a bank, credit union, or brokerage house account as a Quicken account:

- If you don't have any deposits into or withdrawals from the account other than interest income or bank service fees, your monthly statement will suffice for your financial records.

- If you have only a handful of transactions a month (fewer than a dozen) and none represents an account transfer from or to an account for which you will use Quicken, you probably don't need to track the account in Quicken. This choice, however, is a matter of personal preference.

- If you otherwise don't track an account, you probably shouldn't bother to put the account into Quicken—even if you have the best of intentions about becoming more diligent in your record-keeping.

CPA Tip: Measuring Your Net Worth

If you want to measure your *net worth* (assets minus liabilities), you should add a Quicken account for each of your assets and liabilities. You can have, for example, an account with only a few transactions per month but with a large balance. If you don't set up a Quicken account to record these transactions, the account balance (which represents an asset or a liability) isn't reflected in your net worth in Quicken Net Worth reports.

Adding an Account

You need to define or identify accounts for each account you want to track with Quicken. You defined only a checking account, savings account, and/or credit card account when you set up your Quicken system, but you can have as many as 64 accounts in a single Quicken file, and you can have multiple files. (Chapter 21, "Managing Your Quicken Files," discusses files in more detail.) Quicken stores all your accounts in the Account List (see fig. 3.1), which you can access by clicking the Acct button on the Iconbar. If you have more than one Quicken file, a separate Account List is included in each file. The Account List is explained in more detail later in this chapter.

> **Note**
>
> In a Quicken file, you can store up to 64 accounts, however, if you need to increase the number of accounts (up to a maximum of 255), you can copy your file into a new Quicken file. Refer to Chapter 21, "Managing Your Quicken Files," to learn how to copy files.

Fig. 3.1
The Account List window shows all the accounts added to your Quicken file. Quicken can store up to 64 accounts in the Account List.

Accounts are sorted alphabetically by account type. The Account List tabs at the top of the list allow you to display All Types, Bank, Credit, Other, or Invest (Investment) accounts in the Account List. You learn how to use Account List tabs in the section "Sorting the Account List," later in this chapter.

When you add an account, you define it by entering the account name, the balance in the account as of the date that you add the account, and a brief description of the account. You can add even more information about an account, such as the bank name, bank account number, and contact person.

If you want more help as you're creating accounts, Quicken 4 for Windows provides the Guide Me option. When you select the Guide Me option, as you create an account, Quicken interviews you along the way to help you enter the correct information.

Defining the Account

When you add an account to the Account List in your Quicken file, you must define the account by entering the account name, account balance, the date of the account balance, and (optionally) a brief description.

To define and add an account to the Account List, follow these steps:

1. Click the Accts button on the Iconbar, and then choose the **N**ew button in the Account List window (see figure 3.1); or choose the Create **N**ew Account command from the Acti**v**ities menu. Quicken displays the Create New Account dialog box, shown in figure 3.2.

Fig. 3.2

The Create New Account dialog box includes the eight account types in Quicken.

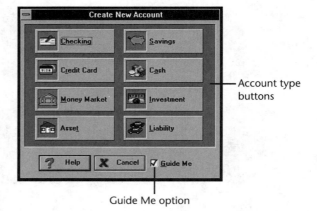

Account type buttons

Guide Me option

2. (Optional) If you want Quicken to "guide" you through the account setup process, click the **G**uide Me check box at the bottom of the Create New Account dialog box. If you feel that you don't need help, don't select this option.

3. Select the account type you want to add by choosing the appropriate button in the Create New Account dialog box. To create a checking account, for example, choose the **C**hecking option. Quicken displays the Create Account dialog box (see fig. 3.3) with the name of the account that you selected in the title bar. For example, if you select to create a checking account, Quicken displays the Create Checking Account dialog box.

   If you selected the **G**uide Me option, Quicken displays a series of dialog boxes that asks you to enter the appropriate information. (Fig. 3.4 shows the first dialog box displayed when you choose to create a checking account). Because these Quicken instructions are straight forward and self-explanatory, the discussion that follows covers adding an account without the **G**uide Me option.

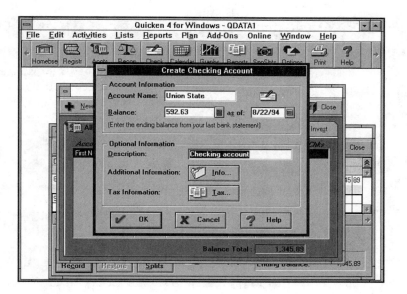

Fig. 3.3
Use the Create Account dialog box to enter information about the new account you are creating.

Learning Quicken

Fig. 3.4
Quicken displays an interview dialog box when creating an account using the Guide Me option.

4. In the **A**ccount Name text box, type the new account name using up to 15 characters. You can use letters, spaces, and any symbols in the account name except the following:

    :] [/ | ^

5. Press Tab to move to the **B**alance text box and type the starting account balance. For bank accounts, like checking, savings, and money market accounts, this dollar amount is the ending balance from your last bank statement.

Don't use commas or dollar signs when you type the balance. If the balance for an account is zero, you must type **0**.

Tip
For best results, use the ending balance from your last bank statement as the balance in a new bank account.

CPA Tip: Naming Accounts

Remember that you have only 15 spaces for the account name. Use an abbreviation of the bank's name; *First National* could become *1stNatl*, for example. This way, you have room for the last four digits of the account number. You then can distinguish accounts easily, as the following example shows:

1stNatl-1234 for a checking account

1stNatl-3272 for a savings account

1stNatl-7113 for CDs

Note

Although you can enter a balance for an account from any source (not just your bank statement), Quicken recommends that you use the ending balance from your last bank statement as the balance you add the account. Make sure, however, that you reconcile your account with that statement before you rely on the amount the bank states you have in the account.

Caution

When you enter the ending balance from your last bank statement as the starting balance in a new account, you must enter all uncleared transactions in the Register for the account. In other words, you must include all transactions that haven't cleared through your bank account by the date of your last statement. If you overlook these transactions, you will have difficulty reconciling your account. Chapter 6, "Using the Register," explains how to enter transactions in the Register.

Tip
To enter dates quickly in date text fields, press the + (plus) and – (minus) keys to move the current date ahead and back one day.

6. Press Tab to move to the A**s** Of text box and type the date on which the balance you entered is correct, using the *mm/dd/yy* format. You can also enter the date by clicking the drop-down button and selecting a date from Quicken's minicalendar. (Refer to Chapter 7, "Using Quicken Shortcuts," to learn more about the minicalendar.) If you use the ending balance from your last bank statement in step 5, enter the statement date (the ending or cutoff date) in the A**s** Of text box.

7. (Optional) If you want to, press Tab to move to the **D**escription text box and type a description of the account, using up to 21 characters.

Descriptions of accounts appear in the Account List window and in reports.

8. (Optional) You can enter additional information for the account that you add to store information about the account, like the account number, contact person, and telephone number. Select the **I**nfo button to display the Additional Account Information dialog box, as shown in figure 3.5.

Fig. 3.5
The Additional Account Information dialog box enables you to enter extra detail for an account.

9. (Optional) Press Tab to move to the text box that you want to complete in the Additional Account Information dialog box. How much information you enter here is up to you. Enter as little or as much as you like.

10. After you enter the information that you want to add for the account, choose OK or press Enter to save the information and return to the Create Account dialog box.

11. (Optional) If the earnings on the account that you are adding are not subject to income tax until a later year, select the **T**ax button so that you can designate the account as tax deferred. Quicken displays the Tax Schedule Information dialog box. Select the **T**ax-Deferred check box. Quicken does not include the earnings from this account in tax reports. Chapter 12, "Estimating and Preparing for Income Taxes," discusses Quicken's tax reports.

12. (Optional) If you want to designate a tax schedule to assign to transfers in or out of the account that you are adding, click the drop-down arrow in the T**r**ansfers In or Transfers **O**ut boxes and select the appropriate tax schedule. (You learn more about assigning tax schedules to accounts and categories in Chapter 12, "Estimating and Preparing for Income Taxes.") Choose OK when the information in the Tax Schedule Information dialog box is complete. Quicken returns to the Create Account dialog box.

> **Note**
>
> The Transfers In and Transfers Out options are not available in the Tax Schedule Information dialog box unless the Use Tax Schedules option is selected from the General Options dialog box. Refer to Chapter 22, "Customizing Quicken," to learn how to set this option.

13. When the information in the Create Account dialog box is complete, choose OK or press Enter. Quicken adds the account to the Account List window.

14. If you want to add more accounts, repeat steps 1 through 13.

Editing Existing Accounts

Tip
If you need to change the starting balance or date for an account, you can edit the Opening Balance transaction that Quicken enters in the Register for the account. Chapter 6 explains how to edit transactions in the Register.

After you add an account to the Account List in your Quicken file, you can change the account name, the account description, or any of the additional information about the account that you entered. You may want to make such changes if, for example, you originally described the account incorrectly. Or you may want to edit an account name and description if you have transferred the account in total to a new account number, or even a new bank.

> **Note**
>
> If you need to change the account type for an account that you have added, for example, change a checking account to a savings account type, you first must export the old account to a QIF file; then create the new account; and then import transactions from the QIF file into the new account. You cannot, however, change an investment account to another type of account. To learn how to export accounts, refer to Chapter 21, "Managing Your Quicken Files."

To edit an account, follow these steps:

1. Select Account from the Lists menu or choose the Accts button on the Iconbar. Quicken displays the Account List window (refer to fig. 3.1).

2. (Optional) If your list of accounts is large, you may want to limit the Account List to make it easier to find the account that you want to edit. To limit the Account List, click the appropriate Account List tab to display only those accounts that include the account that you want to edit. For example, if you want to edit a savings account, select the **B**ank tab so that Quicken displays only bank accounts in the Account List window.

3. Highlight the account you want to edit.

4. Choose Ed**it** from the Account List button bar. Quicken displays the Edit Account Information dialog box for the account that you selected (see fig. 3.6).

Tip
You also can display the Account List window by pressing Ctrl+A.

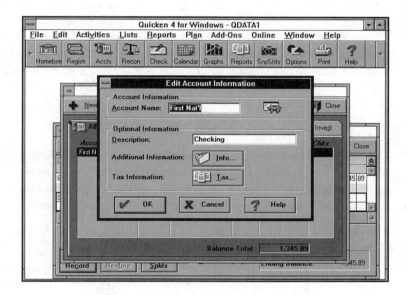

Fig. 3.6
The Edit Account Information dialog box contains the account information that you can edit.

5. Press Tab to move to the text box you want to edit. Type over the existing characters or use the Backspace or Delete key to remove characters.

6. If you want to edit any additional information you may have entered for an account, choose the **I**nfo button. Make the necessary changes in the Additional Account Information dialog box (refer to fig. 3.5) and choose OK. Quicken returns to the Edit Account Information dialog box.

7. Choose OK or press Enter to save your changes to the account and return to the Account List window.

To edit additional accounts, repeat steps 2 through 7.

Deleting Accounts

You can delete an existing account from the Account List. Perhaps you closed an account or decided that an account wasn't worth tracking with Quicken. To delete an account, follow these steps:

1. Select **A**ccount from the **L**ists menu or choose the Accts button on the Iconbar. Quicken displays the Account List window (refer to fig. 3.1).

2. (Optional) If your list of accounts is large, you may want to limit the Account List to make it easier to find the account that you want to delete. To limit the Account List, click the appropriate Account List tab to display only those accounts that include the account that you want to delete. For example, if you want to delete a savings account, select the **B**ank tab so that Quicken displays only bank accounts in the Account List window.

3. Highlight the account you want to delete.

4. Choose **D**elete from the Account List button bar. Quicken displays the Deleting Account dialog box with the name of the account you are deleting (see fig. 3.7). Quicken requires typed confirmation to ensure that you don't mistakenly delete an account with important data.

Fig. 3.7
Quicken displays
the Deleting
Account dialog
box when you
select to delete an
account.

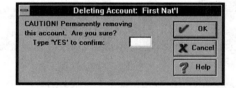

5. To delete the selected account, type **yes** and then choose OK or press Enter.

If you don't want to delete the account, choose Cancel or press Esc; Quicken displays an information dialog box telling you that the account was not deleted. Choose OK to return to the Account List window.

Caution

When you delete an account, you delete the account description and any transactions you recorded in the account. Make sure that you really want to delete the account before taking the steps to do so. Deleting an account with current balances will affect your total net worth. Refer to Chapter 11, "Managing Your Assets and Other Liabilities," to learn how your net worth is calculated.

Sorting the Account List

Quicken 4 for Windows provides tabs in the Account List window (see fig. 3.1) that enable you to sort the list by account type. When you select one of the following Account List tabs, Quicken displays in the list only those accounts that belong to the account group that you select:

Account List Tab	Accounts Displayed
All Types	All accounts
Bank	All checking, savings, and money market accounts
Credit	All credit card accounts, including IntelliCharge accounts
Other	All cash, asset, and liability accounts
Invest	All investment accounts

Selecting an Account to Use

When you start working with multiple accounts, you need to tell Quicken which account you want to use. Suppose that you decide to use Quicken to track a savings and a checking account. Whenever you enter a savings account deposit, you need to make sure that you record the deposit in the savings account and not in the checking account. Similarly, if you withdraw money from the checking account, you need to make sure that the withdrawal is correctly recorded in your checking account and not in the savings account. To record account activity correctly, you first must select the appropriate Quicken account to use.

There are four ways to select an account to use, described here:

- Access the Account List window (see fig. 3.1), highlight the account that you want to use, and select **O**pen from the Account List button bar.

- If you've already worked in the account in your current Quicken session, the account is still open. To activate the Register for the account, click the title bar of the account Register window.

- If the account is still open, but if the account Register window is not visible in your Quicken desktop, select **W**indow from the Main menu to display the **W**indow menu. Quicken lists all active windows in the

Tip

Entering all transactions for an account at one time is more efficient than entering them randomly. Consider collecting several transactions for an account and then recording them at once.

bottom of the **W**indow menu. Select the account name from the **W**indow menu by clicking the account name or pressing the number key that corresponds to the account in the **W**indow menu.

■ Quicken 4 for Windows includes the Account Selector Bar in each Register (see fig. 3.8) and in the Write Checks window. The Account Selector Bar is used to select other accounts directly from a Register. To use the Account Selector Bar, simply click the account button for the account that you want to use. Quicken then displays the Register for the account that you selected.

Fig. 3.8
Account Registers include the Account Selector Bar so that you can easily switch among accounts.

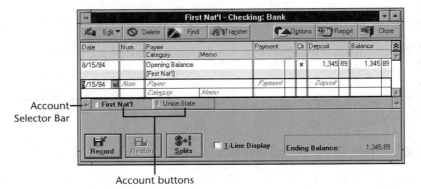

Account Selector Bar

Account buttons

From Here...

You've learned all about accounts, but you still need to know about the categories that Quicken uses to classify your transactions. Refer to the following chapters for more information:

■ Chapter 4, "Organizing Your Finances," contains important information about setting up categories in Quicken. All of the transactions that you enter in Quicken should be assigned to a category so that you can track your income, expenses, and tax items, create budgets, estimate your tax liability, and generate financial reports.

■ Chapter 5, "Writing and Printing Checks," shows you how to write checks from your Quicken accounts.

■ Chapter 6, "Using the Register," explains how to use Quicken's account Register to enter transactions.

Chapter 4

Organizing Your Finances

Before you can manage your finances successfully, you need a system that tracks your income and expenses. To help you track these elements, Quicken uses *categories*. By classifying your income and expenses in categories, you see exactly where your money comes from and where it goes. This information is a vital component of effective financial management and planning. You must know your sources of income and your spending habits before you can gain control of your finances.

You also can use *subcategories* in Quicken to divide a category into smaller categories that provide a more detailed accounting of your income and expenses.

Categories and subcategories, therefore, enable you to monitor the money flowing into and out of accounts. By assigning categories and subcategories to transactions, you can summarize the information in a Register and track tax deductions easily.

Classes are used to organize your finances by more than just income and expenses. Using classes in Quicken enables you to specify the information a transaction covers. Classes are an extension of categories and specify who, where, what, and when. If, for example, you want to track expenses for a rental property you own, you can create and assign a class for expense transactions relating to the property.

This chapter goes into depth on the subject of categories, subcategories, and classes, and how you can use categories to organize your finances and track your income and expenses.

More specifically, you learn how to do the following:

- Add categories and subcategories to the Category & Transfer List
- Rearrange categories and subcategories
- Merge categories and subcategories
- Work with classes and subclasses

Note

This chapter shows you how to assign a category, subcategory, class, or subclass to a transaction. Beginning in Chapter 5, "Writing and Printing Checks," you learn how to enter transactions as you write checks or use the Register.

Working with Categories

Categories enable you to group *income* and *expense* items that flow into and out of accounts. Income or deposits into an account can stem from earned wages from a full-time job, interest income, dividends, revenues from a part-time business, and so on.

Expenses or payments can stem from rent, food, transportation, clothing, part-time business expenses, and so on. By grouping each payment from and each deposit into an account, Quicken easily adds the totals for each type of payment and deposit. You then can see exactly how much each category contributes to the cash flow.

CPA Tip: Cash Inflows Aren't Always Income

Not all cash inflows represent income, and not all cash outflows represent an expense. If you sell stock, for example, the proceeds from the sale aren't considered income. Income from the sale is determined by subtracting the cost basis of the stock from the net sales proceeds (if the result is negative, you incur a loss).

Medical insurance reimbursements also aren't considered income; instead, they offset your medical expense. If you pay $100 to a doctor, for example, you enter a transaction in the Register for $100 and assign the Medical category to the transaction. If you later receive $80 reimbursement from your medical insurance company, the $80 isn't income; instead, it offsets the $100 medical expense transaction that you previously entered. Your net medical expense is $20 ($100–$80).

CPA Tip: Cash Outflows Aren't Always Expenses

If you pay $15,000 for a car, this amount isn't considered an expense. You should enter a transaction in your Bank Account Register for the $15,000 check you write to the car dealer, but rather than assign a category to the transaction, assign an account. In this example, you probably would set up an Asset account for your new automobile (perhaps called *Auto*) and enter the Asset account in the Category field. In essence, this transaction transferred funds from your bank account to another asset account (the account called *Auto*). Transfer transactions like this are explained in Chapter 6, "Using the Register."

Categories enable you to do the following:

- Track and tally income tax deductions for individual retirement accounts, mortgage interest deductions, charitable contributions, and so on.

- Break down checking account deposits and payments into groups of similar transactions so that you can summarize income and expenses.

- Budget income and expenses and compare budgeted amounts with actual amounts.

If you want to use Quicken for a business, the predefined categories enable you to prepare most of the reports you need for managing business finances. These reports include the following:

- A business profit-and-loss statement that resembles and performs most of the calculations required to complete the federal income tax form Schedule C (which reports the profits or losses from a business or profession)

- Income and cash-flow statements on a monthly and annual basis that enable you to understand cash flows and measure business profits or losses

- Accounts receivable reports by customer so that you can track how much each customer owes

- Accounts payable reports by vendor so that you can track how much you owe to each vendor

- Job/project reports that show you the net income for each job or project you set up in Quicken

- Employee payroll reports that track wages paid to each employee and related payroll deductions

- Comparison reports so that you can analyze your progress from period to period

If any of the reports listed look like benefits you want to enjoy as part of using Quicken, you will want to use Quicken's categories. How involved or complicated the use of these categories becomes depends on your goals.

Quicken doesn't require that you assign categories to transactions. If you want to make sure that you assign a category to all your transactions so that your income and expenses are accurately accounted for, you can turn on the **W**arn Before Recording Uncategorized Transactions option. When this option is turned on, Quicken displays a message each time you try to record a transaction in the Register or Write Checks window without a category. You must confirm that you don't want to assign a category to the transaction before you can record the transaction. To learn how to turn on the **W**arn Before Recording Uncategorized Transactions option, refer to Chapter 6, "Using the Register."

CPA Tip: Assign Categories to Every Transaction

If you want your Quicken system to track each item of income and each expense, make sure that you assign a category, subcategory, or other Quicken account to every transaction you enter. Turning on the **W**arn Before Recording Uncategorized Transactions option helps you remember to do so.

Tip
For Canadian users of Quicken, the predefined list of categories includes categories for GST (Goods and Service Tax) and PST (Provincial Sales Tax).

Quicken includes two sets of predefined category lists in the program; Home and Business. You choose the category list that you want to use when you create a new file in Quicken. Consider these lists as starting points. The predefined Home category list provides a long list of income and expense categories that you may find useful for your home finances. Depending on the situation, some categories you don't need may be provided, and other categories you do need may be missing. Similarly, the predefined Business list provides income and expense categories you may find useful in business accounting. If you apply the rules described earlier for devising categories, you should have no problem when using the predefined lists as starting points for constructing a category list that works well for you.

Categories act as building blocks in classifying data the way you want it. You can use the following categories to calculate the tax deduction and budgeted items shown in table 4.1:

Mortgage interest

Mortgage principal

Mortgage late-payment fees

Credit card late-payment fees

Property taxes

Table 4.1   Personal Budget and Tax Categories

Items	Categories Used
Late fees (a budgeted amount)	Mortgage late-payment fees Credit card late-payment fee
Housing (a budgeted amount)	Mortgage principal Mortgage interest Property taxes
Mortgage interest (deduction)	Mortgage interest Mortgage late-payment fees
Property taxes (deduction)	Property taxes

Setting Up Categories

When you create a new file in Quicken, you can choose to use the defined Home or Business categories from the Create Quicken File dialog box as the foundation of the Category & Transfer List (see fig. 4.1). Chapter 21, "Managing Your Quicken Files," describes how to create new files.

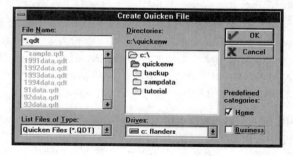

Fig. 4.1
In the Create Quicken File dialog box, you can specify which predefined category list you want to set up in your new file: Home, Business, or both.

If you select the **H**ome option, Quicken copies its predefined list of Home categories to the Category & Transfer List in your file. If you select the **B**usiness option, Quicken copies its predefined list of Business categories to your list.

Note

Quicken enables you to specify which categories are tax-related (a taxable income item or a tax-deductible expense) so that you easily can summarize your tax items to prepare your income tax return. Setting up categories as tax-related also enables you to export your Quicken data to a tax preparation program. See Chapter 12, "Estimating and Preparing for Income Taxes," to learn how to make tax time easier with Quicken.

Tip
Access the Category & Transfer List by choosing **C**ategory & Transfer from the **L**ists menu.

Quicken stores the predefined categories that you select to use (**H**ome or **B**usiness) in the Category & Transfer List (see fig. 4.2). The Category & Transfer List also is where Quicken stores all the subcategories and accounts in your Quicken file. Accounts are listed after the alphabetical listing of income and expense categories (income categories are listed before expense categories). Quicken provides a separate Category & Transfer List for each file.

Fig. 4.2
The Category & Transfer List stores the categories and subcategories that you use to classify transactions.

Button bar   QuickReport button   Scroll bar

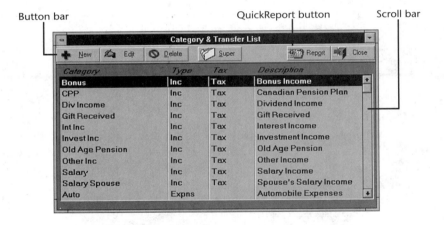

The Category & Transfer List not only lists the categories, subcategories, and accounts, but also shows the category type (income or expense), the account type (bank, cash, investment, and so on), the category or account description, and whether the category or subcategory is tax-related.

You can use the Category & Transfer List to select a category, subcategory, or transfer account to assign to a transaction. You also can use the list to add, edit, or delete categories and subcategories, change a category to a subcategory (and vice versa), and create a QuickReport that lists all transactions assigned to the highlighted category or subcategory.

Adding a Category

You can add categories to the Category & Transfer List by accessing the list and adding a category directly to the list, or you can type the new category name in the Category field while entering a transaction in Quicken.

> **Note**
>
> This chapter describes the steps to add a category directly to the Category & Transfer List. Because you don't learn about entering transactions until the next few chapters, wait until then to learn about adding categories while entering transactions. (See Chapter 5, "Writing and Printing Checks," and Chapter 6, "Using the Register.")

To add a category to the Category & Transfer List, follow these steps:

1. Choose **C**ategory & Transfer from the **L**ists menu (or press Ctrl+C) to access the Category & Transfer List (refer to fig. 4.2).

2. Choose **N**ew to display the Set Up Category dialog box, shown in figure 4.3.

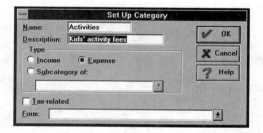

Fig. 4.3
In the Set Up Category dialog box, you can set up income or expense categories or a subcategory.

3. Type the category name you want to use in the **N**ame text box. Category names can contain up to 15 characters and can include any character except the following:

    :] / [| ^

4. (Optional) Press Tab to move to the **D**escription field and type a brief description of the category that you are adding. You can use up to 25 characters to describe the new category.

5. In the Type section, select the appropriate option to designate the category as an income or expense category. Select the **I**ncome option for income categories or the **E**xpense option for expense categories. If you're adding a subcategory, select the S**u**bcategory Of option (adding subcategories is covered later in this chapter).

6. (Optional) If you need to specify the category as tax-related, select the **T**ax-Related check box. The **T**ax-Related check box determines whether the category you are adding is a taxable income or tax-deductible expense item.

   If you specify that a category is tax-related by selecting the check box, Quicken includes that category in tax reports. You then can use tax reports to accumulate transactions that are assigned to tax-related categories to help you prepare your personal or business income tax return.

   If you want to assign a tax form to your tax-related category, continue with step 7; otherwise, skip to step 8.

7. (Optional) If you are setting up a category to report a specific kind of taxable income or tax deduction, click the arrow next to the **F**orm drop-down list box to display the list of tax forms and schedules that you can assign to this category (see fig. 4.4). Scroll the list and select the tax form or schedule that the category pertains to. If, for example, you're adding a category for an itemized deduction, such as tax preparation fees, select Schedule A: Tax preparation fees.

Fig. 4.4
From the Form drop-down list box, select the tax form or schedule to assign to the category that you are adding.

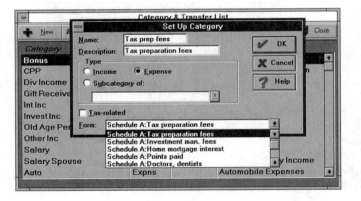

Note

Quicken does not display the **F**orm drop-down list box in the Set Up Category dialog Mbox automatically. You first must select the Use **T**ax Schedules with Categories option in the General Options dialog box. (Access the General Options dialog box by clicking the Options button on the Iconbar and then choosing the **G**eneral option.)

8. When the Set Up Category dialog box is complete, choose OK to save the category information and add the category to the Category & Transfer List. Quicken inserts the new category name in its proper alphabetical order. If you want to change the order of the Category & Transfer List, refer to the section, "Rearranging Categories and Subcategories," later in this chapter.

Note

Generally, you have plenty of room for as many categories as you need. The precise maximum number, however, depends on the computer's available memory, the length of the category names and descriptions, and the other information stored in memory. You usually have room for about 150 categories with 384K of memory and more than 1,000 categories with 512K of memory.

Deleting a Category

You also may want to delete categories, because you don't use a particular category or because you added the category incorrectly. Deleting categories is even easier than adding categories.

To delete a category, follow these steps:

1. Choose **C**ategory & Transfer from the **L**ists menu or press Ctrl+C to access the Category & Transfer List (refer to fig. 4.2).

2. Use the scroll box to move up and down in the Category & Transfer List and highlight the category that you want to delete.

   You also can select a category by typing the first letter of the category name to move the section of the list that contains all categories starting with that letter. For example, to move to the category Subscriptions, press S.

   Tip
   To move quickly to the top or bottom of the Category & Transfer List, press Home to move to the beginning of the list or End to move to the end of the list.

3. When the item you want to delete is highlighted, choose **D**elete. Quicken displays a warning, telling you that you are about to delete a category permanently.

Caution

You can't delete a category that has subcategories. If you need to delete a category with subcategories, first change its subcategories into categories or move the subcategories to another category. Changing and moving subcategories is explained later in this chapter.

4. To remove the category from the category list, choose OK. If you don't want to remove the category, press Cancel.

After you delete a category, you can't use the category unless you add it again. If you assigned previous transactions to the deleted category, Quicken removes the category from the Category field in the transaction (that Category field becomes blank). Transactions assigned to the category that you delete are not deleted. You need to return to the Register and assign a new category to any blank Category field. (Chapter 6 explains how to use the Register.)

Editing a Category

You also can edit a category. Suppose that you run a business and use Quicken to account for, among other things, the wages you pay. Further, suppose that the Wages category was always used for employees working in Washington state. If you create a new category named OR_WAGES to account for the wages you pay to employees working in Oregon, you may want to change the name of the Wages category to WA_WAGES to reflect the change in the significance of the account.

The steps for editing a category roughly parallel the steps for adding one. To edit a category, follow these steps:

1. Choose **C**ategory & Transfer from the **L**ists menu or press Ctrl+C to access the Category & Transfer List (refer to fig. 4.2).

2. Use the scroll box to move up and down in the Category & Transfer List and highlight the category that you want to edit.

3. Choose Ed**i**t to display the Edit Category dialog box, shown in figure 4.5.

Fig. 4.5
The Edit Category dialog box shows the category information that you can edit.

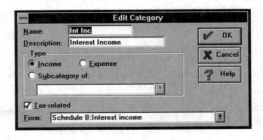

4. Press Tab to move to the text box that you want to edit and then type over the existing information. If necessary, change the **I**ncome, **E**xpense, or S**u**bcategory setting by selecting the appropriate option in the

Type section. You also can change a category's tax status by selecting the **T**ax-Related check box to enter or remove the check mark. Change the tax form or schedule by selecting a new form or schedule from the **F**orm drop-down list box.

5. To save the changes to the category, choose OK or press Enter.

Using Subcategories

If you decide to use categories as building blocks to classify your income and expenses, you need to know about subcategories. Taking the first row of the data from table 4.1, suppose that you create a category called LateFees to track late-payment fees. You then can set up two subcategories of the category LateFees called LMortgage for late mortgage fees and LCredit for late credit-card fees (the *L* stands for *late*.) Then, when you record a transaction to pay late fees on your mortgage, you can assign the subcategory LMortgage to the transaction. When you record a transaction for late fees on your credit card, assign the subcategory LCredit to the transaction. You can design reports so that all your subcategories are shown or just the categories are shown.

When only categories are shown, Quicken shows the sum of all transactions assigned to their subcategories as the category total. In the example, you can show a subcategory line for LMortgage and LCredit to see just how much was spent on late fees for each, or you can lump the LMortgage and LCredit subcategories together and show their total in the category line LateFees.

Adding a Subcategory

You add a subcategory to the Category & Transfer List in much the same way you add a category. To add a subcategory to the Category & Transfer List, follow these steps:

1. Choose **C**ategory & Transfer from the **L**ists menu or press Ctrl+C to access the Category & Transfer List (refer to fig. 4.2).

2. Choose **N**ew to display the Set Up Category dialog box (refer to fig. 4.3).

3. Type the subcategory name you want to use in the **N**ame text box. Subcategory names can contain up to 15 characters and can include any character except the following:

   :] / [| ^

Learning Quicken

4. (Optional) If you want, press Tab to move to the **D**escription field and then type a brief description of the subcategory that you are adding. You can use up to 25 characters to describe the new category.

5. In the Type section, select the S**u**bcategory Of option.

6. Click the arrow next to the S**u**bcategory Of drop-down list box to display the list of categories. Scroll the list to select the category to which you are adding the subcategory.

7. (Optional) Subcategories can be specified as tax-related in the same way as categories. If you need to specify the subcategory as tax-related, refer to steps 6 and 7 in the section "Adding a Category" earlier in this chapter.

8. When the Set Up Category dialog box is complete, choose OK to save the subcategory information and add the subcategory to the Category & Transfer List.

Quicken inserts the new subcategory name under the category to which it pertains, or its parent category. If a category has more than one subcategory, Quicken places the new subcategory within the other subcategories in its proper alphabetical order.

Editing and Deleting Subcategories

You can edit a subcategory at any time. When you change a subcategory name, all previous transactions assigned to that subcategory also are changed. To edit a subcategory, follow the same steps for editing a category, as explained earlier in this chapter.

You also can delete a subcategory if you no longer need it. When you delete a subcategory, Quicken permanently removes it from the Category & Transfer List. Previous transactions assigned to the subcategory that you subsequently delete are merged into the parent category. If, for example, you assign transactions to the subcategory Movies, under the category Entertainment, and then delete the Movies subcategory, Quicken assigns all those transactions to the category Entertainment.

To delete a subcategory, follow the same steps for deleting a category, as explained earlier in this chapter.

Rearranging Categories and Subcategories

After you establish your category list and add categories and subcategories, you can change categories to subcategories and vice versa. You can change a category to a subcategory (*demote* a category), change a subcategory to a category (*promote* a subcategory), or move a subcategory under another category (so that it has a different parent category). You may decide, for example, to make the category, Auto Fuel, a subcategory of the category Auto. You can make this change so that Quicken changes the previous transactions assigned to these categories.

Changing Categories and Subcategories

To change a category to a subcategory (demote a category), or to change a subcategory to a category (promote a subcategory), follow these steps:

1. Choose **C**ategory & Transfer from the **L**ists menu or press Ctrl+C to access the Category & Transfer List (refer to fig. 4.2).

2. Use the scroll box to move up and down in the Category & Transfer List and highlight the category or subcategory that you want to change.

3. Choose Ed**i**t to display the Edit Category dialog box.

4. To change a category to a subcategory, select the S**u**bcategory Of option. Then choose the arrow in the drop-down list box to display the list of categories and subcategories and select the new parent category.

   To change a subcategory to a category, select the **I**ncome option or the **E**xpense option.

5. Choose OK or press Enter.

Moving a Subcategory to Another Category

You can change the parent category for a subcategory by moving the subcategory to another category. You may want to move a subcategory called Auto Lease, for example, from the Auto category to the Lease Expense category.

To move a subcategory to another category, follow these steps:

1. Choose **C**ategory & Transfer from the **L**ists menu or press Ctrl+C to access the Category & Transfer List.

2. Use the scroll box to move up and down in the Category & Transfer List and highlight the subcategory that you want to move.

3. Choose Edit to display the Edit Category dialog box.

4. Choose the arrow in the Subcategory Of drop-down list box to display the list of categories and subcategories and select the new parent category.

5. Choose OK or press Enter. Quicken repositions the subcategory under the new parent category in the Category & Transfer List.

Merging Categories and Subcategories

You can merge one category or subcategory into another. You may want to merge the Int Inc (Interest Income) category into the Invest Inc (Investment Income) category if you find that you aren't really using the former category, for example. When you merge two categories or subcategories, Quicken assigns the category or subcategory name that you retain (in this case, Invest Inc) to each transaction assigned to the merged category or subcategory (Int Inc).

Before you can merge a category into another category, you first must change the category that you want to merge into a subcategory. To merge a subcategory into another, move the subcategory so it's a subcategory of the subcategory that you want to retain. If the subcategory you are merging has its own subcategories, they follow the parent subcategory as you move to another subcategory. (Quicken enables you to create a subcategory of another subcategory, a subcategory of a subcategory of a subcategory, and so forth!) If, for example, you have a subcategory named Condo Exp and want to merge it with a subcategory named Condo Repairs, you first must make the subcategory Condo Exp a subcategory of Condo Repairs.

Figure 4.6 shows how categories and subcategories are listed in the Category & Transfer List. Notice how categories and subcategories appear in outline format with a category listed first, followed by its subcategory (indented to the right). A subcategory of a subcategory is indented to the right a little further.

To merge a category or subcategory, follow these steps:

1. Choose Category & Transfer from the Lists menu or press Ctrl+C to access the Category & Transfer List (refer to fig. 4.6).

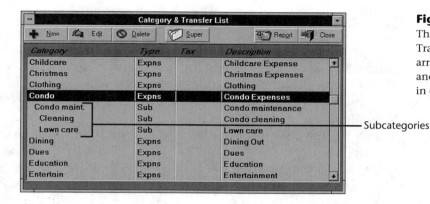

Learning Quicken

Fig. 4.6
The Category &
Transfer List
arranges categories
and subcategories
in outline format.

2. Use the scroll box to move up and down in the Category & Transfer List
   and then highlight the category or subcategory that you want to merge.

3. Choose Edit to display the Edit Category dialog box.

4. If you are merging a category into another category, change the category that you don't want to retain into a subcategory of the category
   that you want to keep. Follow the steps given earlier in the section
   "Changing Categories and Subcategories."

   If you are merging a subcategory into another subcategory, change the
   subcategory that you don't want to retain into a subcategory of the
   subcategory that you want to keep.

5. After you change the category or subcategory in step 4, highlight the
   subcategory that you don't want to keep.

6. Choose Delete. Quicken displays a message asking if you want to merge
   the subcategory with its parent.

7. Choose Yes to merge the subcategory with its parent.

Note

Occasionally, you may want a printed copy of the Category & Transfer List. You also
may want to review the list with a tax advisor at her or his office to verify that you are
tracking all tax deduction categories, or you may want to keep a paper copy of the
list as an aid to entering transactions. You can print the Category & Transfer List by
choosing Print List from the File menu (or pressing Ctrl+P while the Catagory &
Transfer List is open).

Recategorizing Transactions

With Quicken 4 for Windows, you can search your transactions for those assigned to a specific category or subcategory and replace them with another category or subcategory. Assume, for example, that you've been entering transactions in Quicken for six months and have been assigning the category *Utilities* to all utility expenses; gas, water, electric. Now, however, you want to break out your utilities expense into subcategories for each type. You would first have to create the subcategories *Gas, Water,* and *Electric* as subcategories of the category *Utilities*. Then, you can use the Recategorize command to search your transactions for those assigned to the *Utilities* category and change the category for these transactions to the appropriate subcategory. This new feature is quick and easy and prevents you from having to look through the Register and change each transaction, one by one.

To recategorize transactions, follow these steps:

1. Choose Recategorize from the Activities menu. Quicken displays the Recategorize window shown in figure 4.7.

Fig. 4.7
The Recategorize window lets you search for transactions assigned to a category and then change the category to another.

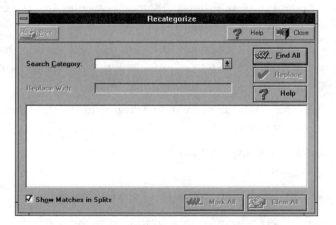

2. In the Search Category drop-down list box, select the category or sub-category that you want to search for. If you want to find transactions that are unassigned, leave the Search Category drop-down list box blank.

3. Select the Find All button. Quicken searches your transactions and lists all of those assigned to the category or subcategory that you specified in the Search Category drop-down list box. Quicken displays the date, account, check number, payee, category, memo, clear status, and amount for each transaction. To display each line in a split transaction, select the Show Matches in Splits option check box at the bottom of the Recategorize window.

4. To replace the category or subcategory in all transactions, select the Mark All button, Quicken enters a check next to each transaction. To select the transactions to recategorize, select the Clear All button (Quicken removes the check from all transactions) and then click each transaction that you want to recategorize.

5. Next, select a replacement category or subcategory in the Replace With drop-down list box. Quicken replaces the category in each selected transaction with the category or subcategory that you select.

6. To recategorize the marked transactions, select the Replace button.

Working with Classes

Categories and subcategories group revenues and expenses by the type of transaction. You can categorize income transactions, for example, as gross sales, other income, and so on. You can categorize expense transactions as car and truck expenses, supply expenses, utilities, and so on. But you may want to slice the data in other ways. You also may want to see income or expenses by job or project, by salesperson or product line, and by geographic location or functional company areas.

Classes add a second dimension to the income and expense summaries that categories provide. Nonbusiness use of Quicken probably doesn't require this second dimension. Business owners, however, can find Quicken's classes a powerful way to view financial data from a second perspective.

In addition to using two categories (Product and Service) to track income, you can use classes to determine which salespeople actually are booking the orders. With three salespeople, use these three classes: Joe, Bill, and Sue. In addition to seeing the sales of company products and company services, you also can see things such as the sales Bill made, the product sales Joe made, and the service sales Sue made. In effect, you have two perspectives on this income—the type of income (which appears as a product or service) and sales-people (which appear as Joe, Bill, or Sue). Table 4.2 shows these perspectives.

Table 4.2   Two Perspectives on Income

Kind of	Salespeople Booking Orders		
Income	Joe	Bill	Sue
Product	Joe's product sales	Bill's product sales	Sue's product sales
Service	Joe's service sales	Bill's service sales	Sue's service sales

Note

The basic problem with classes is that they don't give you a way to budget. You can't budget by classes, for example. This problem may not seem too important to you right now, but before you begin to use classes, review Chapter 17, "Budgeting with Quicken."

Defining a Class

The first step in using classes is to define the classes you want to use. The classes you choose depend on how you need or want to view the financial data you collect with Quicken. Unfortunately, giving specific advice on picking appropriate classes is difficult, and Quicken doesn't provide predefined lists of classes (as it does for categories). Classes usually are specific to the particular personal or business finances. You can follow one rough rule of thumb, however; look at the kinds of questions you now ask but can't answer by using categories alone.

A real-estate investor may want to use classes that correspond to individual properties. A law firm may want to use classes that represent each partner or each client. Other businesses have still different views of financial data. After you define the classes you want to use, you are ready to add the classes in Quicken. You can add as many classes as you want.

To add a class, follow these steps:

1. Choose Class from the Lists menu (or press Ctrl+L) to display the Class List (see fig. 4.8). The Class List includes an alphabetical listing of all classes set up in Quicken.

2. Choose New to display the Set Up Class dialog box, shown in figure 4.9.

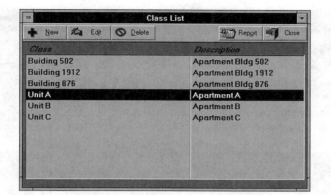

Fig. 4.8
You can select to
use a class, add a
new class, edit a
class, or delete a
class from the
Class List.

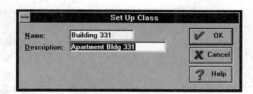

Fig. 4.9
The Set Up Class
dialog box is used
to define a new
class.

3. In the **N**ame text box, type the name you want to use for the class.
Class names can contain up to 15 characters, including spaces. You
can't use the following characters:

    :] / [| ^

4. (Optional) Press Tab to move to the **D**escription text box and type a
description for the class.

5. Choose OK or press Enter. Quicken adds the class to the Class List in
alphabetical order.

You also assign a class to a transaction as you enter the transaction in
Quicken (see Chapters 5 and 6). The class that you want to assign to a transaction is entered in the Category field, after the category name. Note, however, that you don't have to assign a category to a transaction to assign a class
to the transaction.

To assign a class to a transaction, access the Class List (as explained in the
preceding steps) and select the class name from the list, or type a forward
slash (/) in the Category field for the transaction and begin typing the class
name. Note that as you begin typing the class name, Quicken's QuickFill
feature searches the Class List for the class name that matches the first few
characters that you type and then enters the rest of the class name for you.

Note

You can add a class to the Class List *on the fly*, or as you enter a transaction in Quicken. Just type the new class name in the Category field (after the forward slash). When the name isn't found in the Class List, Quicken asks whether you want to add it. You then can define the new class and immediately return to the transaction so that you can assign the new class to the transaction.

Note

If you want a quick report of all transactions assigned to a category or subcategory, you can use Quicken's QuickReport feature. When you use QuickReport, Quicken lists all transactions (in all accounts) assigned to the selected category or subcategory through the current date. Quicken shows the date, account, check number (if applicable), description, memo, category or subcategory name, cleared status, and amount for each transaction in the list. To see a QuickReport, highlight a category or a subcategory in the Category & Transfer List and click Report in the button bar. To remove the QuickReport from your screen, choose **C**lose at the top of the report. You can also create a QuickReport of all transactions assigned to a class in the Class List by clicking the Rep**o**rt button.

Editing and Deleting Classes

If you start defining classes, you also need to know how to edit and delete these classes. The classification scheme you use undoubtedly can change over time. Suppose that you are a real-estate investor and use classes to track properties. You probably buy and sell properties over a period of time. Alternatively, if you are a bookkeeper for a law firm, the lawyers working at the firm probably change over a period of time. Both examples indicate a need for editing classes. The steps for editing and deleting are simple and familiar if you previously edited or deleted categories.

To edit a class, follow these steps:

1. Choose C**l**ass from the **L**ists menu (or press Ctrl+L) to display the Class List (refer to fig. 4.8).

2. Use the scroll box to move through the Class List and highlight the class that you want to edit.

3. Choose Ed**i**t to display the Edit Class dialog box, which includes the class name and description.

4. Press Tab to move to the text box that you want to change and then type over the existing information.

5. Choose OK or press Enter to save the changes to the class.

To delete a class, follow these steps:

1. Choose Class from the Lists menu (or press Ctrl+L) to display the Class List (refer to fig. 4.8).

2. Use the scroll box to move through the Class List and highlight the class that you want to delete.

3. Choose Delete. Quicken warns you that you are about to delete a class permanently.

4. Choose OK or press Enter to complete the deletion; choose Cancel or press Esc to cancel the deletion.

Using Subclasses

If you use classes to add another dimension to the reporting and recording process, you also may want to use subclasses. *Subclasses* are classes within classes. If you use a geographical scheme to create classes, the classes may be states. Within each state, you may choose to use subclasses corresponding to portions of the state. A class called Washington, for example, may have the subclasses E. Washington and W. Washington. California, another class, may have the subclasses N. California (excluding the Bay Area), Bay Area, S. California (excluding Los Angeles County), and Los Angeles County.

You don't actually add subclasses to the Class List. Instead, you set up a class name for each item that you want to function as a subclass. Then, when you assign a subclass to a transaction (see Chapter 5 and Chapter 6), type the class, a colon (:), and then the subclass. When assigning the class California and the subclass Bay Area to a transaction, for example, enter the following in the Category field:

California:Bay Area

You edit and delete subclasses by following the same procedures as you do for classes.

Caution

If you have assigned a subclass to transactions, you may not be able to display a QuickReport when you select that transaction from the Class List and then choose the Report button.

CPA Tip: Using Subclasses for Sales Tax

Subclasses are helpful for sales taxes based on a state, county, or city with different tax rates for each jurisdiction or if you must report sales within each jurisdiction.

From Here...

Now that you've learned how to use categories, you're ready to learn how to enter transactions in Quicken by reviewing the following chapters:

- Chapter 5, "Writing and Printing Checks," shows you how to enter information in the Write Checks window and assign categories to check transactions.

- Chapter 6, "Using the Register," explains how to use Quicken's Registers to enter transactions and assign categories.

Chapter 5

Writing and Printing Checks

With Quicken's check-printing feature, you can write checks and pay bills faster and more efficiently than you ever thought possible. You can pay bills faster because Quicken provides a collection of shortcuts and time-saving techniques that automate and speed up check writing and bill paying. You can pay bills more efficiently because Quicken helps you keep track of the bills coming due and provides categories with which you can classify the ways you are spending your money.

The check-writing feature in Quicken is one of the program's most powerful tools. Writing checks with Quicken not only saves you valuable time, but spares you from having numerous opportunities to make clerical errors. When you write a check using Quicken, you simply enter the information in a check facsimile window (the Write Checks window), and Quicken takes it from there. The program records the check in the Check Register, adjusts your account balance, and adds the transaction amount to the appropriate category, which you specify when you write a check. From this point, you must print the check, sign it, put the check in an envelope (Intuit even provides window envelopes for checks), and mail it.

This chapter describes the basics of writing and printing checks with Quicken. The following topics are discussed:

- Using the Write Checks window

- Adding artwork to on-screen checks

- Writing and recording checks

- Reviewing and editing checks

- Deleting and voiding checks

- Splitting a check transaction by assigning more than one category

- Printing checks

Displaying the Write Checks Window

You need to display the Write Checks window when you want to do the following:

- Write checks

- Review checks that you haven't printed

- Edit or delete checks that you haven't printed

- Print checks

If you use Quicken to print checks, use the Write Checks window to enter check information. Manual checks that you write are entered in the Check Register (see Chapter 6, "Using the Register").

Note

You can't write a check from any other type of account other than a bank account. The bank account that you normally use is your checking account, but may also be savings accounts or money market accounts with check-writing features.

To display the Write Checks window, shown in figure 5.1, use one of the following methods:

- Choose **W**rite Checks from the **A**ctivities menu.

- Choose the Check button on the Iconbar.

- Press Ctrl+W.

Write Checks button bar

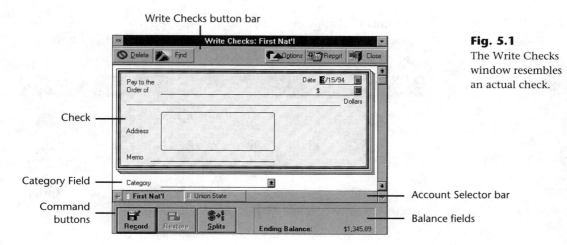

Check

Category Field

Command
buttons

Account Selector bar

Balance fields

Fig. 5.1
The Write Checks
window resembles
an actual check.

Reviewing the Write Checks Window

You use the Write Checks window to collect the information you use to print
checks. After you collect the information, Quicken records the check in the
Register for the bank account you're using.

The Write Checks window includes the following items:

- *Write Checks button bar.* This new Quicken 4 for Windows feature includes buttons at the top of the Write Checks window that you can use
  to perform the following activities:

Button	Description
Delete	Deletes the check currently displayed
F**i**nd	Finds a check
O**p**tions	Displays the Check Options dialog box so that you can change check settings
Rep**o**rt	Generates a QuickReport that lists all transactions that contain the same payee as the currently displayed check
Close	Closes the Write Checks window

- *The actual check.* Enter the date, payee, amount, and memo (optional).
  If you select the Allow **E**ntry of Extra Message on Check option, an

additional field appears on the check so that you can enter an informational message. (You learn how to select this option later in the section "Setting Check Options.")

> **Note**
>
> Check numbers aren't entered in the Write Checks window; you specify the check numbers when you print checks. The steps for completing checks are described later in the section "Writing a Check."

- *Category field.* Assign a category, subcategory, class, subclass, or transfer account to a check transaction in this field.

- *Account Selector Bar.* Use the Account Selector Bar to select the checking account from which you want to write a check.

- *Command buttons.* Use the command buttons to record the check, restore the information in an edited check, or open the Splits window so that you can assign more than one category to the check.

- *Balance fields.* These fields show the total amount of the checks that you have written but not yet printed, the current balance in the checking account (as of the current date) before checks are printed, and the ending balance in the account after the checks are printed. You can't make entries to the balance fields in the Write Checks window.

Moving Around the Write Checks Window

You easily can move from check to check in the Write Checks window using the scroll bar on the right side of the window. Just click the down arrow to move to the next check, or click the up arrow to move to the preceding check.

Use the scroll box to move quickly through checks in the Write Checks window. First, point the mouse pointer at the scroll box. Then press and hold down the left mouse button as you drag the scroll box (move up or down) the scroll bar. As you are scrolling, Quicken displays a date box to the left of the scroll box. The date shown in the date box represents the date of the check displayed when you release the scroll box.

You also can use the keyboard to move from check to check and from field to field in the Write Checks window.

Learning Quicken

The following keys help you move around the Write Checks window quickly and easily:

Press	To Move
Tab	Forward one field
Shift+Tab	Backward one field
Home	Beginning of current field
Home Home	Beginning of first field in current check
End	End of current field
End End	End of last field in current check
Ctrl+→	Forward one word within a field
Ctrl+←	Backward one word within a field
PgUp	To the preceding check written
PgDn	To the next check written or a blank check
Home (3 times)	To the first check written (but not yet printed)
End (3 times)	To a blank check
End (3 times)	To the last check written and PgUp

Displaying Check Artwork On-Screen

To make writing checks a little more fun and easier on the eyes, Quicken 4 for Windows includes artwork that you can display in the Write Checks window. The artwork is displayed on the check image and *does not* print on your checks. You can, however, print logos on your preprinted checks which you learn about later in this chapter in the section, "Setting Up Quicken to Print Checks."

To display check artwork in the Write Checks window, follow these steps:

1. Select the Options button in the Write Checks button bar. Quicken displays the Check Options dialog box (see fig. 5.8).

2. Select the Checks tab.

3. Move to the Artwork on Check Entry Screen option. Click the option check box.

4. Select the graphic that you want displayed in the Write Checks window. You can select one of seven, including Sea Scape, Skyline, City Nights, and so forth.

5. Choose OK to save the Artwork on Check Entry **S**creen option setting. Figure 5.2 displays City Nights artwork in the Write Checks window.

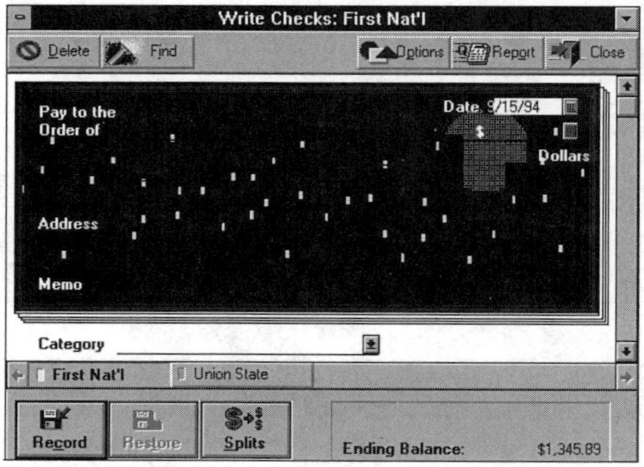

Fig. 5.2
Adding artwork to the Write Checks window.

Writing a Check

The mechanics of writing a check with Quicken closely resemble those for manually writing a check. The only real difference is that Quicken's Write Checks window makes the process easier. With Quicken, writing a check means you simply complete the Write Checks window. You fill in as many as seven fields: Date, Pay to the Order of, $ (Amount), Address, Memo, Category, and Message. After you write the check, you're ready to record and print the check.

Tip
In the Write Checks window, press Ctrl+R to switch to the Register for the current checking account. To switch from the Register to the Write Checks window, press Ctrl+W.

To write a check, follow these steps:

1. Display the Write Checks window (refer to fig. 5.1).

2. If the checking account that you want to use isn't shown in the Write Checks window title bar, select the correct account from the Account Selector Bar. If the checking account that you want to use isn't shown, use the right and left arrow buttons to scroll through the Account Selector Bar to display the account that you want to use.

3. Press Tab to move to the Date field and type the date of the check. Enter the date in the *mm/dd/yy* format, but typing the slashes isn't

necessary (such as **511** for 5/11/95). Note that Quicken automatically enters the current year, so you don't have to enter it.

> **Note**
>
> The first time you write a check in the current Quicken session, the program fills the Date field with the system date (the current date according to your computer's internal memory). After you write your first check using the Write Checks window, Quicken fills the Date field with the last date used.
>
> You can change the date by typing over the existing date or by pressing the + (plus) and – (minus) keys to change the date one day at a time. To change the existing date of 5/11/95 to 5/13/95, for example, press the + key twice.

Tip

To use Quicken's pop-up calendar to enter dates in the Write Checks window, just click the calendar button in the Date field.

4. Press Tab to move to the Pay to the Order Of field, where you enter the name of the person or business (called the *payee*) that the check pays. Type the name you want to appear on the check. Because you have space for up to 40 characters, you shouldn't have any problem fitting the payee's name.

Tip

Quicken also provides a drop-down list box in the Pay to the Order Of field that you can use to select a payee. Quicken adds a payee's name to the list each time you write a check or enter a transaction for a new payee.

> **Note**
>
> The QuickFill feature makes entering payees and transactions fast and easy. When you type a few characters of the payee name, Quicken searches all previous entries in the Check Register, plus your memorized transactions, for a transaction with a payee name that begins with the characters you type. (Memorized transactions represent stored transaction information from previously entered transactions.) When a transaction is found, QuickFill fills in the rest of the payee name for you. If this payee is the one you want, press Tab; QuickFill fills in the rest of the check for you—the check amount; memo (if used); and category, subcategory, or transfer account. Chapter 7, "Using Quicken Shortcuts," explains how to use QuickFill and memorized transactions.
>
> If the check that QuickFill completes for you is the way you want it, you're ready to record the check (go to step 10). If the amount is different, continue with step 5 to learn how to enter or edit check amounts.

5. Press Tab to move to the $ (Amount) field and enter the check amount. You can use up to 10 characters to enter the amount. Characters can consist of only numbers, commas, and decimal points. Quicken enters commas if you don't and if room is available for them.

The largest value you can enter in the Amount field is 9999999.99. Because this number is difficult to read without commas (the number is $9,999,999.99), you probably want Quicken to have enough room to insert commas. If you use some of the 10 characters for commas, the largest value you can enter is 999,999.99.

> **Note**
>
> If you need to add several amounts together for a check, Quicken's pop-up calculator can help. Click the calculator button in the $ (Amount) field to display a calculator you can use to compute the check amount. Chapter 7, "Using Quicken Shortcuts," explains how to use this feature.

When you complete the $ (Amount) field and press Tab, Quicken writes out the amount on the next line of the check just as you do when writing a check manually. To save space, Quicken may abbreviate hundred as *Hndrd*, thousand as *Thsnd*, and million as *Mill*.

6. (Optional) Press Tab to move the cursor to the first line of the address block. The optional Address field provides five 30-character lines. If you use envelopes with windows and enter the payee's address in this field, the address shows in the envelope window. This field saves time that otherwise is spent addressing envelopes.

   When using the Address field, you need to type the payee's name on the first line. Quicken provides a shortcut for you. If you type ' (apostrophe) or " (quotation marks) and then press Enter, Quicken copies the name from the Pay to the Order Of field. (Because the Pay to the Order Of field has space for 40 characters and the address lines have only 30 characters, this shortcut may cut off up to the last 10 characters of the payee's name.)

   Press Tab to move to the second line of the address block. Type the street address or post office box and press Tab. Then type the city, state, and ZIP code. Press Tab to type any additional address information on the fifth address line.

7. (Optional) Press Tab to move to the Memo field, which you can use to describe the check further (such as **April rent**) or to tell the payee your account or loan number.

8. Press Tab to move to the Category field, in which you can assign a category or subcategory to a check so that you know what the check covers, such as utilities expense, interest expense, or entertainment. You also can use the Category field to describe the class into which a check falls. (Chapter 4, "Organizing Your Finances," describes categories and classes.) To learn about the Category field, refer to the later section "Assigning Categories and Classes to Checks."

You can use the Category field to enter another Quicken account if the check you are writing represents a transfer of funds between your checking account and another account. (Chapter 6, "Using the Register," explains transfer transactions.) Quicken provides a listing of the most typical categories for home or business use to enable you to categorize your most frequent transactions quickly.

9. After the check is complete, record the check by choosing Record at the bottom of the Write Checks window, or press Enter if the cursor is positioned in the last field in the Write Checks window.

After Quicken records the check, your computer beeps, and the recorded check scrolls off screen. A new, blank check hidden by the preceding check is left on-screen, ready to be completed. Once a check is recorded it is ready to print. Refer to the section, "Printing Checks," to learn how to print checks.

> **Note**
>
> You can turn off the beep through the **B**eep When Recording and Memorizing check option. Turning off the beep is particularly attractive if you are entering several checks at a time and become annoyed with the constant beeping. The section, "Setting Check Options " later in this chapter, explains how to select general options and turn off the beep.

Quicken enables you to add an additional message to checks. If you select the Allow **E**ntry of Extra Message on Check options, Quicken displays the Message field, as shown in figure 5.3, on the check. (See "Setting Check Options," later in this chapter.) To enter a message, press Tab after you assign a category to the check in the Category field to move to the Message field.

Fig. 5.3

The Write Checks window displays a Message field if you select the check option that enables you to enter an extra message on checks.

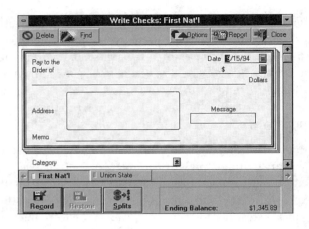

The message field gives you another 24 characters for additional information you want printed on the check, such as an account number for a credit card or a loan number for a mortgage. Because this information doesn't show through an envelope window, don't use the line for address information.

Assigning Categories and Classes to Checks

To help you track how you spend your money, Quicken uses categories, subcategories, classes, subclasses, and accounts to classify your expenses. In the Write Checks window, Quicken has designated the Category field for this purpose.

When you press Tab to move to the Category field in the Write Checks window and then click the down arrow, Quicken displays the list of categories, classes, and accounts from the Category & Transfer List. From this list, highlight the category that you want to assign to the check. Then choose the category name (or subcategory, class, or account name) or press Enter. Quicken inserts the category name in the Category field in the Write Checks window.

The QuickFill feature in Quicken also works from the Category field in the Write Checks window. When you type the first characters in a category name, Quicken searches the Category & Transfer List to find the first category that begins with the characters you type. Suppose that you have a category named Entertainment, and that it's the only category name that starts with the letters Ent. If you type **Ent**, Quicken searches the Category & Transfer List until it finds a category that begins with Ent. When Quicken finds Entertainment, the QuickFill feature fills in the remaining letters of the category name.

You also can use QuickFill to enter an account name in the Category field when transferring money to another account. You learn more about using QuickFill to write checks in Chapter 7, "Using Quicken Shortcuts."

You also assign subcategories, classes, and subclasses to checks in the Category field. Subcategories, classes, and subclasses are explained in Chapter 4, "Organizing Your Finances."

To assign a subcategory, click the drop-down list box to display the Category & Transfer List and select the subcategory from the list. Quicken enters the parent category name and the subcategory name in the Category field. You also can use the QuickFill feature to enter a subcategory in the Category field. Type or enter the category first; then type a **:** (colon) and begin typing the subcategory name. QuickFill enters the rest of the subcategory when it finds the matching subcategory name in the Category & Transfer List.

To assign a class to a check transaction, type a **/** (slash) after the category or subcategory name in the Category field. Then type the class name or press Ctrl+L to display the Class List and select a class from the list. To assign a subclass to a check transaction, type a **:** (colon) after the class name. Then type the class that you want to function as a subclass, or press Ctrl+L to display the Class List and select the class from the list.

Tip
The QuickFill feature also works with classes. After you type a few characters after the slash, QuickFill enters the rest of the class when it finds the matching class in the Class List.

> **Note**
>
> You can add categories, subcategories, and classes to the Category & Transfer List and the Class List (respectively) as you enter checks, or *on the fly.* Just type the new category, subcategory, or class, and Quicken displays the appropriate dialog box to enter information about the new subcategory or class.

Quicken doesn't require that you assign categories to transactions. If you want to track your income and expenses so that you know where your money comes from and where it goes, however, you should assign a category to each transaction that you enter in Quicken. To ensure that you do assign a category to each transaction, you can select the **W**arn Before Recording Uncategorized Transactions check option. When you select this option, Quicken displays a warning message each time you record a transaction without an assigned category. In the section "Setting Check Options," later in this chapter, you learn how to select this option.

Learning Quicken

Note

Quicken provides defined Home, Business, or Home and Business categories, which you select when you create your Quicken data file. The Home Category list provides categories for most general household expenses, and the Business Category list includes general business income and expense categories. Home and Business categories combine both sets of categories into the category list. To access these categories, click the drop-down list box in the Category field or press Ctrl+C.

Changing the Date Field Display

You can change the way dates are entered and displayed in the Write Checks window by setting the option that controls how dates are entered. By default, Quicken displays dates as *mm/dd/yy*; however, you can change the way dates are displayed (to *dd/mm/yy*) by changing the date option. If you change the date option, dates are entered and displayed with the day first, followed by the month. August 18, 1995, for example, is entered and displayed as 18/08/94 instead of 08/18/95. See the section "Setting Check Options," later in this chapter, to learn how to set the date option.

The way dates are entered has no impact on the way dates are printed on checks. To change the date format on printed checks, also see the section "Setting Check Options" later in this chapter.

CPA Tip: Paying Early to Receive Discounts

Businesses and individuals often receive discounts for paying bills early, so consider early payment when writing checks. In effect, not taking early payment discounts is an extremely expensive way to borrow money from the vendor. Suppose that a vendor normally requires payment within 30 days but gives a two percent discount for payments received within 10 days. If you pay within 30 rather than 10 days, you pay the vendor a two percent interest charge for paying 20 days later. Because one year contains roughly 18 20-day periods, the two percent for 20 days equals approximately 36 percent annually.

Although you may need to borrow this money, you probably can find a much cheaper lender. As a rule of thumb, if a vendor gives you a one percent discount for paying 20 days early, you are borrowing money from her or him at about an 18 percent annual interest rate if you don't pay early. A three percent discount works out to a whopping 54 percent per year.

Reviewing and Editing Checks

From the Write Checks window, you can return to, review, and edit the checks you write. You can correct errors in a payee's name, for example, change the check amount, or change the category or subcategory assigned to the check. Suppose that you write a check to pay several bills to the same person or business, such as the bank where you have your mortgage, your car loan, and a personal line of credit. If you receive another bill from the bank, you may need to change the check amount.

> **Note**
>
> When you write and record a check in the Write Checks window, Quicken enters the check transaction in the Check Register; however, the check remains accessible from the Write Checks window until you print the check. Quicken doesn't store checks in the Write Checks window after they are printed. To review checks that have been printed, you must access the Check Register and then locate the checks by using the Find window. Chapter 7, "Using Quicken Shortcuts," explains how to locate checks and transactions.

You can use the scroll bar on the right side of the Write Checks window to move through the checks that you have written but not yet printed. Click the up arrow on the scroll bar to display the preceding check; click the down arrow to display the next check. You also can press PgUp to display the preceding check, press PgDn to display the next check, press Home three times to display the first check, or press End three times to display the last check.

Quicken arranges by date the checks you have written at the Write Checks window but haven't printed. Those checks with the earliest dates are listed first, followed chronologically by later checks. Checks with the same date are arranged in the order you entered them. To edit a check you already have recorded, display the check you want to change, and then edit the appropriate fields.

Deleting and Voiding Checks

You can delete, at any time, checks that you have written but not yet printed. Checks that you already have printed, however, must be voided so that you have a complete record of every check number in your Check Register. The following sections explain how to delete and void checks in Quicken.

Caution

You shouldn't delete a check that you have written and printed with Quicken. When you delete a check, Quicken removes all record of the transaction. Deleting the check removes the check information and leaves a gap in your check-numbering sequence. Instead, you need to void a check transaction that you want to remove because of a lost check, a check that you have stopped payment on, or an improperly printed check, but don't delete such checks. Information for voided transactions remains in the Check Register so that you can track each prenumbered check.

Deleting Checks

You can delete a check that you have written at the Write Checks window as long as you haven't printed the check. You may want to delete a check that you have written if, for example, you discover that you have already paid the bill or if you decide against making the payment at all.

Note

After checks are printed, Quicken no longer stores them in the Write Checks window. Printed check information is saved in the Check Register. Chapter 6, "Using the Register," teaches you how to use the Check Register.

To delete a check from the Write Checks window, follow these steps:

1. Use the scroll bar or the PgUp or PgDn keys to display the check that you want to delete.

2. Choose **D**elete from the Write Checks button bar or press Ctrl+D.

3. Quicken displays the message OK to Delete transaction? (see fig. 5.4). Choose OK to delete the check.

Fig. 5.4
Quicken confirms whether you want to delete a check.

When you delete a check, Quicken removes all check information from the Write Checks window and the Check Register.

Voiding Checks

You may need to void a check when you want to stop payment, when you lose a check and write another one to replace it, or when a check prints incorrectly and you must print another. To void a check, go to the Check Register, highlight the transaction, and then choose **V**oid Transaction from the **E**dit menu (or press Ctrl+V). You learn more about voiding transactions in the Check Register in Chapter 6, "Using the Register."

> **Note**
>
> Because you never need to void a check that you haven't yet printed, you don't void checks from the Write Checks window.

Splitting Check Transactions

The Write Checks window provides a field for assigning a category or subcategory to the check transaction. You can assign a check written to the electric company, for example, to the Utilities category. You can assign a check written to pay for office supplies to the Supplies category. Many transactions, however, fit into more than one category, like the payment to your credit card company or a department store. When you need to assign a check to more than one category, use the **S**plits command button at the bottom of the Write Checks window. When you choose **S**plits, Quicken displays the Splits window, which provides additional category fields and more space to assign categories and subcategories to a check (see fig. 5.5).

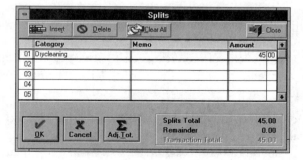

Fig. 5.5

The Splits window provides additional category fields so that you can assign more than one category to a check transaction.

CPA Tip: Tracking Income and Expenses with Split Transactions

When you want to track your income and expenses closely, enter split transactions for payments to department stores and discount stores where you buy different types of items. If you don't split the transaction to record a check to pay your Sears charge for tools, clothing, and cosmetics purchases, for example, and instead lump the total check transaction into one category, your expenses aren't accurately reflected.

To split a check transaction, follow these steps:

1. Enter the date, payee, check amount, address (if applicable), and memo (if applicable) for the check, as explained earlier in this chapter.

2. Choose **S**plits. Quicken displays the Splits window (refer to fig. 5.5).

Tip
You also can display the Splits window by pressing Ctrl+S.

3. In the first Category field, type the category name or click the drop-down list box to select a category from the Category & Transfer List.

Note

Quicken includes the **D**rop Down Lists Automatically option that automatically displays drop-down lists for some fields when you move to those fields. If this option is selected, the drop-down list in the Category field in the Splits window automatically appears. If this feature annoys you because the list covers the command buttons in the Splits window, you can change the **D**rop Down List Automatically option. Refer to the section, "Setting Check Options," later in this chapter, to learn how to change this option.

Use the Category field in the Splits window in the same way that you use the Category field in the Write Checks window. You also can use the Category field to record transfers to other accounts. Up to 30 lines are available in the Splits window to assign categories, subcategories, or transfer accounts.

4. (Optional) Press Tab to move to the Memo field. Type a description of the category or the amount. The Memo field provides a 27-character space that you can use to describe a transaction, to explain why you selected a category, or to detail how you calculated the amount.

5. Press Tab to move to the Amount field. You can use the Amount field in two ways, depending on whether you accessed **S**plits before or after you enter the amount on the Write Checks window.

If you chose the **S**plits button *before* you make an entry in the $ (Amount) field on the Write Checks window, Quicken adds each amount you enter in the Splits window's Amount field and then enters this total in the $ (Amount) field in the Write Checks window.

If you chose the **S**plits button *after* entering a check amount in the Write Checks window, Quicken shows this amount in the first Amount field in the Splits window and in the Splits Total at the bottom of the Splits window. If you then enter a number in the first Amount field in the Splits window, Quicken calculates the difference between the check amount in the Write Checks window and the new amount you entered, and then places this difference in the second Amount field in the Splits window.

Quicken keeps track of the amounts that you have assigned to transactions in the Splits window. Notice the Transaction Total field, which shows the difference between the Splits Total and the Remainder amount (refer to fig. 5.5).

> **Note**
>
> You can enter percents in the Splits window's Amount fields. If you enter a check for $1,200 and 25 percent of this amount is to be entered in the first Splits field, move to the Amount field, type **25%**, and press Tab. When you press Tab to move to the next field, Quicken calculates the number that equals 25 percent of $1,200 and enters this value in the Amount field.

6. Press Tab to move to the next line of the Splits window. Repeat steps 3 through 5 for each category and amount combination you want to record. You can record up to 30 category and amount combinations. Figure 5.6 shows a completed Splits window.

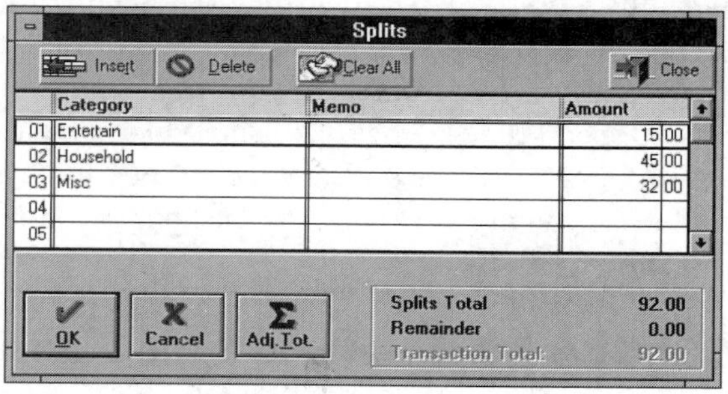

Fig. 5.6
Use the Splits window for a check transaction to assign more than one category.

If you use all 30 split transaction Amount fields, Quicken has nowhere to make the Write Checks window amount equal to the total Splits Total amount. You manually must adjust the Write Checks window amount or one of the Splits window amounts. You also can choose Adj. **T**ot. (Adjust Total) to total the Amount fields in the Splits window and insert the total into the $ (Amount) field in the Write Checks window.

7. To record the categories and amounts in the Splits window, choose OK. Quicken returns to the Write Checks window and indicates the split transaction with the word —SPLITS— in the Category field (see fig. 5.7). Quicken also displays a check mark and an X in the Category field. Click the check mark to reopen the Splits window; click the X to clear all lines in the Splits window and assign only one category or subcategory to the check transaction.

8. Choose Re**c**ord to record the check with the split transaction amounts.

Fig. 5.7
Quicken enters the word —SPLITS— in the Category field of the Write Checks window when you assign more than one category or subcategory to a check.

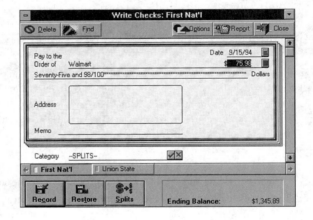

If you use check forms with *vouchers* (the additional sheets that appear with the checks detailing who and what they are for) and enter individual invoices and invoice amounts in the Splits window, Quicken prints this information on the voucher. Vendors then can record your payments correctly, and you no longer have to spend time trying to explain which invoice a check pays. Remember that room is available on the voucher only for the first 15 lines in the Splits window. If you use all 30 lines in the Splits window, only half of the split transaction detail appears.

Calculating Check Amounts in Split Transactions

You can calculate the amount that you want to write a check for by using the Splits window. Perhaps you have several invoices from the same vendor, but each invoice represents a different type of expense that you want to assign to different categories. You can use the Splits window to assign the categories, enter the amounts, and calculate the total amount to enter as the check amount in the Write Checks window.

To have Quicken calculate the check amount in a split transaction, follow these steps:

1. Fill out the Write Checks window as usual, except for the amount.

2. Choose **S**plits (or press Ctrl+S) to display the Splits window (refer to fig. 5.5).

3. Enter the information in the Splits window. As you enter amounts, Quicken keeps track of the split transaction amounts in the Transaction Total field at the bottom of the window.

4. After you finish entering lines in the Splits window, choose Adj. **T**ot. (Adjust Total). Quicken adds the entries in the Amount fields in the Splits window and enters the total in the $ (Amount) field in the Write Checks window.

5. Choose OK or press Enter to return to the Write Checks window.

6. (Optional) If you need to return to the Splits window to make a change, choose **S**plits or click the check mark in the Category field, make the necessary changes, and then choose Adj. **T**ot. again to recalculate the check amount.

7. At the Write Checks window, choose Re**c**ord to record the check.

Editing Split Transactions

You can change the information in the Splits window just as you can change any other transaction. To edit a split transaction, follow these steps:

1. Display the check whose split transaction information you want to edit.

2. Choose **S**plits or click the check mark in the Category field to display the Splits window.

3. Press Tab to move to the field in the Splits window that you want to edit and select a new category, type a new memo, or enter a new amount.

You also can use the following buttons from the Splits window button bar to edit information:

Insert	Inserts a line between two other lines in the Splits window
Delete (Ctrl+D)	Deletes the highlighted line in the Splits window
Clear All	Clears all lines in the Splits window

> **Note**
>
> If you change an amount in a split transaction, the Splits window may not balance (the Splits Total won't equal the Transaction Total). If necessary, you can choose Adj. Tot. to recalculate the transaction amount. Don't choose Adj. Tot. to recalculate if the amount in the $ (Amount) field in the Write Checks window is the correct amount and you're just reallocating amounts to categories or subcategories in the Splits window.

4. After making changes in the Splits window, choose OK to save the changes and return to the Write Checks window.

5. Choose Record to record the changed split transaction.

> **Note**
>
> Just as you can delete checks with only one category or subcategory assigned to it, you also can delete split transactions. Use the same discretion when deleting a split transaction that you use for deleting a check assigned to only one category or subcategory, as explained earlier in this chapter.

Undoing Split Transactions

After you split a check transaction, you can go back, undo the split, and assign only one category or subcategory to the transaction. Follow these steps to undo a split transaction:

1. Display the check whose split transaction you want to undo.

2. Click the X in the Category field. Quicken asks whether you want to Delete all split lines.

3. Choose **Y**es. Quicken enters the first category from the Splits window in the Category field and deletes the remaining categories and amounts from the Splits window.

4. Change the category in the Category field, if necessary, and select Re**c**ord.

Setting Check Options

Quicken enables you to set check options so that you can fine-tune the check-writing features in the program to work the way you want them.

To set check options, follow these steps:

1. Choose O**p**tions from the Write Checks button bar. Quicken displays the Check Options dialog box, shown in figure 5.8. The Check Options dialog box includes tabs to select **Ch**ecks, **Mi**scellaneous, and Quic**k**Fill options. Figure 5.8 shows the general **Ch**ecks options that control how checks are printed. To display miscellaneous check options shown in figure 5.9, click the **Mi**scellaneous tab. To display the options that control the way QuickFill works, as seen in figure 5.10, click the Quic**k**Fill tab.

Tip

You can change any of the check option settings at any time.

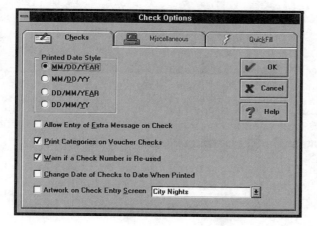

Fig. 5.8

The Check Options dialog box for Checks includes the areas in which you can set options for printing checks.

Margin (right side): **Learning Quicken**

Fig. 5.9
The Miscellaneous settings included in the Check Options dialog box control how you enter information in the Write Checks window.

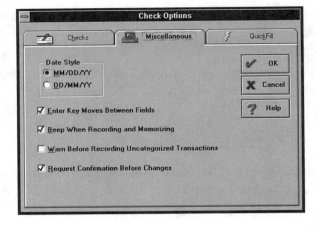

Fig. 5.10
The QuickFill settings included in the Check Options dialog box control the way the QuickFill feature works when entering checks.

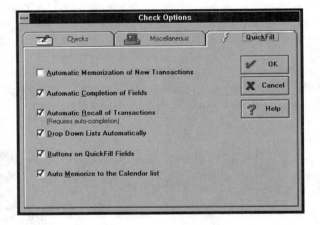

3. Move to the check option that you want to change and turn it on or off. Turn an option on by selecting the blank button or check box for that option. Turn an option off by selecting it again.

Tip
Aligning checks in your continuous-feed printer is easy with Intuit's automatic on-screen alignment feature; you no longer have to align by trial and error.

4. When you're finished setting options, choose OK to save the check option settings and return to the Write Checks window.

Printing Checks

Before you can begin to print checks, you must choose the proper printer settings so that Quicken knows the printer that you are using, the check format, and so forth. After you have the correct printer settings to print checks, you need to position them in your printer properly before you start printing.

Before you begin to print checks with Quicken, make sure that your printer is set up in Windows to print in Windows applications. Refer to Chapter 1, "Preparing to Use Quicken for Windows," to learn how to set up Windows to use your printer. Also, review your checks to make sure that you've entered the correct spellings for payees and correct check amounts.

CPA Tip: Reviewing Checks for Errors

After you receive your checks from Intuit, review them carefully to ensure that they are free of printing errors. Most importantly, examine the bank account number to make sure that it is correct. If you find an error, return the checks immediately and have them reprinted. Unless the printing error was caused by wrong information you submitted, your checks are reprinted at no charge.

Setting Up Quicken to Print Checks

Before you can begin printing checks, you must enter information about your printer and the style of checks you are using.

Note

Don't try to print checks with Quicken until you enter the information about your printer. Checks don't print properly unless Quicken knows the type of printer you are using, the paper feed your printer uses, the style of checks you use, and the printing style (print left, print centered, or print portrait style).

Tip
You can print a logo on your checks if the logo comes from artwork in a Windows bitmap (.BMP) file and is not larger than one-inch square.

To set up Quicken to print checks, follow these steps:

1. Choose Printer **S**etup from the **F**ile menu.

2. From the Printer Setup submenu, choose **C**heck Printer Setup. Quicken displays the Check Printer Setup dialog box (see fig. 5.11).

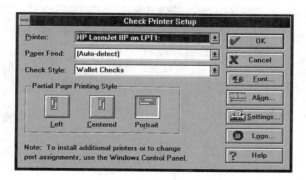

Fig. 5.11
Use the Check Printer Setup dialog box to tell Quicken about your printer and the check style that you are using.

3. If your installed printer doesn't appear in the Printer drop-down list, select the correct printer from the list.

4. Quicken uses the Auto-detect option to determine whether your printer is continuous-feed or page-oriented. If the paper feed isn't correct, choose the **P**aper Feed drop-down list to select the appropriate paper feed for your installed printer.

5. Choose the Check St**y**le drop-down list box to display a list of check styles. Select the check style that matches the checks you ordered.

> **Note**
>
> Entering the correct check style is extremely important when you set up Quicken to print checks. The information on checks doesn't print the same for different check styles. If you don't enter the correct check style when you set up Quicken to print checks, you can change the check style when printing checks.

6. In the Partial Page Printing Style section, choose the position that matches the way you load a partial page of checks in your printer.

> **Note**
>
> The partial page printing style applies only to page-oriented printers.

7. (Optional) Select the **F**ont command button to display the Check Printing Font dialog box (see fig. 5.12). Here, you can change the font, font style, and size that Quicken uses to print information on checks. Quicken shows a sample of the font, style, and size in the Sample area. If you don't see a sample, choose Regular from the Font St**y**le list box.

Fig. 5.12
The Check Printer Font dialog box to set the font, font style, and size that Quicken uses to print information on checks.

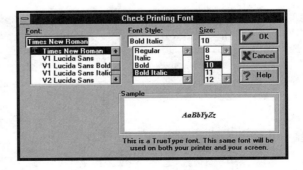

Choose OK to save your font selections. Quicken returns to the Check Printer Setup dialog box.

8. You can change other print settings, such as the paper tray, paper size, orientation, and number of copies by choosing **S**ettings. Quicken displays a dialog box for your installed printer. Figure 5.13 shows the dialog box for a Hewlett-Packard LaserJet IIP printer.

   Set the correct resolution, paper size, and source. If you are using a printer that supports different memory configurations, specify how much memory is available for your printer. (Notice that the **M**emory text box isn't available if your printer doesn't support different memory configurations.) Choose the appropriate paper position for printing: **P**ortrait or **L**andscape. Leave the **C**opies setting at 1 for check printing. If your printer supports cartridge fonts (built into the printer drive for your printer), choose a cartridge from the Car**t**ridges list box.

   When the settings in the printer dialog box are the way you want them, choose OK to return to the Check Printer Setup dialog box.

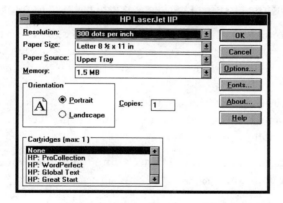

Fig. 5.13
The HP LaserJet IIP dialog box shows the default settings for the Hewlett Packard LaserJet IIP printer. You can change any of the default settings.

9. Choose OK to save the printer settings in the Check Printer Setup dialog box.

From the Check Printer Setup dialog box, you can align your preprinted checks.

> ### Note
>
> From the printer dialog box (refer to fig. 5.11), you can choose **O**ptions to change the dithering and intensity control options. *Dithering* determines how detailed the graphic images appear in printed documents. Choosing coarse dithering, for example, produces graphic images at 300 dpi (dots per inch). *Intensity control* increases or decreases the darkness of graphics. You shouldn't need to change these options, as they aren't relevant to check printing.
>
> You also can install fonts for your printer by choosing **F**onts from the printer dialog box shown in figure 5.13. Installing fonts is beyond the scope of this book. If you want to venture out and install new fonts to use in Quicken, refer to your Windows and printer manuals to learn how to install new fonts.

Aligning Checks

Before you start printing checks, you should print a sample check to ensure that your checks are properly positioned and aligned in your printer and that the vertical and horizontal print settings are correct. Use the sample checks that were enclosed in your Quicken software package to print a test check.

After you go through the process of aligning checks by entering the vertical and horizontal print settings, the alignment settings in Quicken remain and you don't need to repeat this process each time you print checks.

Aligning Continuous-Feed Checks

To print a sample check and adjust the printer alignment for a continuous-feed printer, follow these steps:

1. Insert the continuous-form checks into the printer as you would insert continuous-form paper.

2. Choose Printer **S**etup from the **F**ile menu.

3. Choose **C**heck Printer Setup from the Printer Setup submenu. Quicken displays the Check Printer Setup dialog box.

4. Choose Al**i**gn. Quicken displays the Alignment for Continuous Feed Printers dialog box.

5. The Alignment for Continuous Feed Printers dialog box includes two methods for aligning checks; **C**oarse and **F**ine. If you want to adjust your printer alignment by one line or more, select **C**oarse and proceed to step 6. If you want to make small horizontal or vertical alignments, select **F**ine and proceed to step 9.

6. If you use the **C**oarse method to align continuous-feed checks, Quicken tells you not to adjust your printer now. Select OK to print a sample check.

7. Quicken prints the sample check and then displays the Type Position Number dialog box. If the sample check printed correctly, choose OK.

   If the sample check did not print correctly, enter the number from the check form's pin-feed strips that the pointer arrow points to. (*Pin-feed strips* are the strips of holes on the sides of the check forms. Your printer uses these holes to move the check forms through your printer.) Only even numbers show on the pin-feed strips. The odd numbers are identified by hash marks. Choose OK after you enter the pointer line number.

8. Quicken prints another sample check. Review the sample check to make sure that it is properly aligned. If so, choose OK. If not, repeat step 7.

9. If you use the **F**ine method to align continuous-feed checks, Quicken displays the Check Printer Alignment dialog box shown in figure 5.14.

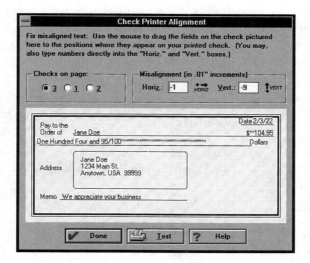

Fig. 5.14
You can make small horizontal or vertical adjustments in the Check Printer Alignment dialog box.

Note

For continuous-feed checks, disregard the Checks On Page section of the Check Printer Alignment dialog box.

10. Choose **T**est. Quicken prints a test check to Jane Doe. Review the test check to make sure that Quicken printed the information in the proper positions on the check. If the check information was printed in the correct positions, you don't need to change the alignment settings and you're ready to print checks in Quicken.

    If the check information isn't printed in the correct positions, you need to enter alignment settings so that Quicken knows where to print the information on your checks.

11. You can enter the approximate values, measured in .01-inch increments, that the printed information was off from the correct positioning on the check. For information that is printed too far to the left or right on the check, enter the approximate distance in the **H**oriz text box. For information that is printed up or down too far, enter the approximate distance in the **V**ert text box.

    Using the alignment cursor, however, to move the text on the check in the Check Printer Alignment window is much easier. Just hold down the left mouse button as you move (drag) the text around in the on-screen check until it looks the same as the printed test check. Then, release the left mouse button to leave the text where you placed it. Quicken automatically enters the appropriate values in the **H**oriz and **V**ert text boxes.

> **Note**
>
> If the printing needs only a small adjustment vertically or horizontally, increase or decrease the values in the **H**oriz or **V**ert text boxes by one or two. Repositioning the text by extremely small increments is difficult when using the mouse.

12. When the text in the on-screen check in the Check Printer Alignment dialog box matches the positioning on the test check, choose **T**est to print another test check. Quicken uses the alignment of the text in the on-screen check to adjust the text on the printed check.

13. Review the test check for proper positioning. If the information on the test check is printed in the correct positions, choose OK to return to the Check Printer Setup dialog box. Choose OK again to save your check alignment settings.

If the text on the test check didn't print in the correct positions, repeat steps 11 and 12.

Aligning Single Sheet Checks

If you're using a laser, inkjet, PostScript, or other page-oriented printer, you also need to print a test, or sample, check to determine the proper alignment settings. To print a test check and adjust the alignment for a page-oriented printer, follow these steps:

1. Load regular paper into your page-oriented printer.

2. Choose Printer **S**etup from the **F**ile menu.

3. Choose **C**heck Printer Setup from the Printer Setup submenu. Quicken displays the Check Printer Setup dialog box.

4. Choose Al**i**gn. Quicken displays the Check Printer Alignment dialog box (see figure 5.14).

5. Choose **T**est. Quicken prints a test check to Jane Doe. Figure 5.15 shows the test check (on plain paper) printed by Quicken on a page-oriented printer.

Review the test check to make sure that Quicken printed the information in the proper positions on the check. If the check information was printed in the correct positions, you don't need to change the alignment settings, and you're ready to print checks in Quicken. Choose OK to return to the Check Printer Setup dialog box and then choose OK again to save your check alignment settings.

6. If the check information isn't printed in the correct positions, you need to enter alignment settings so that Quicken knows where to print the information on your checks. In the Checks on Page section of the Check Printer Alignment dialog box (see figure 5.14), choose the number of checks on the preprinted check form page that you are aligning.

Tip

Use plain paper when printing a test check on page-oriented printers so that you don't waste any pre-printed checks. You can overlay the plain-paper test check on your preprinted checks to see how the print lines up.

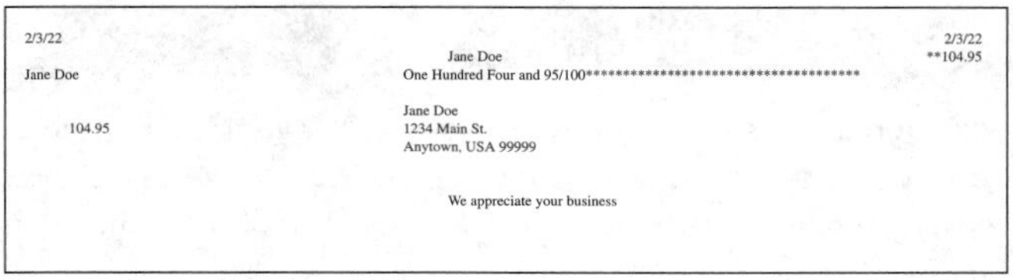

Fig. 5.15

A test check printed on plain paper on a page-oriented printer. Match the printed text to a blank check.

Learning Quicken

> **Note**
>
> You must enter alignment settings for partial pages of checks. Therefore, you must enter alignment settings for a page with two checks and enter alignment settings for a page with one check.

7. In the **H**oriz and **V**ert text boxes, you can enter the approximate values, measured in .01-inch increments, that the printed information was off from the correct positioning on the check. For information printed too far to the left or right on the check, enter the approximate distance in the **H**oriz text box. For information that is printed up or down too far, enter the approximate distance in the **V**ert text box.

    Using the alignment cursor to move the text on the check in the Check Printer Alignment window is much easier, however. Just hold down the left mouse button as you move (drag) the text around the on-screen check until it looks the same as the printed test check. Then, release the left mouse button to leave the text where you placed it. Quicken automatically enters the appropriate values in the **H**oriz and **V**ert text boxes.

> **Note**
>
> If the printing needs only a small adjustment vertically or horizontally, increase or decrease the values by one or two in the **H**oriz or **V**ert text boxes. Repositioning the text by extremely small increments is difficult when using the mouse.

8. When the text in the on-screen check in the Check Printer Alignment dialog box matches the positioning on the test check, choose **T**est to print another test check. Quicken uses the alignment of the text in the on-screen check to adjust the text on the printed check.

9. Review the test check for proper positioning. If the information on the test check is printed in the correct positions, choose OK to return to the Check Printer Setup dialog box. Choose OK again to save your check alignment settings.

If the information on the test check didn't print in the correct positions, repeat steps 7 and 8.

Printing Checks

After your checks are aligned properly, you're ready to print a check. Printing checks with Quicken is fast, easy, and even fun. Just don't forget to sign your checks after they are printed. Signing checks is the one task that Quicken can't perform for you.

To print checks, follow these steps:

1. Load the blank checks into your printer.

If you are using a page-oriented printer, place the check form sheets in the printer paper tray, as you place regular sheets of paper. If your printer prints on the face-down side of the paper, for example, make sure that your checks are inserted face down. Also, make sure that your checks are positioned in the proper order according to check number (the sheet with check number 3456 comes before the sheet with check number 3459).

2. With the Write Checks window on-screen, choose **P**rint Checks from the **F**ile menu, press Ctrl+P, or click the Print button from the Iconbar to display the Select Checks to Print dialog box (see fig. 5.16). At the top of the dialog box, Quicken tells you how many checks you need to print and the total dollar amount of the checks to be printed.

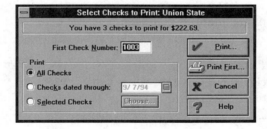

Fig. 5.16
The Select Checks to Print dialog box shows you how many checks you need to print and the total dollar amount of checks to be printed.

3. Quicken displays the number of the next check in the First Check **N**umber text box. If the number Quicken displays isn't the same as the number that appears in the upper-right corner of the next check, type the correct check number. You also can press the + (plus) and – (minus) keys to change the number.

4. In the Print section, select which checks you want to print, as follows:

■ To print all checks, choose **A**ll Checks.

■ Choose Chec**k**s Dated Through if you have postdated checks that you want to print. (Unless you specify a date through which to print checks, Quicken prints only those checks dated on or before the current date.) In the date text box, select the date through which you want Quicken to print postdated checks.

■ To select the checks that you want to print, select S**e**lected Checks, and then choose **C**hoose. Quicken displays the Select Checks to Print window (see fig. 5.17).

Fig. 5.17
Quicken lists all checks written, but not yet printed, in the Select Checks to Print window.

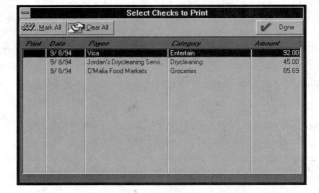

To select a check to print, click the check in the Select Checks to Print window or highlight press the spacebar. Quicken puts a check mark next to the check that you want to print.

To deselect a check previously marked for printing, click the check to remove the check mark or highlight the check and press the spacebar. To select all checks for printing or to deselect all checks for printing, choose **C**lear All.

After you finish selecting checks to print, choose Close to return to the Select Checks to Print dialog box (refer to fig. 5.16).

5. If you're printing a group of checks, choose the Print **F**irst button to print only the first check so that you can check the alignment. If you select to print only the first check and it prints correctly, you can then choose the **P**rint button and Quicken will print the remaining checks.

6. Choose **P**rint. Quicken displays the Print Checks dialog box, shown in figure 5.18.

Fig. 5.18
After you select
which checks you
want to print,
Quicken displays
the Print Checks
dialog box.

7. If the check style that appears in the Check Style drop-down list box isn't correct, select the correct one from the drop-down list.

8. For page-oriented printers, choose the Three, Two, or One check icon to match the number of checks that are on the first page of checks.

9. For voucher-check styles, an extra text box—Additional Copies—appears in the Print Checks dialog box. Type the number of additional check copies that you want to print.

10. Choose OK to begin printing checks. Quicken displays a message that checks are printing.

    If you are printing on a partial page of checks and selected to print partial pages in landscape printing style (checks are inserted vertically in your printer), Quicken displays the message Do the Checks Have a Tear-Off Strip? If the partial page of checks you are printing still have the tear-off strip attached, choose Yes. Otherwise, choose No. Quicken begins printing checks on the partial page.

11. After the checks are printed, Quicken displays the Did check(s) print OK? message. Review the printed checks carefully.

    If your checks printed correctly, choose OK. Quicken returns to the Write Checks window.

    If one or more of your checks printed incorrectly, perhaps the alignment wasn't right or the check forms jammed in the printer. Type the number of the first check that printed incorrectly and then choose OK. Quicken returns to the Select Checks to Print dialog box. Repeat steps 3 through 11 to reprint the checks that printed incorrectly.

CPA Tip: Voiding Misprinted Checks

Write **VOID** in large letters across the face of checks that Quicken incorrectly prints. This precaution prevents anyone from later signing and cashing the checks.

Reprinting a Check

If you decide later, even after leaving the Print Checks dialog box, that you want to reprint a check, you can. Suppose that the original check somehow gets lost or destroyed. Because you still must pay the person, you need to reprint the check. Rather than reenter all the same information, you can reprint the original information. (If you lose a check, consider placing a stop-payment order with your bank.)

When you enter checks you plan to print using the Write Checks window, Quicken records the checks in the Check Register. Because Quicken hasn't assigned check numbers, however, the word *Print* is entered in the Num (Check Number) field in the Check Register to indicate that the check is one that you have set up to print using the Write Checks window. When Quicken prints the checks, it replaces the word *Print* with the actual check number.

By itself, this bit of information isn't all that exciting, but it does enable you to trick Quicken into reprinting a check. All you need to do is change a check's number to the word *Print*. Quicken then assumes that the check is one you want to print. To print the check after you change the number to the word *Print*, follow the steps earlier in the section, "Printing Checks."

After you reprint a check, Quicken enters the new check number in the Num (Check Number) field for the check transaction in the Check Register. You then must enter a voided transaction for the original check number so that each check is accounted for in the Check Register. Chapter 6, "Using the Register," explains how to enter transactions in the Register and how to void transactions.

From Here...

After learning how to use Quicken to write and print checks, you may want to review the following chapters:

- Chapter 6, "Using the Register," describes how checks that you write in the Write Checks window are entered in the Check Register. From the Register, you can edit, delete, or void check transactions.

■ Chapter 7, "Using Quicken Shortcuts," shows you how to use shortcuts in Quicken to save even more time writing checks.

■ Chapter 13, "Paying Your Bills Electronically," explains how to set up and use Quicken to pay bills electronically through CheckFree.

Learning Quicken

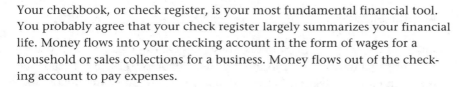

Chapter 6

Using the Register

Your checkbook, or check register, is your most fundamental financial tool. You probably agree that your check register largely summarizes your financial life. Money flows into your checking account in the form of wages for a household or sales collections for a business. Money flows out of the checking account to pay expenses.

Moving your check register to Quicken provides two major benefits. First, Quicken does the arithmetic of deducting checks and withdrawals and adding deposits—a trivial contribution until you remember the last time an error in your arithmetic caused you to bounce a check. Second, Quicken records each checking account transaction in the Register so that you can use Quicken's Reports feature to summarize and extract information from the Register— information that helps you plan and control your finances more effectively.

Quicken's Register is the program's major component. Every other program feature that writes checks, reconciles accounts, and prints reports depends on the Register. Every user works with Quicken's Register directly by entering transactions into the Register and indirectly by using the information stored in the Register. In fact, you can enter any of the financial transactions you record directly into the Quicken Register.

Note

If you don't print checks using Quicken, you probably will enter all your checking account transactions in the Register. If you do print checks with Quicken, you should enter check information in the Write Checks window (although you also can print checks from information entered in the Register). When you enter and record a check in the Write Checks window, Quicken records the transaction in the Register and updates the account balance. The steps for entering check information in the Write Checks window are outlined in Chapter 5, "Writing and Printing Checks." The steps you take to record a transaction in the Register screen are described in this chapter.

This chapter describes the basics of using Quicken's Register, including the following:

- Displaying and understanding the Register window

- Recording checks, deposits, withdrawals, and other transactions in the Register

- Recording transfers between accounts

- Assigning more than one category to a transaction by splitting the transaction

- Reviewing and editing transactions

- Setting Register Options

Chapter 7, "Using Quicken Shortcuts," describes Quicken features that you can use to speed up your work in the Register. Chapters 9, 10, and 11 describe how you can use the Register to track assets, credit card purchases, loans, and other liabilities. Chapter 16, "Monitoring Your Investments," describes a special set of tools that Quicken provides for managing your investments. To track and monitor your investments, Quicken provides the Investment Register.

Note

This chapter focuses on the Register for a bank account. Although all Quicken Registers work basically the same, a few slight differences exist. You learn about Credit Card, Cash, Asset, Liability, and Investment Registers in later chapters.

Displaying the Register

Display the Register when you want to do the following:

- Enter checks that you write manually

- Enter deposits and ATM withdrawals

- Enter other types of transactions, such as interest earned from your bank account and service charges

- Review transactions

- Edit or delete transactions

■ Void a transaction

■ Locate a specific transaction

■ Print the Register

> **Note**
>
> Each account that you set up in Quicken has its own Register. You must select the account that you want to work with to display its Register. Quicken's new Account Selector Bar in each Register helps you select an account quickly and easily.

To display the Register (shown in fig. 6.1), follow these steps:

1. Choose **A**ccount from the **L**ists menu, press Ctrl+A, or click Accts on the Iconbar to display the Account List.

2. Scroll the Account List to highlight the account whose Register you want to use, and then choose **O**pen. If you want to enter transactions for your checking account, for example, highlight your checking account in the Account List and choose **O**pen.

Quicken displays the Register for the account that you selected.

Tip
While working in the Write Checks window, you quickly can display the Register for your checking account by pressing Ctrl+R. To switch back to the Write Checks window, press Ctrl+W.

Fig. 6.1
The Register appears when you select an account to use from the Account List.

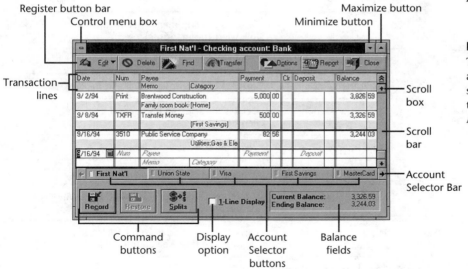

Note

You also can click Registr on the Iconbar to display the Register; however, when you select the Registr button, Quicken displays the Register for the account in which you were last working. For example, if you're reconciling your credit card account and click Registr on the Iconbar, Quicken displays the Register for the credit card account. Similarly, if you're writing checks in the Write Checks window and click Registr, Quicken displays the Register for the checking account from which you are writing checks.

You can easily change the Register to the account that you want to work in by selecting the account from the Account Selector Bar. Just click the appropriate account button and Quicken opens the Register for that account.

Reviewing the Register

The displayed Register looks similar to the manual check register that you use (refer to fig. 6.1).

The Register window includes the following:

■ *Register button bar*. This new Quicken 4 for Windows feature includes buttons at the top of the Register that you can use to perform the following activities:

Button	Description
Edit	Displays the Edit menu that includes the following commands:
New transaction	
Insert transaction	Inserts a blank transaction line in the Register
Delete transaction	Deletes the selected transaction from the Register
Void transaction	Voids the current transaction
Memorize transaction	Memorizes the current transaction
Copy transaction	Copies the selected transaction to the Windows clipboard
Paste transaction	Pastes a transaction from the Windows clipboard to the selected transaction line
Go to Other End of Transfer	
Go to A Specific Date	

Button	Description
Delete	Deletes the selected transaction from the Register
Find	Finds a transaction in the Register
Transfer	Creates a transfer transaction between the current account and another account
Options	Displays Register options
Report	Generates a QuickReport that lists all transactions that contain the same payee as the selected transaction
Close	Closes the Register window

■ *The transaction lines of the Register.* Transaction lines include fields to enter the following information:

Field	Records
Date	The date of the transaction.
Num	The check number. You also can use this field to enter **ATM** (for automatic teller machine transaction) or any other descriptive term for transactions that don't involve checks.
Payee	The person or firm you are paying, or, in the case of a deposit, the source of the deposit.
Memo	An optional field to enter a check memo or description of the transaction.
Category	The category or subcategory assigned to the transaction. You also use the Category field to assign a class and subclass to a transaction. (Refer to Chapter 4, "Organizing Your Finances," for more on categories and classes.)
Payment	The amount of the check or withdrawal.
Clr (Cleared)	Indicates whether the transaction has cleared the bank. You learn more about cleared transactions in Chapter 8, "Reconciling Your Bank Account."
Deposit	The amount of the deposit or bank credit.
Balance	Quicken calculates the balance in your account after the current transaction and enters the result here. You can't make an entry in the Balance field.

- *Account Selector Bar.* Use the Account Selector Bar to select the account whose Register you want to display and work in.

- *Command buttons.* The buttons at the bottom of the Register perform the following activities:

Button	Description
Record	Records the selected transaction. Choose Record when you are finished entering a transaction in the Register.
Restore	Reverts the transaction you are editing to the way it was before you started editing.
Splits	Opens the Splits window so that you can assign more than one category, subcategory, class, or subclass to a transaction. (You learn more about splitting transactions later in this chapter.)

- *Display option check box.* If you want to display more transactions at a time, select the **1**-Line Display check box to condense the Register to one line for each transaction.

- *Balance fields.* If you enter postdated transactions in the Register (transactions whose dates are later than the current system date), Quicken displays two balance fields; the Current Balance field and the Ending Balance field. If displayed, the Current Balance field shows the balance in the account based on all transactions entered with dates through the current date. The Ending Balance field shows the balance of all entered transactions. If no postdated transactions are in the Register, Quicken displays only the Ending Balance field.

CPA Tip: Using Balance Fields to Confirm Account Balances

Before you start recording transactions in the Register, use the balance fields to gauge the effect of the transactions you want to record (does your account have enough money to cover the checks you need to write?).

Note

You can't make entries to or edit the Current Balance or the Ending Balance fields. Quicken calculates these fields based on the transactions entered in the Register.

Moving Around the Register

As you get up to speed with Quicken, you will want to move through the Register quickly so that you can enter transactions as fast as possible or review prior transactions without having to move through the Register line by line.

You easily can move from transaction to transaction in the Register window using the scroll bar on the right side of the window. Just click the down arrow to move to the next transaction, or click the up arrow to move to the preceding transaction.

You also can use the scroll box to move quickly through transactions in the Register window. To move through the Register window using the scroll box, follow these steps:

1. Put the mouse pointer on the scroll box (review fig. 6.1).

2. Press and hold down the left mouse button as you drag (move) the scroll box up or down the scroll bar.

As you drag the scroll box, Quicken displays a date and check number in a box to the left of the scroll box. This information represents the date and check number of the transaction that will be at the top of the Register window when you release the scroll box.

You also can use the keyboard to move from transaction to transaction and from field to field in the Register window. The following keys help you move around the Register window quickly and easily:

Press	To Move
↑	To the same field in the preceding transaction
↓	To the same field in the next transaction
Tab	To the next field in the same transaction
Shift+Tab	To the preceding field in the same transaction
Home	To the beginning of the current field
End	To the end of the current field
Home Home	To the first field in the current transaction
End End	To the last field in the current transaction
Ctrl+Home	To the first transaction in the Register

(continues)

Press	To Move
Ctrl+End	To the first blank transaction line in the Register
PgUp	Up one window of transactions
PgDn	Down one window of transactions
Ctrl+PgUp	To the first transaction in the current month
Ctrl+PgDn	To the last transaction in the current month

> **Note**
>
> If you want to find a specific transaction, such as a check written to a particular payee or a check written on a certain date, you an use the Find window to locate the transaction. Finding transactions in the Register is explained in Chapter 7, "Using Quicken Shortcuts."

Changing the Number of Lines Displayed in the Register

When you start using Quicken, the Register is displayed using two lines of text for each transaction (other than the highlighted transaction). Figure 6.1 shows the Register in normal, or two-line, view. You can change the Register display so that each transaction takes up only one line in the Register; that way, Quicken compresses each transaction line into one line and increases the number of transactions shown in the window. Don't worry, your data is safe—some of it is just hidden from view.

To change the Register display to one-line, select the **1**-Line Display check box at the bottom of the Register. Quicken enters a check mark in the check box and condenses the Register, as shown in figure 6.2.

To change the Register display back to two-line, select the **1**-Line option check box again. The Register now appears with two lines for each transaction.

> **Note**
>
> Quicken doesn't provide the one-line display in the Investment Register. A transaction line in an Investment Register contains more information than can be condensed into one line.

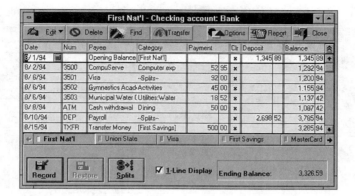

Fig. 6.2
Quicken increases
the number of
transactions
displayed in the
Register window
when you select
the 1-Line Display
option.

Resizing the Register

You can resize, maximize, or minimize the Register just as you can in other Windows applications. When you maximize the Register window, Quicken enlarges the window to fill the screen. When you minimize the Register window, Quicken reduces the Register to an icon at the bottom of the Quicken application window.

To resize the Register window, follow these steps:

1. Point to any corner of the Register window. The mouse pointer changes to a two-headed arrow, which indicates that the window can be sized.

2. Press and hold the left mouse button and drag the corner of the Register window to enlarge it or reduce its size.

3. Release the mouse button when the Register window is sized the way you want it.

To maximize the Register window, click the upward-pointing triangle (the Maximize button) in the upper-right corner of the window. Figure 6.3 shows the Register window after it's maximized. To restore the Register window to its original size, click the Restore button (with the two triangles) in the upper-right corner of the window.

To minimize the Register window, select the downward-pointing triangle (the Minimize button) in the upper-right corner of the window. Figure 6.4 shows the Register as an icon after the Register window is minimized. To restore the Register window to its original size, double-click the Register icon.

Restore button

Fig. 6.3
You can enlarge
the Register
window to fill the
screen by clicking
the Maximize
button in the
upper-right corner
of the Register
window.

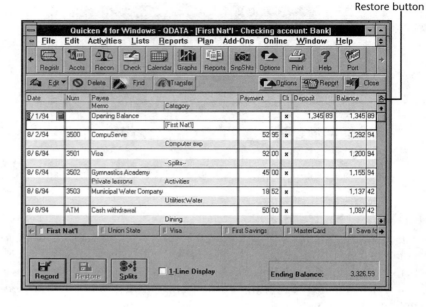

Fig. 6.4
The Register icon
appears at the
bottom of the
Quicken applica-
tion window when
you minimize the
Register window.

Using the Register Button Bar

Quicken displays a button bar at the top of the Register so that you quickly
can select a few of the more common Quicken commands. The Register button bar includes the Edit, Delete, Find, Transfer, Options, Report, and Close
buttons.

To use the button bar to perform operations, select the appropriate button by
clicking it. You also can press the Alt key in combination with the underlined
letter in the button name. To select the Transfer button, for example, press
Alt+N.

Closing the Register Window

If you don't need to use the Register window any longer, you can close the
Register so that it's removed from the Quicken application window. You can
reopen the Register window at any time.

To close the Register window, choose Close on the Register button bar or
double-click the Control menu box in the upper-left corner of the window.

Recording Transactions in the Register

Recording a check transaction in the Quicken Register closely parallels recording a check by hand in a paper checkbook register. The Register screen, however, makes the whole process easier. You can record any check in the Register, including checks you want to print. Typically, however, you record checks you wrote previously by hand directly into the register. You record checks you want to print in the Write Checks window, which is described in Chapter 5.

As you may expect, recording a deposit in the Quicken Register is like recording a deposit in your checkbook's paper register. Recording other withdrawals such as automated teller machine transactions, electronic fund transfers, and automatic payments parallel the steps for recording a check. (Quicken includes several references for other types of transactions, such as ATM, EFT, and XMIT.) You enter the date, reference, payee, payment amount, and (optionally) a memo description and a category. Record the withdrawal by choosing Re**c**ord after you double-check the transaction's accuracy.

To record a transaction in a Quicken bank account Register, follow these steps:

1. Choose **A**ccount from the **L**ists menu, press Ctrl+A, or click the Accts button on the Iconbar to display the Account List.

2. Scroll the Account List to highlight the bank account you want to use, and then select **O**pen. Quicken displays the Register for the bank account you selected.

3. Enter the check date in the *mm/dd/yy* format, but typing the slashes isn't necessary (such as **511** for 5/11/95). Note that Quicken automatically enters the current year, so you don't have to enter the year.

   The first time you enter a transaction in the Register in the current Quicken session, the program fills the Date field with the system date (the current date according to your computer's internal memory). After you enter your first transaction in the Register, Quicken fills the Date field with the last date used.

   To edit the date, you can move the cursor to the part of the date (month, day, or year) that you want to change and type over the date already on-screen. Alternatively, you can use the + (plus) and – (minus) keys to change the date one day at a time. To change the existing date

Tip

You can hide the button bar from the Register window if you want to display more transactions or don't want to use the button bar. See the section "Setting Register Options," later in this chapter, to learn how to set the option that controls whether the button bar is displayed.

Tip

You can use the new pop-up calendar to enter dates in the Date field. Click the calendar button in the Date field to display a minicalendar that you can use to enter the date. Chapter 7, "Using Quicken Shortcuts," explains how.

Learning Quicken

of 5/11/95 to 5/13/95, for example, press the plus key twice. To change the date of 5/11/95 to 5/9/95, press the minus key twice.

> **Note**
>
> You can change the way dates are entered and displayed by setting the option that controls how dates are entered. By default, Quicken displays dates as *mm/dd/yy*; however, you can change the way dates are displayed (to *dd/mm/yy*) by changing the date option. If you change the date option, for example, dates are entered and displayed with the day first, followed by the month. August 18, 1995, for example, is entered and displayed as 18/08/95 instead of 8/18/95. See the section, "Setting Register Options," later in this chapter, to learn how to set the date option.

4. Press Tab to move to the Num field. If you're entering a check transaction, enter the number of the check in this field. You can use the + (plus) key to enter the next check number or the – (minus) key to enter the check number before the last check number used. If the check number from the preceding transaction was 1892, for example, press the plus key to enter 1893 as the check number in the next transaction line or press the minus key to enter 1891 as the check number.

   Checks you recorded in the Write Checks window but haven't printed show the word *Print* in the Num field. If you want to enter a check that you want to print later, you can type **Print** in the Num field.

   If you're entering a deposit transaction, type **DEP** in the Num field.

   For other withdrawals, enter the appropriate reference in the Num field. Quicken includes several references for other types of transactions, such as **ATM**, **Transfer**, and **EFT**.

Tip
The Write Checks window provides a more convenient method of writing and printing checks. Chapter 5 explains how to write checks in the Write Checks window.

> **Note**
>
> QuickFill works from the Num field in the Register. When you Tab to the Num field, Quicken displays a list of references, (ATM, Deposit, Next Chk #, and so forth). Select a reference from the list or begin typing the reference in the Num field. Quicken enters the selected reference or completes the reference that you begin to type.

5. Press Tab to move to the Payee field. For checks or other payments, type the name of the person or business that you wrote the check to. You have space for up to 31 characters.

For deposits, enter a description of the deposit transaction. A business recording a deposit from a customer, for example, can describe the deposit by using the customer name, such as **Acme Manufacturing**. A home user recording a payroll deposit can describe the deposit as **Payroll Check**. You could describe interest as **October Interest Income**.

6. Press Tab to move to the Payment field. If you're entering a check transaction or other withdrawal, enter the amount, using up to 10 characters. You can enter an amount as large as $9,999,999.99. The decimal point counts as one of the 10 characters but the commas do not.

> **Note**
>
> If you need to add several amounts together for a check you're entering in the Register, Quicken's pop-up calculator can help. Just click the calculator button in the Payment (or Deposit) field to display a minicalculator that you can use to compute the transaction amount. Refer to Chapter 7, "Using Quicken Shortcuts," to learn how to use the new pop-up calculator to enter amounts.

7. Press Tab to reach the Clr (Cleared) field, which shows whether a transaction has been recorded by the bank. Use this field as part of *reconciling*, or explaining the difference between your check register account balance and the balance the bank shows on your monthly statement. To mark a transaction as cleared, enter an asterisk (*), the only character Quicken accepts here in the Clr field. During reconciliation, Quicken changes the asterisk to an X (see Chapter 8, "Reconciling Your Bank Account").

8. If you're entering a deposit, press Tab to move to the Deposit field. As with the Payment field, Quicken enables you to enter only numbers, with amounts under $9,999,999.99.

9. (Optional) Press Tab to move to the Memo field, where you can use up to 31 characters to describe a transaction. If you are making several payments a month to the bank, the Memo field enables you to specify the house payment, the school loan, the hot tub, the boat, and so on.

10. Press Tab to move to the Category field, which you can use to assign a category, subcategory, transfer account, or class to a transaction. You use the Category field to classify expenses and income.

When you move to the Category field, Quicken displays a drop-down list with the list of categories, subcategories, and accounts from the Category & Transfer List. (If the drop-down list doesn't appear automatically, click the arrow in the Category field to display the list.) From the list, select the category, subcategory, or transfer account that you want to assign to the check transaction and press Enter. Quicken inserts the category, subcategory, or account name in the Category field in the Register.

> ### Note
>
> You can assign more than one category to a single transaction. This procedure is called *splitting a transaction*. You may need to split a transaction if, for example, you are writing one check to a department store to pay for clothing, computer supplies, and cosmetics. Obviously, no one category describes these different expenses. By splitting the transaction, you can assign three categories to the check transaction so that each expense is properly classified in your records. You learn how to split a transaction later in this chapter.

Tip

You also can use QuickFill to enter an account name in the Category field when transferring money to another account.

Quicken's QuickFill feature also works from the Category field in the Register. When you type the first characters in a category name, Quicken searches the Category & Transfer List to find the first category that begins with the characters you type. Suppose that you have a category named Utilities, and it's the only category name that starts with the letter *U*. If you type a **U** in the Category field, Quicken searches the Category & Transfer List until it finds a category that begins with *U*. When Quicken finds Utilities, the QuickFill feature fills in the remaining letters of the category name for you: *tilities*. You learn about using QuickFill to fill in the Category field in Chapter 7, "Using Quicken Shortcuts."

To use the QuickFill feature to enter a subcategory in the Category field, type or enter the category name, type a **:** (colon), and then begin typing the subcategory name. QuickFill enters the rest of the subcategory when it finds the matching subcategory name in the Category & Transfer List.

Tip

You can add classes to the Class List as you enter transactions. Type the new class; then enter information about the new class in the dialog box that appears.

To assign a class to a check transaction, type a **/** (slash) after the category or subcategory name in the Category field. Then type the class name or press Ctrl+L to display the Class List and select a class from the list. The QuickFill feature also works for entering classes. When you type a few characters after the slash, QuickFill enters the rest of the class when it finds the matching class name in the Class List.

> **Note**
>
> If the category or subcategory that you want to assign to a check transaction isn't included in the drop-down list, you can add it *on the fly* as you enter a transaction in the Register. Just type the new category name in the Category field. When Quicken doesn't find the category in the Category & Transfer List, the Set Up Category dialog box appears so that you can enter the information about the new category. Choose OK when the Set Up Category dialog box is complete; Quicken returns to the Register window with the new category name in the Category field. You learn more about adding categories and subcategories in Chapter 4, "Organizing Your Finances."

To assign a subclass to a check transaction, type a **:** (colon) after the class name. Then type the class that you want to function as a subclass, or press Ctrl+L to display the Class List and select the class from the list.

> **Note**
>
> Quicken doesn't require that you assign categories, subcategories, or classes to transactions. If you want to track your income and expense so that you know where your money comes from and where it goes, however, you should assign a category to each transaction that you enter in Quicken. To ensure that you do assign a category to each transaction, you can select the **W**arn Before Recording Uncategorized Transactions Register option. You learn how to select options later in this chapter in the section, "Setting Register Options."

11. Record the transaction by choosing Re**c**ord. Figure 6.5 shows transactions recorded in the Register.

Quicken calculates the new balance in the account each time you record a transaction and enters the amount in the Balance field for each transaction. If the balance is too large for a positive or negative number to display, Quicken displays asterisks in the Balance field. Quicken uses negative numbers to indicate that you have overdrawn your account. If you have a color monitor, Quicken displays negative amounts in red.

After you enter a few transactions in the Register, you can use Quicken's QuickFill feature. QuickFill makes entering payees and transactions fast and easy. When you Tab to the Payee field, Quicken displays a drop-down list with previously entered transactions plus the transactions from the Memorized Transaction List. (You learn about the Memorized Transaction List in

> **Tip**
>
> So that Quicken is silent when you record transactions, you can turn off the beep by turning off the **B**eep When Recording and Memorizing option. Refer to the section, "Setting Register Options," later in this chapter to learn how to turn off this option.

Chapter 7, "Using Quicken Shortcuts.") If you begin typing a few characters of the payee name, Quicken moves through the list and highlights the first transaction that matches what you type.

Fig. 6.5

Use the Register to record checks that you write manually. Quicken saves all the check information and updates your account balance.

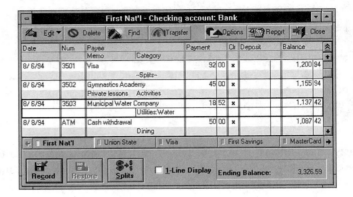

If you want to use the information for that transaction, just press Tab; QuickFill fills in the rest of the payee name for you, plus the other information for the selected transaction (amount, memo, category, and so forth). If you don't want to use the information for the transaction that Quicken highlights from the list, you can type a few more characters in the Payee field or select the transaction from the drop-down list that you do want to use to enter your new transaction. Refer to Chapter 7, "Using Quicken Shortcuts," for more detailed information on QuickFill.

If the transaction that QuickFill completes for you is the way you want it, you're ready to record the check, deposit, or other withdrawal. If the amount is different, you can edit the transaction before choosing Record.

Note

If you want an instant report of all transactions that contain the same payee, you can use Quicken's QuickReport feature. When you select Report from the Register button bar, Quicken lists all transactions (in the current account) that contain the same payee as the selected transaction through the current date. Quicken shows the date, check number (or other reference), description, memo, category or subcategory name, cleared status, and amount for each transaction in the list.

CPA Tip: Reviewing Bank Fees

Consider the monthly service fees a bank charges when choosing a bank and in keeping minimum balances. Most banks charge monthly service fees of about $5. Some banks waive the $5 fee if you keep an average balance of $200 at all times in your account. The $5 a month translates into $60 a year. Because $60 in fee savings equals $60 in interest, the interest rate the bank pays people who keep their minimum balance at $200 is $60 divided by $200, or 30 percent. The return is even better than that for most people because the interest income gets taxed, but the fee savings don't. Probably no other $200 investment in the world is risk-free and pays 30 percent "interest."

Recording Transfers Between Accounts

Quicken 4 for Windows makes it easy to record a transfer from one account to another. Suppose that you are recording a check drawn on your checking account for deposit to your account with First Savings. The check isn't an expense, so it shouldn't be categorized as utilities, medical, insurance, or something else. It's a transfer of funds from one account to another.

To record a transfer from one account to another, follow these steps:

1. From the Register, select Transfer from the Register button bar. Quicken displays the Transfer Money Between Accounts dialog box shown in figure 6.6.

Fig. 6.6
The Transfer Money Between Accounts dialog box is used to enter a transfer transaction in the Register.

2. Quicken enters the current date in the **D**ate field and enters the description *Transfer Money* in the Description text box. You can change both the date and description, if necessary.

> **Note**
>
> You can also record a transfer transaction by entering the information about the transfer in a transaction line in the Register. Enter the date, **TXFR** in the Num field (for transfer), description, and the amount. In the Category field, enter or select the account to which you want to transfer funds. Quicken enters brackets around the account name in the Category field to indicate that the transaction is a transfer from the current account to the account shown in the Category field.

3. In the $ (Amount) field, enter the amount that you want to transfer from one account to another. If you need to calculate an amount, click the calculator button to display Quicken's minicalculator.

4. In the Transfer Money From drop-down list box, Quicken enters the name of the account in which you are currently working. If necessary, select a different account.

5. In the To drop-down list box, select the account to which you want to transfer money.

6. Choose OK. Quicken records the transaction in the Registers for both accounts. In the transaction shown in figure 6.7, a payment of $500 is recorded in the checking account and, at the same time, a deposit of $500 is recorded in the First Savings account. Figure 6.8 shows the Register for the First Savings account with the $500 deposit.

Fig. 6.7
Quicken encloses brackets around the account name in the Category field when you record a transfer transaction.

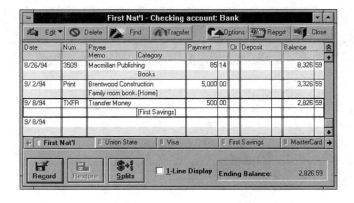

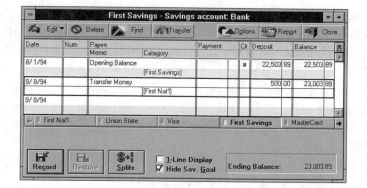

Fig. 6.8
Press Ctrl+X to go to the corresponding transfer transaction.

Learning Quicken

> **Note**
>
> You quickly can move to the corresponding transfer transaction in the other account Register if you want to review the transaction to make sure that it was recorded correctly. To go to the corresponding transaction, highlight the transfer transaction in the account Register where you recorded the transfer transaction and then choose **G**o To Transfer from the **E**dit menu (or press Ctrl+X). You can also choose the **G**o to Other End of Transfer option from the **E**dit menu displayed when you click **E**dit from the Register button bar.

Entering Uncleared Transactions

You learned in Chapters 1 and 3 that you enter the ending balance from your last bank statement as the starting balance in your Quicken bank account. This makes reconciling easy the next time you receive your bank statement and start to reconcile your bank account with Quicken.

Using the balance from your last bank statement, however, doesn't account for transactions that occurred before you started using Quicken, but that haven't cleared your bank. To reflect your account balance accurately in Quicken, you must enter all uncleared transactions from the date of your last bank statement to the date that you start using Quicken. If your last bank statement was dated 2/15/95, for example, and you started using Quicken on 3/01/95, you must enter all transactions that occurred between 2/15/95 and 3/01/95 in addition to those transactions that occurred prior to 2/15/95 but didn't show up on your last statement.

This section shows you how to enter check, deposit, and other withdrawal transactions in the Register, which is all you need to know to enter uncleared transactions. Just move to a blank transaction line in the Register and begin entering uncleared transactions like you enter any other transaction.

Make sure that you enter the correct date and check number for each transaction. After you record the transaction by choosing Record, Quicken sorts your transactions in the Register and places the transactions that you just entered in order by date.

Splitting Transactions

Earlier in this chapter, you learned how to enter transactions in the Register and how to assign a single category to a transaction. But what happens when you write a check for an expense that covers more than one category, such as the check you write to the bank to pay a mortgage payment that pays principal, interest, insurance, and property taxes? In this case, you need to split the transaction, or assign more than one category or subcategory to the transaction. (Subcategories further divide a category into second-, third-, fourth-, and so on levels.) You may want to divide the Utilities category so that you can track expenses for electricity, gas, and water, for example. Subcategories are explained in more detail in Chapter 4, "Organizing Your Finances."

> **Note**
>
> You can split transactions when you write a check from the Write Checks window or enter a manual check in the Register. Quicken enables you to assign up to 30 categories or subcategories to a single transaction.

A transaction line in the Register window provides one field to assign a category or subcategory. Occasionally, however, you need to be able to break down a transaction into multiple categories, such as in the mortgage payment example. By splitting the transaction, Quicken provides additional Category fields so that you can assign more than one category to a transaction or further describe a transaction.

The steps for splitting a transaction in the Register are the same for splitting a transaction in the Write Checks window. Refer to the section, "Splitting Check Transactions," in Chapter 5 to learn how to split a transaction.

CPA Tip: Tracking Income and Expenses with Split Transactions

When you want to track your income and expenses closely, enter split transactions for payments to department stores, discount stores, and so on where you buy different items. If you don't split the transaction to record a check to Wal-Mart where you buy hardware, cleaning supplies, office supplies, and so on, for example, and instead lump the total check transaction into one category, your expenses aren't reflected accurately.

Note

If you try to delete a transaction that is part of a split transfer transaction (where one part of the split transaction transfers funds from one Quicken account to another), you must delete the transaction from the account where the transaction originated; in other words, the account that you entered the split transfer transaction in. Press Ctrl+X to locate the split transfer transaction. After you find the split transfer transaction, highlight the transfer transaction and click the Delete button from the Register button bar (or press Ctrl+D) to delete the transaction. Quicken then deletes the corresponding transaction in the other account.

Reviewing and Editing Register Transactions

You can review and edit transactions by accessing the Register at any time. You may want to review a transaction to make sure that you recorded the transaction correctly. You also may want to review a transaction to see whether you received a deposit or remembered to pay a particular bill.

You can move from transaction to transaction in the Register window by using the scroll bar on the right side of the window or by using the keyboard. (You learned about moving around the Register earlier in this chapter.)

To edit a transaction in the Register, follow these steps:

1. Highlight the transaction in the Register that you want to change.

2. Click the field that you want to edit or press Tab to move to the field.

3. Type over the existing information or select a new item from the drop-down list.

Tip
To correct a mistake made while editing a field in a transaction, choose **U**ndo from the **E**dit menu or press Alt+Backspace.

If you decide that you want to cancel changes that you have made to a transaction, choose Restore. Quicken restores the transaction to the way it was before you began editing.

4. Choose Record to save the changes to the transaction.

By default, Quicken selects the Register option that requests confirmation when changing a transaction in the Register. The confirmation message appears when you go to another transaction or a new window without first recording the changes in the transaction. Therefore, if you don't choose Record after editing a transaction, Quicken displays a message asking you to confirm the change to the transaction. Choose **Y**es to change the transaction. If the transaction you are editing is a reconciled transaction (the transaction has cleared the bank and has been marked as cleared against your bank statement), Quicken asks you to confirm that you want to change a reconciled transaction. Choose **Y**es to change the reconciled transaction.

CPA Tip: Printing the Register

At the end of each month, print a copy of the Register for the transactions you entered in that month. Store the Register with the bank statement for the month. That way, if you ever have questions about a previous month or have the bad luck of losing your Quicken data file, you can reconstruct transactions from previous months. You can discard the now redundant individual Registers that show each group of transactions for the month. You don't need these with a copy of the entire month.

Deleting a Transaction from the Register

Quicken enables you to delete a transaction that you inadvertently entered twice, entered in the wrong account Register, and so on. When you delete a transaction, it's removed permanently from the Register.

CPA Tip: Voiding Checks versus Deleting Checks

You shouldn't delete transactions for manual checks or for checks you have written with Quicken. When you delete a transaction, Quicken removes all record of the transaction. If the transaction involves a check, deleting the transaction removes the check information and leaves a gap in your check-numbering sequence. Void a check transaction that you want to remove because of a lost check, a check that you have stopped payment on, or an improperly printed check, but *don't delete* such checks. Information for voided transactions remains in the Register so that you can track each prenumbered check. You learn how to void a transaction later in this chapter.

You should delete a recorded transaction only under the following conditions:

- *You inadvertently enter a transaction that shouldn't be entered.* If you enter a deposit transaction in the Register and subsequently don't make the deposit, for example, you should delete the transaction. Or if you enter a transaction for a bank fee in the Register that the bank later rescinds, delete the bank fee transaction.

- *You duplicate transaction information.* If you withdraw funds from an automatic teller machine and enter the transaction twice in the Register, for example, you should delete one of the two transactions.

- *You enter a transaction in the wrong Quicken Register* (Quicken provides a Register for each account that you set up). If you enter a credit card payment (that you make manually) in the Register for your checking account but want to track your credit card purchases in the Credit Card Register, you should copy the transaction to the Credit Card Register and then delete the transaction from the Checking Account Register. You learn how to copy transactions in Chapter 7, "Using Quicken Shortcuts."

In all other cases, you should void or reverse transactions in the Register so that you have complete records of all your check numbers and have established a proper audit trail (a history of each and every transaction) in the Register.

If you need to delete a transaction, follow these steps:

1. Display the Register for the account from which you need to delete the transaction.

2. Highlight the transaction that you want to delete.

3. Choose Delete from the Register button bar, choose **D**elete Transaction from the **E**dit menu, or press Ctrl+D.

4. Quicken displays the Delete the Current Transaction? dialog box, shown in figure 6.9. Choose **Y**es to delete the current transaction. If the transaction that you are editing is a reconciled transaction (the transaction has cleared the bank and has been marked as cleared against your bank statement), Quicken asks you to confirm that you want to delete a reconciled transaction. Choose **Y**es to delete the reconciled transaction.

When you delete a transaction, Quicken removes all transaction information from the Register.

Fig. 6.9
Quicken confirms that you want to delete a transaction before the transaction is removed from the Register.

If you delete a transaction from one Quicken account that is part of a transfer transaction (where you transferred funds from one Quicken account to another), the corresponding transaction in the other account also is deleted. To quickly find the corresponding transfer transaction, press Ctrl+X.

If you try to delete a transaction that is part of a split transfer transaction, you must delete the transaction from the account where the transaction originated—in other words, the account in which you entered the transfer transaction.

Voiding a Transaction

You may need to void a check when you want to stop payment, when you lose a check and write another one to replace it, or when a check prints incorrectly and you must print another.

> **Note**
>
> If you void a transaction that is part of a transfer from one account to another, voiding any part of the transaction also voids the other parts of the transaction that are recorded in the other Registers.

To void a check from the Checking Account Register, follow these steps:

1. Display the Register for your checking account.

2. Highlight the transaction for the check that you want to void. If you are voiding a manual check that you haven't yet entered in the Register, enter the date and check number in a blank transaction line. Keep this transaction highlighted as you move to the next step.

3. Choose **V**oid Transaction from the **E**dit menu (or press Ctrl+V). Quicken enters **VOID** in the Payee field before the payee name and marks the transaction with an X in the Clear column so that the transaction isn't considered an uncleared item when you perform your account reconciliation.

4. Choose Re**c**ord.

Figure 6.10 shows the Register with a voided check transaction. When you void a check, Quicken erases the amount of the transaction and adjusts your checking account balance. Quicken also subtracts the amount of the voided check from the category originally assigned to the check transaction.

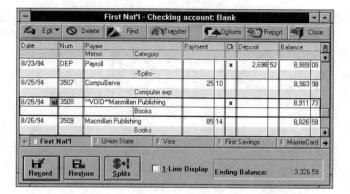

Learning Quicken

Fig. 6.10
Quicken inserts
VOID in the
Payee field of a
transaction that
you void in the
Register.

> **Note**
>
> You can insert a blank transaction line anywhere in the Register. When you insert a line, Quicken inserts the transaction line above the currently highlighted transaction line. To insert a transaction, just select E**d**it from the Register button bar and then select **I**nsert Transaction, or press Ctrl+I.

Setting Register Options

Quicken enables you to fine-tune the Register features in the program to work the way you want them to.

To set Register options, follow these steps:

1. Choose O**p**tions from the Register button bar. Quicken displays the Register Options dialog box, shown in figure 6.11. The Register Options dialog box includes tabs to select Dis**p**lay, M**i**scellaneous, and Quic**k**Fill options. Figure 6.11 shows the Dis**p**lay options that control how the Register is displayed. To display miscellaneous Register options shown in figure 6.11, click the M**i**scellaneous tab. To display the options that control the way QuickFill works, as seen in figure 6.13, click the Quic**k**Fill tab.

Fig. 6.11
The Register Options dialog box for Display includes the areas in which you can set options for displaying the Register on-screen.

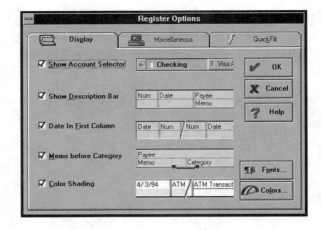

Fig. 6.12
The Miscellaneous settings included in the Register Options dialog box control how you enter information in the Register.

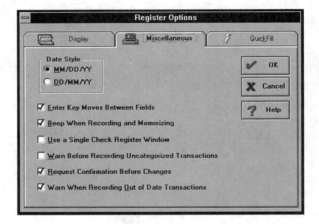

Fig. 6.13
The QuickFill settings included in the Register Options dialog box control the way the QuickFill feature works when entering transactions in the Register.

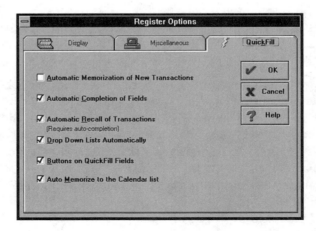

2. Move to the Register option that you want to change and turn it on or off. Turn an option on by selecting the blank button or check box for that option. Turn an option off by selecting it again.

3. When you're finished setting options, choose OK to save the Register option settings and return to the Register.

From Here...

After learning how to use the Register, you may want to review the following chapters:

■ Chapter 7, "Using Quicken Shortcuts," shows you how to save even more time using shortcut features in Quicken to enter transactions.

■ Chapter 8, "Reconciling Your Bank Account," explains how to reconcile your Quicken Register with your bank account statement.

■ Chapter 11, "Managing Your Assets and Other Liabilities," describes the Registers used for cash, asset, and liability accounts.

Tip

If you prefer to enter dates in Quicken using the Canadian or European date style, select the DD/MM/YY option under Miscellaneous settings in the Register Options dialog box.

Chapter 7

Using Quicken Shortcuts

You learned how to write a check at the Write Checks window in Chapter 5, "Writing and Printing Checks." In Chapter 6, "Using the Register," you learned how to use the Register to record transactions. This chapter describes how you can use Quicken shortcuts to make check writing and using the Register faster and easier. These features can help you write checks and enter transactions quickly, save and reuse information you record repeatedly in transactions, or search through the Register for specific transactions.

In this chapter, you learn how to use the following shortcuts:

- The pop-up calendar to enter dates

- The pop-up field calculator to calculate amount fields

- Quicken's on-screen calculator to perform calculations

- QuickFill to have Quicken enter transaction information for you

- Memorized transactions to save checks and other transactions that you frequently record

- The Find command to locate a specific transaction

Using the Minicalendar to Enter Dates

Quicken includes a pop-up calendar, or minicalendar, that you can display from the Date field in the Write Checks window and the Register, and other Date fields in dialog boxes and windows. When the calendar is displayed, you quickly can select the date that you want to enter for a transaction, report, or graph.

To use the minicalendar to enter dates, simply click the calendar button when it is displayed. From the minicalendar, click the date you want to enter. Figure 7.1 shows the minicalendar displayed from the Date field in the Register.

Fig. 7.1

Quicken displays a minicalendar when you click the calendar button in the Date field of the Register. Use the calendar to enter a date in the Date field.

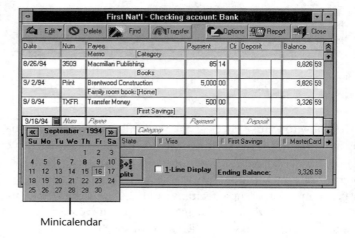

Minicalendar

Tip

To move quickly from month to month in the calendar, click the left-arrow button to move to the previous month and the right-arrow button to move to the next month.

To remove the minicalendar without selecting a date, click outside the calendar or press Esc.

Using the Minicalculator in Amount Fields

The minicalculator that pops up from the $ (Amount) field in the Write Checks window, in the Payment and Deposit fields in the Register, and in the Amount fields in the Splits window is very handy for adding several amounts that you want to include in one check, deposit, or other transaction. The minicalculator is used just like a regular calculator. When you're finished with a calculation, Quicken enters the result in the amount field where the calculator was displayed.

To use the minicalculator to enter amounts, click the calculator button in the $ (Amount) field in the Write Checks window or the Payment or Deposit field in the Register. If you're splitting a transaction, click the calculator button in the Amount field in the Splits window. Quicken displays the minicalculator, shown in figure 7.2.

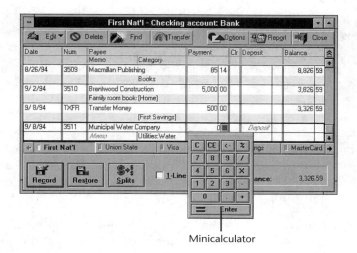

Minicalculator

Fig. 7.2
Quicken displays a
minicalculator
that you can use to
calculate entries in
amount fields.

Perform your calculation. As you enter a number in the calculator, Quicken displays the number in the amount field.

After you perform the calculation, click = (equal) on the calculator, press the = (equal) key on the keyboard, or press Enter. Quicken enters the result of your calculation in the amount field.

Using Quicken's On-Screen Calculator

A convenient tool that Quicken offers is its on-screen calculator (see fig. 7.3). Quicken's calculator is accessible from any Register, the Write Checks window, or from reports. You can access the calculator during bank account reconciliation as well. The calculator operates like most other regular calculators. To access the on-screen calculator, choose Use Calculator from the Activities menu.

Fig. 7.3
The on-screen
calculator is always
accessible and
handy as you work
in Quicken.

If you need to perform a calculation for a field that does not include the calculator button, you can perform the calculation with the on-screen calculator and then select the Paste button on the calculator. Quicken enters the result of your calculation in the current field (the field that you were in before you accessed the calculator).

After you perform calculations, remove the calculator from the screen by double-clicking the Control menu box (in the top-left corner of the calculator) or by pressing Esc.

Using QuickFill

Writing checks in the Write Checks window and entering transactions in the Register are faster and easier with Quicken's improved QuickFill feature. QuickFill is available when editing existing checks and transactions. And, you now see more transaction information displayed as you fill in fields that use QuickFill.

When you type a few characters in a field, Quicken searches previous transactions in the Register and the Memorized Transaction List to find a matching entry in that particular field. (You learn about the Memorized Transaction List later in this chapter.) When Quicken finds a match, the QuickFill feature fills in the rest of the check or transaction with the information that it finds.

QuickFill works when you make an entry in the Pay to the Order of field or the Category field in the Write Checks window and in the Num, Payee, and Category fields in the Register. QuickFill also works when you edit an existing check or transaction.

When you install Quicken 4 for Windows, QuickFill is set to do the following:

- Automatically complete the field in a transaction as you type.

- Recall a memorized or previously entered transaction when you press Tab to leave the Payee field.

■ Automatically display the drop-down list when you press Tab to move to a field where QuickFill works.

■ Place down-arrow buttons beside fields in which you can use QuickFill (click the button to display the drop-down list).

■ Automatically add new transactions to the Calendar list. (The Calendar list of transactions is used to scheduled transactions in the Financial Calendar. Refer to Chapter 14, "Scheduling Future Transactions," to learn about the Financial Calendar.)

You can change the way QuickFill works by setting the Check and Register options for QuickFill. You also can set a QuickFill option to have Quicken automatically memorize each new transaction that you enter in Quicken. (This option isn't selected when you install Quicken 4 for Windows.) See the section "Setting QuickFill Options" to learn how to change the way QuickFill works.

Using QuickFill in Fields

QuickFill works in the following fields:

■ The Num field in the Register

■ The Pay to the Order of field in the Write Checks window

■ The Payee field in the Register

■ The Category field

When you press Tab to move to the Num field and begin typing a reference, Quicken completes the reference that you begin to type. For example, if you type **A**, Quicken enters *ATM* in the Num field because *ATM* is the only reference that Quicken recognizes that begins with the letter A. If you type **N** (for check number), Quicken adds 1 to the previously entered check number.

When you begin typing a few characters in the Pay to the Order of field in the Write Checks window or the Payee field in the Register, Quicken searches the Memorized Transaction List and previous transactions entered in the Register. When Quicken finds a transaction with the same payee name, QuickFill fills in the rest of the payee name from the transaction it found in the Memorized Transaction List or the previous transactions in the Register.

For example, if you type **Ca** in the Pay to the Order of field in the Write Checks window, Quicken searches the Memorized Transaction List and the

Register for a payee name that starts with *Ca*. When Quicken finds the first transaction with the payee *Carmel Boy Scouts*, for example, QuickFill fills in the rest of the payee name and shows you the rest of the transaction that it found (amount and category) above the Pay to the Order of field.

If the payee name (or in this example, *Carmel Boy Scouts*), is indeed the payee that you want to enter in the transaction, press Tab. QuickFill fills in the rest of the transaction information for that payee—the transaction amount, the memo field (if used), and the category or subcategory—exactly like the transaction that Quicken found.

If QuickFill doesn't fill in the payee information that you want, keep typing characters until QuickFill finds the payee that you want. You also can select the payee that you want from the field's drop-down list box.

> ### Note
>
> If more than one payee name exists in the Memorized Transaction List or more than one previous transaction exists in the Register that begins with the characters you type, QuickFill enters the transaction information for the first payee name found.

Figure 7.4 shows the payee name filled in by QuickFill.

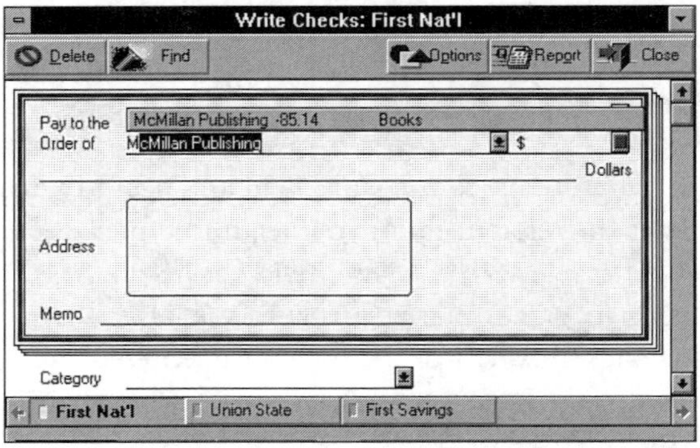

Fig. 7.4
QuickFill fills in the payee name from a matching transaction from the Memorized Transaction List or the Register.

After QuickFill fills in transaction information from a previously entered transaction, you can edit any of the transaction fields necessary. When the correct entries are made to all fields, record the transaction as usual by choosing Record.

QuickFill also works when you type a few characters in the Category field of a check or transaction in the Register. QuickFill searches the Category &

Transfer List and searches for the first category or transfer account that begins with the characters you type. Quicken searches the Category & Transfer List for the first category or transfer account that matches the characters you type. When Quicken finds a matching category or transfer account, QuickFill fills in the rest of the category or transfer account name. If this category or transfer account is the one you want to assign to the transaction, press Tab to accept it. If the category or transfer account name filled in by QuickFill isn't the one that you want, type a few more characters or press Ctrl+down arrow or Ctrl+up arrow until Quicken finds the right name.

If you want to enter a subcategory, you can type a colon (:) after the category name is filled in. Quicken searches the subcategories under that particular category and enters the first one that it finds. If you want to enter a class, you can type a slash (/), and a few characters after the category or subcategory name is filled in. Quicken then searches the Class list and enters the first class it finds that begins with the characters you type. (Refer to Chapter 4, "Organizing Your Finances," for more information on classes.)

Note

If the category or class that you want to assign to a check or transaction in the Register isn't in the Category & Transfer List or the Class list (because it is new), you can add a new category or class by typing the new name in the Category field. When you press Tab after you enter a new category or class name in the Write Checks window or the Register, Quicken displays the appropriate dialog box for you to enter information to set up the new category or class. Follow the usual steps for adding categories and classes. Refer to Chapter 4, "Organizing Your Finances," for information on how to add a category and class.

Setting QuickFill Options

If you don't want to use the QuickFill feature in the way that Quicken sets it up at installation, you can change the options so that QuickFill works the way you want.

To change QuickFill options, follow these steps:

1. From the Write Checks window or the Register, select Options from the button bar. Quicken displays either the Check Options dialog box or the Register Options dialog box.

2. Click the QuickFill tab to display the QuickFill options, as shown in figure 7.5.

Tip

You can change QuickFill options at any time. QuickFill options don't change the way Quicken processes your data.

Fig. 7.5
If you want to change the way QuickFill works, change one or more of the QuickFill options.

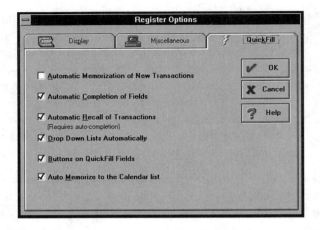

3. Click the appropriate check box to turn on or off a QuickFill option.

4. When the QuickFill options are set as you want them, choose OK to save the settings.

Copying Part of a Transaction

Quicken provides fast and easy ways to copy information between transactions. If you want to add the same memo to several transactions, you can copy the text in the Memo field and paste it to the Memo field in another transaction.

To copy transaction information, follow these steps:

1. In the Register, highlight the transaction that you want to copy.

   Drag the mouse pointer to highlight the information you want to copy, or press Shift+← or Shift+→ to highlight the information to the left or right of the cursor, respectively (see fig. 7.6).

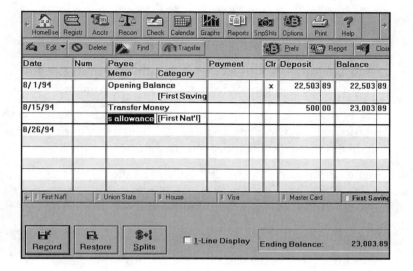

Fig. 7.6
Highlight
information in a
transaction that
you want to copy
to another
transaction.

2. From the **E**dit menu, choose **C**opy (or press Ctrl+Ins). Quicken copies the highlighted text to the Windows clipboard.

3. Highlight the transaction to which you want to copy the information. Press Tab to move to the field to which you want to copy the transaction information.

4. From the **E**dit menu, choose **P**aste (or press Shift+Ins) to copy the information to the field in the other transaction.

Copying Entire Transactions

If you enter a transaction in the wrong account Register, you can copy the information to the correct account and then delete the transaction from the wrong account. If you enter a transaction for a deposit in your checking account Register, for example, but the deposit was actually made in your savings account, you can copy the deposit transaction to the savings account Register and then delete the transaction from the checking account Register.

You also can copy transactions within the same account. If you have a transaction that mirrors another transaction, simply copy the transaction to a blank transaction line in the Register.

To copy a transaction, follow these steps:

1. In the Register, highlight the transaction that you want to copy.

2. Choose E**d**it from the Register button bar and then select **C**opy Transaction. Quicken copies the entire transaction to the Windows clipboard.

3. Move to a new transaction line within the same Register, or access another account Register and move to a new transaction line. (Moving around the Register is explained in Chapter 6, "Using the Register.")

4. Choose E**d**it from the Register button bar and then select **P**aste Transaction. Quicken enters the copied transaction information from the Windows clipboard to the new transaction line.

Be sure to delete the old transaction to avoid duplication.

Using Memorized Transactions

To speed the check-writing process, you can have Quicken memorize recurring checks from the Write Checks window. For quick entry in the Register, you also can have Quicken memorize recurring transactions. A memorized check or transaction is information you save from one transaction so that you can recall it for other checks or transactions.

Many transactions you enter probably are similar from week to week and month to month. For a household, you may write a mortgage check, a car loan check, a utility bill check, and so on. For a business, you may write weekly payroll checks to employees and monthly checks to major vendors. Because transactions often are similar, Quicken enables you to store transaction information in a special list known as the *Memorized Transaction List*. Rather than reenter the same information, you can reuse transaction information.

Tip
Memorizing checks is valuable if you address checks, because you don't have to reenter the payee's address every time you write a check.

By default, Quicken memorizes all new transactions that you enter. Memorizing new transactions is a QuickFill option (explained in the section "Setting QuickFill Options," earlier in this chapter). If you turn off this option, you can still select to memorize a transaction and add it to the Memorized Transaction List. The following discussion assumes that you have turned off the **A**utomatic Memorization of New Transactions option (see fig. 7.5).

You can recall a memorized transaction from the Memorized Transaction List. Quicken enters the transaction information in the Write Checks window or the Register. You can edit or delete a memorized transaction directly from the memorized lists.

CPA Tip: Memorizing Transactions to Save Time

Memorized transactions provide a quick way to enter lengthy, split transactions that you always assign to the same categories or subcategories. A transaction to record your paycheck, for example, involves several split lines because you must assign categories for federal withholding, state withholding, FICA withholding, Medicare withholding, and so on, to each paycheck transaction. If you have Quicken memorize a paycheck transaction and then recall the transaction, Quicken enters the categories for you. Then, if necessary, you simply change the amounts assigned to the categories.

Memorizing a Transaction

When you have Quicken memorize a transaction, Quicken stores the payee name, amount, address (if applicable), memo, and category for the transaction in the Memorized Transaction List. Later, you can recall the memorized check to a blank check or transaction line, and Quicken automatically fills in the same information as the memorized transaction.

To memorize a transaction, follow these steps:

1. In the Write Checks window, display the check, or in the Register, highlight the transaction that you want to memorize. If you are entering a new transaction, you can enter as little or as much of the transaction that you want Quicken to memorize. If you want Quicken to memorize only the payee and the category, for example, enter only that information and continue with steps 2 through 4.

2. From the **E**dit menu, choose **M**emorize Transaction (or press Ctrl+M).

3. If you have Quicken memorize a split transaction, Quicken displays a message window that asks whether you want to memorize the split amounts as percentages of the transaction amount. Choose **Y**es to memorize the percentages, or choose **N**o if you want the actual amounts memorized. This feature is handy if a memorized transaction amount varies, but the split is always based on the same percentages.

4. Quicken displays a message that it is about to memorize the transaction. Choose OK to save the transaction information in the Memorized Transaction List.

> **Note**
>
> Quicken stores memorized investment transactions in a separate Memorized Transaction List. (Refer to Chapter 16, "Monitoring Your Investments," to learn about memorized investment transactions.) In this section, you learn how to memorize and recall transactions in all other account Registers.

> **Note**
>
> Quicken doesn't memorize the date of a transaction or the check or transaction number. When you recall a memorized transaction, Quicken enters the current date. You assign the check number when you enter or print a check transaction.

Recalling a Check or Transaction

Tip
Press Ctrl+T to display the Memorized Transaction List to use a memorized transaction from the list.

If the QuickFill option that controls whether transactions are automatically entered is on, Quicken automatically recalls a memorized transaction when you begin typing the payee (see the sections, "Using QuickFill in Fields," and "Setting QuickFill Options," earlier in this chapter). If this option is not on, you can still recall a memorized transaction from the Memorized Transaction List. Suppose that you have Quicken memorize a check to L.L. Department Store for a montly service agreement. When you need to pay L.L. Department Store again, you recall the memorized check from the Memorized Transaction List, shown in figure 7.7.

Fig. 7.7
The Memorized Transaction List includes the transactions that you have had Quicken memorize.

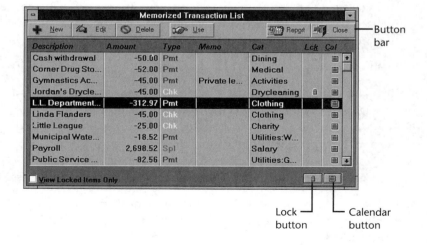

The Memorized Transaction List shows all memorized transactions (except memorized investment transactions). For checks, you want to recall only those transactions that show Chk in the Type column. Chk indicates that the transaction was memorized from the Write Checks window. Check transactions include information that appears only in the Write Checks window, such as the address data and the extra message line.

Figure 7.7 shows some of the information saved as part of the Memorize Transaction operation. The address information and message also are saved, but the address and message don't appear in the Memorized Transaction List.

The Memorized Transaction List is sorted by payee. For each payee, Quicken shows the transaction amount, the transaction type (Chk, Pmt, Dep, and so on), the memo (if any), the category assigned to the memorized transaction, whether the memorized transaction is locked, and whether the transaction is a scheduled transaction. You learn about locked transactions later in this chapter. Chapter 14, "Scheduling Future Transactions," describes scheduled transactions.

To recall a memorized transaction, follow these steps:

1. Access the Write Checks window and display a blank check, or access the Register and move to a blank transaction line.

2. From the **L**ists menu, choose Memorized **T**ransaction (or press Ctrl+T) to display the Memorized Transaction List (refer to fig. 7.7).

3. Use the scroll bar or press the up- and down-arrow keys to highlight the memorized transaction you want to recall.

4. Choose the **U**se button, double-click the transaction, or press Enter to select the memorized transaction. Quicken uses the memorized transaction to fill in the check in the Write Checks window or the transaction line in the Register.

5. Edit the transaction information, if necessary.

6. Choose Re**c**ord to record the check.

Caution

If you recall a memorized transaction into a transaction line with a recorded transaction, Quicken replaces the existing transaction information with the recalled memorized transaction. Be careful not to recall a memorized transaction to a valid transaction line in the Register. You can remove the memorized transaction by choosing the Restore button before recording the transaction.

Locking a Memorized Transaction

Quicken 4 for Windows allows you to lock a memorized transaction so that it doesn't change if you memorize another transaction with the same payee. For example, assume that you enter a new transaction for a payment to Jordan's Drycleaning Service for $45 and assign the category *Drycleaning*. Then, the transaction is automatically memorized by Quicken or you memorize the transaction (as explained in the previous section). The next time that you enter a transaction for Jordan's Drycleaning Service, QuickFill automatically enters the amount of $45 and assigns the *Drycleaning* category. If you change the transaction amount from $45 to $50, Quicken changes the amount of the memorized transaction to $50. If you lock the memorized transaction, however, Quicken allows you to enter a different amount ($50) for the amount but it does not change the amount in the memorized transaction (which remains at $45).

To lock a memorized transaction, follow these steps:

1. Access the Memorized Transaction List (as explained previously).

2. Highlight the memorized transaction that you want to lock.

3. Click the Lock button (see fig. 7.7). Quicken displays a Lock icon in the Lck column of the memorized transaction. Notice that in figure 7.7, the check transaction to Jordan's Drycleaning Service is locked.

To unlock a transaction, follow the same steps above. When you click the Lock button for a locked transaction, Quicken unlocks the memorized transaction and removes the Lock icon from the transaction.

Note

If you want to show only locked transactions in the Memorized Transaction List, select the **V**iew Locked Items Only check box (in lower-left corner of figure 7.7).

> **Note**
>
> Quicken shows all transactions in the Financial Calendar on the date that they are recorded or the date that they are scheduled for in the future. The Memorized Transaction List shows a calendar button next to each transaction that is also entered in the Financial Calendar (see fig. 7.7). If you don't want to show a transaction in the Financial Calendar, remove the calendar button by highlighting the transaction in the Memorized Transaction List and clicking the Calendar button at the bottom of the Memorized Transaction List.

Editing a Memorized Transaction

Over time, the transaction information that Quicken has memorized may need to be updated. Updating transaction information doesn't present a problem. To edit a memorized transaction, follow these steps:

1. From the Memorized Transaction List (refer to fig. 7.7), highlight the memorized transaction that you want to edit.

2. Choose Edit from the button bar. Quicken displays the Edit Memorized Transaction dialog box with the memorized transaction information.

3. Make the necessary changes to the transaction information. To change the cleared status, click the Cleared check box. To change the information for a memorized split transaction, choose **S**plits to display the Splits window. Edit the information in the Splits window and choose OK to return to the Edit Memorized Transaction dialog box. To change the address and message line (if applicable) for printed checks, choose Add**r**ess. Quicken displays the Printed Check Information dialog box. Choose OK to return to the Edit Memorized Transaction dialog box.

4. Choose OK to save the changes to the memorized transaction.

Deleting a Memorized Transaction

At some point, the original reasons you had for memorizing a transaction may no longer apply. Eventually, you may pay off the mortgage or car loan, children may outgrow the need for day care, or you may decide to stop spending money on an item, such as club dues or cable television.

At any time, you can delete memorized transactions from the Memorized Transaction List. To delete a memorized transaction from the list, follow these steps:

1. From the Memorized Transaction List (refer to fig. 7.7), highlight the memorized transaction that you want to delete.

2. Choose **D**elete.

3. Quicken displays a message that you are about to delete a memorized transaction. To delete the memorized check, choose OK. If you decide not to delete the memorized transaction, choose Cancel or press Esc.

> **Note**
>
> To get a quick report listing of all transactions containing the payee name for a specific memorized transaction in the Memorized Transaction List, select the Rep**o**rt button. When you select QuickReport, Quicken lists all transactions (in all accounts) with the same payee name as the highlighted memorized transaction in the Memorized Transaction List.

Finding Transactions

You may write only a handful of checks and make only one or two deposits a month. Even with such low volume, however, you soon have several dozen transactions in a Register. As you write more checks and make additional deposits, searching through your Register for specific transactions becomes more and more difficult. You eventually may want to know whether you recorded a deposit or paid a bill, or when you last paid a vendor.

Tip
You also can use the Find window to search for a check that you have written, but not yet printed, from the Write Checks window.

You easily can locate the transaction in the Write Checks window or in the Register by using Quicken's Find window. You can look for transactions where the payee is Stouffer's Office Supplies, where the category is Utilities, or where the amount is $88.44, for example.

> **Note**
>
> If you want to search for transactions in the Register by date, select E**d**it button from the Register button bar and then choose Go to A **S**pecific Date. Quicken displays the Go to Date dialog box. Enter or select the date that corresponds to the transaction that you are searching for and choose OK.

One way to search through transactions is to use an exact match. An *exact match* means that you look for a transaction that has a payee, an amount, a category, or another piece of transaction information exactly equal to what you want.

To search through transactions in the Register, follow these steps:

1. Select **F**ind from the Register button bar or the Write Checks button bar. Or, choose **F**ind from the **E**dit menu (or press Ctrl+F). Quicken displays the Find window, shown in figure 7.8.

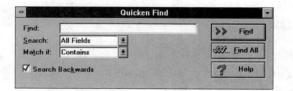

Fig. 7.8
Use the Quicken Find window to locate a transaction.

2. In the **F**ind text box, type the information you are looking for. If you are looking for a check transaction to CompuServe, for example, type **CompuServe** in the **F**ind text box. If you are looking for a check for $100 but don't know who it was made to, type **100** in the **F**ind text box.

3. Next, tell Quicken where to look for the information that you entered in the **F**ind text box. From the **S**earch drop-down list, select one of the following search options:

All Fields	Searches every field in every transaction in the Register
Amount	Searches the Payment or Deposit fields (or the Amount field in the Splits window)
Cleared Status	Searches only those transactions with the specified cleared status
Memo	Searches only the Memo field
Date	Searches only the Date field
Category/Class	Searches only the Category field
Check Number	Searches only the Num (Check Number) field
Payee	Searches only the Payee field

4. Tell Quicken how you want to match the information you entered in the Match text box. You may want to find only transactions that match the exact text you entered in the Find box, or you may want to find all transactions that are greater than the amount you entered in the Find text box.

Use match characters to search for transactions based on a field that includes or excludes certain letters, characters, or series of characters. Match characters include three special characters: the question mark (?), double periods (..), and the tilde (~). The question mark can represent any one character. Double periods represent any character at the beginning, middle, or end of what you type. The tilde identifies a word, character, or group of characters to exclude from the search.

To search for transactions whose date is the first 9 days in July 1995, type **7/?/95** in the Find text box. To search for transactions whose date is after July 9, 1994, type 7/??/95.

Type **..computer..** to find checks to payees with the word *Computer* in the name. Quicken finds Computer Superstore, Jones Computers, and A-1 Computer Stores.

To find transactions assigned to categories other than the *Interest* category, type **~interest** in the Find text box. Then specify the field that you want Quicken to search in the **S**earch drop-down list.

> **Note**
>
> You can use search characters together. For example, you can type **~..Smith..** to find transactions to payees other than those with the name Smith in the name.

5. To search backwards through the Register or the Write Checks window, select the Search Backwards check box.

6. Begin the search by selecting the Find button. If Quicken finds a transaction that matches the search request that you entered in the Find window, it highlights the transaction (the Find window remains open for additional searches). To repeat the search, select Find again. When Quicken reaches the first or last transaction in the Register, it displays a message asking whether you want to continue the search from the beginning or end of the account. Choose **Y**es to continue or **N**o to stop the search. If no transactions are found that match your search request,

Quicken displays a message that no matching transactions were found. Choose OK to stop the search.

To display a list of all transactions that match the Find criteria, select Find All. Quicken displays the Quicken Find window, as shown in figure 7.9, with a list of all transactions that match the Find criteria. If you want to show split detail for the transactions in the Quicken Find window, select the Show Matches in Splits check box.

To go to a transaction listed in the Quicken Find window, highlight the transaction and click the Zoom button. Quicken goes to the Register and highlights the transaction. If you want to print the list of transactions, select the Print button.

Select Zoom to go to
transaction in the Register

Transactions
that match
the Find
criteria

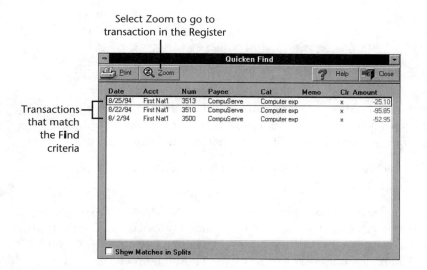

Fig. 7.9
The Quicken Find window is displayed and lists all transactions that match the Find criteria when you select the Find All button.

Searching and Replacing Data in Transactions

New to Quicken 4 for Windows is the Find/Replace command that enables you to search for one or more transactions and make a change to fields in the transactions. For example, if you notice that you've misspelled the payee name in several transactions in the Register, you can quickly locate the transactions and replace the payee name with the correct spelling.

To search and replace data in transactions, follow these steps:

1. Select Find/Replace from the **E**dit menu. Quicken displays the Find and Replace window shown in figure 7.10.

Fig. 7.10
Use the Find and Replace window to replace information in transactions.

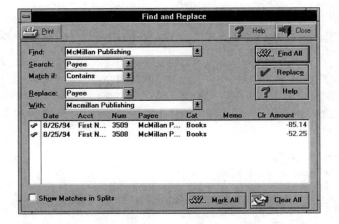

2. In the F**i**nd text box, type the information you are looking for. For example, if you're looking for transactions to the payee whose name you misspelled, enter the misspelled name in the F**i**nd text box.

3. Tell Quicken where to look for the information that you entered in the F**i**nd text box.

4. Next, tell Quicken how you want to match the information you entered in the Ma**t**ch text box. You may want to find only transactions that match the exact text you entered in the F**i**nd box, or you may want to find all transactions that are greater than the amount you entered in the F**i**nd text box.

   Use match characters to search for transactions based on a field that includes or excludes certain letters, characters, or series of characters. Match characters include three special characters: the question mark (?), double periods (..), and the tilde (~). The question mark can represent any one character. Double periods represent any character at the beginning, middle, or end of what you type. The tilde identifies a word, character, or group of characters to exclude from the search.

5. Select the **F**ind All button. Quicken searches the Register and displays the transactions that it found in the Find and Replace window. If you want to show the split detail in transactions, select the Sh**o**w Matches in Splits check box.

6. You can replace information in all transactions listed or in selected transactions. To mark a transaction to replace, highlight the transaction and click. To mark all transactions, select the M**a**rk All button. To unmark all transactions, select the C**l**ear All button.

7. After you have selected the transactions to replace, tell Quicken which field to enter the replacement information in. Select the field from the **R**eplace drop-down list box.

8. In the **W**ith text box, enter the exact information that you want entered as a replacement for the field selected in the Replac**e** drop-down list box.

9. Select the Replac**e** button to have Quicken replace the information in the selected transactions.

10. Quicken tells you the number of items that it is about to replace. Choose OK.

11. Choose OK again when Quicken confirms that it replaced the items.

From Here...

In this chapter, you learned shortcut methods for using Quicken. You may want to review the following chapters to learn when to use these shortcuts:

- Chapter 5, "Writing and Printing Checks," shows you how to enter information in the Write Checks window. Use the shortcuts you learned to make writing checks even easier.

- Chapter 6, "Using the Register," explains how to use Quicken's Registers to enter your financial transactions. The shortcuts that you learned can speed up your work in any Register.

- Chapter 16, "Monitoring Your Investments," shows you how to shortcut your work in investment account Registers by memorizing investment transactions.

Chapter 8

Reconciling Your Bank Account

Reconciling your bank account regularly is one of the most important steps you can take to protect your cash and the accuracy and reliability of your financial records. Most people, however, probably don't reconcile their bank account—unless they feel guilty or frustrated. The work is tedious and usually aggravating as you search, often in vain, for the transaction that explains the difference between the bank's records and your personal records. Fortunately, Quicken provides a fast and easy method of reconciliation.

In this chapter, you learn how to do the following:

- Reconcile a bank account using Quicken

- Mark transactions as cleared

- Print and use Reconciliation Reports

- Create balance-adjustment transactions

Reconciling Your Bank Account with Quicken

Reconciling a bank account isn't difficult. You probably already understand the mechanics of the reconciliation process. To reconcile a bank account, you perform three basic steps:

1. Review the bank statement for new transactions and errors. You want to verify that you have recorded each transaction correctly.

2. Find the transactions not recorded by the bank or cleared, and total these transactions.

3. Verify that the difference between your checkbook balance and the bank balance equals the total of the uncleared transactions. If the totals don't agree, you need to repeat steps 1 and 2.

> ### CPA Tip: Reviewing Canceled Checks
>
> Carefully review each canceled check for authenticity. If a check forger successfully draws a check on your account, you can discover the forgery by reviewing canceled checks. You need to find forgeries if you hope to recover the money.

Quicken makes reconciling a bank account easier by automating the steps and doing the arithmetic for you. To reconcile an account, follow these steps:

1. Select the bank account that you want to reconcile from the Account List or select the account from the Account Selector Bar in the Register or the Write Checks window.

2. Choose Reconcile from the Activities menu, or click the Recon button on the Iconbar. Quicken displays the Reconcile Bank Statement dialog box, with the name of the account that you are reconciling on the title bar (see fig. 8.1).

Fig. 8.1
The Reconcile Bank Statement dialog box includes on the title bar the name of the account that you are reconciling.

3. Quicken automatically enters the bank statement's opening balance in the **B**ank Statement Opening Balance text box. Quicken uses the ending balance from the last reconciliation as the opening balance for this reconciliation. If this is the first time you have reconciled your bank account with Quicken, the opening balance that you entered when you added the account to your system is entered in the **B**ank Statement Opening Balance text box.

4. If the bank statement's balance at the start of the period that the bank statement covers is different than the opening balance entered by Quicken, type the correct opening balance from your statement. (Be sure to read the section "Adjusting Opening Balance Differences" later in this chapter to learn how to handle differences in the bank statement's opening balance.)

> ### Note
>
> Quicken strongly recommends that you use the ending balance from your last bank statement as the opening balance in a new bank account. Therefore, if you used the ending balance as your opening balance, the opening balance that Quicken enters in the Bank Statement Opening Balance field should be correct.

5. Move to the Bank **S**tatement Ending Balance text box and type the bank statement balance shown at the end of the period that the bank statement covers. This amount also appears on the bank statement.

6. Move to the Service **C**harge text box. If you didn't record monthly service fees, record them now by entering the appropriate amount in the Service **C**harge text box. Then enter the service charge transaction date in the **D**ate text box, or click the calendar button to display the minicalendar and select a date. (You learn how to use the minicalendar to enter dates in Chapter 7, "Using Quicken Shortcuts.")

7. (Optional) Move to the Cate**g**ory drop-down list box for the service charge transaction. If you entered an amount in the Service **C**harge drop-down box and want to assign the service charge to a category, select from the drop-down list box the category or subcategory that you want to assign to the service charges.

8. Move to the **I**nterest Earned text box. If you haven't recorded monthly interest income in this account yet, record this amount now by entering the appropriate amount. Type the date that the interest was credited to your bank account in the Da**t**e text box, or click the calendar button to display the minicalendar and select a date. (You learn how to use the minicalendar to enter dates in Chapter 7, "Using Quicken Shortcuts.")

Tip
Use the Service **C**harge text box to enter check charges, ATM charges, or any other fees that your bank assesses.

CPA Tip: Reviewing Canceled Checks

If you normally keep a large account balance, you should have an interest-bearing checking account. You shouldn't keep your money in an account that doesn't earn interest.

Before you close your current account and open a new one, however, review the fees that your bank charges for each type of account. Weigh the interest factor against the fee schedule to determine the most beneficial account type for your business. If your bank doesn't offer interest-bearing accounts to businesses, you may want to deposit excess cash into a savings or money market account. Remember that you can set up savings and money market accounts in your Quicken system and use the Reconcile feature to balance each account.

9. (Optional) Move to the Category drop-down list box for the interest transaction. If you entered an amount in the Interest Earned text box and want to assign the interest income to a category, select from the drop-down list the category or subcategory that you want to assign to the interest income.

10. (Optional) If you didn't print a copy of the Reconciliation Report the last time that you reconciled your bank account, you can print a copy of the report now by choosing the Report command button.

11. Choose OK when the Reconcile Bank Statement dialog box is complete. Quicken displays the Reconcile Bank Statement window, shown in figure 8.2.

Fig. 8.2

The Reconcile Bank Statement window lists all uncleared payments and checks on one side of the window and all uncleared deposits on the other side of the window.

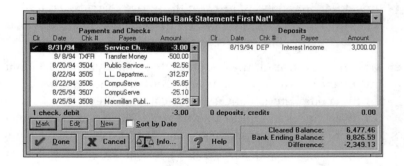

The Reconcile Bank Statement window lists all uncleared transactions (transactions that aren't marked as cleared in the Clr (Cleared) field in the Register), with the Payments and Checks list on the left and the

Deposits list on the right side of the window. The Reconcile Bank Statement window shows the total number and total amount of payments, checks, and deposits marked as cleared during the reconciliation process. This window also shows the cleared balance in your account, the bank's ending statement balance, and the difference. When the difference is zero, you've successfully balanced your bank account.

12. (Optional) If your bank statement lists transactions in date order, you can reorganize the uncleared transactions in the Reconcile Bank Statement window so that they are in date order (instead of check number order). To reorganize uncleared transactions by date, select the **S**ort by Date check box. To return the uncleared transaction to check number order, select the **S**ort by Date check box again to remove the check mark.

13. Mark payments, checks, and deposits that have *cleared* (were recorded by) the bank. To mark a payment or check as cleared, click the payment or check that you want to mark as cleared. You can also mark an item as cleared by highlighting the payment or check and then selecting the **M**ark command button or pressing the spacebar. (To highlight the payment or check, use the scroll bar on the side of the Payments and Checks list or the up and down arrow keys to move through the transaction list.) Follow the same procedure to mark a deposit as cleared in the Deposits list.

Quicken enters a check mark in the Clr (Cleared) column and shows the cleared transaction in darker type.

Tip

If you accidentally mark the wrong transaction as cleared, change its status by clicking the transaction, or by highlighting it and then choosing **M**ark or pressing the spacebar.

> **Note**
>
> To mark a range of transactions as cleared, click the first transaction in the range to highlight it; then Shift+click the last uncleared transaction within the range that you want to mark as cleared (press the Shift key and simultaneously click). Quicken highlights the range of transactions and enters a check mark in the Clr column for each transaction within the range. To mark checks 3405 through 3425 as cleared, for example, click check number 3405, and then Shift+click check number 3425.
>
> You also can mark a range of transactions as cleared by dragging your mouse through the range. Just point to the first transaction in the range and then drag the pointer through the other uncleared transactions in the range that you want to mark as cleared. Release the mouse button at the last uncleared transaction within the desired range. Quicken enters a check mark in the Clr column for each transaction as you drag the mouse pointer through the range of transactions.

As you mark transactions as cleared, Quicken adds the total number of cleared transactions and the total amount of the transactions marked as cleared. These totals are shown below the Payments and Checks list and the Deposits list.

14. (Optional) To correct transactions entered incorrectly in the Register, select the transaction that you want to change and then choose the Edi**t** button. Quicken displays the Register window and highlights the selected transaction. Edit the transactions in the Register in the usual manner. (Chapter 6 describes how to edit transactions in the Register.) Then return to the Reconcile Bank Statement window by clicking the Recon button on the Iconbar or selecting the Reconcile Bank Statement window from the **W**indow menu.

15. (Optional) If you need to enter a new transaction in the Register while you are reconciling, select the **N**ew button. Quicken returns to the Register to the next blank transaction line so that you can enter a new transaction. Return to the Reconcile Bank Statement window by clicking the Recon button on the Iconbar or selecting the Reconcile Bank Statement window from the **W**indow menu.

    If you need to return to the Reconcile Bank Statement dialog box to revise the bank statement information (see fig. 8.1), select the **I**nfo button.

16. When the difference between the Cleared Balance and the Bank Ending Balance is zero, choose **D**one to indicate that you are finished with the reconciliation. Quicken changes each asterisk in the Clr (Cleared) field in the Register to an x. Then Quicken congratulates you and asks whether you want to create a Reconciliation Report, as shown in figure 8.3. (Refer to the next section, "Printing Reconciliation Reports," to learn how to print a Reconciliation Report.)

Note

If the difference between the Cleared Balance and the Bank Ending Balance isn't zero, you may need to make a balance adjustment. The section "Creating Balance Adjustment Transactions" later in this chapter shows you how to adjust your account so that it balances with your bank statement.

Fig. 8.3
Quicken congratulates you when your bank account balances with your bank statement and asks whether you want to create a Reconciliation Report.

CPA Tip: Understanding Debits and Credits

If you understand double-entry bookkeeping, you probably recognize that Quicken uses the labels *debit* and *credit* incorrectly from your perspective. Don't be confused by this usage. The reconciliation summary uses the terms from the bank's perspective to help people who don't understand double-entry bookkeeping.

You can leave the reconciliation process at any time by choosing Cancel or pressing Esc. When you choose Cancel, Quicken asks whether you want to save the items that you have marked in the Reconcile Bank Statement window. Choose **S**ave to leave the reconciliation process and save the work that you have done so far (such as the bank statement ending balance, service charges, interest income, and transactions marked as cleared). If you don't want to save the work you have done so far, choose **D**on't Save. Quicken returns to the Register you were in before you began reconciliation. If you save your work, when you return to the reconciliation process you can pick up where you left off.

Printing Reconciliation Reports

Many people like to keep printed records of their reconciliations. Printed copies of the Reconciliation Report show how you reconciled your records with the bank, indicate all checks and deposits still outstanding, and show all transactions that cleared the bank in a given month. This information may be helpful if you subsequently discover that the bank made an error or that you made a reconciliation error.

To print a Reconciliation Report, follow these steps:

1. From the Reconciliation Complete dialog box shown in figure 8.3, choose **Y**es. The Reconciliation Report Setup window appears (see fig. 8.4).

Fig. 8.4

The Reconciliation Report Setup dialog box appears when you opt to print a Reconciliation Report.

2. (Optional) In the **R**eport Title text box, enter the title that you want printed on the Reconciliation Report. You may want to use the month and year to distinguish one report from another.

3. In the Show Reconciliation to **B**ank Balance As Of drop-down list box, type the date that you performed the reconciliation. Alternatively, click the calendar button to select a date from the minicalendar. (Refer to Chapter 7, "Using Quicken Shortcuts," to learn how to use the minicalendar to enter dates.)

4. In the Transactions to Include section, select the level of detail that you want included in the Reconciliation Report. Select **A**ll Transactions if you want to print all the details of every transaction (cleared and uncleared). Select **S**ummary and Uncleared to summarize transactions marked as cleared and to show detail of uncleared transactions.

5. If you want the transactions from a savings goal account to appear in the Reconciliation Report, select the Show Savings **G**oal Transactions check box. You learn about savings goal accounts in Chapter 18, "Saving for the Future with Quicken."

6. Choose the **P**rint button. Quicken displays the Print Report dialog box.

7. To print to your printer, select the P**r**inter option in the Print To section.

The printed Reconciliation Report includes three distinct components: the Reconciliation Summary, the Cleared Transaction Detail, and the Uncleared Transaction Detail. If you select to print **A**ll Transactions in the Reconciliation Report (refer to fig. 8.4), Quicken prints all three components. If you select to print **S**ummary and Uncleared transactions in the Reconciliation Report (refer to fig. 8.4), only the first and third parts print.

Creating Balance Adjustment Transactions

If you can't *reconcile* an account—that is, if the difference amount shown in the Reconcile Bank Account window equals any number other than zero (refer to fig. 8.2)—the difference may be due to a difference in the opening balance that Quicken shows in the Reconcile Bank Statement dialog box (refer to fig. 8.1) and the opening balance shown on your bank statement. Quicken handles these differences by adjusting the opening balance difference. Quicken handles any other differences (not arising from an opening balance difference) by creating a balancing adjustment.

Adjusting Opening Balance Differences

If you changed the amount in the **B**ank Statement Opening Balance text box in the Reconcile Bank Statement dialog box to match the opening balance on your bank statement, Quicken shows the opening balance difference in the Reconcile Bank Account window.

The following three reasons can cause your Quicken opening balance to differ from your bank statement's opening balance:

■ You are reconciling your account with Quicken for the first time, so Quicken is using the opening balance you entered when you set up your checking account as the bank statement opening balance. If the opening balance that you entered when you set up your checking account didn't account for uncleared checks written before you started your Quicken system (because you didn't enter previous transactions), your bank's opening balance differs from the opening balance in your account by the amount of uncleared checks.

Assume that you set up your checking account on January 1 and entered the opening balance shown in your manual checkbook register—$3,500. If, however, you had written three checks totaling $500 that hadn't cleared the bank by January 1, your opening bank statement balance would be $500 greater, or $4,000.

The opening balance difference remains until you enter all uncleared transactions and adjust Quicken's opening balance to agree with the amount that actually was in your checking account the day you started using Quicken (in this example, you adjust the opening balance to $4,000). You can enter uncleared transactions without leaving the reconciliation by choosing the Edit button to access the Register.

> ### Note
>
> Quicken can do an automatic opening balance adjustment at the end of the reconciliation process; however, don't let Quicken make this adjustment unless you agree with the amount. In this section, you learn how to make opening balance adjustments when you complete the reconciliation process.

- You didn't enter previous transactions before you began using Quicken. When you later entered these previous transactions, you changed the opening balance in the Bank Account Register to reflect your checking account's balance on the first day of the year. The opening balance difference remains until you mark previous transactions as cleared. To do so, leave the reconciliation and go to the Register.

  For each cleared transaction, type an **X** in the Clr (cleared) field. Because all previous transactions may not have cleared the bank, you should review your bank statements, beginning with the first of the year, to account for all numbered checks and deposits.

- You aren't using the most current bank statement, or you haven't reconciled a previous month's statement. Reconcile your account first against the earliest monthly statement, and then reconcile your account against each subsequent statement.

When you choose **D**one to finish a reconciliation when an opening balance difference exists, Quicken displays the Create Opening Balance Adjustment dialog box (see fig. 8.5).

If you have exhausted all your efforts at locating the opening balance difference, you can have Quicken create an adjustment to your opening balance. Enter the date for the opening balance adjustment in the **D**ate for Adjustment text box. Choose **Y**es to create the adjustment; choose **N**o if you don't want to adjust the opening balance but want to proceed with the reconciliation. Choose Cancel if you don't want to adjust the opening balance and want to return to the Reconcile Bank Statement window to review cleared transactions.

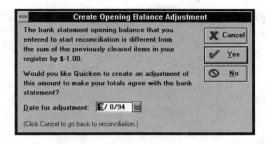

Fig. 8.5
In the Create
Opening Balance
Adjustment dialog
box, you can
adjust your
opening balance if
the reconciliation
difference results
from a difference
in the opening
balance.

Adjusting for Other Differences

If other differences arise (other than an opening balance difference) at the completion of the reconciliation, as a last resort you may want to make a *balance adjustment*. A balance adjustment means that Quicken creates a transaction that forces the difference amount to zero.

When you finish the reconciliation (by selecting **D**one) when the difference between the Cleared Balance and the Bank Ending Balance isn't zero, Quicken displays the Adjust Balance dialog box, shown in figure 8.6.

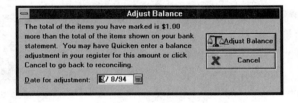

Fig. 8.6
The Adjust Balance
dialog box enables
you to tell Quicken
whether you want
to make a balance
adjustment.

In the Adjust Balance dialog box, Quicken informs you of the magnitude of the reconciliation difference. To create the balance adjustment, follow these steps:

1. In the **D**ate For Adjustment box, type or select the date that you want Quicken to use for the balance adjustment transaction.

2. Choose the **A**djust Balance button. Quicken enters a balance adjustment transaction to your account and displays the Reconciliation Complete: Balance Adjusted dialog box.

3. If you want to create a Reconciliation Report, choose **Y**es and follow the steps for printing a Reconciliation Report earlier in this chapter. To finish the reconciliation process and return to the Register without printing a Reconciliation Report, choose **N**o.

Figure 8.7 shows a balance adjustment transaction in the Register.

Fig. 8.7
Quicken creates a balance adjustment transaction in the Register for the account that you are reconciling.

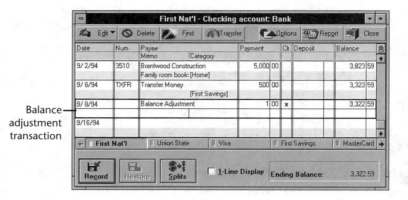

Balance adjustment transaction

CPA Tip: Finding Reconciliation Differences

Although Quicken provides the adjustment feature, you probably shouldn't use it because it camouflages errors in the Register. As a result, you never really can be sure where the error occurred. The difference amount equals a number other than zero because you are missing one or more transactions in the Register, you incorrectly marked a transaction as cleared, or perhaps you transposed some numbers (such as typing **$87.00** as **$78.00**).

If you've spent hours to locate a $1 difference, obviously, you should not waste any more time and select to make the adjustment.

The difference also may occur because someone forged checks or embezzled from your account. If you can't reconcile the account, make sure that the previous month's reconciliation resulted in a difference equal to zero. If the previous month's reconciliation shows a difference other than zero, you must reconcile that month (and perhaps the months before that one) before you can get the current month's difference to be displayed as zero.

From Here...

You may want to review the following chapters:

■ Chapter 3, "Defining Your Accounts," describes accounts and how to select an account to use.

■ Chapter 6, "Using the Register," shows you how to edit and delete transactions in the Register.

■ Chapter 7, "Using Quicken Shortcuts," shows you how to use the pop-up calendar to select dates in fields.

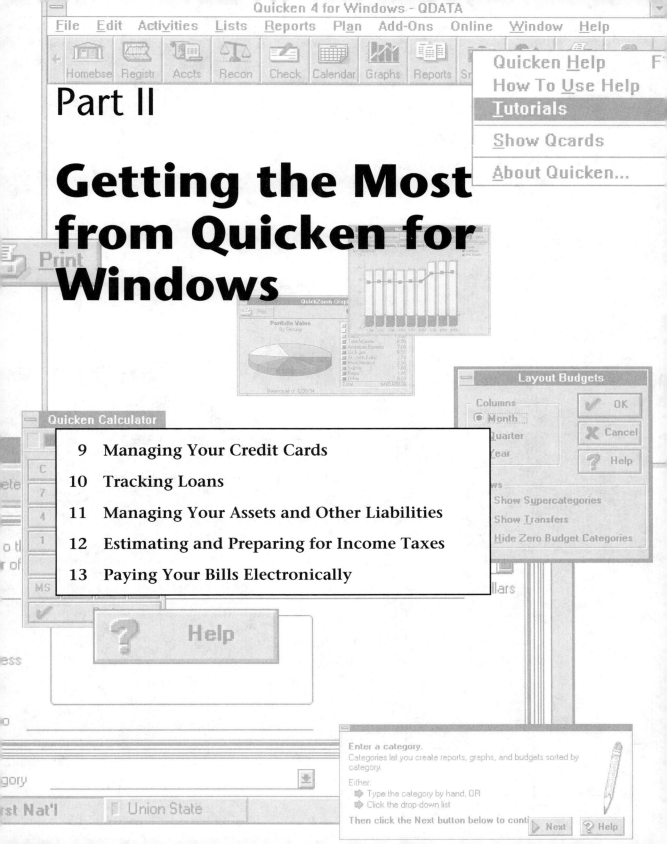

Part II

Getting the Most from Quicken for Windows

Quicken 4 for Windows - QDATA

File   Edit   Activities   Lists   Reports   Plan   Add-Ons   Online   Window   Help

Homebse   Registr   Accts   Recon   Check   Calendar   Graphs   Reports   Sr

Quicken **H**elp
How To **U**se Hel
Tutorials
Show Qcards
About Quicken...

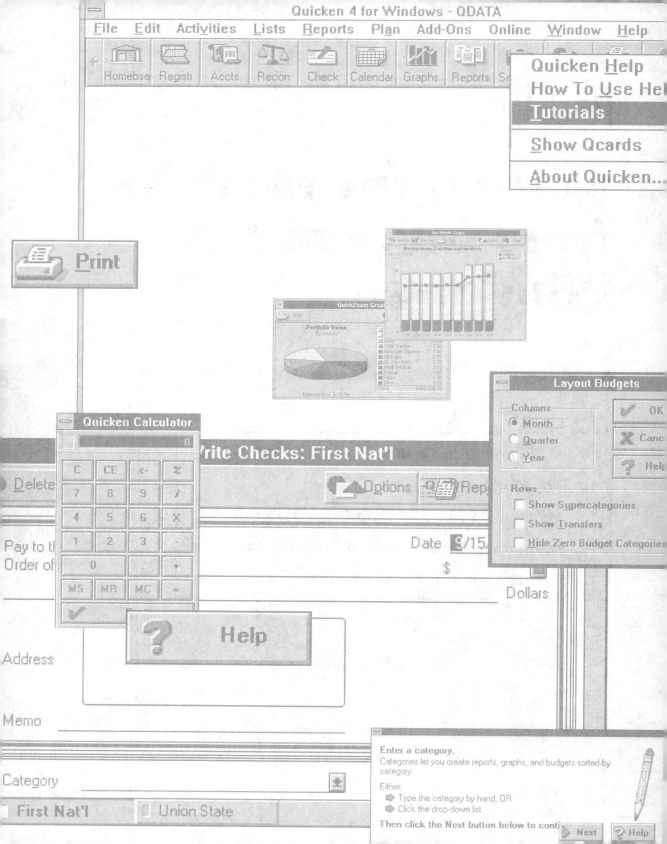

Print

Net Worth Graph
Monthly Assets, Liabilities, and Net Worth

QuickZoom Graph

Print

Portfolio Value
By Security

Dean	0.00
Time Warner	0.93
American Express	7.06
Oil & gas	6.51
St. John Knits	3.78
Mead Medical	2.50
Siskus	1.88
Pitou	1.46
Other	8.08
Total	**$460,608.09**

Balance as of 6/30/94

Layout Budgets

Columns
- ⦿ Month
- ◯ Quarter
- ◯ Year

Rows
- ☐ Show **S**upercategories
- ☐ Show **T**ransfers
- ☐ **H**ide Zero Budget Categories

✔ OK
✘ Canc
❓ Help

Quicken Calculator

```
                          0
  C    CE   <-    %
  7    8    9     /
  4    5    6     X
  1    2    3     -
     0         +
  MS   MR   MC    =
  ✔
```

rite Checks: First Nat'l

Options   Rep

Delete

❓ Help

Pay to tl
Order of

Date ☰/15,

$

Dollars

Address

Memo

Category   ⬇

First Nat'l   Union State

Enter a category.
Categories let you create reports, graphs, and budgets sorted by category.

Either:
➡ Type the category by hand, OR
➡ Click the drop-down list

Then click the Next button below to conti   ▶ Next   ❓ Help

Chapter 9

Managing Your Credit Cards

If you're like most people, you use several credit cards to buy merchandise. Now that many service providers such as doctors, lawyers, and dentists are accepting credit cards as payment, you may be making even more credit purchases.

The more you buy on credit and the more credit cards you use, the more important managing your credit becomes. With Quicken, you can set up individual credit card accounts that help you record and keep track of purchases, payments, and finance charges. Credit card accounts can also help you track a line of credit from your bank (such as a line of credit for working capital to set up your new business).

You can use an IntelliCharge account with your Quicken VISA card. The Quicken VISA card is like any other credit card, except that the name Quicken appears on the card and the card is issued to Quicken users only. *IntelliCharge* is an Intuit-provided service that updates your Credit Card Register automatically by disk or modem.

Tip
If you're interested in obtaining a Quicken credit card, fill out the application form enclosed in your Quicken 4 for Windows package.

If you don't pay your credit card balance each month, setting up a credit card account helps you manage your credit transactions.

If you do pay the balance on your credit card bills each month, you probably don't need to set up a credit card account. Instead, enter the payment transaction in the Register for the account that you use to pay your credit card bill and split the transaction to assign multiple categories to it (Chapters 5 and 6 discuss how to split transactions). The categories that you assign to a credit card transaction classify the purchases that you make.

CPA Tip: Show Credit Card Liabilities on a Balance Sheet

The balance carried on your credit cards is a liability. If you want all liabilities reflected in your net worth, set up a credit card account so that these liabilities appear in your Net Worth Reports or balance sheet statements.

This chapter shows you how to do the following:

- Set up a credit card account
- Track credit card activity in a credit card account
- Reconcile your credit card account
- Pay your credit card bills
- Use an IntelliCharge account

Using a Credit Card Account

If you pay your credit card bill in full every month (good for you!), you don't need to set up a credit card account unless you want to track exactly where and when charges are made. Your credit card spending is recorded in your checking account when you write your check to pay the credit card company. And because your credit card balance is reduced to zero each month, you don't need to keep track of that balance.

But for those of you who might carry a credit card balance, set up and use the Register of a credit card account to keep records of your credit card spending. Follow the same steps you do for using any other Register: set up an account, enter transactions, and then reconcile the account.

Setting Up a Credit Card Account

First, you need to set up the account and record the beginning balance. (Because you are working with a liability, the beginning balance is what you owe.) To set up a credit card account, follow these steps:

1. Click the Accts button on the Iconbar, and then choose the **N**ew button in the Account List window; or choose the Create **N**ew Account command from the Acti**v**ities menu. Quicken displays the Create New Account dialog box.

2. Select the Credit Card Account option. The Create Credit Card Account dialog box appears (see fig. 9.1).

> **Note**
>
> If you want Quicken to "guide" you through the credit card account set up process, click the **G**uide Me option check box at the bottom of the Create New Account dialog box. If you feel that you don't need help, don't select this option. Because these Quicken instructions are straightforward and self-explanatory, the discussion that follows covers adding a credit card account without the **G**uide Me option.

Fig. 9.1
Use the Create Credit Card Account dialog box to enter information about the credit card account you are creating.

II

Getting the Most

3. In the **A**ccount Name text box, type the credit card account name (**MasterCard**, **VISA**, or **Discover**, for example). You can use up to 15 letters, spaces, and any symbols in the account name except the following:

    :] [/ | ^

4. Type your outstanding credit card balance in the **B**alance text box. If the credit card balance is zero, you must enter **0** in the **B**alance text box (you can't leave it blank). If you need to calculate your balance, click the calculator icon to display the pop-up calculator.

5. In the As Of text box, type or select the date (in *mm/dd/yy* format) that corresponds with the balance you entered.

Tip
Use the + (plus) and – (minus) keys to move the date forward or backward one day. Also, try clicking the calendar icon and selecting a date from the minicalendar, as explained in Chapter 7.

6. (Optional) In the **D**escription text box, type a description of the credit card account, using up to 21 characters.

7. (Optional) Type your credit limit in the Credit **L**imit text box.

8. (Optional) To enter more detail for the credit card account, such as the bank name, account number, contact person, telephone number, and interest rate, click the **I**nfo button. The Additional Account Information dialog box appears. Add the desired details, and then choose OK to return to the Create Credit Card Account dialog box.

9. (Optional) If you want to designate a tax schedule for transactions in this credit card account, select **T**ax. Quicken displays the Tax Schedule Information dialog box. Click the drop-down arrow in the T**r**ansfers In or Transfers **O**ut boxes and select the appropriate tax schedule. (You learn more about assigning tax schedules to accounts and categories in Chapter 12, "Estimating and Preparing For Income Taxes.") Click OK to return to the Create Credit Card Account dialog box.

> **Note**
>
> The T**r**ansfers In and Transfers **O**ut options are not available in the Tax Schedule Information dialog box unless the Use **T**ax Schedules option is selected from the **G**eneral Options dialog box. Refer to Chapter 22, "Customizing Quicken," to learn how to set this option.

10. After entering the necessary information in the Create Credit Card Account dialog box, choose OK or press Enter to add the credit card account to the Account List. The Credit Card Register for the account that you just created appears.

> **Note**
>
> If you choose the **N**ew button from the Account List to set up a new account, Quicken displays the Account List—not the Register—after you add account information to the Create Credit Card Account dialog box.

Figure 9.2 shows the Register for the account named MasterCard.

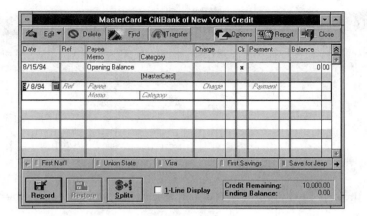

Fig. 9.2
Use the Credit
Card Register to
enter credit card
purchases.

Tracking Credit Card Activity

To track your credit card activity, enter all your credit card transactions into
the Credit Card Register. Credit card purchases are entered directly into your
credit card account; payments are entered into the Bank Account Register
that you use to pay bills when you reconcile your credit card statement.

Although the process of entering transactions is the same in all Quicken Registers, some minor differences exist between the Bank Account Register and
the Credit Card Register. You record each use of your credit card in the
Charge field in the Credit Card Register. Payments to the credit card company appear in the Payment field. If you filled in the Credit **L**imit text box
when you set up the credit card account, Quicken shows the credit remaining
in the lower-right corner of the Register window (above the Ending Balance
field). Figure 9.3 shows a Credit Card Register containing several credit card
purchase transactions.

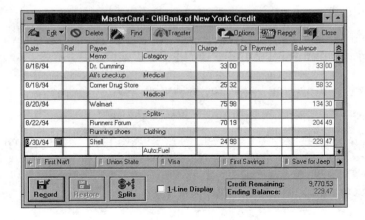

Fig. 9.3
Enter credit card
purchases in the
Charge field in the
Credit Card
Register.

II

Getting the Most

> **Note**
>
> You can enter, edit, and delete credit card transactions the same way that you enter transactions in the Bank Account Register. Refer to Chapter 6, "Using the Register," to review the techniques for entering, editing, and deleting transactions in the Bank Account Register.

If you receive a cash advance from your credit card, record it in the Charge field. If you also use a Cash account to track your cash expenditures, enter the name of that account in the Category field for the transaction. This step enters the cash advance in your Cash account. Chapter 11, "Managing Your Assets and Other Liabilities," gives you some instructions for using a Cash account.

> **CPA Tip: Paying Back Cash Advances**
>
> If you can get cash advances with your credit card, don't make the mistake of assuming that the cash you receive is interest-free for 30 days. Cash advances begin accruing interest on the day the cash is advanced to you. Also, on each cash advance, banks usually charge an additional fee of as much as 1.5 percent. If you are in a bind for cash, get that cash advance—but pay it back as soon as possible to avoid excessive interest charges.

Reconciling Your Credit Card Account

When you receive your credit card statement each month, review it carefully to make sure that you have entered all credit purchases in the Credit Card Register. Reviewing your statement also can help you uncover unauthorized uses of your credit card. You may find that the statement contains credit purchases that you or your spouse didn't make.

Before you pay your credit card bill, reconcile your statement balance with the balance in your Quicken Credit Card Register. After you successfully reconcile your credit card statement, Quicken gives you the option of paying the entire credit card account balance or making a partial payment.

To reconcile your credit card account, follow these steps:

1. While in the Credit Card Register, choose Pay Credit Card Bill from the Activities menu or click the Recon button on the Iconbar. The Credit Card Statement Information dialog box appears, with the name of the credit card account in the Title bar (see fig. 9.4).

Fig. 9.4
The Credit Card
Statement
Information dialog
box.

2. Type the sum of the charges and cash advances shown on your state-ment in the **C**harges, Cash Advances text box.

3. In the **P**ayments, Credits text box, enter the sum of the payments and credits shown on your credit card statement.

4. In the **N**ew Balance text box, type the balance due as shown on your credit card statement.

5. Enter any finance charges that appear on your credit card statement in the **F**inance Charges text box (in the Transaction To Be Added section). Quicken enters a credit card transaction in your Credit Card Register for finance charges.

6. Enter the date on which the finance charges were assessed in the Date text box, or click the calendar icon and select the date from the minicalendar.

7. Move to the C**a**tegory text box. If you entered an amount in the **F**inance Charges text box and want to assign the finance charge to a category, from the drop-down list select the category or subcategory that you want to assign to the finance charge transaction that Quicken enters (you may enter Int Exp for interest expense, for example).

CPA Tip: Avoid Credit Card Interest

Avoid credit card interest and finance charges. The Tax Reform Act of 1986 disallowed deductions for consumer or personal interest on federal and most state income tax returns. More importantly, credit card annual interest rates are usually 18 percent to 21 percent (if you are considered a high risk, even more). Consequently, with the lost tax deduction and high interest costs, carrying credit card balances that accrue interest just doesn't make sense.

8. Choose OK after entering all the necessary information in the Credit Card Statement Information dialog box. The Pay Credit Card Bill win-dow appears (see fig. 9.5).

II

Getting the Most

Fig. 9.5
The Pay Credit Card Bill window lists all uncleared charges on one side of the window; all uncleared payments are listed on the other.

The Pay Credit Card Bill window shows the total number and total dollar amount of charges and payments marked as cleared during the reconciliation process. All uncleared transactions also are listed in the Pay Credit Card Bill window. The Charges list appears on the left side and the Payments list appears on the right side of the window.

The Pay Credit Card Bill also shows the cleared balance in your credit card account, the credit card statement's balance, and the difference. When the difference is zero, you've successfully balanced your credit card account.

9. Mark as cleared the charges and payments that appear on your credit card statement. (Refer to Chapter 8, "Reconciling Your Bank Account," to learn how to mark transactions as cleared.)

   To change the cleared status of a transaction, simply repeat the marking process.

   As you mark transactions as cleared, Quicken adds the total number of cleared transactions and the total amount of the transactions marked as cleared. These totals are shown below the Charges list and the Payments list.

10. (Optional) To enter a new credit card transaction or correct a transaction, select the **N**ew or Edi**t** buttons. Quicken returns to the Credit Card Register so that you can add a new transaction or edit a transaction. Click the Recon button on the Iconbar to return to the Pay Credit Card Bill window.

11. When the difference between the Cleared Balance and the Statement Balance is zero, choose **D**one to indicate that you are finished with the reconciliation. The Make Credit Card Payment dialog box appears. The next section of this chapter explains how to pay your credit card bill.

If the difference between the Cleared Balance and the Statement Balance in the Pay Credit Card window doesn't equal zero when you choose **D**one to complete the reconciliation, an Adjusting Register to Agree with Statement dialog box appears. To accept Quicken's opening balance or missing charges adjustments, select categories to assign to the adjustment transactions in the appropriate Category text boxes. Then choose the **A**djust Balance button. Quicken enters a Balance Adjustment Transaction in the Credit Card Register. If you don't want to make the adjustments, choose Cancel. Quicken returns to the Pay Credit Card Bill window.

To leave the reconciliation process at any time, choose Cancel. Quicken asks whether you want to save the items you marked as cleared. Choose **S**ave to save the work that you have done so far before leaving the reconciliation. If you prefer not saving the work you have done so far, choose **D**on't Save to return to the Register you were in before you began the reconciliation. If you save your work, you can proceed from that point when you return to the reconciliation. Otherwise, you must start over.

CPA Tip: Monitoring Your Credit Card Statements

Balancing your credit card account helps you avoid unauthorized credit transactions. Because you don't need to give your signature when you use your credit card number for purchases made by telephone, all that an unauthorized user needs is your account number, expiration date, and current address to make a credit purchase by telephone.

If you don't monitor your credit card statements on a timely basis, you may not be aware of fraudulent usage until several thousand dollars are charged. Most credit card companies protect you against unauthorized credit transactions, but you must inform the company within a certain time period for its safeguards to take effect.

Paying Your Credit Card Bill

Now that you have reconciled your credit card account with your credit card statement, you're ready to pay your credit card bill. You can write a check in Quicken that pays the entire balance or makes a partial payment, or you can choose to pay nothing at this time. If you don't use Quicken to write checks, a transaction is entered in the Bank Account Register from which you write manual checks for the credit card payment.

II

Getting the Most

To pay your credit card bill, follow these steps:

1. In the Make Credit Card Payment dialog box (see fig. 9.6), select the bank account to use for paying your credit card bill from the **B**ank Acct drop-down list.

Fig. 9.6

The Make Credit Card Payment dialog box appears when you complete your credit card account reconciliation.

Note

If you don't want to pay your credit card bill at this time, choose Cancel in the Make Credit Card Payment dialog box. Quicken returns you to the Credit Card Register.

2. In the Payment Will Be section, select **P**rinted if you want to write and print a check using Quicken. Select **H**and Written if you want to write a manual check and have Quicken enter the check transaction in the Register.

3. Choose OK.

   If you chose to write a computer check, the Write Checks window appears. The check is initially filled in with the outstanding balance amount in the $ (Amount) field. To make a partial payment rather than pay the outstanding balance, move to the $ (Amount) field and change the amount to whatever you want to pay. Choose the Re**c**ord button to record the check in the Write Checks window, the Credit Card Register, and the Bank Account Register.

   If you chose to write a manual check, Quicken displays the Register and fills in the transaction with the outstanding balance amount in the Payment field. If you plan to make a partial payment rather than pay the full balance, change the dollar amount in the Payment field to the amount you want to pay. Then choose the Re**c**ord button to record the transaction in the Register. Quicken also records the payment in the Credit Card Register.

Using the IntelliCharge Account

IntelliCharge is a service that you can use in Quicken to track your Quicken VISA card activity. With IntelliCharge, you receive your monthly credit card statements on disk or by modem, thus enabling you to record your credit card activity in your IntelliCharge account instantly. Your credit transactions not only are recorded but are assigned automatically to categories (according to Intuit's standard list).

Tip

To obtain a Quicken VISA card, complete the application form enclosed in your Quicken 4 for Windows package.

If you want to receive your statements by modem, you must use the local access number for CompuServe where Quicken downloads statement information. You don't need a CompuServe membership to use IntelliCharge, however. Call CompuServe at (800)848-8980 to get the local access number where Quicken downloads information.

> **Note**
>
> If you don't have a Quicken VISA card, don't set up an IntelliCharge account; IntelliCharge accounts work only with Quicken credit cards.

Before you can begin using IntelliCharge to record your credit card transactions, you must set up a credit card account as an IntelliCharge account. Setting up an IntelliCharge account is much like setting up a regular credit card account. Just select the Enable IntelliCharge check box in the Create Credit Card Account dialog box (see fig. 9.1). The Description text box changes to the Credit Card Number text box where you enter the 13- or 16-digit account number of your Quicken VISA card. Make sure that you enter the correct account number from your card or your latest Quicken VISA statement.

After you enter information about your IntelliCharge account, you must tell Quicken whether you want to receive your statements by disk or modem. If by modem, you must also enter your social security number and a password for Quicken to use when accessing your IntelliCharge statement (of up to eight characters, but at least four nonblank characters).

Quicken adds your IntelliCharge account to the Account List. A lightning bolt character appears in the Type column to designate that this credit card account is an IntelliCharge account.

II

Getting the Most

> **Note**
>
> If you have already set up a credit card account for your Quicken VISA card, you can easily convert the account to an IntelliCharge account if you want to receive your statements on disk or by modem. Just edit the credit card account information and select the Enable IntelliCharge check box.

Updating your IntelliCharge credit card account is the same as entering credit card transactions in a regular credit card account, except that IntelliCharge enters the transactions for you (by way of disk file or modem transmission). Every month, Intuit sends you your Quicken VISA card statement. When you receive your statement and are ready to update your IntelliCharge account, select **G**et IntelliCharge Date from the Online menu.

If you choose to receive your statements on disk, Intuit mails you a file that contains your credit card activity (purchases, cash advances, finance charges, credit, and payments) during the current statement period.

If you choose to download your statement information by modem, Intuit makes an electronic statement available each month for you to download to your Quicken system. After Quicken reads credit card transactions from the IntelliCharge statement, the transactions are displayed in the IntelliCharge Statement window so that you can review and mark any transactions for edit or further review in the Register. After your review, transactions are recorded in the Credit Card Register.

> **Note**
>
> The first time that you use IntelliCharge to update your credit card account, IntelliCharge categorizes transactions according to Intuit's standard category list. (The standard category list is contained in the file INTELLIC.CAT on your Quicken 4 for Windows program disks and copied to your hard disk when you install Quicken.) If you later change any of the assigned categories, IntelliCharge picks up the changes in subsequent updates by scanning the Credit Card Register.

> **Note**
>
> If a transaction appears in your IntelliCharge statement that doesn't match your records, you can dispute the item by contacting Primerica Bank immediately at (800) 772-2221. You also must notify the bank, in writing, of any disputed item.

From Here...

After learning about credit card accounts, you may want to review the following chapters:

- Chapter 6, "Using the Register," explains the basics of Quicken Registers. The credit card Register works the same way as other Registers.

- Chapter 7, "Using Quicken Shortcuts," shows you how to save time entering transactions using Quicken's shortcut features. You can use these same shortcuts when entering credit card transactions.

- Chapter 8, "Reconciling Your Bank Accounts," describes the reconciliation process for bank accounts, which is similar to that of credit card accounts. Refer to this chapter to learn how to mark transactions as cleared.

II

Getting the Most

Chapter 10

Tracking Loans

With Quicken, setting up and tracking your outstanding loans is easy. With Quicken's loan features, you can keep accurate records of your amortized loans, outstanding loan balances, and loan payments. An *amortized loan* is a loan where a specified rate of interest is charged to the outstanding principal portion of the loan.

Your home mortgage, car loan, and student loan are examples of amortized loans that you can set up accounts for in Quicken. Part of a payment on an amortized loan reduces the principal balance; the other part is the interest charge. Quicken keeps track of the principal and interest portion of loan payments and even can alert you when loan payments are due.

Quicken can handle many different types of loans, including variable interest-rate loans, loans with balloon payments, negative-amortization loans, and even loans based on Canadian compounding methods. For each of these types of loans, you can generate a payment schedule that shows each payment, the portion of the payment that reduces the principal balance, the interest portion of the payment, and the outstanding principal balance.

You can use Quicken's Loan Planner at any time to compare loan alternatives. If you are thinking about buying a new home, for example, you can use the Loan Planner to calculate your new monthly payment based on different interest rate scenarios. You also can use the Loan Planner to determine what your monthly mortgage payments would be if you extended the loan period, and to generate a payment schedule to learn how much you will owe on a loan in 5 years, 10 years, and so on.

Quicken enables you to create liability accounts to record your other liabilities (other than amortized loans). Examples of other liabilities for which you may want to set up a liability account include personal loans, taxes payable, accounts payable, insurance premiums, and so forth. You can set up a separate liability account for each liability, or you can group related liabilities into one account. Quicken also helps you remember to make timely payments on your loans. Chapter 11, "Managing Your Assets and Other Liabilities," shows you how to set up accounts to track other liabilities.

In this chapter, you learn how to do the following:

- Set up a fixed-rate loan, a variable interest-rate loan, and a loan with a balloon payment due

- Make loan payments and undo loan payments recorded by mistake

- Make principal prepayments on a loan

- Edit loan information, delete a loan, or pay off a loan

- Refinance a loan, using the Refinance Planner

- Use the Loan Planner

Setting Up Loans

For each outstanding amortized loan, you should set up a separate loan account in Quicken. Be sure to have your loan documents handy before you begin setting up loan accounts. You need the following information:

- *Original balance of loan.* The amount you borrow at the time you take out a loan. If you borrow $20,000 to buy a new automobile, for example, $20,000 is the principal portion of the loan.

> **Note**
>
> You can use the Loan Planner to calculate any one loan variable. If you know the principal balance, loan term, and payment on a loan, for example, you can use the Loan Planner to calculate the interest rate. If you know the interest rate, loan term, and payment, you can use the Loan Planner to calculate the original principal balance.

- *Current interest rate.* The amount you pay to use the principal. The longer you use the money, the more interest you pay the lender.

- *Original length of loan.* The period or length of the loan (usually 30 years—or 360 months—for home mortgages).

CPA Tip: Reviewing Canceled Checks

Interest is computed periodically (monthly, quarterly, or annually, for example) as a percentage of the outstanding principal balance of the loan. In the automobile loan example, you will pay back the $20,000 plus the interest computed during the loan term. The interest portion of a loan is a future cost and isn't considered a liability for purposes of your net worth. In other words, a liability listed on your statement of net worth represents the outstanding principal portion of the loan and doesn't include the interest portion.

- *Principal and interest payment.* The payment required by the terms of the loan agreement. Make sure that the payment amount you use is only for principal and interest and doesn't include amounts for real estate or insurance escrow.

- *Escrow amounts.* Portions of your loan payment may be for real estate taxes, insurance, and so forth. The bank *escrows* (holds) these funds for you until payment is due and then makes the payment for you.

Note

You also can set up a loan in Quicken for a *receivable*—a loan that you make to another individual or company. To set up a loan receivable, be sure to select the **L**end Money option when you begin to set up the loan.

Quicken handles several types of loans, including fixed-rate loans, variable-rate loans, and loans with a balloon payment due. The next several sections explain how to set up each of these loan types in Quicken.

Setting Up a Fixed-Rate Loan

A *fixed-rate loan* charges the same interest rate throughout the loan period. If you have a fixed-rate 30-year mortgage at 8.5 percent, for example, your interest rate through the 30-year term of the loan remains constant at 8.5 percent.

To set up a fixed-rate loan in Quicken, follow these steps:

1. Choose **L**oans from the Acti**v**ities menu (or press Ctrl+H). Quicken displays the View Loans window, shown in figure 10.1.

   The View Loans window is the main information window for all loans set up in Quicken. You can view a payment history and projected payments for the loan by selecting the loan in the Loan drop-down list. You learn more about the View Loans window later in this chapter.

Fig. 10.1

The View Loans window appears when you choose Loans from the Activities menu.

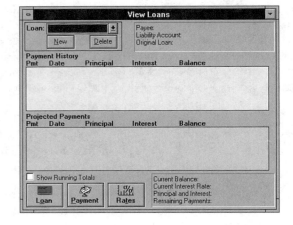

2. To set up a new loan, choose the **N**ew button in the upper-left corner of the View Loans window. Quicken displays the Set Up Loan Account dialog box, shown in figure 10.2.

Fig. 10.2

The Set Up Loan Account dialog box appears when you choose to set up a new loan.

3. In the Loan Type section of the dialog box, indicate the type of loan you are setting up. Select **B**orrow Money for a loan made to you, or **L**end Money for a loan made by you to someone else.

4. In the Liability Account area, do one of the following:

  ■ Select **N**ew Account if you want to define a new liability account for the loan you are setting up. Then press Tab to move to the **N**ew Account text box and type a name for the new account—for example, **Mortgage** or **Car Loan**.

■ Select **E**xisting Account if you have manually tracked a loan in Quicken and therefore already have a liability account established. From the drop-down list, select the existing liability account.

5. Choose OK to close the dialog box and set up the loan account.

Quicken adds the loan account as a liability account in the Account List and displays the Set Up Loan dialog box so that you can enter information about the loan, such as the loan's length, original loan balance, interest rate, and so forth (see fig. 10.3). Note that the account name you entered or selected in the Set Up Loan Account dialog box now appears in the Loan/Account Name field of the Set Up Loan dialog box.

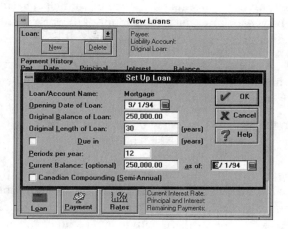

Fig. 10.3
In the Set Up Loan dialog box, you enter specific information about an outstanding loan.

Getting the Most

To enter information about the loan, follow these steps:

1. In the Opening Date of **L**oan option, select the date from the pop-up calendar. Select today's date or the date that you want to use to start tracking the loan.

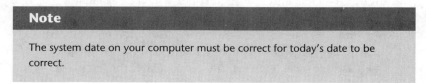

Note

The system date on your computer must be correct for today's date to be correct.

2. For existing loans, type the original principal balance of the loan in the Original **B**alance of Loan text box. If you are setting up a new loan (one for which you haven't made previous payments), leave this text box blank.

3. In the **O**riginal Length of Loan text box, specify the original loan term, in years. Type **5** for a five-year loan, **30** for a 30-year loan, and so forth.

4. If you are setting up a loan with a balloon payment, use the **D**ue In text box to specify the number of years until the balloon payment is due. For all other types of loans, leave this text box blank. (You learn about loans with balloon payments later in this chapter.)

5. In the **P**eriods per Year text box, type the number of payments you make each year. For monthly payments, type **12**. For semiannual payments, type **2**.

6. In the **C**urrent Balance text box, type the principal balance of the loan. For a new loan, enter the total amount of the loan. In the **as** of text box, enter or select the date to which the current balance relates.

7. (Optional) Canadian users who need to calculate interest based on semiannual compounding can select the Canadian Compounding (**S**emi-Annual) check box.

8. When the Set Up Loan dialog box is complete, choose OK. Quicken displays the Set Up Loan Payment dialog box.

Tip

For variable-rate loans, type the interest rate that is now being charged. You learn more about variable-rate loans later in this chapter.

Next, you must enter information about the loan payments that you will be making, such as the escrow amounts included in a loan payment (if any), whether you write checks with Quicken or write them manually, the payee's name, and so forth. Follow these steps to enter loan payment information in the Set Up Loan Payment dialog box (see fig. 10.4):

1. In the Current **I**nterest Rate text box, type the interest rate that applies to the loan as of today's date. If your loan rate today is 7 percent, for example, type **7** (Quicken enters the percent sign automatically).

2. In the **P**rincipal and Interest text box, Quicken calculates the regular payment amount (principal plus interest), based on the interest rate, the principal balance, and the term information entered earlier. You can change the regular payment amount in the **P**rincipal and Interest text box; however, Quicken then recalculates the length of the loan in the Set Up Loan dialog box (refer to fig. 10.3).

3. If other amounts or fees are included in your loan payment—real estate taxes, home insurance premiums, and so on—choose the **S**plit button to display the Splits window, shown in figure 10.5.

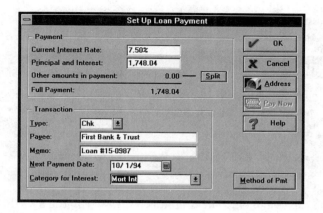

Fig. 10.4
Enter details about loan payments in the Set Up Loan Payment dialog box.

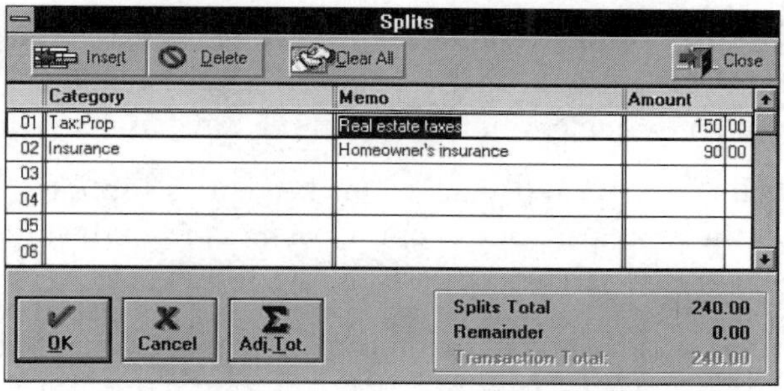

Fig. 10.5
Use the Splits window to enter other amounts or fees included in your loan payment and assign a category to each.

II

Getting the Most

4. In the Splits window, enter the category, a description (optional), and the amount for each fee included in the loan payment. If insurance premiums and real estate taxes are included in the loan payment, for example, enter a separate line for each in the Splits window and assign the appropriate categories.

   Choose OK when the Splits window is complete. Quicken returns to the Set Up Loan Payment dialog box (refer to fig. 10.4).

5. In the **T**ype drop-down list, indicate the type of transaction you want to enter when you make a loan payment. If you plan to use Quicken to write checks for the loan payments, for example, select *Chk*.

6. In the Pa**y**ee text box, type the name of the payee to whom you make the loan payment. The payee is normally the creditor who granted the loan.

7. (Optional) If you want, you can type a memo for the loan payment transaction in the M**e**mo text box. If you print checks with Quicken,

including the loan account number in the Memo field of the check
helps the lender match your check with the loan file.

> **Note**
>
> If you write checks with Quicken for your loan payment, you can print the
> payee's address on the check automatically. Choose the **A**ddress command
> button in the Set Up Loan Payment dialog box, enter the payee's address, and
> then choose OK. Quicken saves the payee's address and prints it on each loan
> payment check. You can also specify a message to print on checks.

8. In the **N**ext Payment Date drop-down list, specify the date that the next
   loan payment is due.

9. In the **C**ategory for Interest drop-down list, indicate the category that
   you want to assign to the interest portion of the payment. For a mortgage loan, for example, you may assign the category Mort Int.

   When you make a loan payment, Quicken enters a split transaction and
   separates the principal portion of the payment from the interest portion.

10. Now that you have entered the information about your loan, you need
    to indicate the payment method that you want to use. Select the
    Method of Pmt button from the Set Up Loan Payment dialog box.
    Quicken displays the Select Payment Method dialog box, shown in
    figure 10.6.

Fig. 10.6
Select the
payment method
that you want to
use to make loan
payments.

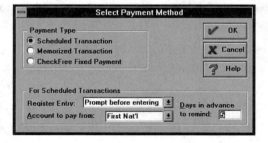

11. Select the appropriate payment type. You can choose from the follow-
    ing three methods for making loan payments:

    ■ *Scheduled Transaction.* Select this option if you want Quicken to
      enter the loan payment in your Register (or in the Write Checks

window, if you choose to write the loan payment check with Quicken).

Quicken knows when loan payments are due (from the **N**ext Payment Date setting in the Set Up Loan Payment dialog box) and how often to make loan payments (from the **P**eriods per Year setting in the Set Up Loan dialog box). You learn more about scheduled transactions in Chapter 14, "Scheduling Future Transactions."

■ *Memorized Transaction*. Select this option if you want to memorize the loan payment transaction and then recall the transaction in the Write Checks window or the Register each time a loan payment is due. Refer to Chapter 7, "Using Quicken Shortcuts," to learn how to memorize a transaction.

■ *CheckFree Fixed Payment*. When you select this option, you can set up the loan payment as a fixed (recurring) payment if you use CheckFree to make your payments. See Chapter 13, "Paying Your Bills Electronically," to learn how to use CheckFree services with Quicken.

12. If you selected the Scheduled Transaction option, fill in the For Scheduled Transactions section at the bottom of the Select Payment Method dialog box. The options are described as follows:

■ In the **R**egister Entry drop-down list, indicate whether you want Quicken to enter the loan payment in your Register with or without asking you to confirm the transaction.

■ In the **A**ccount to Pay From drop-down list, specify the checking account into which the loan payment should be entered.

■ In the **D**ays in Advance to Remind text box, type the number of days ahead of time that you want Quicken to enter loan payments in your Register.

13. When the Select Payment Method dialog box is complete, choose OK to return to the Set Up Loan Payment dialog box (refer to fig. 10.4).

14. If you want to make a loan payment now, choose the **P**ay Now button; otherwise, go to step 15.

Quicken displays the Choose Account To Pay From dialog box. Select the checking account that you want to use to make the loan payment and choose OK.

15. Choose OK in the Set Up Loan Payment dialog box to return to the View Loans window and display the new loan (see fig. 10.7). If all the scheduled payments don't appear in the Projected Payments list, you can use the scroll bar to display the rest of the payments.

Fig. 10.7
The View Loans
Window displays
the new loan and
its scheduled
payments.

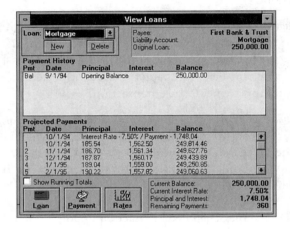

Tip
You can change
the details of a
loan at any time
by selecting the
appropriate com-
mand button from
the View Loans
window. You learn
how to change
loan details later
in the section
"Editing a Loan."

16. Close the View Loans window by double-clicking the Control menu box.

Setting Up a Variable-Rate Loan

A *variable-rate loan* charges a different, or *variable*, interest rate throughout the loan period. If you have a six-month variable-rate loan, for example, your rate is adjusted every six months throughout the loan period.

To set up a variable-rate loan in Quicken, follow the steps for setting up a fixed-rate loan as described in the preceding section. In the Set Up Loan Payment dialog box (refer to fig. 10.4), type the rate that you now are being charged for the Current **I**nterest Rate.

When the interest rate changes on your loan, change the current interest rate that Quicken uses to amortize the loan, using one of the following two methods:

■ Change the interest rate, effective today, by entering the new interest rate in the Current **I**nterest Rate option in the Set Up Loan Payment dialog box.

■ If you know in advance when the interest rate changes take effect, you can program rate changes in Quicken, as discussed later in this section.

> **Note**
>
> If your loan agreement expressly states the effective dates for interest rate changes and the new rates, you can enter those changes as you set up your loan. For most variable-rate loans where the rate is adjusted on a periodic basis (semiannually, annually, biannually, and so forth), you probably won't know the new interest rate until you are notified by your lender.

To access the Set Up Loan Payment dialog box so that you can enter the new interest rate, choose the **P**ayment button in the View Loans window when the loan name is displayed in the Loan list box.

To program a rate change, follow these steps:

1. Choose Set Up L**o**ans from the **A**ctivities menu to display the View Loans window. Make sure that the loan for which you want to change the interest rate appears in the Loan drop-down list box.

2. Choose the Ra**t**es button. Quicken displays the Loan Rate Changes dialog box, as shown in figure 10.8.

Fig. 10.8
The Loan Rate Changes dialog box shows a history of rate changes for the selected loan.

3. Choose the **N**ew button to display the Insert an Interest Rate Change dialog box.

4. Enter the interest rate and the date that the new rate is effective. Quicken calculates the new regular payment amount. You can increase or decrease the regular payment amount.

> **Note**
>
> When you change the interest rate, Quicken calculates the regular payment based on the original length of the loan. If you increase the regular payment amount, however, Quicken reduces the loan term. When you decrease the regular payment amount, Quicken doesn't change the loan term, but adds the unpaid amount of the loan to the last payment amount.

Tip
You can edit and delete interest rate changes in the Loan Rate Changes dialog box by choosing the Ed**i**t and **D**elete buttons.

5. Choose OK to add the new interest rate and date to the Loan Rate Changes dialog box.

6. Choose Close to save the interest rate change.

Setting Up Loans with Balloon Payments

A *balloon-payment loan* requires that the unpaid principal balance of a loan be paid at the end of the payment period. The balance payment (*balloon payment*) is due when specified by the loan contract. If the provisions of your loan are "30 due in 5," for example, the loan is amortized over 30 years. The unpaid principal balance, however, is payable at the end of the fifth year.

To set up a loan with a balloon payment, follow these steps:

1. Follow the steps for setting up a fixed-rate loan as described earlier in the section "Setting Up a Fixed-Rate Loan."

2. In the **O**riginal Length of Loan text box in the Set Up Loan dialog box (refer to fig. 10.3), type the period over which the loan is amortized. If the loan is amortized over 30 years, for example, type **30**.

3. In the same dialog box, select the **D**ue In check box and type the number of years in which the balloon payment is due. Type **5**, for example, if the loan calls for the balloon payment in five years.

4. Fill in the rest of the Set Up Loan dialog box and then choose OK.

> **Note**
>
> If payments on your balloon-payment loan don't reduce the principal balance of the loan (payments cover only interest), don't set up the loan in Quicken to track payments. Instead, memorize a regular transaction for the loan payment and assign the entire amount of the transaction to interest expense. See Chapter 7, "Using Quicken Shortcuts," to learn how to memorize transactions.

Setting Up Loans You Make

As noted earlier in this chapter, you can set up a loan in Quicken for which you receive payments (you make the loan). To set up a loan that you make, select the **L**end Money option in the Set Up Loan Account dialog box (refer to fig. 10.2) and specify the asset account that you want to set up to track the loan. (Accounts for loans you make to others assets because they represent a receivable, or an amount, due to you). In the Set Up Loan Payment dialog box (refer to fig. 10.4), enter the name of the borrower in the Pa**y**ee text box and select an income category to assign to deposit transactions in the **C**ategory for Interest text box.

When you set up a loan for which you are receiving payments, Quicken creates a memorized loan deposit transaction and also creates an asset account as the account it uses to track the outstanding balance of the loan.

Making Loan Payments

After your loan is set up in Quicken, you are ready to enter or make loan payments when they are due. The method used to make loan payments depends on the method you chose in the Select Payment Method dialog box (refer to fig. 10.6). If you selected the Scheduled Transaction or the CheckFree Fixed Payment option, your loan payment transactions are entered automatically. If you chose to memorize loan payments, however, you must recall the memorized loan payment in the Write Checks window or the Register, as described in the following section.

Tip
For more details on scheduled transactions, see Chapter 14, "Scheduling Future Transactions." Details about using CheckFree are in Chapter 13, "Paying Your Bills Electronically."

When you make a loan payment, Quicken enters the principal and interest portion of the payment—and any other charges and fees—in the Splits window, and assigns the appropriate category to each part of the payment. Quicken uses the payment schedule (or amortization schedule) in the View Loans window to enter the appropriate principal and interest amounts for each payment. Each time you make a payment, Quicken updates the loan balance.

You can make regular loan payments or make an additional principal payment and add it to a regular payment. Later sections of this chapter describe how to make prepayments and how to undo loan payments made in error.

Recalling a Memorized Loan Payment

When you set up a loan in Quicken and select the Memorized Transaction option as the payment method, Quicken memorizes the loan payment information and adds it to the Memorized Transaction List. (You learn about the Memorized Transaction List in Chapter 7, "Using Quicken Shortcuts.")

When the time comes to make a loan payment, follow these steps to recall the memorized loan payment:

Tip
You also can recall a memorized loan payment by pressing Ctrl+T to display the Memorized Transaction List. Then highlight the loan payment transaction in the list and choose the **U**se button.

1. If you're writing a check for the loan payment with Quicken, display the Write Checks window. If you're writing a manual check, display the Register for the checking account that you use to write checks.

2. In the Payee field in the Register or the Pay to the Order Of field in the Write Checks window, begin typing the payee name. QuickFill completes the full name of the payee. Press Tab to accept the payee when it is correct. Quicken displays the Confirm Principal and Interest dialog box, as shown in figure 10.9.

Fig. 10.9
Review the principal and interest portions of a loan payment in the Confirm Principal and Interest dialog box.

3. If you want to change the principal or interest amount, type the new amount over the existing amount.

Note that any changes affect only this payment. All future loan payments are separated into principal and interest based on the payment schedule in the View Loans window.

4. When the principal and interest amounts are correct, choose OK.

> **Note**
>
> If you *increase* the principal amount of a loan payment, you are making an additional principal payment. When you prepay the principal of a loan, Quicken recalculates the payment schedule in the View Loans window. The adjustment to the payment schedule may shorten the term of the loan.
>
> If you *decrease* the principal amount of a loan payment, Quicken recalculates the payment schedule in the View Loans window. The adjustment to the payment schedule doesn't change the loan term; however, an extra balance may be shown at the end of the repayment period.

5. Choose OK to return to the Write Checks window or the Register.

6. (Optional) Remember that if your loan payment includes any charges or fees, Quicken enters those amounts and categories in the Splits window, following the principal and interest amounts. If you want to review the amounts, choose the **S**plits button to open the Splits window. Then choose OK to return to the Write Checks window or the Register.

7. Choose Re**c**ord to record the loan payment.

Undoing Loan Payments

If you accidentally record a loan payment you didn't actually make, you can delete the loan payment transaction from the Register. Follow these steps to undo a loan payment transaction:

1. Highlight the loan payment transaction in the Register for the bank account that you use to make loan payments.

2. Choose the Delete button on the Register button bar (or press Ctrl+D).

3. Quicken asks you to confirm that you want to delete the transaction. Choose **Y**es.

Quicken removes the transaction from the Bank Account Register and the Liability Account Register, and from the payment schedule in the View Loans window.

Making Principal Prepayments

By making additional principal payments during the term of your loan, you reduce the loan term and pay less total interest on the loan.

To make a principal prepayment, follow these steps:

1. Recall the loan payment in the Write Checks window or the Register, as explained earlier in the section "Recalling a Memorized Loan Payment."

2. When Quicken displays the Confirm Principal and Interest dialog box (refer to fig. 10.9), type the increased amount in the **P**rincipal Amount text box. This action tells Quicken that you are making an additional principal payment.

3. Choose OK to return to the Write Checks window or the Register. Quicken recalculates the loan payment amount to include the additional principal payment.

4. Choose Re**c**ord to record the loan payment.

II

Getting the Most

Note

If you make a separate principal payment (not with your loan payment), don't recall the loan payment. Just enter a transaction for the principal payment in the Write Checks window or the Register and enter the liability account in the Category field.

CPA Tip: Cutting Your Mortgage Loan Term

By making one extra mortgage payment each year, you can cut some years off your loan term. If your regular payment amount each month is $1,000, for example, just make one extra payment of $1,000 and apply it to the principal of your loan. (Be sure to indicate when you submit the extra payment that you want the total amount applied to the principal balance.)

Editing a Loan

At any time, you can change any of the loan details from the View Loans window, except for the loan name. The loan name is the name Quicken assigns to the principal account that it uses to track your loan balance. The principal account is set up as a liability account. You can change the name of an account from the Account List, however. Refer to Chapter 3, "Defining Your Accounts," to learn how to change account names.

To change loan details, follow these steps:

1. From the Loan drop-down list in the View Loans window (see fig. 10.1), select the loan that you want to change.

2. To change the details of the loan, choose from the following options (in any order):

   ■ To change the length of the loan, balloon-payment date (if applicable), original and current balances, periods per year, or opening date of the loan, choose the L**o**an button. Quicken displays the Set Up Loan dialog box.

   ■ To change the loan payment details, choose the **P**ayment button. Quicken displays the Set Up Loan Payment dialog box.

   ■ To change the future interest rates that Quicken uses to amortize the loan, choose the Ra**t**es button. Quicken displays the Loan Rate Changes dialog box.

3. Make the necessary changes in the dialog box or window and then choose OK or Done to return to the View Loans window. Then repeat step 3 as necessary until all changes are complete.

> **Note**
>
> If you need to change only the payment information for a loan, select the loan in the Memorized Transaction List and choose the Edit button. Quicken displays the payment information for the memorized loan payment. Make the necessary changes and choose OK.

Deleting a Loan

If you have paid off a loan, you need to delete the loan from the View Loans window. If you have mistakenly set up a loan in Quicken, you must also delete it. When you delete a loan, Quicken removes all loan information from the View Loans window, the Memorized Transaction List, the Scheduled Transaction list (if applicable), and the Electronic Payee list (if applicable), however, the Liability account remains in the Account List.

To delete a loan, follow these steps:

1. From the Loan drop-down list in the View Loans window (see fig. 10.1), select the loan that you want to delete.

2. Choose the **D**elete button.

3. Quicken asks you to confirm that you want to delete the amortized loan. Choose OK.

> **Note**
>
> When you delete a loan, Quicken deletes the loan from the View Loans window but doesn't delete the liability account from the Account List. Refer to Chapter 3, "Defining Your Accounts," to learn how to delete accounts.

Paying Off a Loan

It's a happy day when you finally pay off a loan—especially a home mortgage that you may have been paying for 30 years!

CPA Tip: Paying Off a Loan

When paying off a loan, check with your lending institution for the exact payoff for the loan on the date that you will be making the payment. Make sure that you are specific about the date for which you want payoff information. Just one or two days makes a difference in the amount of interest that has accrued on your loan.

To pay off a loan, follow these steps:

1. Record the last payment on the loan, as usual. This should reduce the principal balance on the loan to zero (see the payment schedule in the View Loans window).

2. From the Loan drop-down list in the View Loans window (see fig. 10.1), select the loan that you paid off.

3. Choose the **D**elete button.

4. Quicken asks you to confirm that you want to delete the amortized loan. Choose OK. Quicken removes the loan from the View Loans window; however, the liability account remains in the Account List.

Refinancing a Loan

With fluctuating mortgage rates, many homeowners refinance home mortgages to take advantage of lower interest rates. If you refinance a loan that you have set up in Quicken, you first must set up a new loan and then pay off—or delete—the old loan.

Follow the steps in the earlier sections of this chapter for setting up a loan. Be sure to make these specific changes:

1. Specify a new name for the refinanced loan—for example, type **Refinance**.

2. In the Set Up Loan dialog box (refer to fig. 10.3), enter the total term of the new loan in the Original Length of Loan text box. Enter the amount that you are refinancing in the Original **B**alance of Loan text box.

    Quicken sets up your loan and creates a new liability account for the new loan.

3. Display the Register for the new liability account. If your new loan account is called Refinance, for example, display the Register for the Refinance account.

4. Highlight the Opening Balance transaction.

5. Change the description in the Payee field in the Register from Opening Balance to the name of the new lender who is refinancing your loan.

6. Choose the **S**plits button to display the Splits window.

7. In the first line of the Splits window, type the name of the old loan in the Payee field. Then, type the outstanding balance on the old loan in the Amount field. This transaction pays off the balance in the old loan and transfers the balance to the new loan.

8. If the new loan includes any closing costs, enter those in the next line of the Splits window.

9. If the new loan amount is greater than the outstanding balance of the old loan, you may receive cash from the new lender. If so, enter the account in which you want to deposit the money (checking, savings, and so forth) in the Category field and enter the amount of cash received in the Amount field.

10. When the Splits window is complete, choose OK to return to the Register.

11. Choose Re**c**ord to record the edited opening balance transaction. Quicken enters a corresponding transaction in the old loan account Register that wipes out the balance.

12. Now that the old loan account balance is zero, you can delete the loan from the View Loans window. To delete the loan, select the loan in the View Loans window and choose the **D**elete button.

13. Choose OK to confirm that you want to delete an amortized loan. Note that the Liability account for the loan remains in Quicken with a zero balance.

Note

When you delete the loan that you have refinanced, Quicken doesn't delete the liability account. The liability account, with a zero balance, remains in the Account List. You should not delete the Liability account from the Account List because it contains the historical payment data for the loan.

Using the Refinance Planner

Although refinancing your mortgage may save on your monthly payment, refinancing is rarely achieved without incurring additional costs (closing costs and mortgage points). Don't be fooled into thinking that refinancing is the answer just because you can secure a lower interest rate. Mortgage lenders usually charge closing costs and points to refinance a mortgage. If your existing mortgage isn't very old and you incurred closing costs to obtain your mortgage, refinancing may not be prudent unless the refinance rate is significantly less than your current rate. You may find, though, that refinancing makes a great deal of sense and results in significant savings.

Quicken's Refinance Planner can help you determine whether refinancing your current mortgage is cost-effective. The Refinance Planner shows your new monthly payment amount (based on the refinance rate), how much you save per month by refinancing, the total closing costs you will incur if you refinance, and the amount of time necessary to recoup those closing costs with monthly savings from refinancing.

CPA Tip: Refinancing Your Mortgage

Many mortgage lenders will refinance only 80 percent of your home's current market value—or less. If the value of your home hasn't appreciated and your current mortgage balance is greater than 80 percent of the market value of your home, you may not be able to find a lender to refinance your mortgage.

To use the Refinance Planner, follow these steps:

1. Choose Financial **P**lanners from the Pl**a**n menu. Quicken displays the Financial **P**lanners submenu.

2. Choose Re**f**inance. Quicken displays the Refinance Planner, as shown in figure 10.10.

3. In the Existing Mortgage section, type your current payment amount in the Cu**r**rent Payment text box; type the escrow amount for insurance, property taxes, and so on in the Impound/**E**scrow Amount text box.

   Quicken subtracts the escrow amount from your current payment and enters the result as the Monthly Principal/Int. This amount is the portion of your monthly payment that relates to the principal balance of your mortgage loan and the mortgage interest due.

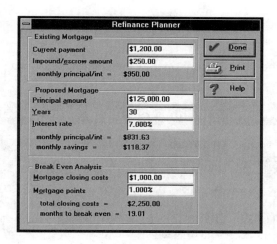

Fig. 10.10
The Refinance
Planner can
calculate how
much you will save
if you refinance
your mortgage at a
lower interest rate.

4. In the Proposed Mortgage section, type the data for the new mortgage. In the Principal **A**mount text box, type the amount that you are planning to refinance. Remember that this amount isn't the same amount as your original mortgage because you have paid down some principal since the beginning of the mortgage.

    In the **Y**ears text box, type the number of years that you plan to extend the refinanced mortgage loan—usually 30 or 15 years.

    In the **I**nterest rate text box, type the refinancing rate. Type 8.75% as **8.75**, for example; don't type a percent sign.

    Quicken calculates the new monthly principal and interest payment and your monthly savings (your old monthly principal and interest payment minus the new monthly principal and interest payment).

5. In the Break Even Analysis section, type any costs you will incur by refinancing. In the **M**ortgage Closing Costs text box, type the amount that the mortgage bank is charging to refinance your mortgage. In the M**o**rtgage Points text box, type the percentage point(s) that you are being charged. Usually, this amount is from 1 percent to 4 percent, but can vary from lender to lender and also is based on the size of the loan.

    Quicken calculates the total closing costs to refinance and determines how many months you will need to break even (how many months to recover the closing costs, using the monthly savings from refinancing).

    Figure 10.10 shows a monthly savings of $118.37 when refinancing a mortgage of $125,000 at 7 percent. With closing costs of $2,250, it will

II

Getting the Most

take 19 months to break even, or recover the closing costs using the monthly savings.

6. Choose the Done button to remove the Refinance Planner from the screen.

CPA Tip: Weighing Income Tax Implications of Refinancing

When you refinance your mortgage, in essence, you're giving up deductible interest by refinancing at a lower interest rate. Now, mortgage interest on up to two residences is generally fully deductible (subject to the three percent reduction for itemized deductions if your adjusted gross income is greater than $100,000, or $50,000 if filing separately). You may end up paying more in taxes a few years down the road than you would if you hadn't refinanced. Consider the income tax implications before you make the decision to refinance.

Using the Loan Planner

If you want to calculate "what-if" scenarios to determine how much a loan payment would be if you borrowed *x* amount at *x* interest rate over *x* period of time, you can use Quicken's Loan Planner to calculate the loan. The Loan Planner also can produce a payment (amortization) schedule. An amortization schedule shows what portion of your payments goes to paying interest and what portion goes to reducing the principal balance of the loan.

You can select the type of calculation to make with the Loan Planner. You can calculate the payment per period when you know the loan amount, the annual interest rate, the number of years the loan will be outstanding, and the number of payments made each year. You can calculate the loan amount when you know the annual interest rate, the number of years the loan will be outstanding, the number of payments made annually, and the payment per period amount.

To calculate loan amounts or payments per period of a loan and produce a payment schedule, follow these steps:

1. Choose the Financial **P**lanners option from the Pl**a**n menu. Quicken displays the Financial **P**lanners submenu.

2. Choose **L**oan. Quicken displays the Loan Planner dialog box, as shown in figure 10.11.

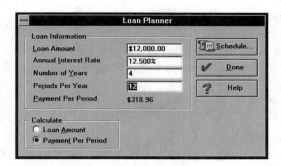

Fig. 10.11
The Loan Planner
can help you
determine the
payment amount
of a loan or the
principal amount
of a loan.

3. Specify the type of calculation that you want to make. To have Quicken calculate the loan amount, select the Loan **A**mount option. Quicken enters the word CALCULATED in the **L**oan Amount text box.

To have Quicken calculate the payment amount, select the Paymen**t** per Period option. Quicken enters the word CALCULATED in the **P**ayment per Period text box.

4. If you're calculating the payment per period, type the amount of the loan in the **L**oan Amount text box. Otherwise, go to step 5.

5. In the Annual **I**nterest Rate text box, type the annual interest rate. If the annual loan interest rate is 12.5 percent, for example, type **12.5**.

Caution

Don't mistake the annual *percentage* rate (APR) for the annual *interest* rate. The APR encompasses all the costs of obtaining credit and includes not only interest charges but loan fees and other borrowing costs. The APR, which is required by truth-in-lending laws, provides a way to compare the overall costs of obtaining loans. The APR, however, shouldn't be used to calculate the loan payment.

---

6. In the Number of **Y**ears text box, type the number of years you must make payments. If the loan is a five-year car loan, for example, type **5**. If the loan is a 30-year mortgage, type **30**.

7. In the Perio**d**s per Year text box, type the number of payments you must make each year. Typically, because most payments must be made monthly, this number is **12** and appears by default.

8. If you are calculating the loan amount, enter the payment amount in the **P**ayment per Period text box.

II

Getting the Most

9. Press Tab after you enter the value for the last text box in the Loan Planner. Quicken calculates the payment per period amount and enters the result in the **P**ayment per Period text box, or calculates the loan amount and enters the result in the **L**oan Amount text box.

   Earlier, figure 10.11 showed the payment per period on a $12,000 loan at 12.5 percent interest with four years of monthly payments to be $318.96.

10. (Optional) To produce a payment schedule for the loan, choose the **S**chedule button after you finish calculating the loan amount or the payment per period.

    Quicken displays the Approximate Future Payment Schedule window, shown in figure 10.12. The Approximate Future Payment Schedule window shows the approximate interest and principal portions of each loan payment and the loan balance after the payment. Choose Close to return to the Loan Planner.

Fig. 10.12
The Approximate Future Payment Schedule window shows the approximate interest and principal portions of each loan payment.

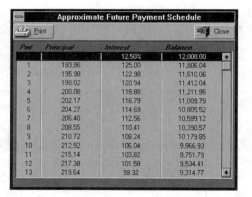

Pmt	Principal	Interest	Balance
		12.50%	12,000.00
1	193.96	125.00	11,806.04
2	195.98	122.98	11,610.06
3	198.02	120.94	11,412.04
4	200.08	118.88	11,211.96
5	202.17	116.79	11,009.79
6	204.27	114.69	10,805.52
7	206.40	112.56	10,599.12
8	208.55	110.41	10,390.57
9	210.72	108.24	10,179.85
10	212.92	106.04	9,966.93
11	215.14	103.82	9,751.79
12	217.38	101.58	9,534.41
13	219.64	99.32	9,314.77

Note

To print a copy of the payment schedule, choose the **P**rint button from the Approximate Future Payment Schedule window. Quicken displays the Print Report dialog box. Indicate where you want to print the Approximate Future Payment Schedule and the pages that you want to print. Choose OK to print the report.

11. Choose the **C**lose button when you are finished using the Loan Planner.

CPA Tip: Reviewing Canceled Checks

If you are uncertain how big a mortgage you can afford when buying a home, use the Loan Planner to help you determine what amount you can afford. To calculate the principal amount, enter in the appropriate Loan Planner text boxes the amount you decide that you can spend for housing from your monthly income (Payment per Period) and the current Annual Interest Rate.

If you want to pay less interest over the life of the mortgage and pay off the mortgage balance sooner, use 15 years as the total years to pay. If you can't afford the monthly mortgage payments for a 15-year loan, use 30 years. With this information, you can calculate the total loan amount, which gives you a better idea of what to look for in a mortgage.

From Here...

After learning how to set up loans in Quicken, you may want to review the following chapters:

- Chapter 11, "Managing Your Assets and Other Liabilities," shows you how to set up other liability accounts to track unamoritized loans.

- Chapter 14, "Scheduling Future Transactions," explains how to use the Financial Calendar to review the loan payments you've set up as scheduled transactions.

- Chapter 18, "Saving for the Future with Quicken," describes how to use the other financial planning calculators in Quicken.

II

Getting the Most

Chapter 11

Managing Your Assets and Other Liabilities

Quicken originally was designed as an electronic check register for writing and recording checks. The newer releases of Quicken, however, can do much more than keep track of your checking account. You can maintain financial records for any asset or liability by using Quicken's familiar Register format.

Assets are personal or business resources that have lasting value. For individuals, assets include such items as a house, cars, furniture, and investments. For businesses, assets include money owed by customers (accounts receivable), inventory held for resale, and any fixtures or equipment used in the business.

Liabilities are debts—any money you owe others. For individuals, liabilities include mortgages, car loans, credit card debts, and income taxes. For businesses, liabilities include amounts owed to suppliers (accounts payable), wages payable to employees, and loans from banks and leasing companies.

Using Quicken to track all your assets, as well as your liabilities, gives you a complete picture of your entire financial state in one place. You not only have a powerful record-keeping tool for your cash inflows and outflows, but also all the information you need to determine your overall financial health, or *net worth*, within easy access.

This chapter teaches you how to do the following:

- Set up accounts for other assets and liabilities

- Record assets and liabilities and track their values

- Record assets and liabilities using transfer transactions

- Use a cash account to keep track of your cash expenditures

- Update account balances

- Measure your net worth by creating a net-worth report, or balance sheet

Setting Up Accounts for Other Assets and Liabilities

You must set up a Quicken account for each asset or liability for which you want to keep computer records. You can track any asset or liability you want. Only one limit or restriction exists: you can keep a maximum of only 255 accounts in a single Quicken file. You must remember, however, that any accounts you want grouped on a single balance sheet must be set up in the same file. Typically, this restriction means that all your business accounts must be kept in one file and all your personal accounts in another file.

After you create a Quicken file, take the following steps to set up your accounts:

1. Choose Create New Account from the Activities menu. Quicken displays the Create New Account dialog box.

Tip
For amortized loans, set up a loan in Quicken as explained in Chapter 10, "Tracking Loans." When you set up a loan, Quicken automatically creates a liability account to track the principal balance of the loan.

2. The Create New Account dialog box lists six asset account types: Checking, Money Market, Asset, Savings, Cash, and Investment accounts. If the asset is a bank account, select the Checking, Money Market, or Savings option (you learned about bank accounts in Chapter 3). If the asset is cash, such as that in your wallet or in the petty cash box, select the Cash button. If the account is an investment, select the Investment button. (Refer to Chapter 16 for specifics on defining an investment account.) For any other assets—accounts receivable, real estate, and so on—select the Asset button.

The Create New Account dialog box also lists two liability account types: Credit Card and Liability. If the liability is the balance on your VISA or MasterCard account, select the Credit Card button (Chapter 9 explains credit card accounts). If the liability is an unamortized debt, select the Liability button.

After you select either the Asset or the Liability buttons, Quicken displays the Create Asset Account dialog box or the Create Liability Account dialog box. Figure 11.1 shows the Create Asset Account dialog box.

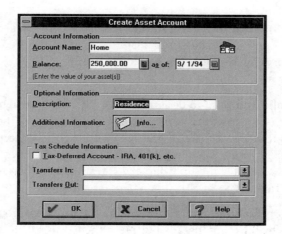

Fig. 11.1
Use the Create Asset Account dialog box to enter information about the new asset account you're creating.

3. In the **A**ccount Name text box, type the new account name. You can use up to 15 letters, spaces, and any symbols in the account name except the following:

   :] [/ | ^

4. In the **B**alance text box, type the starting account balance (as discussed for a bank account in Chapter 3). You can list assets at their original costs or their current market values. Liabilities are listed at their current balances. If the starting balance is zero, you must enter **0** in the **B**alance text box; you can't leave the **B**alance text box blank.

5. In the A**s** Of text box, type the date on which the balance you entered is correct, using the *mm/dd/yy* format, or click the calendar button to select a date from the minicalendar. (Refer to Chapter 7, "Using Quicken Shortcuts," to learn how to use the minicalendar to enter dates.)

6. (Optional) In the Description text box, type a description of the account, using up to 21 characters.

7. (Optional) If you want to enter additional information about an asset or liability account that you are defining (such as a bank name, account

Tip
To enter dates quickly into date text fields, use the + (plus) and – (minus) keys to move the date ahead and back one day.

II

Getting the Most

number, contact person's name, and telephone number), choose the **I**nfo button. Quicken displays the Additional Account Information dialog box. Enter the other information that you want to add to your account and then choose OK to return to the New Account Information dialog box.

8. (Optional)If the earnings on the asset account that you are adding are not subject to income tax until a later year, select the **T**ax-Deferred check box. Quicken does not include the earnings from this account in tax reports.

9. (Optional)If you want to designate a tax schedule to assign to transfers in or out of the asset account that you are adding, click the drop-down arrow in the **T**ransfers In or Transfers **O**ut boxes and select the appropriate tax schedule. (You learn more about assigning tax schedules to accounts and categories in Chapter 12, "Estimating and Preparing for Income Taxes.")

    For liability accounts, you can designate a tax schedule to assign to transfers by selecting the **T**ax button in the Create Liability Account dialog box.

> **Note**
>
> The Transfers In and Transfers **O**ut options are not available in the Create Asset Account dialog box or the Tax Schedule Information dialog box unless the Use **T**ax Schedules option is selected from the **G**eneral Options dialog box. Refer to Chapter 22, "Customizing Quicken," to learn how to set this option.

10. When the information in the Create Asset Account dialog box or the Create Liability Account dialog box is complete, choose OK to add the account. Quicken displays the Register for the account that you just created.

Recording Assets and Liabilities

After you initially set up an account—whether an asset account or a liability account—you can maintain it in one of two ways: by recording transactions directly in the Register, or by using transfer transactions.

Recording Transactions in the Register

Before recording transactions in a Register, you must select the account that you want to use from the Account List (press Ctrl+A). From the Account List, highlight the account that you want to use and select **O**pen from the Account List button bar.

Quicken 4 for Windows includes Account Selector Bars in each Register. The Account Selector Bar is used to select other accounts directly from a Register. To use the Account Selector Bar, simply click the account button for the account that you want to use. Quicken then displays the Register for the account that you selected.

After you select an account, you can use that account's Register to enter transactions that increase or decrease your balance, just as you do in your Quicken Bank account.

Figure 11.2 shows how the Register may look for a major real-estate asset (a personal residence). This Asset Register is almost identical to the regular bank account Register and is used the same way. Transaction amounts that decrease the asset account balance are recorded in the Decrease field of the Register (the Payment field on the bank account version of the Register window). Transaction amounts that increase the asset account are recorded in the Increase field of the Register (the Deposit field on the bank account version). The total real-estate account balance appears in the bottom-right corner of the Register window. If you have *postdated transactions*—transactions with dates in the future—the current balance also is shown.

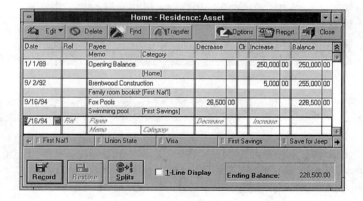

Fig. 11.2
Use an asset account called Home (or another description) to record the value of your personal residence.

Tip
To record the
liability (or mort-
gage) on your
home, set up a
loan in Quicken,
as discussed in
Chapter 10.
Quicken automati-
cally creates a
liability account to
track the principal
balance of the
loan.

In figure 11.2, the opening balance of $250,000 shows what you may have
paid originally for your home. The two subsequent transactions—one for the
addition of a new family room and the other for a new backyard swimming
pool—show what changed the value of your home. By keeping these records,
you can keep better track of the value of your home and any reasons for
changes in its value.

The Register for a liability account, as shown in figure 11.3, also mirrors the
bank account Register in appearance and operation. Transaction amounts
that increase the amount owed are recorded in the Increase field of the Register. (On the bank account version of the Register window, this field is labeled
Payment.) Transaction amounts that decrease the amount owed are recorded
in the Decrease field of the Register. (On the bank account version of the
Register, this field is labeled Deposit.) The total liability balance appears in
the bottom-right corner of the Register window. If you have postdated transactions, the current balance also is shown. You don't use the Clr field when
tracking a liability account.

Fig. 11.3
The liability
account Register is
similar to the bank
account Register.

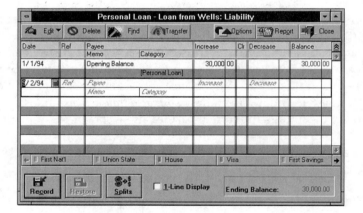

Tip
Set up a liability
account to track
unamortized
debts, such as a
loan to a friend or
accounts payable
to vendors.

Note

Quicken automatically creates a liability account when you set up an amortized loan
(see Chapter 10). When loan payments are made, only the principal reductions are
recorded in the Register for a loan or mortgage. The interest portion is reported as
interest expense and should be assigned to a category set up for mortgage interest
(Mort Int).

Using Transfer Transactions

Entering transactions directly into a Register is one way to maintain correct account balances for another asset or liability account. Quicken also enables you to enter an account name in the Category field in the Write Checks and Register windows. Quicken then uses the information from the checking-account transaction to record the appropriate transaction in one of the asset or liability accounts.

If you write a check to the remodeling company that makes improvements to your home and enter the account name for your home (for example, **House**, **Home**, or **Real Estate**) in the Category field (in the Write Checks window or the Checking Account Register), Quicken records a corresponding increase in the asset account set up to track the value of your home. This increase is equal to the payment made from your checking account. When you enter a transfer that transfers funds from one account to another, Quicken places that account name in brackets ([Home]) to show that the transaction is a transfer transaction. Refer to Chapter 6, "Using the Register," to learn how to enter a transfer transaction in Quicken.

Figure 11.4 shows the transfer transaction that Quicken enters when you write a $5,000 check for a remodeling job. When you record the check, Quicken records a corresponding $5,000 increase in the account that you use to track the value of your home.

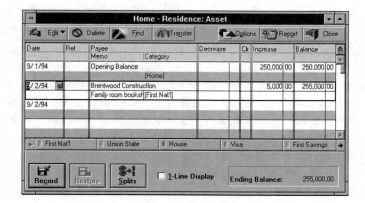

Fig. 11.4

When you pay for improvements, Quicken records a corresponding transaction in the account you use to track the value of your home. Use this account to keep track of the investment in your home.

> **Note**
>
> A convenient way to move between different parts of the same transfer transaction is to press Ctrl+X. After you record a payment in the Check Register, you may want to look at the asset or liability account to see how the account balance was affected.

Tracking Cash Expenditures with Cash Accounts

Cash accounts work well when you want to keep complete, detailed records of miscellaneous cash outlays. (*Miscellaneous cash outlays* are all those paid out of pocket with actual currency rather than with a check, such as $5.80 for stamps, $12 for lunch, or $7.50 for parking.) Often, you don't really need this level of control or detail. But when you do want such detailed records, a cash account gives you just the tool you need for the job.

> **CPA Tip: Keeping Track of Petty Cash**
>
> The Quicken cash account is a convenient way for businesses to keep track of petty-cash expenditures and reimbursements. Even very large businesses can benefit by using Quicken for petty-cash accounting.

Figure 11.5 shows a cash account Register (called Petty Cash), which is almost identical to the bank account Register. Money flowing in and out of the account is recorded in the Spend and Receive fields. (In the bank account Register, money flowing out of the account is recorded in the Payment field and money flowing into the account is recorded in the Deposit field. In the asset and liability account Registers, money flowing into and out of the account is recorded in the Increase and Decrease fields.)

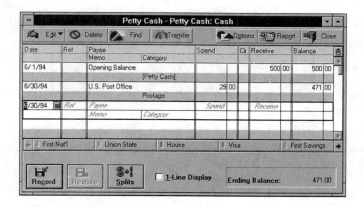

Fig. 11.5
Set up a Petty Cash
account to track
the cash expendi-
tures that your
business makes.
Cash outflows are
entered in the
Spend field;
deposits to the
account are
entered in the
Receive field.

As with the asset and liability account Registers, the Clr field usually isn't used. You can use this column, however, to match receipts against entries to indicate that you have backup records. Press C in this field to show that you have entered a cash transaction from an actual receipt. Quicken enters an asterisk (*) in the Clr field.

Updating Account Balances

If you need to change the account balances in an asset, liability, or cash account, you can reconcile the account, or update the balance. When you update an account's balance, Quicken enters a balance adjustment transaction in the Register.

Suppose that the Register you use to keep track of your petty or pocket cash shows $471.00 as the on-hand cash balance, but the actual balance is $465.00. To reflect the correct cash balance, you must enter a transaction for the difference or update the account balance.

Updating account balances works the same for cash, asset, and liability accounts. To update your account balance, follow these steps:

1. Display the Register for the account whose balance you want to update.

2. Choose **U**pdate Balances from the Acti**v**ities menu, and then choose Update **C**ash Balances. Quicken displays the Update Account Balance dialog box (see fig. 11.6).

Tip
You also can dis-
play the Update
Account Balance
dialog box by
clicking the Recon
button on the
Iconbar.

II

Getting the Most

Fig. 11.6
Enter the amount
that you want as
an ending balance
in an account in
the Update
Account Balance
dialog box.

3. In the **U**pdate This Account's Balance To text box, enter the amount to which the account balance should be adjusted. In the example, you enter **465**.

4. (Optional) From the **C**ategory for Adjustment drop-down list box, select the category to which you want to assign the difference between the old and new account balances. You can use a miscellaneous category or, if you know exactly what the difference stems from, use that category.

5. In the **A**djustment Date text box, enter the date that you want Quicken to use for the balance adjustment transaction in the Register.

6. Choose OK. Quicken makes the adjustment transaction to update the account balance. Figure 11.7 shows the adjustment transaction created by the Update Account Balance transaction so that the account balance is now $465.00.

Fig. 11.7
Quicken enters
an adjustment
transaction in the
Register when you
update your
account balance.

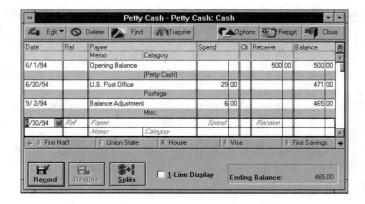

Measuring Your Net Worth

A balance sheet is one traditional tool individuals and businesses use to measure net worth. The balance sheet lists all your assets and liabilities. The difference between assets and liabilities is called *owner's equity*, or *net worth*. A balance sheet differs from reports such as income statements and cash-flow reports, which summarize financial activity occurring over a certain period of time. A balance sheet provides a "snapshot" of your personal or business finances at a particular moment in time.

> **Note**
>
> Before you create a balance sheet, make certain that all your asset and liability accounts are located in the same Quicken file.

Creating a balance sheet with Quicken is a two-step process. First, you must set up an account for each asset, with a beginning balance amount for each asset that is equal to the asset's cost or value. Generally, *assets* are items you have paid for that have lasting value. *Personal assets* include such items as the cash in your wallet, the surrender value of a life insurance policy, any investments, your home, and durable personal items such as your car and furniture. *Business assets* usually include cash, accounts receivable, inventory, and other property and equipment.

The second step in creating a balance sheet is to set up accounts for all your liabilities, recording the balance owed on each liability. *Liabilities* are amounts you now owe other people, banks, or businesses. *Personal liabilities* encompass such items as credit card balances, income taxes, car loans, and mortgages. *Business liabilities* usually include accounts payable, wages and salaries owed to employees, income and payroll taxes, and bank credit lines and loans.

> **CPA Tip: Use Consistent Dates to Determine Market Value**
>
> The cost or market value information must be accurate for your net worth calculation also to be accurate. Use only one method for appraising your assets or liabilities: original cost or fair market value. Mixing the different methods can yield inaccurate results. Note also on your opening balances whether you used original cost or fair market value to determine these appraisals. If you use fair market value, be sure to document the source you used to make your estimate of fair market value.

After you enter the costs or market values of all your assets and liabilities, you can generate a report that calculates your net worth by subtracting your liabilities from your assets. The desired result, of course, is for the difference to be a positive one. Whether you are determining your net worth as a business or an individual, you want the net worth amount to grow larger in time,

II

Getting the Most

because this amount acts as a financial cushion should you ever experience fiscal difficulties.

Figure 11.8 shows an example of a personal balance sheet, or Net Worth Report, created by Quicken. At the top of the page, Quicken lists each asset account and its balance as of a specific date. Below the asset accounts, Quicken lists each liability account and its balance as of a specific date. The difference between assets and liabilities is *total net worth*. In figure 11.8, the net-worth amount is $95,946.27.

Fig. 11.8
A personal Net Worth Report lists your assets and your liabilities. The difference between the two is your net worth.

Net Worth Report (Includes Unrealized Gains) As of 9/2/94	
9/2/94　　　　　　　　　　　　　Page 1 All Accounts	
Account	**Balance (9/2)**
Assets	
Cash and Bank Accounts	
First National	
Ending Balance	3,326.59
plus: Checks Payable	5,000.00
Total First National	8,326.59
First Savings	21,080.82
Petty Cash	465.00
Union State	
Ending Balance	353.65
plus: Checks Payable	120.98
Total Union State	474.63
Total Cash & Bank Accounts	30,347.04
Other Assets	
Home	255,000.00
Save for Jeep	1,923.07
Total Other Assets	256,923.07
Investments	
Merrill Lynch	95,000.00
Total Investments	95,000.00
Total Assets	**382,270.11**
Liabilities	
Checks Payable	5,120.98
Credit Cards	
Mastercard	650.86
Visa	552.00
Total Credit Cards	1,202.86
Other Liabilities	
Mortgage	250,000.00
Personal Loan	30,000.00
Total Other Liabilities	280,000.00
Total Liabilities	**286,323.84**
Overall Total	**95,946.27**

A business balance sheet looks essentially the same, although the assets and liabilities listed usually are different.

Chapter 19, "Creating and Printing Reports," describes how to print a personal Net Worth Report and a business balance sheet, as well as Quicken's other reports.

From Here...

You may want to review the following chapters after learning about tracking your assets and liabilities in Quicken:

- Chapter 3, "Defining Your Accounts," shows you how to create banks accounts and how to edit and delete accounts in Quicken.

- Chapter 6, "Using the Register," explains the use of Registers in Quicken. You learn how to enter, edit, and delete transactions in Registers for any type of account.

II

Getting the Most

Chapter 12

Estimating and Preparing for Income Taxes

A basic accounting requirement for businesses and individuals is to complete the required federal income tax forms at the end of the year to report income and expenses. Although everyone knows that taxes are inevitable, not everyone organizes financial activities so that tax time isn't a surprise. With Quicken, you can designate categories and subcategories as tax-related and accumulate your tax information in seconds. Whether you prepare your own income tax return or hand your tax information to a paid tax accountant, Quicken alleviates the burden of gathering tax data.

Now, with Quicken, you can estimate your income tax liability at any time during the year. With the use of Quicken's new Tax Planner, you can see just how much income tax you'll owe next April 15th. The Tax Planner uses the data that you've entered in Quicken and any other data that you forecast for the remainder of the year. All tax calculations are performed by the Tax Planner, using the current year income tax rates and laws. If you want, you can change the tax rates so that you can estimate next year's tax liability.

In this chapter, you learn how to do the following:

- Set up a category or subcategory as tax-related

- Set up Quicken so that you can assign a tax form or schedule to each tax-related category

- Create reports that summarize your tax-related transactions for the year

- Export tax data in Quicken to a tax preparation program

- Use the Tax Planner to estimate your income tax liability

- Save and print income tax estimates

Using Tax-Related Categories

The basic rule for using categories (and subcategories) to accumulate your tax data is to set up a category or subcategory for each taxable income item or tax deduction you have. The best way to do so is to review your last two income tax returns to determine which items you have. If you make charitable contributions each year and itemize your deductions, you will want to make sure that you have a category set up (and designated as tax-related) to assign to charitable contribution transactions. If you want to track a taxable income item or tax-deduction item in more detail, you can use subcategories and designate the subcategories as tax-related.

CPA Tip: Designating Categories as Tax-Related

If you don't itemize your deductions (because the total of your itemized deductions doesn't exceed the standard deduction amount), designating the categories for charitable contributions, interest expense, real estate taxes, investment fees, and so on as tax-related isn't necessary.

You also need to complete an equivalent state income tax form. Make sure that you or an accountant easily can prepare the tax return with the information Quicken produces. (The more time the accountant takes, the more money you pay to have the accountant prepare the return.)

If you are using Quicken for a partnership or a corporation, you must report asset and liability amounts on the tax return. You also want to verify that Quicken provides the data necessary to complete these lines of the tax return. The easiest approach probably is to set up accounts to track each asset and liability that appears on the tax return. Another approach is to use accounts that you can combine to calculate the total asset or liability figure that needs to be entered on the tax return.

Sole proprietors also must consider one other thing: you may need to complete more than one Schedule C form. You can't aggregate a series of dissimilar businesses and report the consolidated results on one Schedule C. Quicken can handle this situation, but you need to account for each business that needs a separate Schedule C in a separate Quicken file. (Chapter 21, "Managing Your Quicken Files," explains how to set up and select different Quicken files.)

You also can work with categories that you need to combine with other categories to calculate an entry on a tax form. Suppose that you are a sole proprietor of a restaurant. Although total wages go on one line of the Schedule C tax form, you may want to track several categories of wages (subcategories), including waitresses, dishwashers, cooks, bartenders, and so on. Here, you have several wage subcategories that must be added to calculate the wages amount that goes on the tax form. The Tax Schedule report can help you accumulate data from more than one subcategory.

After you understand how to use categories to classify your tax-related items, you must set up categories and subcategories in your Quicken file as tax-related.

For tax-related categories and subcategories, you also can designate the tax form or schedule to which the category or subcategory relates. If, for example, you set up a category for business entertainment expenses (Bus Enter) as tax-related, you also can specify the form or schedule that business expenses should be reported on. Because business expenses are reported on Form 2106, you would select this form when setting up the category. To assign a tax form or schedule to a tax-related category or subcategory, you must set the tax schedule option in Quicken so that the **F**orm text box appears when you set up a new category. The next section shows you how to set this option.

Setting the Tax Schedule Option

If you want to assign a tax form or schedule to a category or subcategory that you're setting up as tax-related, you first must set the tax schedule option so that the appropriate text box appears.

To set the tax schedule option, follow these steps:

1. Choose **O**ptions from the **E**dit menu or click the Options button on the Iconbar. Quicken displays the Options dialog box.

2. Choose the **G**eneral option. Quicken displays the General Options dialog box.

3. Select the Use **T**ax Schedules with Categories option check box.

4. Choose OK to save the tax schedule option setting and return to the Options dialog box and then choose Close.

Setting Up a Tax-Related Category

In Chapter 4, "Organizing Your Finances," you learned how to set up categories and subcategories. If you want to track taxable income items and tax deductions, however, you must set up categories and subcategories as tax-related.

To set up a tax-related category or subcategory, follow these steps:

1. Choose **C**ategory & Transfer from the **L**ists menu or press Ctrl+C to display the Category & Transfer List.

2. If you're setting up a new category in Quicken that you want to designate as tax-related, choose the **N**ew button. Quicken displays the Set Up Category dialog box, shown in figure 12.1.

Fig. 12.1

Use the Set Up Category dialog box to enter information for a new category or subcategory.

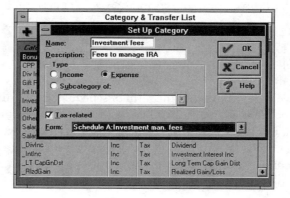

If you want to designate an existing category or subcategory as tax-related, highlight the category or subcategory and choose the Ed**i**t button. Quicken displays the Edit Category dialog box, shown in figure 12.2.

Fig. 12.2

Use the Edit Category dialog box to designate an existing category or subcategory as tax-related.

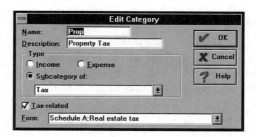

3. For new categories or subcategories, complete the Set Up Category dialog box, as described in Chapter 4. Select the **T**ax-related check box. From the **F**orm drop-down list, select a form or schedule (if the category you are setting up is for real estate taxes, for example, select Schedule A: Real Estate Tax).

   For existing categories or subcategories, select the **T**ax-related check box in the Edit Category dialog box. From the **F**orm drop-down list, select a form or schedule.

4. Choose OK to set up the category or subcategory as tax-related.

Assigning Tax-Related Categories to Transactions

After your categories and subcategories are set up as tax-related, you can start tracking your taxable income items and your tax deductions. Each time that you assign a tax-related category or subcategory to a transaction, Quicken accumulates the amounts as taxable income or a tax deduction. At any time, you can generate a Tax Schedule Report that summarizes your tax-related transactions for whatever period necessary. If, for example, you pay estimated federal income taxes on a quarterly basis, you may need to generate a Tax Schedule Report every three months to determine the income you received in the period.

Assign a tax-related category or subcategory to a transaction in the same manner that you assign any category or subcategory: select the category or subcategory from the drop-down list in the Category field of the Write Checks window or the Register. Just make sure that the transaction to which you are assigning a tax-related category or subcategory is truly taxable income or a tax-deductible item. Don't, for example, assign a tax-related category to a personal entertainment expense or the purchase of furniture for your home, neither of which is tax-deductible.

Summarizing Tax-Related Transactions at Year's End

During the year, you should assign tax-related categories and subcategories to each transaction for taxable income or for a tax-deductible expense (as explained in the preceding section). When you use Quicken's tax-related categories and subcategories, extracting the information you need to complete a tax form is simple. You just print the report that summarizes the categories and subcategories that track taxable income and income tax deductions. This report is called the *Tax Summary Report.*

To create a Tax Summary Report, follow these steps:

1. Choose the Reports button from the Iconbar. Quicken displays the Create Report dialog box with a sample of the Tax Summary Report at the bottom.

2. In the Report Dates section, select the reporting period from the Report Dates drop-down list box or customize the reporting period by selecting the dates that you want the report to cover in the **F**rom and **T**o boxes.

3. Choose OK. Quicken searches all accounts for the period specified in the Create Report dialog box and displays the Tax Summary Report window (see fig. 12.3).

Fig. 12.3
The Tax Summary Report groups and subtotals your tax-related transactions by income and expense categories.

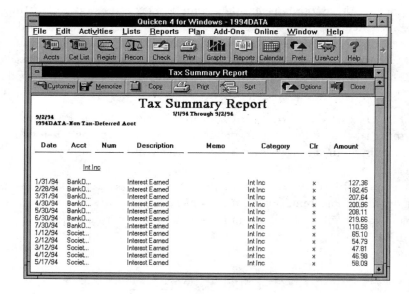

Tip
Refer to Chapter 19, "Creating and Printing Reports," for more information on customizing and printing reports.

4. Choose Pri**n**t on the Report button bar to print the Tax Summary Report.

CPA Tip: Gathering Tax Information

Although tax forms give most of the general information about the kinds of expenses, IRS instructions and regulations may require that you gather additional information. One example is that the business usage of a vehicle owned by a business is subject to different limitations, which aren't necessarily found in Quicken. Consult a tax advisor when you encounter questionable areas.

Another report, the Tax Schedule Report, not only subtotals your tax-related categories and subcategories by taxable income and tax-deductible expenses, but groups and subtotals the transactions by line item, by form, or by schedule. When you choose to create the Tax Schedule Report, Quicken searches all your accounts for transactions assigned to tax-related categories and subcategories. The Tax Schedule Report groups and subtotals the tax-related transactions first by line item, and then by tax form or schedule. Taxable income transactions, by form or schedule, are listed first, followed by tax-deductible transactions.

If you manually prepare your tax return, you can use the Tax Schedule Report to complete tax forms and schedules. If you pay a CPA or tax attorney to prepare your return, you can give her or him a copy of the Tax Schedule Report and save that person time (and yourself tax preparation fees) because the tax information needed already is subtotaled.

If you use a tax preparation software program to prepare your return, you can transfer the data in the Tax Schedule Report directly to that program.

Note

If you use TurboTax for Windows, there's no need to create the Tax Schedule Report to export Quicken data. TurboTax for Windows can read and import Quicken for Windows data with the use of this report.

And with Quicken 4 for Windows, you can easily start your TurboTax for Windows program, right from Quicken. Just select **T**urboTax from the new Add-Ons menu. (Note that you must have already installed TurboTax for Windows on your hard drive).

II

Getting the Most

To create a Tax Schedule Report, follow these steps:

1. Choose the Reports button from the Iconbar. Quicken displays the Create Report dialog box with the sample format for the Tax Schedule Report.

2. In the Report Dates drop-down list, select the reporting period or customize the reporting period by selecting the dates that you want the report to cover in the **F**rom and **T**o boxes.

3. Choose OK. Quicken searches all accounts for the period specified in the Create Report dialog box and displays the Tax Schedule Report window (see fig. 12.4).

Fig. 12.4

The Tax Schedule Report groups and subtotals your tax-related transactions by line item and by tax form or schedule.

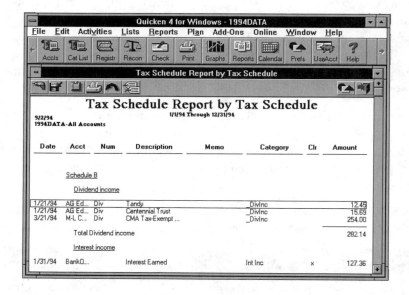

4. Choose Pri**n**t on the Report button bar to print the Tax Schedule Report.

Refer to the next section to learn how to export the report data to a tax preparation program.

Exporting Quicken Data into Tax Preparation Programs

You can transfer the tax data you collect and store in Quicken directly into several popular income tax preparation packages. TurboTax for Windows reads and imports Quicken for Windows data without having to create the Tax Schedule Report. Other tax software programs, including TurboTax for DOS, for example, import Quicken data as well, but through the Tax Schedule Report that you learned about in the last section.

When you export Quicken data, you first must export the data to a tax export file with the TXF (Tax Exchange Format) file extension. After your data is exported to a TXF file, you can start your tax preparation program and import the TXF file to that program.

To export your Quicken data to a tax export file, follow these steps:

1. Create the Tax Schedule Report, as explained in the preceding section. Make sure that the report dates are from January 1 of the prior year to December 31.

2. Choose the Export icon on the Report button bar. Quicken displays the Create Tax Export File dialog box, shown in figure 12.5. Notice that the Tax export files (*.TXF) format type is selected in the Save File as **T**ype drop-down list box.

Fig. 12.5
To export your Quicken tax data to another tax preparation program, use the Create Tax Export File dialog box.

3. In the File **N**ame text box, type the filename that you want Quicken to name the tax export file. Make sure that your filename meets the criteria for filenames.

4. The **D**irectories list box displays the current directory. You can select a different directory. You should probably export the file to the directory where your tax program is located.

5. The Dri**v**es drop-down list box displays the current drive. Select the drive to which you are exporting the Tax Schedule Report.

6. When the Create Tax Export File dialog box is complete, choose OK.

Quicken creates a TXF file with your Tax Schedule Report information ready to be imported to your tax preparation program. Refer to the documentation for your tax preparation program to learn how to import the TXF file to the program.

Estimating Your Income Taxes with the Tax Planner

Quicken 4 for Windows includes a new feature called the Tax Planner that helps you keep one step ahead of the IRS. Quicken's new Tax Planner lets you estimate the amount of tax you'll owe next April 15th, determine whether you are withholding adequate amounts from earnings during the year, determine whether quarterly estimated payments should be made, evaluate the tax impact of major financial decisions (such as buying or selling a home, selling appreciated securities, changing your filing status, and so forth), and analyze your tax liability for 1994 and 1995.

The Tax Planner is easy to use and calculates your tax liability in seconds using tax-related information that you already entered in Quicken. To use the Tax Planner to estimate your tax liability, follow these general steps:

1. Gather your tax information together.

2. Access the Tax Planner window by selecting **T**ax Planner from the Pl**a**n menu.

3. Use Tax Planner to estimate your tax liability using your Quicken data or tax data that you enter manually.

4. (Optional) Change the tax rate the Tax Planner uses.

5. (Optional) Create different tax scenarios.

6. Analyze and print tax estimates.

Gathering Tax Information

Before you start to use the Tax Planner, make sure that you have gathered all of your tax-related documents and information together. This might include paycheck stubs, medical and dental payment records, real estate and personal property tax receipts, interest payment records for mortgages, child care payment receipts, charitable contribution receipts, and perhaps even your prior years' tax returns. Basically, you'll want to have access to all documents that show taxable earnings or tax-deductible expenses.

Accessing the Tax Planner

Once you've accumulated your tax information, you're ready to begin using the Tax Planner. Access the Tax Planner window (shown in fig. 12.6) by selecting **T**ax Planner from the Pl**a**n menu.

Print the tax estimate ———

Use Quicken data ———
in the Tax Planner

——— Calculate tax amounts to enter in fields

——— Reset values in tax scenarios to zero

——— Close the Tax Planner window

Modify 1994
and 1995
tax rates

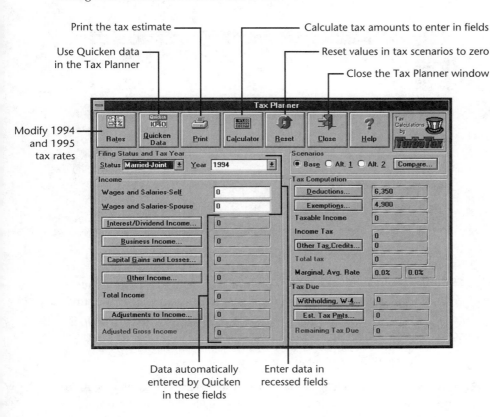

Fig. 12.6
Quicken's Tax
Planner estimates
your tax liability
for 1994 and 1995.

Data automatically
entered by Quicken
in these fields

Enter data in
recessed fields

Estimating Taxes with Quicken Data

The Tax Planner uses tax-related information that you have already entered in Quicken. If you prefer, however, you can manually enter all of your tax-related data in the Tax Planner or use year-to-date Quicken data and then enter the data for the remainder of the year yourself.

To get tax data from Quicken to use in the Tax Planner, follow these steps:

1. From the Tax Planner window (see fig. 12.6), click the **Q**uicken Data button. Quicken searches your data file for transactions that have been assigned to tax-related categories and subcategories for the year-to-date through the end of the previous month. Your Quicken tax data is displayed in the Preview Quicken Tax Data window shown in figure 12.7. The final amounts imported to the Tax Planner, by tax schedule and destination, are listed in the Preview Quicken Tax Data window.

Fig. 12.7
The Preview Quicken Tax Data window displays your year-to-date Quicken data through the end of the previous month.

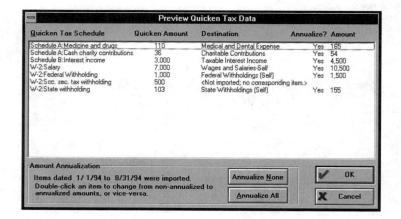

2. Review each line in the Preview Quicken Tax Data window. Then select whether you want Quicken to annualize the year-to-date amounts to reflect a full year. By default, Quicken enters Yes next to each amount in the Preview Quicken Tax Data window. Note, however, that Quicken does not annualize capital gains from Schedule D.

   Double-click a line to change Annualize from Yes to No.

3. After you finish selecting amounts to annualize, select **A**nnualize All to annualize all items marked Yes. Select Annualize **N**one if you don't want Quicken to annualize any of the items in the Preview Quicken Tax Data window.

   Choose OK to go back to the Tax Planner window with the amounts entered in the appropriate fields.

4. In the **S**tatus drop-down list box, select the correct filing status.

5. In the **Y**ear drop-down list box, select the year (1994 or 1995) in which you want to prepare an income tax estimate.

6. The Tax Planner window shows the results of its tax estimate; either a Remaining Tax Due or a Refund Due.

Refer to the section "Analyzing and Printing Tax Estimates," later in this chapter to learn how to evaluate the results of the Tax Planner's tax estimate.

Estimating Taxes with Data Entered Manually

If you don't want to use your Quicken data in the Tax Planner, or if you want to enter data in addition to your Quicken data, you can enter data manually in the Tax Planner.

To estimate taxes with data entered manually, follow these steps:

1. From the Tax Planner window (see fig. 12.6), select the correct filing status in the **S**tatus drop-down list box.

2. In the **Y**ear drop-down list box, select the year (1994 or 1995) in which you want to prepare an income tax estimate.

3. Enter annual wages and salaries for you and your spouse directly in the Tax Planner window.

4. For all other tax data that you want to enter, you must select the appropriate button from the Tax Planner window. When you select a button from the Tax Planner window, Quicken displays the related dialog box so that you can enter the data there. After a dialog box is completed, Quicken totals the amounts from the dialog box and enters the result in the Tax Planner window.

   For example, if you want to enter interest and dividend amounts, select the **I**nterest/Dividend Income button. Quicken then displays the Interest/Dividend Income-Schedule B dialog box that you see in figure 12.8. Here, you enter taxable interest income and dividends for the year. When you choose OK, Quicken totals the amounts in the Interest/Dividend Income-Schedule B dialog box and enters the result in the **I**nterest/Dividend Income field in the Tax Planner window, as shown in figure 12.9.

Fig. 12.8
Enter taxable
interest and
dividend amounts
in the Interest/
Dividend Income-
Schedule B dialog
box.

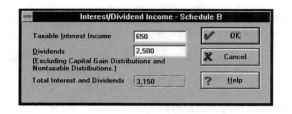

Fig. 12.9
Quicken totals the
amounts in the
Interest/Dividend
Income-Schedule
B dialog box and
enters the result in
the Tax Planner
window.

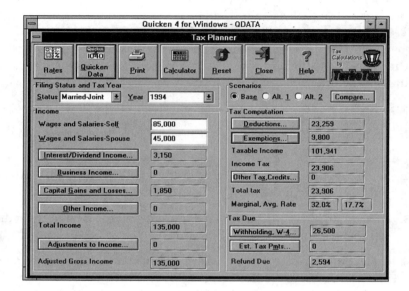

5. Repeat step 4 for data that you want to enter in the fields (except wages and salaries) in the Tax Planner window. Select the Withholding, W-**4** button to display the Withholding and W-4 Allowances dialog box so that you can enter payroll information for yourself and your spouse, such as pay per period, withholdings to date, other withholding per pay period information, and allowances claimed.

> **Note**
>
> If you want the Tax Planner to suggest a withholding amount based on your tax situation, select the **R**ecommend button in the Withholding and W-4 Allowances dialog box.

6. As you enter data in the Tax Planner, you see the results of its tax esti-mate; either a Remaining Tax Due or a Refund Due.

Refer to the section "Analyzing and Printing Tax Estimates," later in this chapter to learn how to evaluate the results of the Tax Planner's tax estimate.

Changing Tax Rates

The Tax Planner includes the tax rates for 1994 and 1995 as of August 1994. If tax rates change after this date, however, you can change the rates to reflect these changes. Tax rates are programmed into the Tax Planner by filing status. Therefore, before you change tax rates, you must first choose the filing status for which you want to change the rates.

> **Note**
>
> For free information about tax changes that affect the Tax Planner, call the Quicken Tax Update Hotline at (415)858-6081 and receive tax update information at any time by fax or by mail.

To change the tax rate in the Tax Planner, follow these steps:

1. From the **S**tatus drop-down list box, select the filing status for which you want to change the tax rate.

2. Next, click the Ra**t**es button. Quicken displays the Tax Rates for Filing Status dialog box shown in figure 12.10.

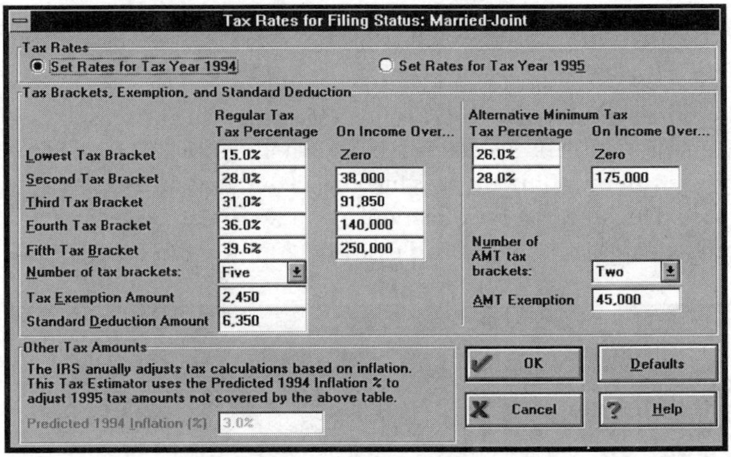

Fig. 12.10
When you select Ra**t**es, Quicken displays the Tax Rates for Filing Status dialog box with the tax rates for the filing status selected in the Tax Planner window.

3. At the top of the Tax Rates for Filing Status dialog box, select the tax year that you want to change.

II

Getting the Most

4. Type new amounts over the original values. Be sure to enter the income threshold amount as well as the percent of tax. When setting 1995 tax rates, you can change the inflation rate that Quicken uses to adjust tax calculations.

5. Choose OK to change the tax rate for the filing status and the year for which you made the changes.

Creating Different Tax Scenarios

The Tax Planner includes two alternative worksheets that you can use to compare different tax scenarios. For example, if you're contemplating selling a security at a substantial gain, you can use one of the alternative worksheets to enter the gain and compare your tax liability with and without it.

To create different tax scenarios, follow these steps:

1. From the Tax Planner window, select the Alt. **1** button or the Alt. **2** button.

2. Quicken asks whether you want to copy the current scenario. If you select Yes, Quicken copies all data from the current scenario (the Base scenario) to the alternative scenario. If you select No, Quicken resets all values to zero in the alternative scenario.

3. Make changes or enter new information in the alternative scenario.

4. (Optional) If you want to reset the values in the alternative scenario to zero, select **R**eset.

5. Compare tax scenarios by selecting Compa**r**e. Quicken displays the Tax Scenario Comparisons dialog box shown in figure 12.11. Quicken shows you the adjusted gross income, deductions and exemptions, taxable income, total tax, marginal tax rate, and average tax rate for each scenario so that you can easily determine which is best.

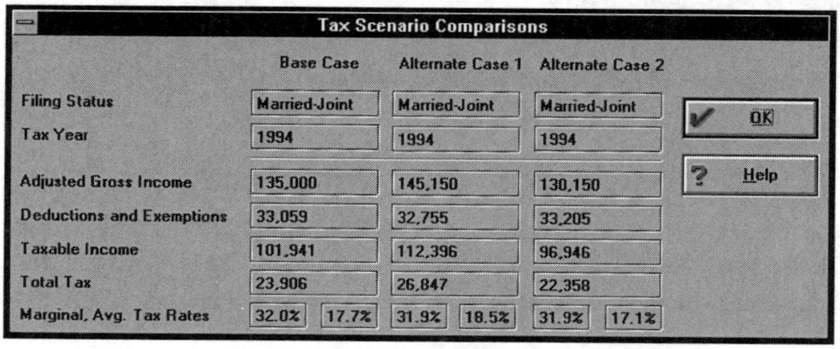

Fig. 12.11
Use the Tax Scenario Comparisons dialog box to compare three tax situations.

	Base Case	Alternate Case 1	Alternate Case 2	
Filing Status	Married-Joint	Married-Joint	Married-Joint	
Tax Year	1994	1994	1994	
Adjusted Gross Income	135,000	145,150	130,150	
Deductions and Exemptions	33,059	32,755	33,205	
Taxable Income	101,941	112,396	96,946	
Total Tax	23,906	26,847	22,358	
Marginal, Avg. Tax Rates	32.0% 17.7%	31.9% 18.5%	31.9% 17.1%	

Analyzing and Printing Tax Estimates

After you've entered tax data in the Tax Planner and your tax liability has been estimated, you'll want to analyze your tax estimate to see whether you're in a tax due or a tax refund situation. Most importantly, you'll want to determine whether your withholdings are adequate or whether you should be making estimated tax payments.

If the Tax Planner window shows a Remaining Tax Due of more than $500, you may be required to make quarterly estimated tax payments or increase your withholding amounts to avoid IRS penalties and interest when you file your income tax return. To begin filing quarterly estimated tax payments, see IRS publication 505 or Form 1040-ES, *Estimated Tax Payments for Individuals* to review the guidelines on how to file and calculate estimated tax payments. To increase your payroll withholdings, contact your employer's human resource department.

If the Tax Planner window shows a Refund Due of a significant amount, you should consider reducing your estimated tax payments or your withholding amounts.

The Tax Planner window also shows you your marginal tax rate and your average tax rate:

- The *marginal tax rate* is the rate of tax on the highest range of your taxable income. If you are married, filing jointly, with a taxable income of $95,000 in 1994, for example, your marginal tax rate is 31%. Your marginal tax rate is determined by the specified tax rates, as set forth by the Internal Revenue Code. In 1994, this rate was 31% for taxable income that exceeds $91,850 (for joint filers).

- The *average tax rate* is the overall rate of tax on your adjusted gross income. If your adjusted gross income is $50,000 and your tax liability is $10,000, for example, your average tax rate is 20% ($10,000/$50,000).

If you want to print a copy of your tax estimate, select the **P**rint button. Quicken displays the Print dialog box where you select which pages to print and the quality of print to use. Set these options and choose OK to print all of your tax information. If you created other tax scenarios, Quicken prints all scenarios along with a comparison of the scenarios.

II

Getting the Most

From Here...

After learning how to prepare for and estimate your income taxes, you may want to review the following:

■ Chapter 4, "Organizing Your Finances," explains how to use categories in Quicken and how to set up categories as tax-related.

■ Chapter 19, "Creating and Printing Reports," shows you how to customize and print reports in Quicken so that you can design the tax reports the way that you want them.

Chapter 13

Paying Your Bills Electronically

With Quicken, you can use CheckFree, an electronic bill payment service, to pay your bills. By using Quicken and a modem, you can send payment instructions to the CheckFree Corporation (located in Ohio). Your payment instructions include all the information CheckFree needs to actually pay the bill: who you owe the money to, when the bill needs to be paid, how much you owe, and so on. CheckFree Corporation then draws a check or electronically transfers funds from your bank account to whomever you owe the money.

Paying bills electronically isn't for everyone. By getting one more party involved in the bill-paying process, you may make this process more complicated. For Quicken users who have a modem and who want to stop printing checks, however, electronic payment is appealing.

This chapter explains how to perform the following tasks:

- Set up your Quicken system for electronic payments
- Pay bills electronically
- Transmit payment information to CheckFree
- Issue stop-payment requests
- Make payment inquiries

> **Note**
>
> If you have been using the CheckFree program (Version 3.0 or later) to make electronic payments, you can't use your CheckFree program again after you use Quicken once to make electronic payments. CheckFree Corporation doesn't let you process payments using their CheckFree software after you use Quicken to transmit payment information. You can't use CheckFree and Quicken concurrently to pay bills.

If you have been using CheckFree (Version 3.0 or later) but now want to use Quicken to transmit electronic payment information to the CheckFree Processing Center, you need to import your CheckFree Register data into Quicken. (You can't import data from earlier versions of CheckFree.) This way, you update your Register in Quicken with any CheckFree transactions that Quicken doesn't include. Refer to your CheckFree manual to learn how to export your CheckFree Register to Quicken.

Setting Up Your System for Electronic Payment

To begin paying your bills electronically, you need to complete four steps:

1. Complete the CheckFree paperwork. The form is self-explanatory. After you provide this basic information, you also need to tell CheckFree which phone lines you are using, specify which account number/security code you plan to use to gain access to the CheckFree system, and sign an authorization so that CheckFree can deduct funds from your bank account. (If you don't choose an account number or security code, CheckFree creates one for you.)

   After you complete the CheckFree Service Form, attach a voided check to the form and mail the form to Intuit.

Tip
For security reasons, use a security code—similar to what you use for automated teller machines—to access your account.

2. Configure your modem by setting the modem options in Quicken. You learn how to set up your modem later in this chapter.

3. Designate the bank account(s) you want to use to make electronic payments from. Setting up bank accounts for electronic payment is explained later in this chapter.

4. Set up the payees (the persons or companies that you want to pay electronically). Later in this chapter, you learn how to set up electronic payees.

Performing these steps is easy. Completing this part of the work should take no more than a few minutes.

Setting Modem Options

Before you can begin paying bills electronically with CheckFree, you must set the modem options in Quicken. Make sure that you have received the confirmation letter from CheckFree before you set modem options because you need to enter the CheckFree access number.

To set modem options, follow these steps:

1. From the Online menu, select **Se**t Up Modem. Quicken displays the Set Up Modem-Intuit Online Services dialog box, shown in figure 13.1.

Fig. 13.1
Enter the information about your telephone and modem in the Set Up Modem-Intuit Online Services dialog box.

2. The easiest way to set up your modem is to select the Auto**c**onfigure button to have Quicken scan your communication ports and automatically configure your modem. If you have special settings that Quicken doesn't recognize, continue to step 3.

3. From the **P**ort drop-down list box, select the port your modem uses in your computer, such as COM1 or COM2.

4. From the **S**peed drop-down list box, select the speed at which your modem operates. If you're unsure about which speed to select, refer to your modem manual for this information.

5. Don't change the number in the **A**ccess Number text; Quicken has already entered the U.S. access number for you.

6. If necessary, select the prefix that must be dialed from your modem line in the **D**ialing Prefix drop-down list box.

7. In the Dial Type section, choose **T**one if the telephone line your modem uses supports touch-tone dialing. Choose P**u**lse if your phone line supports pulse dialing.

> **Note**
>
> If the telephone line that you use supports Call Waiting, you should temporarily disable the service before transmitting to CheckFree. Contact your local telephone company for the code you need to disable Call Waiting, and then enter that code, followed by a comma, before typing the access number for CheckFree.

8. (Optional) If you want to enter advanced modem settings, select Advanced from the Set Up Modem-Intuit Online Services dialog box. Enter modem settings and choose OK.

9. Choose OK to save the modem settings.

Setting Up Bank Accounts for Electronic Payment

After you set up your modem, you are ready to set up the bank account(s) that you will use to make electronic payments. Your bank accounts must already be set up in Quicken. Now you must identify which bank accounts you want to use for electronic payment. You can't use a credit card, asset, liability, or investment account for electronic payment—only bank accounts.

If you haven't set up the bank account in your Quicken file, create it now (see Chapter 3). Then set up a bank account for electronic payment by following these steps:

1. From the Activities menu, choose CheckFree.

2. From the CheckFree submenu, choose Set Up Account. Quicken displays the Electronic Payment Setup dialog box, shown in figure 13.2. Because you can set up only bank accounts for electronic payment, Quicken lists only bank accounts in the Electronic Payment Setup dialog box.

3. Highlight the bank account that you want and then choose Set Up. Quicken displays the Electronic Payment Account Settings dialog box, shown in figure 13.3.

4. Make sure that a check mark appears in the Enable Electronic Payments for Account check box. If a check mark doesn't appear, select the option.

5. Enter your name, address, and home telephone number.

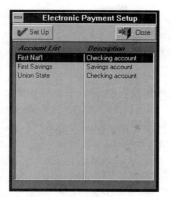

Fig. 13.2
The Electronic
Payment Setup
dialog box lists all
bank accounts in
your Quicken file.

Fig. 13.3
Quicken displays
the Electronic
Payment Account
Settings dialog box
when you select a
bank account to
set up for elec-
tronic payment.

II

Getting the Most

6. Next, type the account number that CheckFree assigned to you.

7. In the CheckFree Security Code text box, enter the account number/ security number or PIN number from the CheckFree confirmation letter.

8. After you complete the Electronic Payment Account Settings dialog box, choose OK. Quicken returns to the Electronic Payment Setup dialog box. The account you set up now is marked as *enabled* (designated with a lightning bolt character) for electronic payment. When you subsequently select the enabled account to use, Quicken adds several more menu options that you can use for processing electronic payments.

9. Repeat steps 3 through 8 for other accounts that you want to set up for electronic payment.

Setting Up Payees for Electronic Payment

To pay a bill electronically, you need to collect and store information about each person or company you plan to pay so that CheckFree Corporation can process payments to the appropriate person or business. To set up a payee, just add the payee to the Electronic Payee List. From the Electronic Payee List, you can edit a payee or delete a payee to whom you no longer make payments.

Quicken enables you to make payments to payees in one of two ways: by variable payments or by fixed payments. Each month, for example, your telephone bill probably isn't the same. To pay the telephone company, you need to write a check for a varying amount each month. Quicken calls this a *normal payment*. Payees that you make ordinary payments to, like your telephone company or your utility company, are called *normal payees*. When you set up a payee to receive a normal payment, you must enter the check in Quicken each time you make payment to the payee.

On the other hand, your check to your landlord for rent is usually the same each month. In this case, you can tell Quicken to pay the same amount each month to the specified payee until you tell Quicken to no longer make the payment. Quicken calls these types of payments *fixed payments*. Payees that receive recurring payments for the same amount at a fixed interval are called *fixed, recurring payees*. When you set up a payee to receive a fixed payment, CheckFree makes the payment for you, based on the intervals that you specify.

Caution

Because many individuals or businesses aren't set up to handle electronic fund transfers, CheckFree mails these kinds of payments from Ohio. If the payee's location is your home town, the payment may take an extra day or two to reach the payee from Ohio. Schedule all CheckFree payments early enough to allow for delays in the mail system.

Setting Up Payees for Normal Payments

To set up an electronic payee to receive normal payments, follow these steps:

1. From the Activities menu, choose CheckFree and then choose Electronic Payee List to display the Electronic Payee List window, shown in figure 13.4.

Fig. 13.4

You can add normal payees or fixed, recurring payees in the Electronic Payee List window.

2. Choose **N**ew. Quicken displays the Choose Type of Electronic Payee dialog box, shown in figure 13.5.

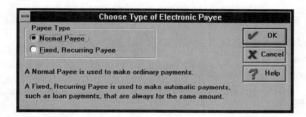

Fig. 13.5

Choose the type of payee you are setting up in the Choose Type of Electronic Payee dialog box.

3. By default, Quicken selects the **N**ormal Payee option. Choose OK to accept the selection. Quicken displays the Set Up Electronic Payee dialog box, shown in figure 13.6.

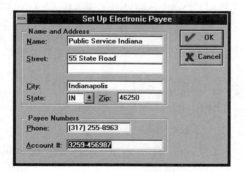

Fig. 13.6

Enter information about a normal payee in the Set Up Electronic Payee dialog box.

4. Enter the payee's name, street address, city, state, and ZIP code.

> **Note**
>
> Entering the payee name, address, phone number, and account number accurately is important because CheckFree uses this information to make payments to the payee.

5. In the **P**hone text box, type the payee's telephone number (the number that you normally call for billing inquiries), including the area code. CheckFree must have the payee's telephone number to route payments correctly.

6. In the **A**ccount text box, type the account number that the person or business uses to identify you.

7. When the Set Up Electronic Payee dialog box is complete, choose OK. Quicken returns to the Electronic Payee List window.

To set up additional normal payees, repeat steps 2 through 7.

Setting Up Payees to Receive Fixed, Recurring Payments

If you have certain monthly payments that don't vary in amount (your rent check or a car loan payment), you can set up the payee as a fixed, recurring payee. You establish a fixed payment schedule, which tells CheckFree to pay the same amount each month to the specified payee until you instruct CheckFree to stop making the payments.

With fixed, recurring payees, you don't have to enter a check each time you make payment—CheckFree automatically transmits a payment to the fixed, recurring payee.

To set up an electronic payee to receive fixed, recurring payments, follow these steps:

1. From the Acti**v**ities menu, choose Chec**k**Free and then choose Electronic Payee **L**ist to display the Electronic Payee List window (refer to fig. 13.4).

2. Choose **N**ew. Quicken displays the Choose Type of Electronic Payee dialog box (refer to fig. 13.5).

3. Choose **F**ixed, Recurring Payee.

4. Choose OK. Quicken displays the Set Up Electronic Payee dialog box for fixed payments, shown in figure 13.7.

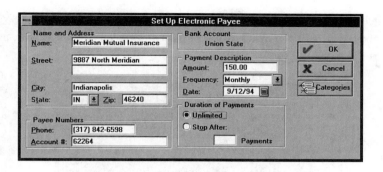

Fig. 13.7
The Set Up Electronic Payee dialog box to enter information about a payee to receive fixed, recurring payments.

5. Enter the name, street address, city, state, and ZIP code for the payee.

6. In the **P**hone text box, type the payee's telephone number (the number that you normally call for billing inquiries), including the area code. CheckFree must have the payee's telephone number to route payments correctly.

7. In the **A**ccount text box, type the account number that the person or business uses to identify you.

8. In the Bank Account area, Quicken displays the name of the bank account that you selected to use for electronic payments. If you set up more than one bank account for electronic payments, a drop-down list is displayed. Select the appropriate account from this list.

9. Type the amount of the fixed payment in the A**m**ount text box.

10. From the **F**requency drop-down list box, select the frequency of payments (weekly, biweekly, monthly, and so forth).

11. In the **D**ate text box, type or select the due date of the next payment.

12. In the Duration of Payments section, choose the **U**nlimited option if you want CheckFree to make regular payments until you give instructions otherwise. Choose St**o**p After to make fixed payments for a specified period of time, and then enter the number of payments to stop after in the Payments text box. For a rent payment, you can choose to have CheckFree make unlimited payments by selecting **U**nlimited. Alternatively, if you make a purchase, and the terms are that you make 12 monthly payments, choose St**o**p After and type **12** in the Payments box.

Tip
Select a date in the Date drop-down list box by clicking the calendar button to display the minicalendar. Chapter 7 explains how to enter dates using the minicalendar.

13. Next, choose Categories to assign category and memo information to fixed payments. Quicken displays the CheckFree Fixed Payment Categories dialog box, shown in figure 13.8.

14. Assign the appropriate category and memo to the fixed payment. To assign more than one category to the fixed payment, choose **S**plits to open the Splits window. Then assign the categories and amounts to the fixed payment and choose OK to return to the CheckFree Fixed Payment Categories dialog box. Choose OK to return to the Set Up Electronic Payee window.

15. Choose OK to return to the Electronic Payee List window. Quicken enters the word FIXED in the Type column for a payee that you set up as fixed and recurring.

To set up additional fixed, recurring payees, repeat steps 2 through 15.

Editing and Deleting Electronic Payees

You can edit or delete a payee from the Electronic Payee List. You can change, for example, the payee's address or even the account number that the payee uses to identify you. Or you can delete a payee to whom you no longer do business with or make payments to.

> **Note**
>
> You can't edit or delete an electronic payee if an untransmitted transaction exists for the payee. You learn more about untransmitted transactions later in this chapter.

To edit or delete an electronic payee, follow these steps:

1. From the Electronic Payee List window (refer to fig. 13.4), highlight the electronic payee that you want to edit or delete.

2. To edit an electronic payee, choose Ed**i**t. Quicken displays the Edit Electronic Payee dialog box, which resembles the Set Up Electronic Payee dialog box (refer to fig. 13.6 or 13.7). Make the necessary changes to the electronic payee information and choose OK.

   To delete an electronic payee, choose **D**elete. Quicken asks you to confirm that you want to delete the payee. Choose OK. If untransmitted payments or scheduled transactions exist for this payee, Quicken displays a warning message and asks whether you want to stop payments. If so, choose OK. Quicken displays another message telling you that CheckFree will continue making payments until the next time you connect to the CheckFree processing center. Choose OK to stop payments.

Paying Bills

Paying bills electronically closely resembles the process of writing and printing checks with Quicken. For this reason, this chapter doesn't repeat the discussions of Chapter 5, "Writing and Printing Checks," which cover how to write and print checks with Quicken. Instead, this section concentrates on different parts of the process. (If you haven't used the Quicken's Write Checks window, you may want to review Chapter 5 before continuing in this chapter.)

You pay bills that aren't set up as fixed and recurring by writing a check in the Write Checks window, recording the check, and transmitting the payment information to CheckFree. For fixed, recurring payments, you don't have to write a check each time a payment is due. After you set up a fixed, recurring payee, enter all the payment information, and transmit to CheckFree, CheckFree makes payments automatically based on the payment schedule that you enter. You receive payment confirmations from CheckFree when fixed payments are made.

Making Regular Payments

After you set up the payees who you will pay electronically in the Electronic Payee List, you can begin paying bills electronically. For each bill you want to pay, follow these steps:

1. From the Write Checks window, select the bank account from which you pay bills electronically using the Account Selector Bar. Quicken displays the electronic version of the Write Checks window, as shown in figure 13.9.

II

Getting the Most

Fig. 13.9
The electronic version of the Write Checks window appears when you select a bank account that you have set up to make electronic payments.

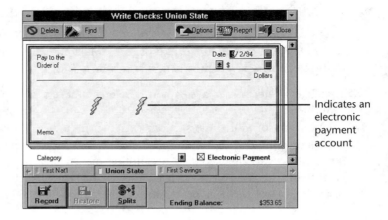

Indicates an electronic payment account

2. If an X doesn't appear in the Electronic Payment check box in the lower-right portion of the Write Checks window, select the option to activate the electronic payment feature.

3. Complete the electronic payment version of the Write Checks window in the same way you complete the regular version of the window.

   In the Date field, you can't enter a date that is less than five business days after the current date. CheckFree needs at least five business days to process payment information and make payments to your payees.

Tip
Use Quicken's minicalendar at the Date field to determine the five-business-day advance date to use for electronic payments.

In the Pay to the Order of field, make sure that you type or select an electronic payee from the drop-down list. Quicken indicates electronic payees with the word <ELECTRONIC PAYEE> next to the payee name in the list.

> **Note**
>
> Rather than track unprinted checks, Quicken shows the total dollar amount of the checks to transmit in the lower-right corner of the Write Checks window.

4. After the Write Checks window is complete, choose Record.

   The check that contains the electronic payment scrolls off the screen, leaving behind an *empty* check that you can use to complete another electronic payment. Until you begin transmitting the electronic payments, you can edit these payments just as you do any other check you write at the Write Checks window.

> **Note**
>
> If you prefer to pay an electronic payee with a manual check or a Quicken check, make sure that an X doesn't appear in the Electronic Payment box in the lower-right portion of the Write Checks window.

Tip
You also can enter and edit electronic payments by using the Quicken Register. Quicken identifies electronic payment transactions in the Quicken Register by displaying XMIT in the Num field.

5. Transmit the payment information to CheckFree. See the section "Transmitting to CheckFree" later in this chapter to learn how to transmit payment information to CheckFree.

Making Fixed, Recurring Payments

After you set up a payee to receive fixed, recurring payments and transmit the payee information to CheckFree, you don't need to do anything when payments are due. CheckFree automatically makes the payments based on the intervals that you enter. If you add your apartment landlord as an electronic payee to receive monthly rent checks in the amount of $750, CheckFree automatically makes those payments on the same day each month.

Editing a Fixed, Recurring Payment

If you want to change the payment information for a fixed, recurring payment, you can do so from the Electronic Payee List:

1. From the Electronic Payee List (refer to fig. 13.4), highlight the fixed payee that you want to change.

2. Choose Edit. Quicken displays the Edit Electronic Payee dialog box, which resembles the Set Up Electronic Payee dialog box in figure 13.7.

3. Make the appropriate changes in the Edit Electronic Payee dialog box. If you need to change the fixed payment amount, for example, move to the Amount text box and type the new amount.

4. After the changes are complete, choose OK.

5. Transmit the changes to the electronic payee to CheckFree (see the later section "Transmitting to CheckFree").

Discontinuing a Fixed, Recurring Payment

If you no longer want to make fixed, recurring payments to a payee, you can discontinue fixed payments in one of two ways: issue a stop payment for the most recent fixed payment, or delete the electronic payee to whom you make

II

Getting the Most

fixed payments from the Electronic Payee List. When you stop payment on the most recent fixed, recurring payment and transmit to CheckFree, any future payments are stopped for this payee; however, the payee information is retained in the Electronic Payee List.

If you choose to delete the payee from the Electronic Payee List, after you transmit the deletion to CheckFree, no future payments are made to the payee. You can't delete an electronic payee, however, that has a payment that already has been made and confirmed (XMIT appears in the Register for these transactions).

To discontinue a fixed, recurring payment by issuing a stop payment on the most recent payment, follow these steps:

1. Make sure that your modem is turned on and properly connected.

2. Display the Check Register for the account that you use to make electronic payments.

3. Highlight the most recent fixed, recurring payment in the Register.

4. From the Activities menu, choose CheckFree, and then choose Stop Payment.

5. Quicken asks you to confirm the stop payment request. Choose OK. Quicken immediately transmits the stop payment request to CheckFree. If the transmission is successful, CheckFree discontinues any future fixed payments. If an error message appears, repeat these steps.

Quicken retains the payee information in the Electronic Payee List, but changes the type from FIXED to INACTIVE.

To discontinue a fixed, recurring payment by deleting the payee, follow these steps:

1. From the Check Register for the account that you use to make electronic payments, access the Electronic Payee List (refer to fig. 13.4).

2. Highlight the payee for the fixed, recurring payment that you want to discontinue or delete.

3. Choose Delete.

4. Quicken asks you to confirm that you want to delete the electronic payee. Choose OK.

5. Transmit the deletion of the payee to CheckFree (as explained later in the section "Transmitting to CheckFree").

Making Loan Payments Electronically

For any amortized loan that you set up in Quicken, you can select CheckFree as the payment method to use to make loan payments. (Chapter 10, "Tracking Loans," shows you how to set up a loan in Quicken.) Before selecting CheckFree as the payment method for an amortized loan, you first must set up the lender as a fixed, recurring payee and then transmit the addition to the Electronic Payee List to CheckFree.

After your lender is set up as an electronic payee to receive fixed, recurring payments (see the earlier section "Setting Up Payees to Receive Fixed, Recurring Payments"), follow these steps to select CheckFree as the payment method for a loan:

1. From the Activities menu, choose Loans. Quicken displays the View Loans window.

2. From the Loan drop-down list box, select the loan for which you want to make loan payments electronically. Quicken displays the payment schedule and payment history for the loan in the View Loans window.

3. Choose Payments. Quicken displays the Set Up Loan Payment dialog box.

4. Choose Method of Pmt. Quicken displays the Select Payment Method dialog box. Choose CheckFree Fixed Payment.

5. Select the lender's name from the Fixed Payee drop-down list.

6. Choose OK.

Each time a loan payment is made by CheckFree and confirmed in Quicken, the payment schedule for the loan is updated to reflect the most recent payment.

Transmitting to CheckFree

After you enter the electronic payments, you need to transmit them so that CheckFree Corporation can pay them. When you transmit to CheckFree, any new payees that you have added to, or deleted from, the Electronic Payee List since the last transmission also are transmitted to CheckFree. Any changes to fixed payments are transmitted at this time.

To transmit electronic payments, electronic payee information, and changes to fixed payments, follow these steps:

1. Turn on your modem.

Quicken first tries to initialize the modem and then retries the modem twice. If a problem is encountered, a message appears that says `Quicken couldn't initialize the modem`. Make sure that your modem is connected properly and turned on. If Quicken continues to have a problem initializing your modem, refer to the user's manual for your modem or call Intuit's technical support staff.

2. From the Acti**v**ities menu, choose Chec**k**Free. Then choose **T**ransmit. Quicken displays the Transmit Payments dialog box, which tells you how many payments you must transmit (see fig. 13.10).

Fig. 13.10
The Transmit Payments dialog box tells you how many payments there are to transmit to CheckFree.

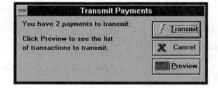

3. If you want to go ahead and transmit payments and payee information (if any), choose **T**ransmit. If you want to review the payments and any other information that can be transmitted, choose **P**review.

4. If you need to make changes to any of the information when you preview transactions, choose Cancel (or Escape) and make the appropriate changes. If the information is correct, choose **T**ransmit.

After you transmit payments, CheckFree sends confirmation numbers back to Quicken for each transmitted payment. Confirmation numbers are stored in the Memo field of each transaction.

> **Note**
>
> If you want to review information about an electronic payment, select the transaction in the Check Register, choose Chec**k**Free from the Acti**v**ities menu, and then choose Electronic Payment I**n**fo. Quicken displays the transmission date, payment date, transmission status, and the confirmation date of each electronic payment. Choose OK after you finish reviewing electronic payment information.

Issuing a Stop Payment

You can use Quicken to issue stop payment requests on electronic payments you transmitted previously. You can stop an electronic payment if the payment date is at least five business days after the current date. Obviously, as with stop payment requests issued directly to the bank, you need to make the request before the transaction is processed.

To issue a stop payment request, follow these steps:

1. Turn on your modem.

2. Display the Register for the account that you use to make electronic payments.

3. Highlight the transaction in the Register on which you want to stop payment.

4. From the Activities menu, choose CheckFree and then choose Stop **P**ayment.

5. Quicken asks you to confirm the stop payment. Choose OK.

Quicken immediately transmits the request to CheckFree. If the transmission is successful, Quicken enters VOID in the transaction line in the Register.

Making Electronic Payment Inquiries

You can ask CheckFree about a payment you transmitted previously. Suppose that you receive a telephone call from someone who wants to know whether you have sent them a check yet. You can make an electronic payment inquiry to check the status of this particular payment.

To make an electronic payment inquiry, follow these steps:

1. Turn on the modem.

2. Access the Register for the account that you use to make electronic payments.

3. Highlight the transaction in the Register that you want to inquire about. Electronic payments are marked with XMIT in the Num field.

4. From the Activities menu, choose CheckFree, and then choose Inquiry. Quicken displays the Electronic Payment Inquiry dialog box, which shows the details of the transmitted payment, including the date the transaction was transmitted to CheckFree, the scheduled payment date, the account number, and the confirmation number you received from CheckFree. Quicken asks whether you want to send an inquiry message to CheckFree regarding the transaction.

> **Note**
>
> This dialog box also indicates whether you can stop payment (if at least five business days still remain between the current date and the payment date).

5. Choose OK to send a payment inquiry. Quicken displays the Transmit Payment Inquiry to CheckFree dialog box, which contains the information about the transmitted payment and provides three lines on which you can make your inquiry.

6. Choose Transmit to send the payment inquiry to CheckFree.

Communicating with CheckFree

You can send messages to CheckFree at any time through your modem. This way, you easily and quickly can make general inquiries about the status of your account or can respond to inquiries from CheckFree. CheckFree also can communicate directly with you by electronic mail.

> **Note**
>
> If you want to issue a stop payment or inquire about a payment that you previously transmitted, you must use the Stop Payment and Inquiry commands from the Activities CheckFree menu. Don't use the E-Mail command to perform these activities. (Refer to the earlier sections "Making Electronic Payment Inquiries" and "Issuing a Stop Payment.")

You can send an electronic message to CheckFree to inquire about your CheckFree account or to respond to an inquiry from CheckFree. Just choose CheckFree and then choose E-Mail from the Activities menu. When Quicken displays the Read E-Mail window (see fig. 13.11), choose Create to display the Transmit Message to CheckFree window where you can type a message to CheckFree. Select Transmit when you're ready to send your message.

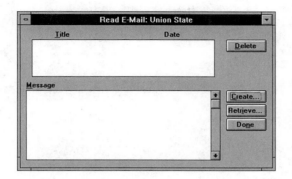

Fig. 13.11
Quicken displays
E-mail messages,
by title, in the
Read E-Mail
window.

CheckFree also can communicate with you by electronic mail. Each message you retrieve from CheckFree is entered, by title and date, in the Read E-Mail window. You can read messages from CheckFree that you already have received at any time from the Read E-Mail window. Quicken saves all messages, in chronological order, until you delete them. To receive electronic mail messages from CheckFree, select the message title from the **T**itle list box in the Read E-Mail window (refer to fig. 13.11). To check for new messages from CheckFree, choose Retrieve. Quicken enters any new messages in the **T**itle list box.

From Here...

After learning about paying bills electronically in this chapter, you may want to review the following:

■ Chapter 3, "Defining Your Accounts," shows you how to create accounts in Quicken. If you haven't already created the bank account that you want to use for electronic payment, you do so in Chapter 3.

■ Chapter 5, "Writing and Printing Checks," describes procedures for filling in check information in the Write Checks window. To make regular payments using CheckFree, you must first enter the payment information in the Write Checks window.

II

Getting the Most

Part III

Planning for the Future with Quicken for Windows

Quicken 4 for Windows - QDATA

File Edit Activities Lists Reports Plan Add-Ons Online Window Help

Homebse Registr Accts Recon Check Calendar Graphs Reports Sr

Quicken **H**elp
How To **U**se He
Tutorials
Show Qcards
About Quicken..

Print

Net Worth Graph

Monthly Assets, Liabilities and Net Worth

QuickZoom Graph

Portfolio Value
By Security

Time Warner   8.98
American Express   7.08
Oil & gas   6.51
St. John Knits   2.70
Mevt Medbol   2.50
Sulcus   1.60
Pepsi   1.46
Other   8.03
Total $489,600.00

Balance as of 6/30/94

Layout Budgets

Columns
- Month
- Quarter
- Year

OK
Cance
Hel

Rows
- Show Supercategories
- Show Transfers
- Hide Zero Budget Categorie

Quicken Calculator

0			
C	CE	<-	%
7	8	9	/
4	5	6	X
1	2	3	-
0			+
MS	MR	MC	=

Write Checks: First Nat'l

Delete

Options Rep

Pay to th
Order of

Date 5/15,
$

Dollars

? Help

Address

Memo

Category

First Nat'l   Union State

Enter a category.
Categories let you create reports, graphs, and budgets sorted by
category.

Either:
➡ Type the category by hand, OR
➡ Click the drop-down list

Then click the Next button below to conti ▷ Next   ? Help

Chapter 14

Scheduling Future Transactions

With Quicken, you may never again forget to pay the light bill, make a rent payment, or send a card on your mother-in-law's birthday. With Quicken's feature to schedule transactions, you can set up bills that you know are coming due, and Quicken not only reminds you to pay them but also enters the transactions for you. All you need to do is print the checks and mail them.

You also can schedule regular deposits (such as your paycheck) so that Quicken enters the deposit transaction in your bank account Register at regular intervals. For groups of recurring transactions that come due at the same time each period, you can set up a transaction group so that Quicken enters all transactions from the group at the same time.

Quicken provides two ways to schedule future transactions: through the Scheduled Transaction List or the Financial Calendar. When you use the Financial Calendar, you "drag and drop" the transaction into its due date in the Calendar. The Calendar resembles any wall calendar you may have at home. To make the Calendar even more helpful, you can add notes to the Financial Calendar to remind you of special events such as birthdays, meetings, and so forth. And in Quicken 4 for Windows, those calendar notes show up in the Quicken Reminders window each time you start the program.

In this chapter, you learn how to do the following:

- Pay bills by scheduling transactions

- Work with transactions in groups

- Use the Financial Calendar to schedule transactions

- Use Quicken Reminders to help remember important payments and events

Scheduling Transactions

You can use Quicken to remind you about upcoming bills and deposits and to schedule those transactions ahead of time. You can schedule transactions that occur only once (such as an a car repair bill) or recurring transactions that occur at regular intervals (such as your rent payment).

This chapter shows you how to schedule future transactions for payments other than amortized loan payments. You must set up loan or mortgage payments through the View Loans window. When you set up a loan, you are setting up the loan payment as a recurring transaction in Quicken. Refer to Chapter 10, "Tracking Loans," to learn how to set up a loan.

When you schedule a transaction in Quicken, you can have Quicken enter and record the scheduled transaction when it's due. You also can have Quicken prompt you before entering the transaction so that you can change the details of the transaction, if necessary, before it's recorded. When Quicken enters scheduled transactions in the Register, you then can go into the Register and edit transactions as necessary.

You can schedule transactions in Quicken in two ways: through the Scheduled Transaction List or in the Financial Calendar. The next section explains how to set up a scheduled transaction through the Scheduled Transaction List. Later in this chapter, you learn how to schedule transactions in the Financial Calendar.

CPA Tip: Scheduling Recurring Transactions

To use Quicken most efficiently, set up a scheduled transaction for each recurring bill or deposit. Recurring *non-business* transactions may include mortgage payments, car payments, insurance premiums, health club dues, and preschool or day-care fees. (Note that you should set up loan payments, such as your mortgage and car payments, in the View Loans window, as discussed in Chapter 10). Recurring *business* transactions may include bank loan payments, workers compensation insurance premiums, payroll taxes, and maintenance contracts.

The amount of a recurring transaction doesn't have to be the same for each period. Your monthly payroll taxes, for example, most likely are different each month because your total payroll isn't the same each month. You can schedule a transaction for payroll taxes, however, and have Quicken prompt you before entering the transaction each period. Then you can change the payment amount before the transaction is entered. You still save time because the payee, memo, category, and subcategory are entered for you, and Quicken reminded you (with plenty of advance notice) to make the payment.

Setting Up a Scheduled Transaction

You can set up a scheduled transaction for a transaction that occurs only once or for a recurring transaction. When you set up the scheduled transaction, you specify the frequency of payments or deposits. To set up a scheduled transaction in the Scheduled Transaction List, follow these steps:

1. Choose Scheduled Transaction from the **L**ists menu, or press Ctrl+J. Quicken displays the Scheduled Transaction List, shown in figure 14.1.

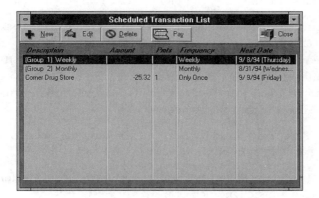

Fig. 14.1
The Scheduled Transaction List includes relative information for each scheduled transaction.

2. Choose the **N**ew button. Quicken displays the Create Scheduled Transaction dialog box, shown in figure 14.2.

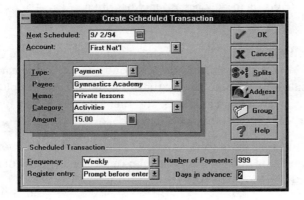

Fig. 14.2
Enter the information about a transaction that you want to schedule in this dialog box.

III

3. Select or enter the date that the next payment is due in the **N**ext Scheduled drop-down list box. For recurring transactions, Quicken updates the next payment date each time a payment or deposit is made.

4. From the **A**ccount drop-down list, select the account in which you want the scheduled transaction entered. For most bills and deposits, you probably will choose your checking account.

5. From the **T**ype drop-down list, select how you want the transaction recorded: as a payment in the Register, as a deposit in the Register, as a printed check from the Write Checks window, or as an electronic payment to be transmitted to CheckFree. (Refer to Chapter 13, "Paying Your Bills Electronically," for more on electronic payments).

For scheduled transactions that you select to record as a check in the Write Checks window, choose the Add**r**ess button to display the Printed Check Information dialog box. Enter the address of the payee and an optional message. Choose OK to return to the Create Scheduled Transaction dialog box. Quicken prints the payee's address and message on the check when you print checks.

6. In the Pa**y**ee drop-down list box, enter or select the payee to whom you make payment or from whom you receive a deposit.

7. (Optional) In the **M**emo text box, type a descriptive memo for the scheduled transaction, such as **Monthly rent**.

> **Note**
>
> The same memo is entered for every transaction, so be careful not to enter a specific date or month, such as **September rent**.

8. Select the category for the scheduled transaction from the **C**ategory drop-down list. To assign more than one category or subcategory to a scheduled transaction, choose the **S**plits button. In the Splits window, assign categories and amounts, and then choose OK to return to the Create Scheduled Transaction dialog box.

9. Enter the amount of the transaction in the Am**o**unt text box. This amount is the one Quicken enters in the Amount field when the transaction is entered each period.

10. Select the payment frequency from the **F**requency drop-down list to tell Quicken how often to enter the scheduled transaction.

11. To record payments indefinitely, such as your rent payment or insurance premium, leave the Num**b**er of Payments text box at 999.

Otherwise, enter the number of payments left to make. If, for example, you originally owed 12 payments to a department store but already made two payments, enter **10** in the Number of Payments text box.

12. From the Register Entry drop-down list, select one of the following options:

- *Automatically enter.* When you start Quicken or open the Quicken file with scheduled transactions, Quicken enters due scheduled transactions. Quicken doesn't display a message or prompt before entering scheduled transactions.

- *Prompt before enter.* When you start Quicken or open the Quicken file with scheduled transactions, Quicken displays the list of due scheduled transactions and asks you to select the transactions to enter. You can change the details of the transaction at this time or select not to enter the scheduled transaction.

13. In the Days in Advance text box, tell Quicken when you want scheduled transactions entered by entering the number of days in advance that you want to be reminded of payments or deposits. If your insurance premiums are due on the 10th day of each month, for example, you may want Quicken to remind you of the payment and enter the transaction at least five days in advance so that you can write or print the check and allow enough time for the payment to arrive in the mail.

14. When the Create Scheduled Transaction dialog box is complete, choose OK. Quicken enters the scheduled transaction in the Scheduled Transaction List (refer to fig. 14.1).

Paying Scheduled Transactions

Quicken reminds you (through Quicken Reminders) when scheduled transactions are due. If you entered a number in the Days in Advance text box when you set up a scheduled transaction, Quicken enters the transaction in the Register (or displays the transaction detail for confirmation) that many days before the payment's due date. Quicken enters the transaction as a postdated transaction. If, for example, the next payment date of a scheduled transaction is 12/15/94 and you entered **5** as the number of days in advance, Quicken enters the transaction in the Register on 12/10/94 but dates the transaction 12/15/94.

You can pay scheduled transactions when they are due or in advance. You also can postpone payment of due bills or skip payment completely.

Paying Bills When Due

After you enter your future bills as scheduled transactions in Quicken, you don't have to worry about forgetting to pay them. Quicken reminds you through Billminder and Reminder messages that scheduled transactions are due. (You learn about Billminder and Reminder messages later in this chapter.)

If you have Quicken automatically enter scheduled transactions without prompting, you don't have to enter anything when scheduled transactions are due. When you start Quicken or open the Quicken file with scheduled transactions, Quicken enters and records the scheduled transactions that are due. If you write manual checks, the transaction is entered in the Register already. Just write the check and record the check number in the Num field in the Register. If you print checks with Quicken, scheduled transactions also are entered in the Write Checks window. Just print them and you're done.

> **Note**
>
> If you write checks manually, it's better to have Quicken prompt you when scheduled transactions are due. That way, you are reminded to write the checks as they get entered in the Register. If Quicken automatically enters scheduled transactions, you must remember to write the checks for the scheduled transactions that are entered.

Tip
After Quicken enters a scheduled transaction in the Register or the Write Checks window, you can make any necessary changes to the transaction.

If you have Quicken prompt you before entering scheduled transactions, follow these steps to pay bills when due:

1. When you start Quicken or open the Quicken file with due scheduled transactions, Quicken displays the Scheduled Transactions Due dialog box (see fig. 14.3) with a list of due transactions.

Fig. 14.3
If you have Quicken prompt you when transactions are due, the Scheduled Transactions Due dialog box appears when you start Quicken.

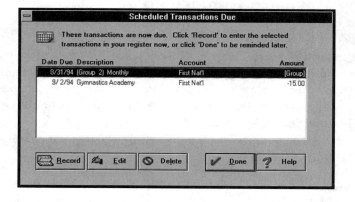

2. Highlight the transaction that you want to pay and select **R**ecord.

    To postpone making payment or entering a scheduled transaction, choose Done in the Scheduled Transactions Due dialog box. The next time you start Quicken, you are prompted again to enter the transaction.

To skip making a payment entirely, choose the **D**elete button in the Scheduled Transactions Due dialog box. If the scheduled transaction was a one-time transaction, Quicken removes it from the Scheduled Transaction List. If the transaction was set up as a recurring transaction, Quicken adjusts the next payment date for the following due date.

CPA Tip: Taking Early Payment Discounts

Take advantage of early payment discounts that vendors offer. Enter the transaction due dates for bills so you can pay invoices by the early payment date. If the terms of an invoice dated 1/31/95 are 2/10-net 30, you can take a two percent discount if you pay the invoice within 10 days of the invoice date (or by 2/10/95).

Paying Bills in Advance

You can pay bills or enter scheduled transactions at any time. If you're going on vacation, for example, you may want to pay bills early if their due date falls in the middle of your vacation.

To pay bills in advance, follow these steps:

1. From the Scheduled Transaction List (refer to fig. 14.1), highlight the scheduled transaction that you want to pay in advance.

2. Choose the **Pa**y button. If you have Quicken entering scheduled transactions automatically, the transaction is entered in the Register. If you have Quicken prompting you before entering scheduled transactions, the Record Scheduled Transaction dialog box appears for the selected transaction.

Review the transaction detail in the Record Scheduled Transaction dialog box. If you need to change any of the transaction details, you can do so now. To change the categories assigned to a split transaction, choose the **S**plits button and make the changes in the Splits window. To change the address to be printed on a check, choose the Ad**d**ress button.

When the information in the Record Scheduled Transaction dialog box is correct, choose the Record button to enter and record the transaction in the Register (and Write Checks window, if necessary). If the scheduled transaction was a one-time transaction (the frequency was set at Only Once), Quicken removes the transaction from the Scheduled Transaction List.

When you pay a scheduled transaction in advance, Quicken enters the transaction in the Register and uses the current date (unless you changed the date in the Record Scheduled Transaction dialog box). For a scheduled transaction set up as a one-time transaction, Quicken removes the transaction from the Scheduled Transaction List after it's entered in the Register. For a recurring scheduled transaction, Quicken adjusts the next payment date for the following due date.

Reviewing Scheduled Transactions

Quicken stores all scheduled transactions in the Scheduled Transaction List, as shown earlier in figure 14.1. For each scheduled transaction in the list, Quicken shows the transaction description, the amount, the number of payments to be made, the frequency of payments, and the next payment due date.

Tip

If you want to print a copy of the Scheduled Transaction List, display the list and press Ctrl+P.

You can edit a scheduled transaction if you need to change any of the transaction details (such as the payment amount, frequency, and so forth). To edit a scheduled transaction, highlight the transaction in the Scheduled Transaction List and choose the Edit button. Quicken displays the Edit Scheduled Transaction dialog box (which resembles the Create Schedule Transaction dialog box shown in figure 14.2), where you can make any necessary changes.

You also can delete a scheduled transaction at any time. To delete a scheduled transaction, highlight the transaction in the Scheduled Transaction List and choose the Delete button. Quicken displays a message that you are about to delete a scheduled transaction. Choose OK to delete the scheduled transaction.

Note

If you want to discontinue making scheduled transactions but want to keep the scheduled transaction information in Quicken, just edit the transaction and change the value in the Number of Payments text box to **0**. You can go back later and activate the scheduled transaction by changing the number of payments.

CPA Tip: Scheduling Deposit Transactions

If the company you work for uses an automatic deposit system to deposit your pay-check each pay period, you should schedule a deposit transaction for your paycheck. If you get paid on a regular basis, you can set the frequency in the **F**requency of Payment drop-down list box so that your deposit is entered in the Register each period. If you are a salaried employee and your paycheck is the same from pay period to pay period, you also can split your payroll deposit transaction so you can allocate to the correct categories federal tax withholding, state tax withholding, FICA (Social Security tax withholding), Medicare tax withholding, 401(k) deductions, medical insurance deductions, and so forth. Then each time Quicken records a deposit trans-action in the Register, the correct categories and amounts are entered.

Using Transaction Groups

A transaction group contains recurring transactions that you simultaneously pay or add to the Register. Transaction groups can consist of one or many transactions. You may, for example, want to set up a transaction group for the bills that you don't receive invoices or statements (such as your rent or loan payments). You also may want to set up a transaction group for bills due at the same time each month (such as quarterly estimated tax payments and insurance premiums).

When you create a transaction group, you assign one or more memorized transactions to a group and then name it. You may set up, for example, a transaction group named *Monthly Bills*.

Note

A transaction must be memorized before you can add it to a transaction group.

Quicken Reminder messages appear when you start your computer and again when you start Quicken or open a Quicken file with due transaction groups.

Quicken treats transaction groups the same as one scheduled transaction. When a transaction group is due, Quicken enters the transactions within the group in the Register, or it prompts you before entering the transactions within the group.

After you set up a transaction group, you can add, delete, or change transac-tions in the group. You also can delete an entire transaction group.

III

Planning for the Future

> **Note**
>
> If you used an earlier version of Quicken for Windows or Quicken DOS and used
> transaction groups, you still can use those same transaction groups in Quicken 4 for
> Windows. When you install Quicken 4 for Windows, transaction groups from previ-
> ous versions are converted automatically and saved to the Scheduled Transaction List.

To set up a transaction group, follow these steps:

1. In the Create Scheduled Transaction dialog box (refer to fig. 14.2), select
   the Grou**p** button. Quicken displays the Create Transaction Group
   dialog box, shown in figure 14.4.

Fig. 14.4

Use the Create
Transaction
Group dialog box
to enter the
information for a
new transaction
group.

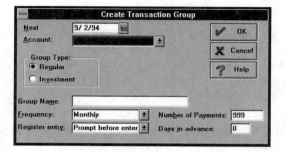

2. Select or enter the date that the next group of payments is due in the
   Next drop-down list box.

3. From the **A**ccount drop-down list, select the account in which you
   want the scheduled transaction group entered. For most bills and deposits, you probably will choose your checking account.

4. In the Group Type section, select Re**g**ular for non-investment transactions or In**v**estment to set up an investment transaction group. Note
   that memorized investment transactions aren't included in the Memorized Transaction List. (The Memorized Investment Transactions List
   contains investment transactions that you have memorized. See Chapter 16, "Monitoring Your Investments," to learn more about memorized
   investment transactions.)

5. In the Group Na**m**e text box, enter a unique, descriptive name for the
   transaction group, such as **First Monthly**. You can include up to 20
   characters in your transaction group names.

6. Select the payment frequency from the **F**requency drop-down list to tell
    Quicken how often to enter the scheduled transaction group.

7. To record scheduled transaction group payments indefinitely, leave the
    Num**b**er of Payments text box at 999. Otherwise, enter the number left
    to be made.

8. From the Register Entr**y** drop-down list, select which type of entry pro-
    cess you want Quicken to use: enter automatically or prompt before
    entering.

9. In the Days **i**n Advance text box, tell Quicken when you want sched-
    uled transaction groups entered by entering the number of days in
    advance that you want to be reminded of due scheduled transaction
    groups.

10. When the Create Transaction Group dialog box is complete, choose OK.
    Quicken displays the Assign Transactions to Group dialog box (shown
    in fig. 14.5), with the list of all memorized transactions. Now select the
    memorized transactions that you want to include in the transaction
    group.

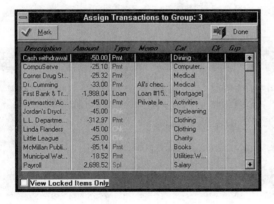

Fig. 14.5
Select the
transactions that
you want to
include in the
transaction group.

11. Highlight each transaction you want to include in the new transaction
    group. Choose the **M**ark button or double-click the transaction to in-
    clude it in the group. Quicken enters the group number in the Grp
    column next to each transaction that you select. To unmark a transac-
    tion, double-click the transaction, or highlight the transaction and
    choose the **M**ark button.

III

Planning for the Future

12. When you finish selecting transactions to include in the new group, choose Done. The new group is listed in the Scheduled Transaction List, as shown in figure 14.6.

Fig. 14.6
Quicken enters transaction groups in the Scheduled Transaction List as single items.

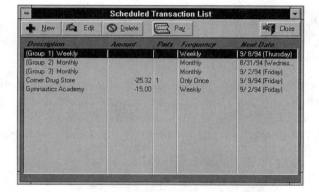

> **Note**
>
> You can delete transaction groups that you no longer use. When you delete a transaction group, Quicken permanently removes the transaction group from the Scheduled Transaction List, but doesn't delete the memorized transactions, which remain in the Memorized Transaction List. To delete a scheduled transaction group, highlight the group in the Scheduled Transaction List and select **D**elete.

Using the Financial Calendar to Schedule Transactions

The second (and easiest) way to schedule transactions is directly into Quicken's Financial Calendar (see fig. 14.7). To display the Financial Calendar, choose Financial Calendar from the Activities menu, press Ctrl+K, or click the Calendar button on the Iconbar. Not only can you schedule transactions directly into the Financial Calendar, you also can edit existing scheduled transactions, delete scheduled transactions, and pay scheduled transactions.

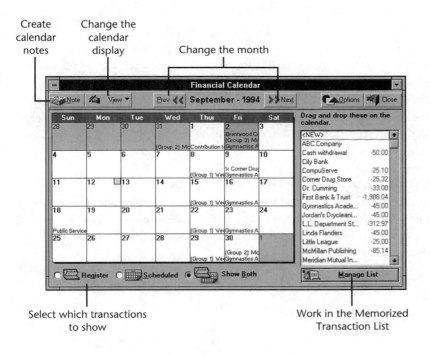

Fig. 14.7

You easily can schedule transactions directly into Quicken's Financial Calendar.

III

Planning for the Future

Quicken shows the current month when you display the Financial Calendar. You can change the month shown using the Pre**v** and **N**ext buttons on the Calendar button bar (at the top of the Financial Calendar). Choose the Pre**v** button once to move to the preceding month; choose the **N**ext button once to move to the next month.

You also can change the Calendar by clicking the date (September - 1994) between the Pre**v** and **N**ext buttons to display the Go To Date dialog box. Then enter the date that you want to change the Calendar to and choose OK. This method works well for dates far into the future or past so that you don't have to click through several months.

The current date box in the Calendar appears in a different color on color monitors, or is shaded on monochrome monitors. Notice that the transactions you entered previously in the Register are noted in the Financial Calendar.

At the bottom of the Financial Calendar, you can select which transactions to show: Register, Scheduled, or Both. To show only scheduled transactions, select the **S**cheduled option. To show only those transactions that you already recorded in the Register, select the Re**g**ister button. Or, select Show **B**oth.

You can see more detail for transactions shown in a date box by double-clicking the date box. For transactions scheduled in the future, Quicken shows the transactions in the Transactions Due window, where you can add a scheduled transaction, edit a scheduled transaction, delete a transaction, go to the Register entry for the transaction, or pay the transaction. You learn more about these activities later in this chapter. For transactions that you already entered in the Register, Quicken shows the transactions in the Transactions On window.

Scheduling Transactions in the Calendar

You learned about scheduled transactions earlier in this chapter and how to set up a scheduled transaction in the Scheduled Transaction List. In this section, you learn how to schedule a future transaction directly into the Financial Calendar.

> **Note**
>
> Quicken treats scheduled transactions entered in the Financial Calendar *exactly* the same as scheduled transactions set up in the Scheduled Transaction List. Regardless of the method you use to set up a scheduled transaction, Quicken shows each scheduled transaction in the Financial Calendar in the date box for the next payment date. Future transactions scheduled in Quicken *are* shown in the Financial Calendar; however, they *aren't* entered in the Register until they become due.

To schedule a transaction in the Financial Calendar, follow these steps:

1. From the Financial Calendar (refer to fig. 14.7), use the Pre**v** and **N**ext buttons to display the month in which you want to schedule a transaction. Or click the date between the Pre**v** and **N**ext buttons and enter the date in the Go To Date dialog box.

2. If the list of transactions isn't displayed on the right side of the Financial Calendar, choose the V**i**ew button from the Calendar button bar and then select Show **M**emorized Txns. Quicken displays a list of transactions that you may want to schedule for the future. This list consists of the memorized transactions from the Memorized Transaction List. The list shown in the Financial Calendar is the same as the drop-down list displayed from the Payee field of the Register or the Pay to the Order Of field in the Write Checks window.

> **Note**
>
> If you want to go to the Memorized Transaction List from the Financial Calendar, select the **M**anage List button. From the Memorized Transaction List, you can add, edit, or delete any of the memorized transactions that appear in the list of transactions in the Financial Calendar.

3. To schedule a transaction from the list into the Calendar, point to the transaction with your mouse. The mouse pointer changes to the shape of a hand to show that the transaction can be picked up. Hold down the left mouse button as you move the mouse pointer to the date box that represents the date in which you want to schedule the transaction.

As you move the transaction to the Calendar, the mouse pointer changes again to a small Calendar icon to show that you can drop the transaction into a day. Release the mouse button when the Calendar icon is positioned in the proper date box in the Calendar. Quicken displays the Drag and Drop Transaction dialog box when you drop a transaction into a date box in the Calendar (see fig. 14.8).

Fig. 14.8

Drop a transaction from the list into a date box to display the Drag and Drop Transaction dialog box.

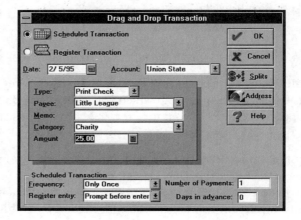

To schedule a new transaction in the Financial Calendar, drag the <New> item from the transaction list to the appropriate date box in the Calendar. When you release the left mouse button in the date box, Quicken displays the Drag and Drop Transaction dialog box that you saw in figure 14.8.

4. For a previously entered transaction, confirm the information in the Drag and Drop Transaction dialog box. You can make any necessary changes to the transaction.

For a new scheduled transaction, complete the Drag and Drop Transaction dialog box the same way you did the Create Scheduled Transaction dialog box (see fig. 14.2), as explained in the section "Setting Up a Scheduled Transaction."

5. Choose OK to schedule the transaction in the Financial Calendar. Quicken shows Only Once scheduled transactions for payments with a red 1x in the date box. Deposit transactions scheduled only once are shown in the date box with a green 1x.

Note

You can schedule a transaction in the Financial Calendar into a date in the past. When you drop a transaction into a past date box, the mouse pointer changes to a Register icon and Quicken displays the Drop & Drag Transaction dialog box with information about the transaction that Quicken is about to enter in the Register. You can change any information in the Drop & Drag Transaction dialog box. See the next section to learn about editing scheduled transactions in the Financial Calendar.

Editing Scheduled Transactions in the Financial Calendar

As you schedule transactions in the Financial Calendar, you can see the transactions due in the future. Each date box in the Financial Calendar can show only about four transactions, however. To review the details or to edit a scheduled transaction in the Financial Calendar, follow these steps:

1. Double-click the date box where the transaction that you want to see or edit is scheduled. Quicken displays the Transactions Due dialog box, with a list of transactions scheduled for that day (see fig. 14.9).

2. You can perform the following operations from the Transactions Due dialog box:

   ■ Set up a new transaction for the selected date by choosing the **N**ew button. Quicken displays the Drag and Drop Transaction dialog box (refer to fig. 14.8).

   ■ Change the details of the highlighted scheduled transaction for the selected date by choosing the **E**dit button. Quicken displays the Edit Scheduled Transaction dialog box, shown in figure 14.10. For recorded transactions in the Financial Calendar, Quicken displays the Edit Register Transaction dialog box, shown in figure 14.11. You edit a recorded transaction in the Financial Calendar just as you do in the Register.

Tip
You also can display the Transactions Due dialog box by clicking the selected date box in the Financial Calendar with the *right* mouse button.

Fig. 14.9
Double-click a date box in the Financial Calendar to display the Transactions Due dialog box for that date.

III

Planning for the Future

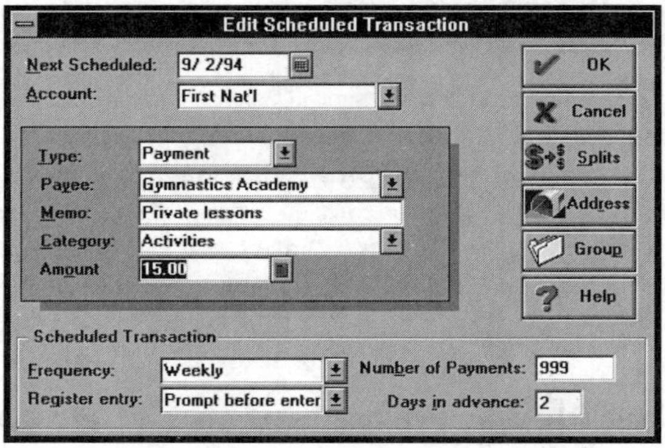

Fig. 14.10
Quicken displays
the details of a
scheduled trans-
action here.

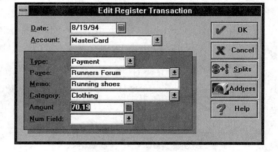

Fig. 14.11
Quicken displays
the details of a
past transaction
here.

- Delete the highlighted scheduled transaction for the selected date by choosing the **D**elete button. Then select OK.

- For recorded transactions, the Transactions Due dialog box includes the **R**egister button, which you can use to go directly to the highlighted transaction in the Register.

- Pay the highlighted scheduled transaction immediately by choosing the P**a**y Now button.

To remove the Transactions Due dialog box without performing an operation, double-click its Control menu box, click anywhere outside the dialog box, or press Esc.

Paying Scheduled Transactions from the Calendar

Quicken reminds you when scheduled transactions in the Financial Calendar are due, just like scheduled transactions that you set up in the Scheduled

Transaction List. If you choose to enter a scheduled transaction automatically, Quicken enters the transaction in the Register when the transaction is due (or ahead of the actual scheduled date if you entered the number of days in advance to remind you when the transaction is due). If you choose to have Quicken prompt you before entering a scheduled transaction, Quicken displays the details of the transaction before entering it in the Register.

You can pay scheduled transactions in the Calendar when they are due or in advance.

Paying When Due

Follow the same steps for paying a transaction when it is due as explained earlier in the section "Paying Bills When Due."

Paying in Advance

To pay transactions in advance from the Financial Calendar, follow these steps:

1. Double-click the date box where the transaction you want to pay in advance is scheduled. Quicken displays the Transactions Due dialog box (refer to fig. 14.9).

2. Highlight the transaction that you want to pay in advance.

3. Choose the Pay Now button. If Quicken prompts you before entering the scheduled transaction, the Record Scheduled Transaction dialog box appears (refer to fig. 14.3). Review the details of the transaction, make any necessary changes, and choose OK to enter the transaction in the Register or the Write Checks window.

If you selected to enter the scheduled transaction without prompting, Quicken enters the transaction in the Register immediately.

Reviewing the Account Graph

The Account Graph is part of the Financial Calendar. To display the graph, select the View button from the Calendar button bar and then select Show Account Graph. Figure 14.12 shows the Account Graph displayed at the bottom of the Financial Calendar.

III

Planning for the Future

Fig. 14.12

The Account Graph appears in the Financial Calendar when you select the View button from the Calendar button bar and then select Show Account Graph.

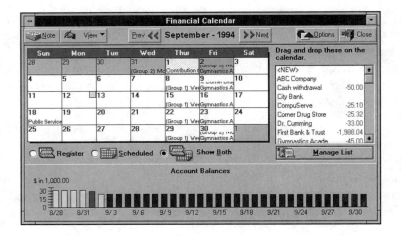

The graph shows a projection of the state of your accounts for the active month. Balances before the current date appear in yellow or a lighter shade. Balances for future dates are shown in blue or appear darker. The balance for the current date appears in green or black.

The graph plots the dates along the horizontal axis and rounded dollar values for the accounts along the vertical axis. To see an exact account balance for a selected date, point to the date on the graph (the shape of the mouse pointer changes to a hand) and then hold down the left mouse button. Quicken shows the exact dollar value of the account in a small box. Release the mouse button to remove the amount box from the graph.

Typically, the Account Graph should show gradual rises or declines in account balances. The first time you display the graph, however, you probably will notice some sharp rises and declines. That's because Quicken doesn't yet have all the information that it needs to reflect the balances accurately in your accounts. The data that Quicken uses in the Account Graph is based on the future transactions you scheduled in the Calendar.

By default, Quicken includes the balances in all your cash flow accounts (bank accounts, cash accounts, and credit card accounts) in the Account Graph. You can, however, show the balance from only one account or select exactly which accounts you want to include in the graph. To change the accounts used in the graph, change the Calendar option that controls the accounts used in the Financial Calendar. Refer to the section, "Changing Calendar Options," later in this chapter to learn how to select accounts included in the Financial Calendar.

Adding Notes to the Financial Calendar

Not only can you schedule your future transactions in the Financial Calendar, but you also can use the Calendar to enter reminder notes just as you do in your wall or desk calendar. Quicken doesn't display the text of a note in the Financial Calendar. Instead, a small square or note box is displayed in the date box for the date in which you enter a note.

In Quicken 4 for Windows, your calendar notes are shown in the Quicken Reminders window when you start Quicken or open a Quicken file with calendar notes.

Note

You can add only one note at a time in any one date in the Financial Calendar.

To add a note to the Financial Calendar, follow these steps:

1. Click the date box in the Financial Calendar in which you want to add a note.

2. Choose the **N**ote button on the Calendar button bar (upper-left corner). Quicken displays the Note window, shown in figure 14.13.

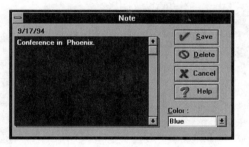

Fig. 14.13
Type your note or reminder in the Note window.

3. Type the text of your note. Press Enter to move to the next line.

4. In the **C**olor drop-down list, select the color in which you want to display the note box in the Calendar. If you're entering a personal note (such as your spouse's birthday), for example, you may select blue. Develop a color scheme that is most useful to you.

5. Choose the **S**ave button to save the note in the Calendar.

III

Planning for the Future

Quicken displays the note as a small square, or note box, in the upper-right corner of the date box for the date in which it was entered. The note box is the color that you selected for the note.

To review a note in the Financial Calendar, click the note box. Quicken displays the Note window with the text of the note. To delete a note in the Financial Calendar, click the note box. At the Note window, choose the **D**elete button.

Changing Calendar Options

Just like Registers and the Write Checks window, the Financial Calendar includes options that you can change to make the Calendar work the way that you want it to. To change Calendar options, follow these steps:

1. Choose **O**ptions from the Calendar button bar. Quicken displays the Calendar Options dialog box. The Calendar Options dialog box includes tabs to select **A**ccounts and Quic**k**Fill options. Figure 14.14 shows the Calendar Options dialog box to change accounts. Figure 14.15 shows the Calendar Options dialog box to change the way QuickFill works.

Fig. 14.14
The Calendar Options dialog box for **A**ccounts includes the accounts from which to show transactions in the Financial Calendar.

2. In the Calendar Options dialog box for **A**ccounts, click the account that you want to select in the Financial Calendar. When you are finished selecting accounts, choose OK.

3. In the Calendar Options dialog box for Quic**k**Fill, move to the QuickFill option that you want to change and turn it on or off. When you're finished setting QuickFill options, choose OK.

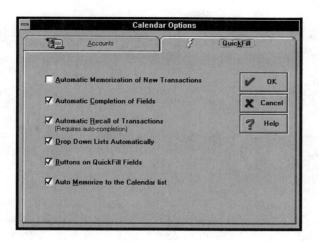

Getting Reminders to Pay Bills

Quicken includes two reminder features that display messages when scheduled transactions or transaction groups are due as well as calendar notes: Billminder and Reminder. Billminder and Reminder messages alert you about other Quicken activities due (such as electronic payments to be transmitted if you use CheckFree).

When you start your computer or when you start Windows, a Quicken Billminder message appears if Quicken finds activities that need to be performed today. When you start Quicken or open a Quicken file, the Quicken Reminders window appears if Quicken detects due activities.

Using Billminder and Quicken Reminders

When you installed Quicken 4 for Windows (see Appendix A), you selected whether or not to use Quicken's Billminder feature. You must install Billminder during installation for Billminder to be active in Quicken. If you didn't, however, you can install Billminder now (see the next section).

When Billminder is active, each time you turn on your computer or start Windows, a Quicken Billminder message, such as the one in figure 14.16, appears if checks need to be printed, or if upcoming bills, scheduled transaction groups, investment reminders, or electronic payments (if you use CheckFree) are due. To remove a Quicken Billminder message from the screen, choose OK or press Enter.

Tip
Quicken's Reminder messages are great for prompting you to pay bills that you don't receive an invoice for (such as rent, payroll taxes, and loan payments).

III

Planning for the Future

Fig. 14.16
The Quicken Billminder message appears if you have upcoming bills or due scheduled transaction groups.

> **Note**
>
> When you installed Quicken 4 for Windows, if you selected the From **D**OS at Boot Time option, a Quicken Billminder message appears when you start your computer. If you selected the At **W**indows start-up option, a Quicken Billminder message appears when you start Windows. The Quicken Billminder icon opens when you display Billminder messages at Windows start-up.

Tip
You can redisplay the Quicken Reminders window at any time by selecting Re**m**inders from the Ac**t**ivities menu.

When Quicken Reminders are active, a Quicken Reminders window appears when you start Quicken or open a Quicken file. When checks are due to print, when scheduled transactions, investment reminders, or electronic payments are due in a Quicken file, or when calendar notes need to be reviewed, the Quicken Reminders window appears (such as the one shown in fig. 14.17). To remove the Quicken Reminders window from the screen, click the Close button.

Fig. 14.17
The Quicken Reminders window appears when you start Quicken or open a Quicken file with due items.

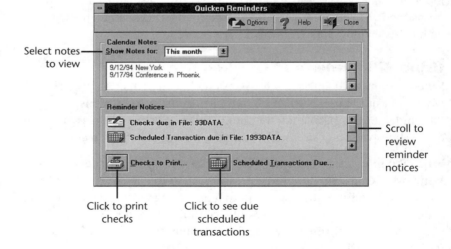

Select notes to view

Scroll to review reminder notices

Click to print checks

Click to see due scheduled transactions

Installing Billminder

Billminder is active after you install Quicken 4 for Windows and select to install Billminder. If you didn't select to install Billminder during installation, you can reinstall the program over your existing program files and select to install Billminder. When you reinstall Quicken, your data files aren't disturbed.

If you don't want to reinstall the program, you can edit your AUTOEXEC.BAT or WIN.INI files, as discussed in the Quicken user's manual.

Caution

Be careful if you decide to edit the AUTOEXEC.BAT or WIN.INI files in your system. These files contain crucial batch files that control how your system works. Making a backup copy of these files before you start to edit them is a good idea, to prevent any damage to the files that can't be remedied.

Setting Reminder Options

By default, Billminder (if it was installed) and Reminder are turned on and are set up to remind you three business days in advance of postdated checks, scheduled transactions, transaction groups, and investment reminders that are due and shows calendar notes that need to be reviewed.

You can turn off Billminder and Reminder, change the number of business days in advance to be reminded of due items, or select whether calendar notes are shown by setting Reminder options.

To set Reminder options, follow these steps:

1. From the **E**dit menu, choose **O**ptions, or click the Options button on the Iconbar. Quicken displays the Options dialog box.

2. Choose the R**e**minder option. Quicken displays the Reminder Options dialog box, shown in figure 14.18.

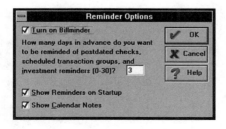

Fig. 14.18
You can deactivate Billminder or Reminder in the Reminder Options dialog box.

3. To turn off Billminder, choose the **T**urn on Billminder check box to remove the check mark.

4. To change the number of business days in advance that you are reminded of items, type over the number in the next text box with a number from 0 to 30.

5. To turn off Reminder messages, click the **S**how **R**eminder Messages on Startup check box to remove the check mark.

6. To not show calendar notes in the Quicken Reminders window, select the Show **C**alendar Notes check box to remove the check mark.

7. Choose OK to save Reminder options and then select Close.

From Here...

Now that you understand how to schedule transactions in Quicken, you may want to review the following:

■ Chapter 15, "Preparing Financial Forecasts," shows you how to create a forecast of your future cash flows. It is similar to using the Account Graph in the Financial Calendar to project the balances in your cash-flow accounts in future periods.

■ Chapter 17, "Budgeting with Quicken," explains how to create a budget and plan for those future scheduled transactions in the Financial Calendar.

Chapter 15

Preparing Financial Forecasts

After you've entered transactions in Quicken Registers and used the Financial Calendar to schedule your future transactions, Quicken 4 allows you to use the Forecasting Graph to project your cash flow for the future. The Forecasting Graph uses data from your Registers, scheduled transactions in the Financial Calendar, and data that you enter manually for purposes of forecasting.

The Forecasting Graph can show your account projections for a month at a time, up to two years in the future. You'll be able to look into the future to determine whether you can afford that trip to Europe, the new car, or just get a feel for your spending patterns.

In this chapter, you learn how to do the following:

- Create a Forecasting Graph

- Change forecast amounts

- Create multiple forecast scenarios

- Compare forecasts

Creating a Forecast

Your Forecasting Graph is made up of two different kinds of amounts: income items and expense items. Both income and expense items can also be *known* or *estimated*. Quicken finds known items from the scheduled transactions in the Financial Calendar. The estimated items come from your Registers or your Budget Spreadsheet.

To create a forecast, you can enter all income and expense items manually. This method, however, does not take advantage of all of the transactions that you already entered in Quicken. Your prior transactions and future scheduled transactions are the best source for projecting your future financial activity. So, it's best to have Quicken automatically create your forecast from the data it already has. You can then modify or add any other data that you want.

To create a forecast automatically, follow these steps:

1. From the Pl**a**n menu, select **F**orecasting. Quicken displays the Automatically Create Forecast dialog box shown in figure 15.1.

Fig. 15.1
In the Automatically Create Forecast dialog box, tell Quicken what range of dates to use to get data when it automatically creates your forecast.

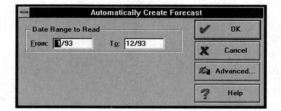

2. In the **F**rom and T**o** text boxes, enter the date range for the transactions that you want Quicken to use in your forecast. Choose OK.

3. (Optional) Select the Advanced button if you want to specify whether you want Quicken to use scheduled transactions, estimated items, or both, whether you want data taken from the Register or from your Budget Spreadsheet, and to select which accounts and categories are included in your forecast. Then choose OK.

4. Quicken displays the Forecasting Graph (see fig. 15.2) that shows the balance of the selected accounts for the time period shown in the bottom of the graph (one month, six months, one year, or two years).

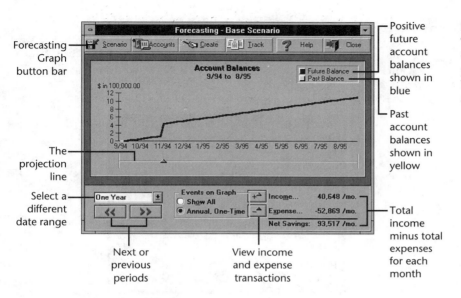

Forecasting Graph button bar

Positive future account balances shown in blue

Past account balances shown in yellow

The projection line

Select a different date range

Next or previous periods

View income and expense transactions

Total income minus total expenses for each month

Fig. 15.2
The Forecasting Graph shows projected future balances in your accounts.

Selecting Which Accounts to Use

By default, Quicken includes all your cash flow accounts (bank accounts, cash accounts, and credit card accounts) in the Forecasting Graph. You can select the accounts that you want to include, however. If you have a credit card account set up in Quicken but don't use it, for example, you may want to select just your checking account. If you're interested in tracking your available funds, you may choose your checking account, savings account, and CD account. If funds exist in accounts that you don't intend to use for spending or for a specific savings goal, don't include that account.

CPA Tip: Excluding Retirement Plan Accounts

You shouldn't include your IRA or 401(k) accounts in cash flow projections. These accounts represent tax-deferred retirement accounts that are heavily penalized if funds are withdrawn before age 59 1/2 and not reinvested in another retirement plan.

III

Planning for the Future

To select accounts to include in your forecast, follow these steps:

1. Choose the Accounts button from the Forecasting Graph button bar. Quicken displays the Select Accounts to Include window, shown in figure 15.3.

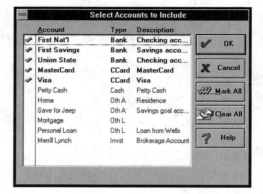

2. Double-click the account that you want to include and then highlight the account and press the spacebar. Choose the **M**ark All button to include all accounts or choose C**l**ear All to deselect all accounts.

4. When you are finished selecting accounts, choose OK to return to the Forecasting Graph. The Forecasting Graph should look much different because other accounts are included.

Changing Forecast Amounts

Even if you automatically created your Forecasting Graph from Quicken data, you can enter new income and expense amounts or modify existing ones at any time.

To enter a new forecast amount, follow these steps:

1. Click the Income or Expense button at the bottom of the Forecasting Graph. Quicken displays the Forecast Income Items dialog box (shown in figure 15.4) or the Forecast Expense Items dialog box. Quicken lists all forecast items by Known Items and Estimated Items.

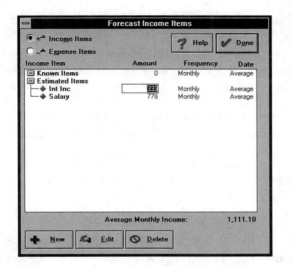

Fig. 15.4
The Forecast
Income Items
dialog box lists all
forecast income
items by Known
Items and Esti-
mated Items.

2. Select **N**ew to display the Create New Income Item dialog box (see fig. 15.5) or the Create New Expense Item dialog box.

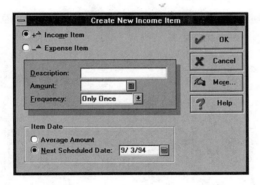

Fig. 15.5
Enter information
about a new
income item in
The Create New
Income Item
dialog box.

3. Enter a description of the item, the amount, the frequency, the average amount, and the next scheduled date. Choose OK to enter the new item.

III

Planning for the Future

> **Caution**
>
> Remember that the Forecasting Graph already includes your scheduled transactions. Don't double-count income or expenses by entering amounts from scheduled trans-actions as new items. If you set up a scheduled transaction for your salary every two weeks, for example, *don't* enter a new income item for salary. Your salary already is accounted for in the Forecast Income Items dialog box.

To edit or delete an income item or expense item, from the Forecast Income Items dialog box (see fig. 15.4) or the Forecast Expense Items dialog box, highlight the item that you want to change or remove and click the **E**dit or **D**elete button.

Creating Multiple Forecast Scenarios

You can save different forecasts so that you can compare what has actually happened to what you anticipated when you created your original forecast or so that you can perform "what-if" analyses to see the effects of hypothetical transactions.

To save a forecast scenario, follow these steps:

1. From the Forecasting Graph, click the **S**cenario button from the button bar. Quicken displays the Manage Forecasts Scenario dialog box shown in figure 15.6.

Fig. 15.6

Create new scenarios in the Manage Forecasts Scenario dialog box.

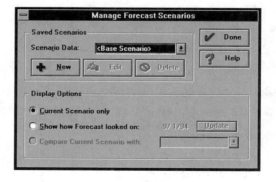

2. Select **N**ew. Quicken displays the Create New Scenario dialog box. Enter a name for the new scenario using up to 21 characters.

3. If you want to copy the data from the current Forecasting Graph, select the Copy Current Scenario check box.

4. Choose OK. Quicken returns to the Manage Forecasts Scenario dialog box (see fig. 15.6).

5. Choose Done to save the new scenario. Quicken displays the Forecasting Graph for the new scenario.

Comparing Forecast Scenarios

If you've created more than one financial forecast, you can compare them. To compare two scenarios, follow these steps:

1. Make sure that the Forecasting Graph is displaying the scenario that you want to make a comparison to. Then select Scenario to display the Manage Forecast Scenarios dialog box (see fig. 15.6).

2. Choose the Compare Current Scenario With option.

3. Then, select the scenario that you want to compare from the drop-down list box.

4. Choose Done. Quicken displays the second scenario's projection line in green, on top of the first scenario's projection line.

From Here...

This chapter showed you how to prepare financial forecasts so that you can project and plan your future cash flows. Now you may want to review or read the following:

■ Chapter 14, "Scheduling Future Transactions," describes the Financial Calendar and how to schedule transactions in the future. The Forecasting Graph uses the scheduled transactions from the Financial Calendar to project account balances.

■ Chapter 17, "Budgeting with Quicken," shows you how to enter budget amounts in the Budgeting Spreadsheet. Quicken uses this spreadsheet to create estimated items in the Forecasting Graph.

Chapter 16

Monitoring Your Investments

Quicken provides a Register specifically for investments. You enter all your security holdings and transactions in the Register for each investment account you set up. The Register not only provides a way to track your investment transactions but also shows you how your investments are performing and the market value of your investments.

In Quicken, you enter investment transactions (such as buying and selling securities, recording dividends and interest, and option trades) in forms that prompt you for the information that Quicken needs to record the transaction. You still can enter investment transactions directly in the Register, but investment forms ensure that your transaction information is complete.

From the Investment Register, you can change the way Quicken displays your securities by switching to the Portfolio View. The Portfolio View gives you a snapshot of your security portfolio. This snapshot shows the current market value, the return on investment, price changes, and other important data. You can use the QuickZoom feature in the Portfolio View of an Investment Register to edit, delete, or set up new securities. You also can use QuickZoom to create a QuickReport that lists the underlying transactions of the security in the Portfolio View.

If you have a modem, you can now update security prices in your investment accounts using Portfolio Price Update. Portfolio Price Update is an online financial service that updates prices of all stocks and mutual funds traded on the New York Stock Exchange, American Stock Exchange, and NASDAQ.

This chapter shows you how to monitor your investments with Quicken and how to track mutual funds and other investments using the Quicken Investment Register.

In this chapter, you learn how to do the following:

- Set up regular and mutual fund investment accounts

- Set up securities

- Use the Investment Register

- Use the Portfolio View window

- Update security prices

Note

To save you from reviewing material you already know, this chapter doesn't explain the parts of the Investment Register that are similar to the other Quicken Registers you have examined in previous chapters. If you aren't well acquainted with the basics of using Quicken, refer to Part I of this book, "Learning Quicken for Windows."

Preparing to Monitor Investments

To monitor investments with Quicken, you need to set up an investment account. When you set up an investment account, you must specify whether the account is a mutual fund account or regular investment account. The basic difference between the two accounts is difficult to grasp. If you learn the difference now, however, you will find deciding when to set up mutual fund accounts and when to set up regular investment accounts is much easier.

A *mutual fund account* is a simplified investment account that keeps track of the market value and number of shares you hold of a single mutual fund. A *mutual fund* is an open-end management company that pools the money of many investors and uses it to establish a portfolio of securities. An investment advisor or a portfolio manager manages the securities of the investors.

The *regular investment account* is a more powerful investment account that you use for other investments and investment groups. The regular investment account keeps track of the market value of multiple securities, the shares, and the cash balance. (The cash balance usually represents the money with which you buy additional stocks, bonds, and so on.)

Given these differences, the easiest approach is to set up a mutual fund account for each mutual fund investment you hold, set up a regular investment account for each brokerage account you hold, and set up a regular investment account for any collection of individual investments you want to track and manage together in one Register. (If, for example, you just want to track your investment in IBM stock, set up a regular investment account named IBM.) As you work with the Quicken investment options, you can fine-tune these suggestions.

CPA Tip: Investing in a Mutual Fund

A mutual fund is an excellent way to diversify your portfolio. When a single company's stock held in the fund declines, the impact on the total value of the mutual fund's portfolio is less because the fund's portfolio is made up of many securities. Also, securities appreciating in value offset security values that decline.

You also can invest in a mutual fund if you don't want to manage your own portfolio by making decisions as to which securities to buy and sell. Large mutual funds usually hire the best investment advisors available.

Another plus for mutual funds: Transaction costs when buying and selling shares in a mutual fund are often less than commission costs when buying and selling individual securities through a broker.

Working with Regular Investment Accounts

As mentioned earlier, you can set up two types of investment accounts in Quicken: a regular investment account and a mutual fund account. In this section, you learn how to set up a regular investment account. You also learn how to set up the securities that you already own and new ones you buy so that Quicken has the information it needs to track your investments accurately. This section also shows you how to enter opening share balances so that your current holdings are reflected in your new investment account.

Setting Up a Regular Investment Account

A regular investment account is designed to track one or more securities in the account. Regular investment accounts may have a cash balance (like a brokerage account). The Register for a regular investment account updates the cash balance after every transaction and also shows the current market value of the account. The Register, however, doesn't show the share balance (total number of shares) of securities held in the account.

To set up a regular investment account, follow these steps:

1. From the Activities menu, choose Create **N**ew Account. Quicken displays the Create New Account dialog box.

2. Select the **I**nvestment option. Quicken displays the Create Investment Account information dialog box, shown in figure 16.1.

Fig. 16.1
Enter the information about the investment account you are adding here.

3. In the **A**ccount Name text box, enter a name for the account. The account name can be up to 15 characters long and can contain any characters except the following:

    :] [/ | ^

You can include spaces in the account name.

4. Make sure that the Account Contains a Single **M**utual Fund check box is blank so that Quicken sets up a regular investment account.

5. (Optional) In the **D**escription text box, enter an investment account description, such as **Brokerage A/C #25345**. You can use 21 characters in this description.

6. To enter additional information about the investment account, choose the **I**nfo button and enter the information in the Additional Account

Information dialog box. Choose OK to save the information and return to the Create Investment Account dialog box.

7. If the earnings from the investment account you are setting up are tax-deferred (the tax is assessed in a later time period than the earnings are received), select the **T**ax-Deferred Account check box. Examples of tax-deferred accounts are IRAs, 401(k) accounts, and annuities.

8. From the **T**ransfers In drop-down list box, select the tax form or schedule to which transfers to the account should be assigned. In the Transfers **O**ut drop-down list box, select the tax form or schedule for transfers from the account.

9. Choose OK. Quicken adds the regular investment account to the Account List. If this investment account isn't the first one in your file, Quicken displays the Register for the new investment account.

If this is the first investment account that you have set up, Quicken displays a dialog box that asks whether you want to add a Portfolio View icon to the Iconbar for updating your investments. Choose **Y**es if you want to add the icon; otherwise, choose **N**o. If you choose to add the icon, Quicken inserts the new Port icon at the end of the Iconbar. Use this icon to switch to the Portfolio View window. (You learn about the Portfolio View window later in this chapter.)

> **Note**
>
> When you set up an investment account, Quicken automatically adds investment categories to your Category & Transfer List. Investment categories all begin with an underline (_DivInc, _IntInc, and so forth). You can't delete an investment category or edit its name, but you can edit its description.

Setting Up Securities

Before you can begin entering investment transactions, you must set up securities in Quicken. When you set up a security, you define the security's symbol, type, goal, and estimated annual income. Quicken saves securities in the Security List.

To set up a security, follow these steps:

1. From the **L**ists menu, choose **S**ecurity (or press Ctrl+Y). Quicken displays the Security List, shown in figure 16.2.

Fig. 16.2
Quicken saves
securities in the
Security List.

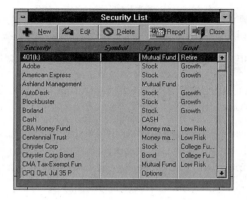

2. Choose the **N**ew button. Quicken displays the Set Up Security dialog box, shown in figure 16.3.

Fig. 16.3
Enter information
about a new
security here.

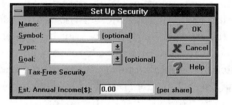

3. In the **N**ame text box, type the name of the security. You can use up to 17 characters, including spaces.

4. In the **S**ymbol text box, enter the symbol for the mutual fund if you plan to export or import price data from a file.

5. From the **T**ype drop-down list, select the type of security that you are setting up (such as Stock, Bond, or CD).

> **Note**
>
> If the security type for the security you are setting up isn't included in the **T**ype drop-down list, you can add a new security type to the Security Types list. Choose Security T**y**pe from the **L**ists menu and then choose the **N**ew button to enter the new security type. You also can edit or delete security types from the Security Types list.

6. (Optional) Select the goal for the security from the **G**oal drop-down list.

A goal enables you to record another piece of information about your investment. Quicken provides several investment goals that you may find valuable, such as Growth, Income, or College funding. You can also create your own goal. The **G**oal drop-down list box is optional and has no effect on the way you track or monitor an investment.

> **Note**
>
> If your goal for investing in a security isn't included in the **G**oal drop-down list, just add your own customized goal to the Investment Goal List. From the **L**ists menu, choose Investment Goal. Choose the **N**ew button to enter the new goal. You also can edit or delete existing goals from the Investment Goal List.

7. If the income from the security is not subject to income tax, select the Tax-**F**ree Security check box.

8. In the **E**st. Annual Income($) text box, enter the income that you project to earn per year from the investment in the security.

9. Choose OK to add the security to the Security List.

Repeat steps 1 through 9 to set up as many securities as you need.

Entering the Opening Share Balances for Securities

After you set up a regular investment account and add securities to the Security List, you must create the opening balance in the account. Three options are available for creating an opening balance in an investment account (regular and mutual fund), as follows:

> **Tip**
> You can edit and delete securities in the Security List by highlighting the security and choosing the Edit or Delete button.

■ *Option 1:* Enter all historical data for each security you now hold. This option entails entering the initial purchase information (date, amount invested, and number of shares) and all subsequent transactions, including acquisitions, sales and gifts, stock splits, returns of capital, dividends, interest, and capital gains distributions.

■ *Option 2:* Set up the opening balance as of the beginning of the current year. This option entails entering all security holdings as of the end of last year and all transactions since the beginning of the current year. For each security, you must enter the number of shares owned at the end of last year, the price per share at the end of last year, and all transactions for the current year.

III

Planning for the Future

■ *Option 3:* Enter current securities as held only. For each security you now hold, enter the number of shares and the current per share price.

If you want complete and accurate data for your investment accounts, you should create an opening balance using the first option. Although you spend much time entering historical data, your reports are more accurate, and Quicken can calculate capital gains or losses for securities that you sell.

To enter the opening share balance for each security in a regular investment account by entering historical data, follow these steps:

1. Choose **A**ccount from the **L**ists menu, press Ctrl+A, or click the Accts button on the Iconbar to display the Account List.

2. Highlight the regular investment account for which you want to enter opening share balances, and then choose the O**p**en button. Quicken displays the Investment Register, shown in figure 16.4. (You learn your way around the Investment Register later in the section, "Using the Investment Register.")

Fig. 16.4
When you select an investment account in the Account List, Quicken displays the Investment Account Register.

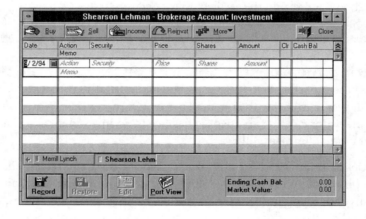

3. Press Ctrl+End, if necessary, to go to an empty transaction line in the Register.

4. To add securities purchased before you started using Quicken, choose the **M**ore button in the button bar. Quicken displays the action list, shown in figure 16.5.

5. Choose the S**h**rsIn (Add shares to Acct) action. Quicken displays the Add Shares to Account dialog box in figure 16.6.

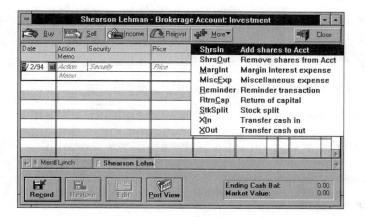

Fig. 16.5
From the More action list, choose the action that you want to record in the Investment Register.

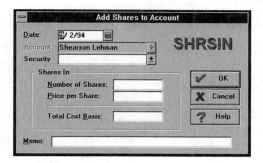

Fig. 16.6
For each security you now hold, enter the number of shares and price per share in the Add Shares to Account dialog box.

Note

The Add Shares to Account dialog box allows you to enter security holdings that you purchased before you started Quicken or set up an investment account. When you enter security holdings in the Add Shares to Account dialog box, you aren't required to deduct funds from the investment account or another bank account to pay for the shares.

6. Enter the date the securities were acquired and the name of the security that you own in the appropriate boxes. In the **A**ccount drop-down list box, Quicken automatically enters the name of the investment account that you now are working in.

7. Enter the number of shares acquired in the **N**umber of shares text box, according to the following rules:

   ■ *Stocks and mutual funds.* Enter the number of shares.

- *Bonds*. Enter the number of bonds multiplied by 10. (If you purchased five bonds, for example, enter 50.)

- *Money market funds or CDs*. Enter their total value.

- *Collectibles* (such as coins). Enter 1 (for $1).

- *Precious metals (such as gold)*. Enter the number of ounces.

8. Enter the price per share in the **P**rice per Share text box. Quicken calculates the total cost in the Total Cost **B**asis text box. Use the following rules to determine the price to enter:

- *Stocks and mutual funds*. Enter the price per share.

- *Bonds*. Enter 1/10 the market value.

- *Money market funds or CDs*. Enter 1 (for $1).

- *Collectibles*. Enter the total value.

- *Precious metals*. Enter the price per ounce.

9. (Optional) Enter a description of the security transaction in the **M**emo text box.

10. Choose OK to record the opening balance transaction.

11. For each security opening balance that you need to add, repeat steps 3 through 10.

12. For each subsequent security transaction, such as dividends, stock splits, and reinvestments, enter a separate transaction. (You learn how to enter transactions in the Register in the section "Entering Investment Transactions.")

13. After you finish entering security transactions, check the ending cash balance against the cash balance shown in your latest brokerage statement. If the cash balance isn't correct, go to the next section.

Tip
To enter a share price with a fraction (for example, 5 3/8), type the whole number, a space, the numerator, a slash (/), and the denominator.

Updating the Cash Balance in a Regular Investment Account

After you enter your security transactions in the Investment Account Register, the ending cash balance in the Register should match the actual cash balance. If the cash balance is incorrect, you must update the balance in the account so that it reflects the actual balance.

To update the cash balance, follow these steps:

1. From the Activities menu, choose **U**pdate Balances.

2. From the Update Balances submenu, choose Update **C**ash Balance. Quicken displays the Update Cash Balance dialog box.

3. Enter the actual cash balance and the date for which you want to adjust the cash balance.

4. Choose OK. Quicken enters a balance adjustment transaction for the difference between the ending cash balance and the balance you entered.

Working with Mutual Fund Investment Accounts

Using Quicken to monitor a mutual fund investment consists of recording your starting balance and periodically recording changes in the balance due to the purchase of additional shares or the redemption of shares within the fund. You record the same information that appears on your mutual fund statements. By recording the information in the Quicken Register, however, you can use the information in several calculations that show how your investments are doing.

Setting Up a Mutual Fund Investment Account

Setting up a mutual fund investment account is similar to setting up a regular investment account. The one difference is that you don't have to set up securities before you enter the opening share balance in the account. Because mutual fund accounts aren't designed for more than one security, the fund itself is considered the one security.

To set up a mutual fund investment account, follow these steps:

1. From the Activities menu, choose Create **N**ew Account. Quicken displays the Create New Account dialog box.

2. Select the **I**nvestment option. Quicken displays the Create Investment Account dialog box (refer to fig. 16.1).

3. In the **A**ccount Name text box, enter a name for the mutual fund account. The account name can be up to 15 characters long.

4. Select the Account Contains a Single **M**utual Fund check box.

5. (Optional) In the **D**escription text box, enter an investment account description of up to 21 characters.

6. (Optional) To enter additional information about the mutual fund account, choose the **I**nfo button and enter the information in the Additional Account Information dialog box. Choose OK to save the information and return to the Create Investment Account dialog box.

7. If the earnings from the mutual fund account you are setting up are tax-deferred (the tax is assessed in a later time period than the earnings are received), select the **T**ax-Deferred Account check box. Examples of tax-deferred accounts are IRAs, 401(k) accounts, and annuities.

8. From the **T**ransfers In drop-down list, select the tax form or schedule to which transfers to the account should be assigned. From the Transfers **O**ut drop-down list, select the tax form or schedule for transfers from the investment account.

9. Choose OK. Quicken displays the Set Up Mutual Fund Security dialog box, as shown in figure 16.7.

Fig. 16.7
You enter information about the mutual fund security in the Set Up Mutual Fund Security dialog box.

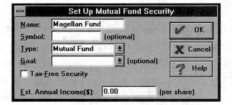

10. In the **S**ymbol text box, enter the symbol for the mutual fund if you plan to export or import price data from a file.

11. In the **T**ype drop-down list, select the mutual fund type.

12. (Optional) Select the goal for the mutual fund investment from the **G**oal drop-down list box. The goal is your purpose for investing in the mutual fund (such as growth, income, or college funding).

13. If the income from the security is not subject to income tax, select the Tax-Free Security check box.

14. In the Est. Annual Income text box, enter the income you project to earn per year from the mutual fund.

15. Choose OK. Quicken adds the mutual fund investment account to the Account List.

When you use this mutual fund account for the first time, Quicken displays the Investment Register for the account along with the Create Opening Share Balance dialog box, shown in figure 16.8.

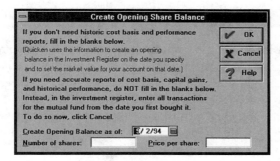

Fig. 16.8
The first time that you open the Investment Register for a mutual fund account, Quicken displays the Create Opening Share Balance dialog box.

If you want to set up historical data for the mutual fund (Option 1 in the section "Entering Opening Share Balances for Securities," earlier in this chapter), choose Cancel to display the Investment Register for the mutual fund investment account. Then enter the opening share balance, using the same steps for entering the opening share balance for each security in a regular investment fund.

If you choose Option 2 (from the section "Entering Opening Share Balances for Securities," earlier in this chapter) for entering opening share balances, select or enter **12/31/xx** (where xx is last year) in the Create Opening Balance As Of drop-down box. Enter the Number of shares owned on 12/31/xx and the Price per share at 12/31/xx.

If you choose Option 3 (from the section "Entering Opening Share Balances for Securities," earlier in this chapter) for entering opening share balances, select or enter today's date, the number of shares you now own, and the current price per share.

Choose OK when the Create Opening Share Balance dialog box is complete. Quicken displays the Investment Register and enters the opening balance.

If you choose Option 2 (from the section "Entering Opening Share Balances for Securities," earlier in this chapter) for entering opening share balances, you now must update the market value of the securities in the account to reflect the current price. See the section "Updating Security Prices" later in this chapter to learn how to update security prices to current prices.

If you choose Option 3 (from the section "Entering Opening Share Balances for Securities," earlier in this chapter) for entering opening share balances, you don't have to enter any other transactions. Your mutual fund investment account is set up with the opening share balance reflected for all current security holdings.

Using the Investment Register

Now that your investment account or accounts are set up, you're ready to start using the Investment Register to track the activity in your account. For each transaction that occurs in your investment account, you enter a transaction in the Investment Register so that all investment activity is accounted for. For example, you must record stock splits so that the number of shares in your Register reflects the number of shares you now hold, and you must enter transactions to record the receipt of dividends.

In earlier chapters, you learned about and worked with Quicken Registers. You probably use the Check Register most of all. Investment Registers work in a similar manner, but a few differences exist.

Although you can enter investment transactions directly in the Investment Register, accessing the appropriate form and entering the transaction data in the form is much easier. When you save a form (by choosing OK), Quicken enters the transaction in the proper fields in the next empty transaction line in the Register.

Because you can use forms to enter transactions, the Investment Register has an Investment button bar with buttons for actions that require a transaction form (see fig. 16.9). When you sell a security, for example, you enter the security sale information in the Sell Shares form, which is accessed by choosing the **S**ell button.

The command buttons at the bottom of the Investment Register are used to record and restore transactions in the Register, edit an investment transaction, and change the view of the Investment Register to Portfolio View. (See the section "Using the Portfolio View of an Investment Account" later in this chapter.) The buttons on the button bar are explained in the next section.

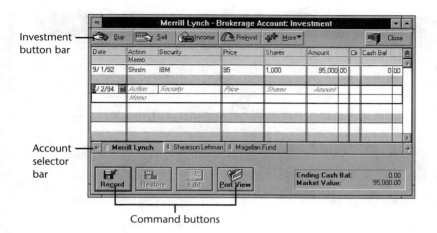

Investment button bar

Account selector bar

Command buttons

Fig. 16.9
In addition to command buttons, the Investment Register has a button bar for actions that require a transaction form.

The Action field in the Investment Register identifies the transaction. If you want to see the various actions you can enter, click the down arrow in the Action field.

Entering Investment Transactions

Each time you buy or sell a security in your investment account, receive dividends or interest, buy or redeem Treasury bills, and so forth, you should enter a transaction in the Investment Register to reflect the activity. Quicken provides forms that make entering investment transaction information easy. To access one of the forms to enter a transaction, choose the appropriate button from the Investment button bar (see table 16.1).

Table 16.1	Buttons on the Investment Button Bar	
Form	**Button**	**Transaction**
Buy Shares	**B**uy	Cash purchase of securities.
Sell Shares	**S**ell	Cash sale of securities.
Record Income	**I**ncome	Cash received from dividends, interest income, miscellaneous income, or capital gains distributions.
Reinvest Income	Rein**v**	Purchase of additional shares of a security with money paid to you by the security as dividends, interest income, or capital gain distributions.

(continues)

III

Planning for the Future

Table 16.1	**Continued**	
Form	**Button**	**Transaction**
Add Shares to Account	**M**ore	Receive shares of a security without paying cash from the investment account or other bank account (for example, a gift). Use this form to enter opening share balances in a new investment account, as explained earlier in this chapter.
Remove Shares from Account	**M**ore	Give shares to someone as a gift.
Margin Interest Expense	**M**ore	Pay interest to your brokerage firm on a margin loan.
Miscellaneous Expense	**M**ore	Incur expenses associated with a security.
Reminder	**M**ore	Enter a reminder message in an investment account.
Return of Capital	**M**ore	Receive cash from an amount paid to you as total or partial payment of the money you originally invested in a security, where you aren't the one who initiated the sale.
Stock Split	**M**ore	Receive additional shares of a security for no additional investment. Quicken recalculates the average cost per share when you enter a stock split transaction.
Transfer Cash In	**M**ore	Transfer cash into an investment account.
Transfer Cash Out	**M**ore	Transfer cash from an investment account.

Note

The Margin Interest Expense, Miscellaneous Income, Return of Capital, Transfer Cash In, and Transfer Cash Out forms aren't available in mutual fund investment accounts.

If you have used previous versions of Quicken and are comfortable using the Investment Register, you can enter investment transactions directly into the Register as you are accustomed to doing. Entering investment transactions is similar to entering other types of transactions in Quicken Registers. When your transaction is complete, choose the Re**c**ord button to record the transaction in the Investment Register.

Buying Securities

When you purchase a security, you enter the transaction in the appropriate investment account in Quicken. If you set up an account to enter transactions through your brokerage firm, enter security purchases in this account. If you buy, sell, and manage securities yourself, you may have an investment account set up for each security you own. If this is the case, enter purchases of additional shares of a security in that security's investment account. For purchases of new securities, set up an investment account for the security and then enter the purchase in that account. (You learned how to set up an investment account earlier in this chapter.)

To enter a transaction to buy securities, follow these steps:

1. In the Investment Register, press Ctrl+End to move to the next empty transaction line.

2. Choose the **B**uy button from the button bar. Quicken displays the Buy Shares form, shown in figure 16.10.

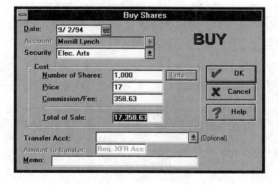

Fig. 16.10
Enter purchases of securities in the Buy Shares form.

3. Enter the date that you purchased the security in the **D**ate text box. Quicken enters the name of the current account in the **A**ccount drop-down list box. Then select the security in the **S**ecurity drop-down list box.

4. Complete the Cost section. Enter the number of shares you bought in the **N**umber of Shares text box, the price paid per share in the **P**rice text box, and the commission or fees charged to you (if explicit) in the **C**ommission/Fee text box. Quicken calculates the total amount of the

purchase. If you don't know the commission or fees charged, leave the **C**ommission/Fees text box blank and enter the total you paid for the shares in the **T**otal of Sale text box. Quicken calculates the commissions or fees.

> **Note**
>
> When you buy a bond after its original date of issue, you pay accrued interest to the previous owner of the bond at the time of purchase. Enter the accrued interest portion of the purchase price as a separate transaction in the Miscellaneous Expense form.

5. If you are buying the security with cash in the current investment account, leave the Trans**f**er Acct drop-down list box blank. If you are buying the security with cash from another investment account or a bank account, select the account in the Trans**f**er Acct drop-down list box. Enter the amount of the transfer in the Amount to transfer box.

6. (Optional) In the **M**emo text box, enter a memo that describes the transaction.

7. When the Buy Shares form is complete, choose OK. Quicken removes the Buy Shares form from the screen and enters the transaction in the next empty transaction line in the Investment Register.

8. Review the information in the Register and choose Re**c**ord to record the transaction. Quicken moves to the next empty transaction line.

> **Note**
>
> Use the Buy Shares form when you purchase securities. If you receive shares of a security by gift, use the Add Shares to Account dialog box.

Selling Securities

When you sell shares of a security, enter the transaction in the investment account where you recorded their purchase. You can identify the shares that you sell if you have purchased shares in different lots. If you bought, for example, 100 shares of IBM on 1/1/88, 200 shares on 6/30/89, and 100 shares on 5/15/90, you have three different lots of IBM stock. If you then sell 50 shares of IBM on 1/1/95, you can select which shares of the stock you are selling. Quicken keeps track of the number of shares remaining and their cost basis in each lot. If you don't specify which shares you are selling, Quicken uses the FIFO (first in, first out) rule, which assumes that the first shares purchased are the first shares sold.

CPA Tip: Specifying Lots

To minimize the capital gain resulting from the sale of securities whose market value has increased, identify the highest per share cost basis as the shares you are selling. Suppose that you bought 100 shares of Electronic Arts at $20 and then bought another 100 shares at $25. If you later sell 100 shares for $30 per share, you should specify the second lot (or the shares purchased at $25) as the shares you are selling because the resulting capital gain is less. If you need to generate a capital loss to offset other capital gains in your portfolio, specify the shares with the highest per share cost basis.

To enter a transaction to sell shares of a security, follow these steps:

1. In the Investment Register, press Ctrl+End to move to the next empty transaction line.

2. Choose the **S**ell button from the Investment button bar. Quicken displays the Sell Shares form, shown in figure 16.11.

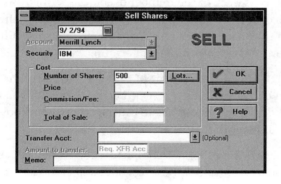

Fig. 16.11
Enter the sale of a security in the Sell Shares form.

3. To complete the Sell Shares form, follow the steps for completing the Buy Shares form as explained earlier in the section "Buying Securities."

4. To specify which lots of securities you are selling, choose the **L**ots button. Quicken displays the Specific Identification of Shares dialog box, shown in figure 16.12.

Fig. 16.12

Specify which shares you are selling in the Specific Identification of Shares dialog box.

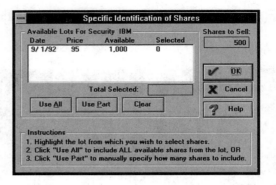

Quicken shows each security lot in the Available Lots for Security List box. Each lot is identified by the date purchased, the price per share, and the number of shares in each lot that you still own.

5. To sell all the shares in a particular lot, highlight the lot in the list box and choose the Use **A**ll button. Choose C**l**ear to deselect lots.

To sell part of the shares from a particular lot, highlight the lot, choose the Use **P**art button, and enter the number of shares you want to sell from the highlighted lot.

Quicken keeps track of the number of shares specified as sold in the Total Selected field. When the total selected is equal to the number of shares in the Shares to Sell text box (entered by Quicken from the Sell Shares form), you have finished allocating shares to lots.

6. Choose OK. If you selected part of the shares to sell in the Specific Identification of Shares dialog box, Quicken asks whether you want to cancel lot allocations. Choose **Y**es to cancel; otherwise, choose **N**o. Quicken displays the Sell Shares form.

7. When the Sell Shares form is complete, choose OK. Quicken removes the Sell Shares form from the screen and enters the sale transaction in the Investment Register.

8. Review the transaction in the Register and choose Re**c**ord to record the sale transaction.

CPA Tip: Planning Security Transactions

Try to plan your security transactions to minimize the amount of net capital gain realized each year. If you are in a net capital gain position, consider selling other securities that are in a loss position. Capital losses offset capital gains dollar for dollar. You may not deduct from your taxable income more than $3,000 in capital losses against ordinary income, however. Be mindful of your net capital loss position before entering into transactions resulting in losses. Capital losses can be carried over to future years.

Recording Investment Income

If you receive dividends, interest income, miscellaneous income, or capital gains distributions from a security, enter the receipt as investment income in the Investment Register.

To enter a transaction to record investment income, choose the **I**ncome button from the button bar and complete the Record Income dialog box.

Recording Reinvestments

When you reinvest dividends, interest income, or capital gains distributions to purchase additional shares of a security, record the reinvestment in the Investment Register.

To record a reinvestment transaction, choose the Rei**n**vst button from the Investment button bar and complete the Reinvest Income form.

Entering Stock Splits and Stock Dividends

You receive additional shares of stock when the company declares a stock split. Suppose that the ABC Company declares a stock split that entitles shareholders to one new share for every share they now hold. Because you own 100 shares, you are issued 100 new shares, for a total of 200.

When you receive additional shares of a security from a stock split, your total cost basis remains the same, but the per share price is adjusted downward. Suppose that you paid $10 per share for the 100 shares you purchased, which is a total investment of $1,000. With the 100 shares you receive in the stock split, your total investment is still $1,000. Your per share cost, however, is now $5.

III

Planning for the Future

Stock splits are entered based on the ratio of new shares issued to existing shares. In the ABC Company example, the ratio is 2:1 (two shares for every one share held).

A stock dividend occurs when a dividend is issued in the form of shares instead of cash. Most stock dividends are nontaxable. For nontaxable stock dividends, enter the transaction as a stock split for the ratio of dividend shares given per shares held. Taxable stock dividends are entered as reinvestment transactions (see the preceding section).

To enter a stock split or nontaxable stock dividend, choose the **M**ore button from the Investment button bar. Then select **S**tkSplit and complete the Stock Split form.

Entering Gifts and Receipts of Securities

When you give or receive shares of stock as a gift, you must enter the activity in the Investment Register so that it reflects the correct number of shares held. Because no funds are transferred when you give shares or receive shares, you use the Remove Shares from Account and the Add Shares to Account forms to enter gift transactions.

You learned how to complete the Add Shares to Account dialog box earlier in the section "Entering Opening Share Balances for Securities." Enter a gift of securities in the same way that you create an opening balance transaction in a new investment account. When you enter the receipt of shares as a gift, Quicken increases your number of shares without subtracting cash from your investment account or any other bank account.

The rules for determining the cost per share of gifted stock are complicated. For now, enter the price per share paid by the giver when the shares were originally purchased. Then consult your tax advisor to determine the cost per share that you should use.

For gifts of stock that you make, choose the **M**ore button from the Investment button bar. Then select Shrs**O**ut and complete the Remove Shares from Account form.

Recording Margin Loans

Brokerage firms enable their clients to borrow money to purchase securities. This type of transaction is called a *margin loan*. The brokerage firm charges interest (*margin interest*) on the loan as a bank or other lending institution does. The cash balance in your brokerage account is negative when you borrow money on margin.

To record the interest you pay on a margin loan, choose the **M**ore button from the Investment button bar, choose **M**argin**I**nt and then complete the Margin Interest Expense form.

Recording Returns of Capital

A return of capital takes place when you receive money as a total or partial repayment of the money you invested in a security. A return of capital is similar to a sale, but the investor isn't the initiator of the return of capital. If you invest in mortgage-backed securities, for example, you receive a return of capital when the underlying mortgages are paid.

To record a return of capital, choose the **M**ore button from the button bar, select Rtrn**C**ap, and complete the Return of Capital form.

Recording Zero-Coupon Bonds

Zero-coupon bonds don't pay interest until the bond matures or is sold. Zero-coupon bonds are purchased at a discount and increase in value due to the accruing of interest. Unfortunately, you must report accrued interest each year as taxable interest (even though you don't receive it). Accrued interest on zero-coupon bonds is reported on Form 1099-OID.

To record accrued interest on a zero-coupon bond, enter the amount as interest in the Record Income form.

To record the increase in value of a zero-coupon bond, enter the accrued interest amount as a negative amount in the Return of Capital form. Negative amounts in the Return of Capital form increase your cost basis in the bond.

Recording Short Sales

A *short sale* is a sale of a security you don't actually own, but rather borrow from your broker. Quicken recognizes short sales because you enter the sale of the security before the purchase.

To record a short sale, follow these steps:

1. Access the Sell Shares form (refer to fig. 16.11), as explained earlier in the section "Selling Securities."

2. Complete the Sell Shares form for the security you are selling short. Then choose OK.

3. When Quicken searches the Investment Register and finds that you don't already own the security, a message is displayed that this

transaction is being entered as a short sale. Choose the Confirm button, and Quicken records the short sale in the Investment Register.

Later, when you actually purchase the security (hopefully at a lower price), enter the purchase in the Buy Shares form (refer to fig. 16.10). Quicken closes the short sale and calculates the gain or loss. Gains from short sales don't appear in the Capital Gains Report but do appear in the Investment Income Report.

Caution

Quicken closes out a short sale before it opens a new position in a security. Therefore, if you record two short sales in the same security before buying the security, you must specify which short sale you are closing when you enter the purchase. Use the **L**ots button in the Buy Shares form to specify short sale lots. (You learned how to specify lots earlier in the section "Selling Securities.")

Entering Option Trades

An *option* is a contract that represents your right or obligation to buy or sell 100 shares of stock at a specified price (called the strike price) at any time during a specified period. Two types of options exist: puts and calls. A *call option* gives you the right to buy shares at a fixed price for a fixed period of time. A *put option* gives you the right to sell shares at a fixed price for a fixed period of time.

Enter the purchase or sale of options as you do any other security in the Buy Shares and Sell Shares forms. (When you set up the security for an option, use a distinctive name so that you can identify options in your Security List.) When you buy calls, use the Buy Shares form to enter the number of calls and the call price. When you exercise calls (buy the shares), enter the exercise in the Sell Shares form for the original purchase price of the calls. (This transaction clears the option position from your investment account.)

Enter the purchase of the shares in the Buy Shares form. Enter the exercise price as the price per share and enter the call price as the commission or fee paid. This adjusts the cost basis of the shares to include the price of the calls.

Recording Miscellaneous Expenses

If expenses incurred in an investment account (for example, broker fees) are paid from your investment account, enter a miscellaneous expense transaction in the account. To enter a miscellaneous expense in the Investment

Register, choose the **M**ore button from the button bar, select Misc**E**xp, and then complete the Miscellaneous Expense form.

> **Note**
>
> You can edit or delete an investment transaction in the Investment Register as you can in other Quicken Registers. You can edit the fields in a transaction in the Investment Register or choose the **E**dit command button to display the transaction form and edit the information in the form. Delete a transaction by highlighting the transaction and pressing Ctrl+D or choose **D**elete Transaction from the **E**dit menu.

Memorizing Investment Transactions

If you enter some transactions in the Investment Register regularly, you can have Quicken memorize the transactions so that the transaction data is saved in the Memorized Investment Transaction list. Each time you need to record the transaction, simply recall it; Quicken enters the memorized transaction in the Investment Register.

> **Note**
>
> Memorizing investment transactions is similar to memorizing regular transactions in the Check Register or any other account Register. However, Quicken stores memorized investment transactions in their own list—the Investment Transaction List. Quicken stores regular memorized transactions in the Memorized Transaction List.

To have Quicken memorize an investment transaction, follow these steps:

1. In the Investment Register, highlight the investment transaction that you want Quicken to memorize.

2. From the **E**dit menu, choose **M**emorize Transaction (or press Ctrl+M).

3. Quicken displays a message that the transaction is about to be memorized. Choose OK to memorize the transaction.

When you're ready to enter a memorized investment transaction in the Investment Register, follow these steps:

1. In the Investment Register, press Ctrl+End to move to the next empty transaction line.

2. From the **L**ists menu, choose Memorized **I**nvestment Trans. Quicken displays the Investment Transaction List, as shown in figure 16.13.

III

Planning for the Future

Fig. 16.13
Quicken lists the
investment
transactions that it
has memorized in
the Investment
Transaction List.

3. Double-click the memorized investment transaction that you want to
   enter. Quicken enters the memorized transaction in the Investment
   Register.

4. Review the transaction and then choose Record to record the memorized investment transaction in the Register.

Using Investment Reminders

You can set up investment reminders so that Quicken alerts you to actions
you want to take with regard to your investment portfolio. You can use investment reminders, for example, to help you remember when a bond or CD
will mature or to remind you to look at a stock's price to determine whether
it's time to sell.

You can use the investment reminders in two ways: to make notes in the
Investment Register and to remind yourself about certain investment transactions through the Quicken Billminder and Reminder features. Investment
reminders are displayed in the Billminder window each time you start your
computer and in the Quicken Reminder window each time you start
Quicken. (Refer to Chapter 14, "Scheduling Future Transactions," to learn
more about how Quicken Reminders work.)

Note

Quicken Reminders are associated with the Billminder feature. Quicken Reminders
(and therefore investment reminders) don't appear if you haven't installed Billminder.
See Chapter 14, "Scheduling Future Transactions," to learn how to install Billminder.

To enter an investment reminder, follow these steps:

1. In the Investment Register, press Ctrl+End to move to the next empty transaction line.

2. Choose the **M**ore button from the Investment button bar and then select **R**eminder. Quicken displays the Reminder form, shown in figure 16.14.

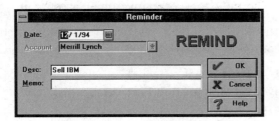

Fig. 16.14
Enter notes or reminders about actions to be taken in your investment account in the Reminder form.

3. Enter the **D**ate you are reminding yourself to take action on in your investment account.

> ### Note
>
> Quicken displays investment reminders every time you turn on your computer or start Quicken, regardless of the date you enter.

4. In the D**e**sc text box, type the text of your reminder, using up to 19 characters.

5. (Optional) Enter additional information in the **M**emo text box.

6. Choose OK. Quicken enters the investment reminder in the transaction line in the Register.

Quicken displays investment reminders in the Billminder or Quicken Reminder window until you turn off the reminder. To turn off an investment reminder, double-click the Clr (Cleared) field to enter an asterisk (*) or an X.

Using the Portfolio View of an Investment Account

Quicken enables you to change the view of the Investment Register so that you can see each of your security holdings (listed alphabetically by security

III

Planning for the Future

type), the number of shares, the current price, the market value, and the return on your investment. When you change the view of the Register to the Portfolio View, you not only can see your securities listed in one place, but also update security prices, create a QuickReport listing all transactions associated with a security, and graph the price history of a security. You also can record investment transactions and edit your list of securities in the Portfolio View of the Register.

To switch to the Portfolio View of an investment account, follow these steps:

1. Display the Register for the investment account for which you want to see the Portfolio View.

2. From the Activities menu, choose **P**ortfolio View (or press Ctrl+U). Alternatively, choose the **P**ort View command button at the bottom of the Investment Register.

Quicken displays the Portfolio View window for the investment account, as shown in figure 16.15.

Fig. 16.15
Choose the Port View command button to display the Portfolio View of an investment account.

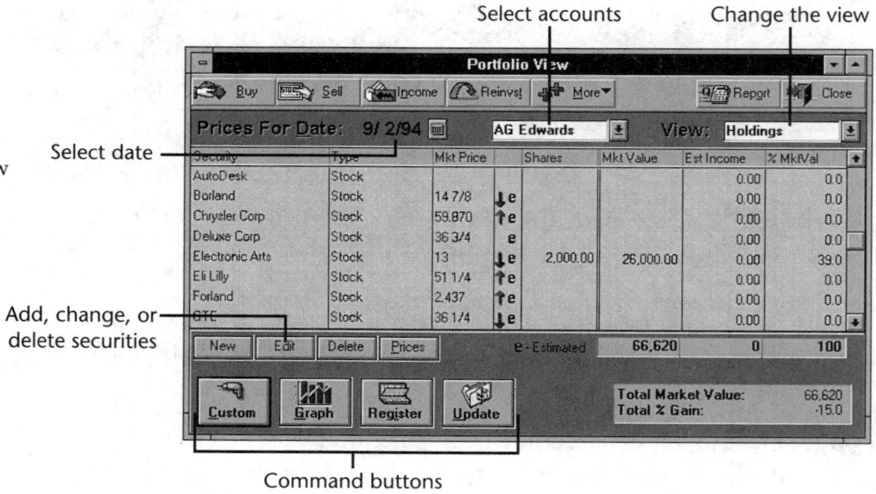

The Portfolio View window has the same buttons as those in the Register Investment button bar, as well as a QuickReport (Rep**o**rt) button for an instant transaction listing for the selected security. In the Portfolio View window, Quicken includes the following command buttons: **C**ustom, **G**raph, Re**g**ister, and **U**pdate.

Updating Security Prices

One of the most common investment record-keeping activities is tracking the market value of your investments. Quicken provides several tools that enable you to update the prices of securities in your portfolio to reflect the current market value. You update security prices in the Portfolio View of the Investment Register. When you enter current prices for securities, Quicken recalculates the market value of each security and the total market value of the investment account.

Now, with Quicken 4 for Windows, updating prices is simple if you have access to a modem and have subscribed to Portfolio Price Update, the online financial service that updates prices of stocks and mutual funds in your Quicken Investment Registers.

Updating Security Prices Online

If you subscribe to Portfolio Price Update and have a modem connected to your computer, you can update your stock and mutual fund prices for any security traded on the New York Stock Exchange, American Stock Exchange, and NASDAQ. When the market is open, stock prices are delayed at least 15 minutes. When the market is closed, stock prices reflect the most recent closing price. Prices for mutual funds are updated only once a day at 5:30 p.m. EST; before 5:30 p.m., mutual fund prices reflect the previous day's closing price.

This online financial service is available 24 hours a day, seven days a week. You can update your security prices up to three times for free with Portfolio Price Update; after the third time, you're asked to sign up. Charges for Portfolio Price Update are billed monthly to your credit card. For current pricing information, call Intuit Online Services Customer Service at (800)245-2164.

To update your security prices using online services, follow these steps:

1. From the Online menu, select **U**pdate Portfolio Prices or click the **U**pdate button in the Portfolio View window.

2. Enter your Portfolio Price Update account number and choose OK.

3. Quicken initializes your modem and dials the phone number to connect to the Portfolio Price Update service.

4. Stock and mutual fund prices are retrieved and entered in the Portfolio View window, at which time Quicken displays a message confirming the price update.

5. Choose OK to return to the Portfolio View window.

Updating Security Prices Manually

To update security prices manually to reflect the current market value, follow these steps:

1. In the Register for the investment account for which you want to update prices, choose the **P**ort View button to display the Portfolio View window.

2. From the View drop-down list box, select Price Update. Quicken changes the view of the Portfolio View window to show the security type, symbol, market price, number of shares, last price, market value, and market value change for each security (see fig. 16.16). Quicken also displays a column to show an estimated price or to show whether the security's price has increased or decreased since the previous price was entered.

Fig. 16.16
Quicken shows information for each security when you select the Price Update view in the Portfolio View window.

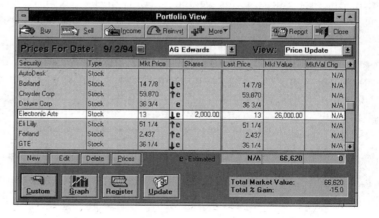

Tip
Use the + (plus) or – (minus) keys to change the security price by 1/8-increments (.125).

3. Highlight the security whose price you want to update.

4. In the Mkt Price column, enter the current market price of the security. To record the price, move out of the Mkt Price column by pressing Tab or by clicking another security.

> **Note**
>
> If a price is unchanged from the last time you entered security prices, press the asterisk (*) key to indicate that the price remains for the current date. Quicken removes the e from the next column. (Quicken enters an e for securities that haven't been updated as of the current date.)

5. Repeat steps 3 and 4 for each security whose price you want to update.

> **Note**
>
> If you want to enter security prices for other dates, change the date in the Prices For **D**ate field as explained earlier in the section "Changing the View Date." Then follow steps 2 through 5 to enter prices for other dates.

> **Note**
>
> You can create a price history for a security so that you can evaluate its performance over time. Quicken automatically stores security prices when you update prices (as explained in the preceding section). You also can add new prices to the price history as well as change and delete prices. To create a price history for a security, highlight the security for which you want to create a price history and then choose the **P**rices button.

From Here...

After learning how to use Quicken to track your investments, you may want to review the following:

- Chapter 6, "Using the Register," shows you the basics for entering transactions in a Quicken Register. Entering transactions in the Investment Register is the same as other Quicken Registers.

- Chapter 19, "Creating and Printing Reports," describes how to create investment reports so that you can analyze the results of your investment strategies.

- Chapter 20, "Using Graphs to Analyze Your Finances," explains how to create graphs to evaluate the performance of your investment portfolio.

III

Planning for the Future

Chapter 17

Budgeting with Quicken

Budgeting has an undeserved bad reputation because people tend to think of a budget as financial handcuffs, an obstacle to enjoyment, and a drag on financial freedom. Actually, nothing is farther from the truth. Budgeting is a simple tool with astonishingly positive benefits for businesses and households. Budgets represent game plans that *calibrate*, or specify, what you need to do to succeed in business or personal financial life.

Because one of Quicken's most significant benefits is the capability to monitor your financial success through budgeting, this chapter describes how Quicken helps you budget more effectively.

In this chapter, you learn how to do the following tasks:

- Enter budget amounts in Quicken's budget spreadsheet

- Automatically create a budget from actual data

- Change the spreadsheet layout

- Save and restore budget data

- Use the Progress Bar to monitor your budget

Using Quicken to Set Up a Budget

Quicken provides three related features that enable you to budget more effectively for personal finances and for small businesses: categories, supercategories, and reporting.

With categories, you can assign each check that you record to a spending category, such as housing, contribution, entertainment, or taxes. You also can assign an income category to each deposit you record, such as wages, gross sales, or interest income. The steps and benefits of using categories are discussed in greater detail in Chapter 4, "Organizing Your Finances."

By assigning the category into which every check and deposit you record belongs, you can produce reports that summarize and total the inflows and outflows by category for a specific period. If you decide to tap the power of budgeting, Cash Flow Reports are invaluable.

Supercategories is a new feature in Quicken 4 for Windows that groups categories into broad levels for budgeting purposes. You learn about supercategories later in this chapter.

Tip
You also can produce graphs that enable you to compare actual dollars visually with budgeted dollars.

Quicken also enables you to enter any amount budgeted for a category. With this information, Quicken calculates the difference, or *variance*, between the total spent on a category and the budgeted amount for a category. Quicken performs the arithmetic related to monitoring how closely you follow the budget and how successfully you are marching toward your life goals.

With Quicken's graphing capabilities, you also can produce a graph that shows the difference between budgeted and actual amounts. Figure 17.1 shows an example of a Quicken Budget Report, and figure 17.2 shows an example of a graph with budget variances. For information on creating a budget report, see Chapter 19, "Creating and Printing Reports." To learn how to create the Budget Variance Graph, refer to Chapter 20, "Using Graphs to Analyze Your Finances."

CPA Tip: Analyzing Budget Differences

When you review the Budget Report, don't worry about immaterial differences; instead, focus on large and unusual differences. Try to find out why a difference is large. Maybe you paid utility bills for the current month and in advance for next month, or perhaps you had some unexpected car repair bills or medical bills. Because some expenses are unexpected and therefore impossible to plan, you always should have a cushion in your budget for those items.

Category Description	8/1/94 Difference	8/31/94 Actual	Budget
Budget Report: 8/1/94 Through 8/31/94			
9/8/94 All Accounts	Page 1		
Income			
Int. Inc.	300.00	300.00	0.00
Salary	7,000.00	7,000.00	0.00
Total Income	**7,300.00**	**7,300.00**	**0.00**
Expenses			
Activities	45.00	25.00	-20.00
Auto:			
Fuel	94.30	120.00	25.70
Total Auto	94.30	120.00	25.70
Bank Chrg	6.00	6.00	0.00
Books	137.39	100.00	37.39
Charity:			
Cash Contr.	0.00	50.00	50.00
Total Charity	0.00	50.00	50.00
Clothing	408.16	500.00	91.84
Computer	173.90	150.00	-23.90
Dining	50.00	100.00	50.00
Education	15.00	15.00	0.00
Entertain	40.00	100.00	60.00
Gifts	71.24	75.00	3.76
Groceries	352.98	400.00	47.02
Household	90.48	90.00	-0.48
Insurance	90.00	90.00	0.00
Medical	110.32	110.00	-0.32
Misc.	78.24	100.00	21.76
Mort. Int.	1,562.50	1,563.00	0.50
Tax:			
Fed	1,000.00	1,000.00	0.00
Prop	150.00	150.00	0.00
Soc. Sec.	500.00	500.00	0.00
State	102.96	103.00	0.04
Total Tax	1,752.96	1,753.00	0.04
Telephone	52.96	50.00	-2.96
Utilities:			
Gas & Elec.	165.12	165.00	-0.12
Water	37.04	32.00	-5.04
Total Utilites	202.16	197.00	-5.16
Total Expenses	**5,333.59**	**5,594.00**	**260.41**
Total Income/Expenses	**1,966.41**	**1,706.00**	**206.41**
Transfers			
To First Nat'l	0.00	0.00	0.00
To Mortgage	-185.54	-186.00	-0.46
From First Nat'l	185.54	186.00	-0.46
From Mortgage	0.00	0.00	0.00
Total Transfers	**0.00**	**0.00**	**0.00**
Overall Total	**1,966.41**	**1,706.00**	**260.41**

Fig. 17.1

You can create a Budget Report for any given period that shows actual data, budgeted data, and the difference between the two.

III

Planning for the Future

Fig. 17.2
The Budget
Variance Graph
shows the
differences
between actual
data and budgeted
data for any given
period.

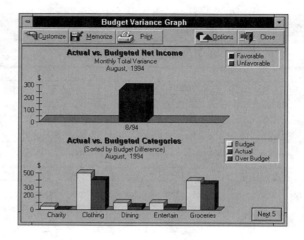

Setting Up a Budget in Quicken

After you determine how much you want to spend on what, you're ready to enter your budget data into Quicken's budget spreadsheet. The budget spreadsheet includes a row for each category set up in the Category & Transfer List. If you want to enter budget amounts for supercategories, you can include supercategories in the budget spreadsheet as well.

CPA Tip: Budgeting for Transfers

You can budget for transfers to other accounts. If you contribute to a 401(k) plan and have an asset account set up in Quicken to track the value of that account, for example, you can enter a budgeted amount each period to be deducted from your salary and transferred to a 401(k) account.

To display the budget spreadsheet, choose **B**udgeting from the Pl**a**n menu. Quicken displays the budget spreadsheet that you see in figure 17.3.

At the top of the budget spreadsheet is the Budget button bar, which makes using the budget spreadsheet quick and easy. Table 17.1 describes each button on the Budget button bar.

Budget button bar

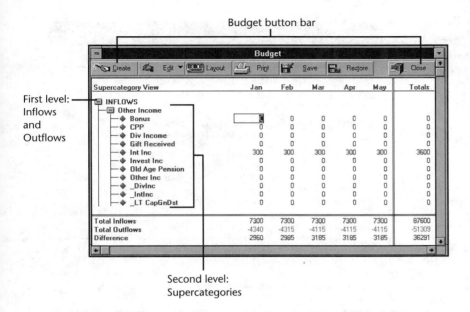

First level:
Inflows
and
Outflows

Second level:
Supercategories

Fig. 17.3
The budget spreadsheet includes a Budget button bar at the top of the spreadsheet so that you can perform budgeting tasks quickly.

III

Planning for the Future

Table 17.1	The Budget Button Bar	
Button	**Function**	
Create	Enters budget information based on actual data.	
E**d**it	Displays the Edit menu, which includes the following options for editing data in the budget spreadsheet:	
	*2-**W**eek*	Sets up a budget for an item that occurs every two weeks (such as a paycheck).
	*Co**p**y All*	Copies the current budget spreadsheet to the Windows Clipboard.
	*Clear **R**ow*	Clears budget data from the current row.
	*Clear A**l**l Budgets*	Clears all budget data from the current spreadsheet.
	*Fill **R**ow Right*	Fills all subsequent periods (to the right) with the same budget amount as the current text box.
	*Fill **C**olumns*	Fills all subsequent categories (below) with the same budget amounts as the current text box.
	***S**upercategories*	Adds, edits, and deletes supercategories; assigns categories and subcategories to supercategories.

(continues)

Table 17.1	**Continued**	
Button	**Function**	
Layout	Displays the Layout Budgets dialog box, which includes the following options for changing the layout of the budget spreadsheet:	
	Columns	Sets the interval on which you base your budget to **M**onth, **Q**uarter, or **Y**ear.
	Rows	Determines the rows that are shown in the budget spreadsheet: Show **S**upercategories, Show **T**ransfers, and **H**ide Zero Budget Cats.
Print	Prints the current budget spreadsheet.	
Save	Saves the data in the current budget spreadsheet.	
Restore	Deletes all changes made to the current budget spreadsheet since the spreadsheet was last saved.	
Close	Closes the budget spreadsheet and gives you the opportunity to save your changes.	

When you display the budget spreadsheet, the income categories appear in the top portion of the spreadsheet, followed by the expense categories. Quicken organizes the budget spreadsheet in outline format. The first level in the budget spreadsheet are INFLOWS and OUTFLOWS. You can click the buttons to the left of INFLOWS and OUTFLOWS to condense the budget spreadsheet data into just those two levels. For example, when you click the INFLOWS button, all categories and subcategories within the INFLOWS level are consolidated into one line—INFLOWS. The same is true of the OUT-FLOWS section.

The second level in the budget spreadsheet is comprised of supercategories (if used). Under each supercategory in the budget spreadsheet are the categories and subcategories assigned to that particular supercategory. You learn how to assign categories and subcategories to supercategories later in this chapter.

Categories and subcategories make up the third level in the budget spreadsheet. You can scroll down the spreadsheet to see all your income and expense categories. If you drag the scroll box in the scroll bar to move through the spreadsheet, Quicken displays a small box to the left of the scroll bar with the name of each category as you scroll through the spreadsheet.

The last three rows of the budget spreadsheet shown in figure 17.3 display the total budget inflows, the total budget outflows, and the difference for

each period. These three rows remain at the bottom of the budget spreadsheet even when you scroll through the spreadsheet. The Total Inflows line
shows the total of all income category budget amounts for each period. At
the end of the expense categories section of the spreadsheet, the Total Outflows line shows the total of all expense category budget amounts for each
period. The Difference line shows the difference between total inflows and
total outflows.

Creating Supercategories for Budgeting

Supercategories are new to Quicken 4 for Windows. Supercategories are used
to group similar categories and subcategories together for budgeting purposes.
Many of your expenses, for example, can be considered discretionary, like
entertainment, clothing, dining, and so forth. They're discretionary because
you can make choices about how much you spend in these areas. Unlike
nondiscretionary expenses such as your mortgage payment, car payment,
child care fees, insurance premiums, and so forth. You can set up a Discretionary and a Nondiscretionary supercategory and group the appropriate
categories in each.

Quicken includes a preset list of supercategories that you can use; Discretionary, Non-Discretionary, Other Income, and Salary Income.

To assign categories and subcategories to supercategories, follow these steps:

1. From the budget spreadsheet, select E**d**it from the button bar and then
   select **S**upercategories. Quicken displays the Manage Supercategories
   dialog box shown in figure 17.4. (You can also display the Manage
   Supercategories dialog box by selecting the **S**uper button from the Category & Transfer List.)

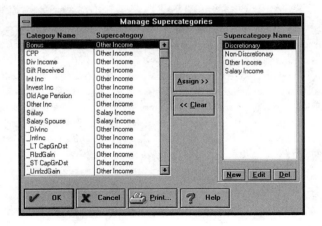

Fig. 17.4
You can assign
categories and
subcategories to a
supercategory in
the Manage
Supercategories
dialog box.

III

Planning for the Future

2. Supercategory names are listed on the right side of the Manage Supercategories dialog box; category names are listed on the left. Highlight the supercategory for which you want to assign categories or subcategories.

3. Next, highlight the category or subcategory name that you want to assign to the supercategory. Then, click the **A**ssign button. Quicken enters the supercategory name next to the category or subcategory name.

4. Repeat steps 2 and 3 for each category or subcategory that you want to assign to a supercategory.

If you want to create your own supercategory, click the **N**ew button in the Manage Supercategories dialog box. You can also edit or delete existing supercategories using the **E**dit and **D**el buttons.

Entering Budget Amounts

One way to enter budget amounts is to enter amounts directly into the budget spreadsheet into a selected cell. Select a cell by moving to the income or expense category for which you want to enter a budget amount, and then moving to the intersection of the appropriate period, such as Childcare for January. Quicken puts a box around the selected cell. You then can type the new budget amount.

To enter budgeted amounts for a particular income or expense category, move to the cell at the intersection of the appropriate period and category in the budget spreadsheet. Type the amount and press Enter to move down one row or press Tab to move to the right one column.

CPA Tip: Keeping Expenses in Line with Your Income

As a general rule, your budgeted expenses shouldn't exceed your budgeted income. If expenses are more than your income, you're deficit spending. People who deficit spend usually rely on credit cards or bank loans to finance their lifestyle, which means they are spending now based on money they plan to make in the future. In most cases, deficit spending doesn't enable you to get ahead of the debt. Before you get in this situation, budget your expenditures wisely. Don't overextend. You should have a good idea of your income each month, each year, and so forth. Don't consistently spend more than that.

The following sections explain how to create a budget automatically from actual data, how to fill in rows and columns quickly, and how to enter biweekly amounts.

Automatically Creating a Budget from Actual Data

A second way to enter budgeted amounts is to copy amounts into the budget spreadsheet by using the **C**reate feature. The **C**reate feature copies actual amounts for categories in a specified period to the budget spreadsheet, or you can fill in one cell or column and have Quicken copy the budget data into other rows or columns. For selected categories, you can enter budget amounts that occur every two weeks, such as a salary paid biweekly.

If you want to set up a budget based on actual income and expense amounts, you can use the **C**reate feature. **C**reate copies actual data from a specified time period into the budgeting spreadsheet. You can tell Quicken to enter rounded values in the budget or to use averages for the period that you specify. When you use **C**reate to enter your budget amounts automatically, Quicken uses information from all accounts in the current file; you can't choose accounts selectively from which to base a budget.

When you use **C**reate to enter budget amounts from actual data in Quicken, you can select the categories for which Quicken enters budget amounts from actual amounts. If, for example, you want to enter budget amounts based on actual amounts for all expense categories but not income categories, you can select only expense categories. Quicken copies actual amounts into the budget spreadsheet for only expense categories and leaves the income categories at zero.

To create a budget automatically from actual data, follow these steps:

1. Choose **C**reate from the Budget button bar. Quicken displays the Automatically Create Budget dialog box, shown in figure 17.5.

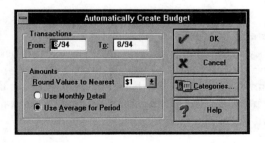

Fig. 17.5
Quicken displays the Automatically Create Budget dialog box when you choose **C**reate from the Budget button bar.

2. Enter the date range of the actual monthly amounts you want to copy in the **F**rom and **T**o text boxes.

3. Then, select how you want values rounded and whether to use actual monthly detail to enter budget amounts or to use average amounts for the period that you select.

4. (Optional) To select the categories for which you want **C**reate to enter budgeted data from actual data, choose the **C**ategories button. Quicken displays the Select Categories to Include dialog box, which lists all categories and subcategories from the Category & Transfer List (see fig. 17.6).

Fig. 17.6
Quicken displays all categories in the Select Categories to Include dialog box when you select the categories to enter budgeted data from actual data.

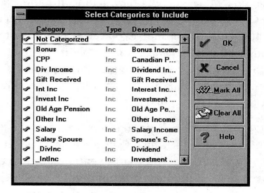

By default, all categories are marked. To clear all categories, choose **C**lear All. To mark all categories, choose **M**ark All. Click a category to mark one category at a time. Choose OK when you are ready; Quicken returns to the Automatically Create Budget dialog box.

5. Choose OK again. Quicken creates the budget (for the selected categories, if applicable).

Filling in Rows and Columns

Quicken enables you to fill in rows and columns of the budget spreadsheet quickly. Based on the amount in the selected cell in the current row, Quicken copies the amount to all cells to the right in the current row. If you fill in $25 in the January entertainment expense budget amount, for example, you can copy the amount to February, March, April, May, and so on.

To copy a budget amount to rows on the right, follow these steps:

1. Select the cell that you want copied.

2. Choose E**d**it on the Budget button bar and then choose Fill **R**ow Right.

3. Quicken asks whether you want to fill rows to the end of the year with the selected cell's budget amount. Choose **Y**es. Quicken copies the budget amount from the selected cell to each cell to the right of the current row.

Filling in columns works the same. To fill in columns, simply follow the previous steps for filling in rows, but choose Fill **C**olumns in step 2.

Budgeting for Biweekly Items

Quicken enables you to budget for items that you receive or pay on a biweekly basis. If you receive your paycheck every two weeks, for example, you can enter a biweekly gross salary budget amount in the Salary category.

To budget for biweekly items, take the following steps:

1. Highlight the category (or transfer account) for which you want to budget on a biweekly basis.

2. Choose E**d**it on the button bar, and then choose 2-**W**eek. Quicken displays the Set Up Two-Week Budget dialog box, shown in figure 17.7. The category for which you want to budget biweekly appears in the Budget For field.

Tip
You also can use the minicalendar in the **E**very Two Weeks Starting date box to determine the starting date for biweekly items.

Fig. 17.7
Use the Set Up Two-Week Budget dialog box to enter a biweekly budget amount for the selected category or transfer account.

3. In the **A**mount box, enter the amount you expect to spend or receive every two weeks.

4. Enter the first date of the first two-week interval in the **E**very Two Weeks Starting date box. If your first biweekly paycheck for the year is paid on January 6, for example, enter **1/6/***yy* in this date box. Then choose OK.

III

Planning for the Future

Clearing the Budget Spreadsheet

You can clear just a row in the budget spreadsheet, or you can clear the whole spreadsheet. To clear budget amounts from one row in the budget spreadsheet, highlight the row that you want to clear. Then choose E**d**it on the button bar and choose Cle**a**r Row. Quicken asks whether you want to clear budget amounts for the category that you have selected. Choose **Y**es. Quicken zeros all budget amounts in the row.

To clear the entire budget spreadsheet, choose E**d**it on the Budget button bar and then choose Clear A**l**l Budgets. When you clear all budgets, Quicken asks you to confirm that you want to clear all budget amounts.

Changing the Budget Spreadsheet

By default, Quicken assumes that you want to budget on a monthly basis, so the spreadsheet displays a column for each month. You also can budget on a quarterly and yearly basis, however.

When you choose La**y**out on the button bar, Quicken displays the Layout Budgets dialog box shown in figure 17.8. You can select the **Q**uarter option to base your budget on quarterly amounts and display a column for each quarter in the spreadsheet, or select the **Y**ear option to base your budget on annual amounts (only one column is displayed for the year).

Fig. 17.8
The Layout
Budgets dialog box
includes options
for changing the
intervals on which
to base your
budget.

If you want to enter budget amounts for supercategories and transfers, you must change the spreadsheet layout so that the spreadsheet displays rows for each supercategory and each account in your Quicken file. You also can remove categories that contain no budget amounts. If, for example, you have a category set up for music lessons but no budget amounts exist for this category, you can hide, or not show, the category in the budget spreadsheet.

Saving and Restoring Budget Data

You can save your budget spreadsheet after you make changes to it. After you work in the budget spreadsheet, just save the data when the budget is the way you want it. If you want to enter what-if scenarios by changing budget amounts for selected categories, you can do so without losing your original budget data. By restoring your budget data, you return to the budget spreadsheet as it was the last time it was saved.

To save budget spreadsheet data, choose Sa**v**e on the Budget button bar.

To restore the budget spreadsheet to the way it was when last saved, choose Re**s**tore on the Budget button bar. Quicken warns you that restoring the budget overwrites the current changes you have made. Choose **Y**es.

> **Note**
>
> When you finish working in the budget spreadsheet, close the spreadsheet by selecting Close from the Budget button bar. Quicken asks whether you want to save the budget data before exiting. Choose Cancel to return to the budget spreadsheet.

Using the Progress Bar to Monitor Your Budget

The Progress Bar is a new feature in Quicken 4 for Windows that you can display at the bottom of your screen to monitor how well you're sticking to your budget for a single category or a single supercategory. If you're trying to cut down on dining out, for example, you can monitor the Dining category in the Progress Bar. The Progress Bar shows you your actual expenditures and also shows you the budgeted amount for the time period that you specify (month, quarter, or year). You can also use the Progress Bar to monitor your savings in a Savings Goal Account. (You learn about Savings Goal Accounts in Chapter 18, "Saving for the Future with Quicken.")

To monitor your budget using the Progress Bar, follow these steps:

1. Select Pr**o**gress Bar from the Pl**a**n menu. Quicken displays the Progress Bar at the bottom of the screen, as shown in figure 17.9. The Progress Bar includes a left and right gauge so that it can monitor two different situations. You can select what is monitored in each gauge.

Fig. 17.9
The Progress Bar is displayed at the bottom of your screen.

2. Select what to monitor by customizing the Progress Bar. Click the Cust button on the right side of the Progress Bar to display the Customize Progress Bar shown in figure 17.10. Here is where you tell Quicken what you want to monitor with the Progress Bar.

Fig. 17.10
Tell Quicken what you want to monitor in the Customize Progress Bar dialog box.

3. Click the drop-down box in the **L**eft Gauge Type or the **R**ight Gauge Type. For budgets, you can monitor a Budget Goal or a Supercategory Budget.

4. If you monitor a Budget Goal, click the **C**hoose Category button to select the category that you want to monitor in the Progress Bar. If you monitor a Supercategory Budget, click the **C**hoose Supercategory button to select the supercategory that you want to monitor.

5. (Optional) You can change the Progress Bar display so that labels are not shown or to place them always on top in the Progress Bar. Select the **S**how Labels or the Always on **T**op options to change the Progress Bar display.

6. Choose OK. Quicken shows the Progress Bar with the situation you selected to monitor.

From Here...

Now that you've mastered budgeting in Quicken, you may want to review the following:

■ Chapter 4, "Organizing Your Finances," explains how to set up categories so that they can be assigned to supercategories for budgeting purposes.

■ Chapter 18, "Saving for the Future with Quicken," where you learn about Quicken's Savings Goal account that you can use to earmark funds for savings.

III

Planning for the Future

Chapter 18

Saving for the Future with Quicken

We all know the sacrifices we need to make to *save*, but what is financial planning? *Financial planning* is the process of setting goals and developing plans to meet those goals. Then, when your goals are set, you must start saving to meet those goals. To retire with enough money to meet expenses (and have a little fun) through the rest of your life, for example, you first must determine how much money you will need, and then develop and implement a financial plan so that you have that amount of money at retirement age. You also need to develop a financial plan for the things that you want to acquire. And if you have children, you will want to plan for college expenses *now*, even if your children are young.

You don't need other software programs to help you with planning your financial needs for the future. Quicken's financial planners are easy to access from anywhere in the program and make calculations as quickly as you can enter the data.

In Chapter 10, "Tracking Loans," you learned about the Loan Planner and the Refinance Planner. In this chapter, you learn about the remaining planners; Investment Savings Planner, College Planner, and Retirement Planner.

What about saving for a trip to Bermuda? Quicken can even help you monitor your savings for the short-term expenditures that you don't necessarily transfer to another bank account. With Quicken's *Savings Goal* account, you can track the money that you want to put aside for a special purpose. This account is handy for gauging the progress you're making toward saving money, for whatever purpose.

And to help you monitor your progress towards meeting that savings goal, Quicken 4 for Windows includes the new Progress Bar that can be displayed at the bottom of your screen and shows you how well you're doing.

In this chapter, you learn how to do the following:

- Set up and use a Savings Goal account

- Monitor savings with the Progress Bar

- Use the Investment Savings Planner to calculate investment earnings

- Use the College Planner to prepare for your children's college tuition

- Prepare for retirement and use the Retirement Planner

Using the Savings Goal Account

With Quicken 4 for Windows, you can create a Savings Goal account that you can use to track money that you want to put aside for a special purpose—perhaps a vacation, a down payment on a new car, or an investment in a new business. Quicken treats transfers to Savings Goal accounts as paper transactions only. Money isn't actually transferred from the bank account to a Savings Goal account. The Savings Goal account is used to track the amount that you are *mentally* saving from your bank account.

The Savings Goal account is set up as an asset account but is treated differently than other asset accounts. With the Savings Goal account, you periodically can make a paper contribution of money, or savings, into the account from a bank account. When you record a contribution transaction from your bank account to a Savings Goal account, the contribution amount increases the balance in the Savings Goal account but never really leaves your bank account. You can choose to show the balance in your bank account, however, with or without the contribution to your Savings Goal account. When you reconcile your checking account, transfer transactions to your Savings Goal account don't appear because money wasn't actually transferred out of your checking account.

Setting Up a Savings Goal Account

To set up a Savings Goal account, from the Pl**a**n menu, select **S**avings Goals. Quicken displays the Savings Goals dialog box, shown in figure 18.1. Then, select **N**ew to display the Create New Savings Goal dialog box (see fig. 18.2). Enter the goal name, the amount that you want to save, and the date by which you hope to have saved the money. Choose OK to add the new Savings Goal account.

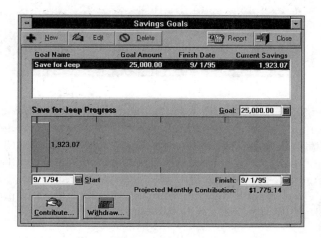

Fig. 18.1
The Savings Goals dialog box shows each Savings Goal account, the goal amount, and the amount saved to date.

Fig. 18.2
Set up a new Savings Goal account in the Create New Savings Goal dialog box.

After you've set up a Savings Goal account, you can be on your way by making regular contributions to the account. The next section shows you how to handle contributions to a Savings Goal account.

Contributing to a Savings Goal Account

After you set up a Savings Goal account, you can make contributions periodically to the account from your checking or other bank account. To make contributions to a Savings Goal account, follow these steps:

1. In the Savings Goals window (see fig. 18.1), highlight the Savings Goal account to which you want to make a contribution; then click the **C**ontribute button. Quicken displays the Contribute to Goal dialog box shown in figure 18.3.

2. Fill out the Contribute To Goal dialog box with the date of the contribution and the account from which you want to withdraw funds.

Fig. 18.3
Enter the amount
that you want to
contribute to a
Savings Goal
account here.

3. In the $ (Amount) box, Quicken has already entered a contribution amount. Quicken calculates this amount based on the goal amount and the finish date that you entered in the Create New Savings Goal dialog box (see fig. 18.2) when you set up the Savings Goal account. This is the amount necessary at the current time for you to reach your goal. You can, however, enter any amount that you want in the $ (Amount) box.

4. Choose OK. Quicken adds the contribution amount to the balance in your Savings Goal account which is shown in the Savings Goal window.

Quicken adds the contribution amount to your Savings Goal account and enters a transaction for a withdrawal in the account from which you took funds. Figure 18.4 shows the Register for a bank account where funds were withdrawn to contribute to a Savings Goal account. Note that this is only a paper reduction of the amount in that account, and, in that account's Register, you can choose whether to show transfers to Savings Goal accounts. Just click the Hide Sav. **G**oal check box (see fig. 18.4) to hide contributions to Savings Goal accounts.

Fig. 18.4
The Register for
the bank account
where funds were
withdrawn to
contribute to a
Savings Goal
account.

Transaction for
contribution to
Savings Goal
account

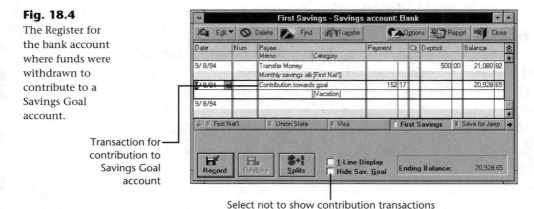

Select not to show contribution transactions

You can make withdrawals from a Savings Goal account by selecting the Withdraw button in the Savings Goal window. Enter the amount of the withdrawal and the bank account in which the funds should be transferred in the Complete the Withdrawal From Goal dialog box. Quicken subtracts withdrawal amounts from the balance in your Savings Goal account.

Using the Progress Bar to Monitor Savings

The Progress Bar is a new feature in Quicken 4 for Windows that you can display at the bottom of your screen to monitor your savings toward a savings goal. The Progress Bar shows you the savings goal amount and your actual savings for the time period that you specify (month, quarter, or year). You can also use the Progress Bar to monitor your budget. (You learn about using the Progress Bar to monitor budgets in Chapter 17.)

To monitor your savings using the Progress Bar, follow these steps:

1. Select Progress Bar from the Plan menu. Quicken displays the Progress Bar at the bottom of the screen, as shown in figure 18.5. The Progress Bar includes a left and right gauge so that it can monitor two different situations. You can select what is monitored in each gauge.

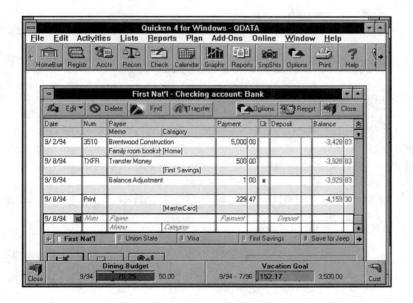

Fig. 18.5
The Progress Bar is displayed at the bottom of your screen.

2. Select what to monitor by customizing the Progress Bar. Click the Cust button on the right side of the Progress Bar to display the Customize

Progress Bar dialog box shown in figure 18.6. Here is where you tell Quicken what you want to monitor with the Progress Bar.

Fig. 18.6
Tell Quicken what you want to monitor in the Customize Progress Bar dialog box.

3. Click the drop-down box in the **L**eft Gauge Type or the **R**ight Gauge Type. Select the Savings Goal option in the **L**eft or the **R**ight Gauge Type boxes.

4. Click the Ch**o**ose Goal button to select the savings goal that you want to monitor in the Progress Bar.

5. Choose OK. Quicken shows the Progress Bar with the Savings Goal you selected to monitor.

Planning Your Investments

Although Quicken can't make your money grow any quicker than the investment vehicle in which it's now maintained, you can monitor your investment growth and play out "what-if" scenarios using Quicken's Investment Savings Planner. You can see how much your investment will grow given different interest rates, inflation rates, and yearly contributions.

Using the Investment Savings Planner

With the Investment Savings Planner, you can calculate the following variables:

■ The expected growth of the money that you now have saved or invested over a certain time period and based on a specific interest rate and expected inflation rate

■ How much money you need *now* to accumulate a certain amount of money in the future

■ How much money you need to save on a regular basis to accumulate a certain amount of money in the future

To access the Investment Savings Planner, choose Financial **P**lanners from the Pl**a**n menu. Then select **S**avings. Quicken displays the Investment Savings Planner, shown in figure 18.7.

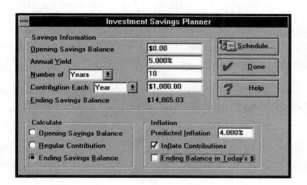

Fig. 18.7
The Investment Savings Planner performs several calculations to help you reach financial goals.

Performing Investment Planning Calculations

To use the Investment Savings Planner, follow these steps:

1. Access the Investment Savings Planner, as explained in the preceding section.

2. In the Calculate section, select the calculation that you want to perform.

To calculate how much money you need to start with to reach a certain goal, select the Opening Sa**v**ings Balance option.

To calculate how much money you need to contribute each period if you start with a certain amount and want to reach a specified goal, select the **R**egular Contribution option.

To calculate how much money you will have at the end of a specified period if you start with a certain amount and make regular contributions, choose the Ending Savings **B**alance option.

3. In the Savings Information section, enter the amounts needed for Quicken to perform its calculation. Use the drop-down lists provided for the **N**umber Of and Contrib**u**tion Each options to identify the type of savings periods you plan to use.

The information you are required to enter in the Savings Information section depends on the calculation that you perform in the Calculate section of the Investment Savings Planner. If you want to calculate the opening savings balance, for example, you must provide the annual yield that you expect to earn on your savings, the number of periods over which you expect to make contributions, the periods you plan to use to make the contributions, and the ending savings balance that you want to attain.

4. In the Inflation section, use the Predicted Inflation text box to enter the current or expected annual inflation rate.

5. Select the Inflate Contributions check box if you want Quicken to adjust the contributions that you make to your investment or savings account based on the inflation rate.

6. Select the Ending Balance in Today's $ check box if you want Quicken to convert the ending savings balance to its purchasing power today.

   As you enter amounts in the various text boxes and select options in the Investment Savings Planner, Quicken performs the calculation according to the option you selected in the Calculate section.

7. If you want to see a schedule of deposits or contributions that you need to make to attain your financial goal, choose the **S**chedule button. Quicken displays the Deposit Schedule, shown in figure 18.8. In figure 18.8, the schedule shows that if you contribute or deposit $1,000 each year, at an annual yield of 5% and an inflation rate of 4%, in 10 years your savings will grow to $14,865.03.

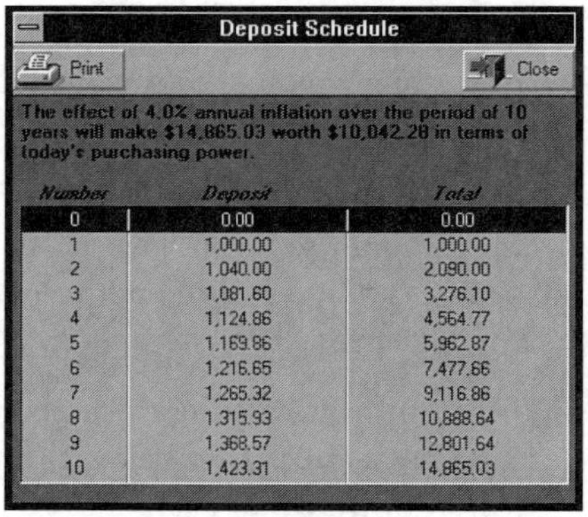

Fig. 18.8

The Deposit Schedule shows how your deposits or contributions to a savings plan grow.

The effect of 4.0% annual inflation over the period of 10 years will make $14,865.03 worth $10,042.28 in terms of today's purchasing power.

Number	Deposit	Total
0	0.00	0.00
1	1,000.00	1,000.00
2	1,040.00	2,090.00
3	1,081.60	3,276.10
4	1,124.86	4,564.77
5	1,169.86	5,962.87
6	1,216.65	7,477.66
7	1,265.32	9,116.86
8	1,315.93	10,888.64
9	1,368.57	12,801.64
10	1,423.31	14,865.03

Choose the **C**lose button to return to the Investment Savings Planner.

> **Note**
>
> If you want to print the Deposit Schedule, choose the **P**rint button. The printed Deposit Schedule lists the data in the Investment Savings Planner (opening savings balance, annual yield, number of years, and so forth), followed by the deposits and a running total for each year contributions are made.

8. When you return to the Investment Savings Planner, perform as many calculations as you want. When you are finished, choose Done.

Quicken doesn't save your calculations when you close the Investment Savings Planner. If you need to retain the calculation information, print the Deposit Schedule, as explained in the preceding note.

Planning for College

Financing a college education is no small investment. You no longer can wait until your kids are in high school to start thinking about where you're going to get the money to send them to college. With rising tuition costs, most people must save and invest for several years to have enough money to pay for college.

With Quicken's College Planner, you can determine how much you need to save each year for college, as well as how much tuition you can afford in the future based on the amount that you can afford to save today. You also can calculate how much you need to have invested or saved now to have enough to pay tuition when your child reaches college age.

> **Note**
>
> Quicken's College Planner assumes that you will continue to save until your child graduates from college. If your child is eight years old, for example, approximately 10 years remain until he or she starts college. But at least 14 years will pass until your child graduates from college. Therefore, the College Planner calculates present savings, current college costs, and yearly payments based on 14 years of savings, not 10.

Using the College Planner

To access the College Planner, select Financial **P**lanners from the Pl**a**n menu and then choose **C**ollege. Quicken displays the College Planner, shown in figure 18.9.

Fig. 18.9
The College Planner calculates how much you'll need for your child's college costs.

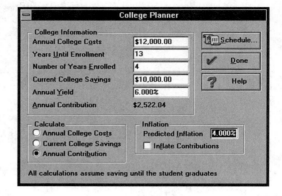

Performing College Planning Calculations

To perform calculations with the College Planner, follow these steps:

1. Access the College Planner, as explained in the preceding section.

2. In the Calculate section of the Planner, select the calculation that you want to perform.

To calculate how much you need to be able to afford annual college costs if you make a specific contribution each period, given that you start with a certain amount of savings, select the Annual College Cos**t**s option.

To calculate how much you need to have saved *now* to have enough for college costs, given an expected contribution each year, select the Cur-rent College Savin**g**s option.

To calculate how much you need to put away each year to have enough to cover all college costs if you start with a certain amount of savings, select the Annual Contri**b**ution option.

3. In the College Information section, enter the amounts needed for Quicken to perform its calculation. Check with the school's bursar's office to find out the current cost of tuition, room and board, and books.

If, for example, you select to calculate annual college costs, you must provide the annual yield you expect to earn on your contributions, the number of years enrolled, the number of years until enrollment, and the annual contribution you intend to make to your college fund.

4. In the Inflation section of the College Planner, enter the current or expected inflation rate in the Predicted **I**nflation text box.

5. Select the In**f**late Contributions check box to have Quicken adjust your contributions by the predicted inflation rate.

   As you enter amounts in the various text boxes and select options in the College Planner, Quicken performs the calculation according to the option you selected in the Calculate section.

6. If you want to see a schedule of deposits or contributions that you need to attain your college tuition goals, choose the **S**chedule button. Quicken displays the Deposit Schedule.

7. Choose the **C**lose button to return to the College Planner.

8. When you return to the College Planner, perform as many calculations as you want. When you're finished, choose Done.

Quicken doesn't save your calculations when you close the College Planner. If you need to retain the calculation information, print the Deposit Schedule as explained in the preceding note.

Planning for Retirement

Most people aspire to stop working some day so that they can enjoy their later years. Just because you stop working, however, doesn't mean your expenses also stop. How do you plan to pay for living expenses after the paycheck stops?

You may believe this topic to be of interest only to readers who are retiring soon, but this isn't the case. The irony is that the easiest time to prepare for retirement is when the time you stop working is still a long way off, and the hardest time to prepare for retirement is when retirement is right around the bend.

Using the Retirement Planner

Now you're ready to use the Retirement Planner to calculate any of the following variables:

- How much your current retirement account will yield annually when you retire based on yearly contributions, expected annual yields, and estimated income tax rates

- How much money you need *now* to accumulate the money you will need when you retire

- How much you need to contribute each year to your retirement account to ensure that you have enough money when you retire

Performing Retirement Planning Calculations

To perform the various retirement calculations, follow these steps:

1. Choose Financial **P**lanners from the Pl**a**n menu and then select **R**etirement. Quicken displays the Retirement Planner, shown in figure 18.10.

Fig. 18.10
Use the Retirement Planner to calculate how much you need to save to retire comfortably.

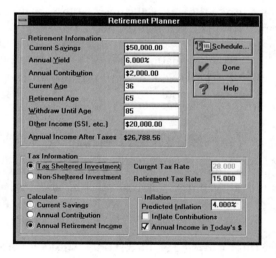

2. In the Calculate section, select the calculation that you want to perform.

   To calculate how much you need to have saved now to meet your annual retirement income goals if you contribute a specified amount, select the Current Savings option.

To calculate how much you need to contribute each year to meet your retirement goals, select the Annual Contribution option.

To calculate how much income you will have each year during retirement if you have a certain amount saved now and make specified contributions each period, select the Annual Retirement Income option.

3. In the Retirement Information box, enter the amounts needed for Quicken to perform its calculations.

4. In the Tax Information section, select the Tax Sheltered Investment option if your retirement investments are invested in a tax-deferred account, such as an IRA or a Keogh. Select the Non-Sheltered Investment option if your retirement investments are taxable.

5. In the Retirement Tax Rate text box, type your estimated tax rate when you retire. This rate may be tough to project because you really don't know where tax rates will be in the future. The best estimate, however, is today's tax rates, given your future level of income.

6. If you are calculating retirement income for nonsheltered investments, enter the applicable tax rate in Current Tax Rate text box. Quicken uses this rate to calculate the income tax effect on the earnings from your yearly contributions if your retirement account isn't tax sheltered. Type your current maximum tax rate without the percent sign. Because tax rates continually change, keep in mind that you may need to modify retirement planning results to take into consideration higher or lower tax rates.

7. In the Inflation section, enter the current or expected inflation rate in the Predicted Inflation text box. The *inflation rate* is the annual percentage rate that prices increase. The $2,000 that you contribute this year won't be the same as contributing $2,000 10 years from now.

8. Select the Inflate Contributions check box if you want Quicken to adjust your yearly contributions for inflation, or leave the check box blank to keep your contributions constant.

9. Select the Annual Income in Today's $ check box to have Quicken adjust the results of the calculation in today's dollars instead of their future value.

As you enter amounts in the various text boxes and select options in the Retirement Planner, Quicken performs the calculation according to the option you selected in the Calculate section.

Tip
If part of your projected retirement income is tax-sheltered and part isn't, make separate calculations using the Retirement Planner.

III

Planning for the Future

10. If you want to see a schedule of deposits or contributions that you need to attain your retirement income goals, choose the **S**chedule button. Quicken displays the Deposit Schedule that shows how your retirement fund balance changes if you make regular contributions.

11. Choose the **C**lose button to return to the Retirement Planner.

Quicken doesn't save your calculations when you close the Retirement Planner. If you need to retain the calculation information, print the Deposit Schedule as explained in an earlier note.

From Here...

After learning about Quicken's features for monitoring savings and planning for the future, you may want to review the following:

- Chapter 10, "Tracking Loans," shows you how to use the other two financial planners; the Loan Planner and the Refinance Planner.

- Chapter 17, "Budgeting with Quicken," explains how to use the Progress Bar to monitor budget categories or supercategories. In this chapter, you learned how to use the Progress Bar to monitor your savings.

Part IV

Analyzing Your Finances with Quicken for Windows

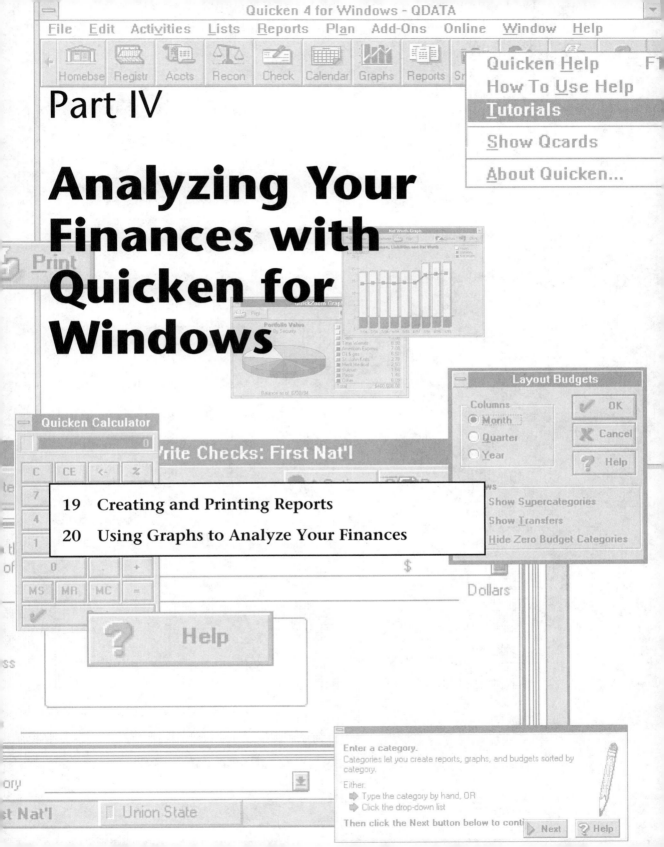

Quicken 4 for Windows - QDATA

File **Edit** **Activities** **Lists** **Reports** **Plan** **Add-Ons** **Online** **Window** **Help**

| Homebse | Registr | Accts | Recon | Check | Calendar | Graphs | Reports | Sr |

Quicken **H**elp
How To **U**se He
Tutorials
Show Qcards
About Quicken..

Print

Net Worth Graph

QuickZoom Grap
Portfolio Value
By Security

Quicken Calculator

| 0 |

C	CE	<-	%
7	8	9	/
4	5	6	×
1	2	3	-
0		.	+
MS	MR	MC	=
✓			

/rite Checks: First Nat'l

Delete

Options Rep

? Help

Pay to t
Order of

Date **5**/15,

$

Dollars

Address

Memo

Category ⊞

First Nat'l Union State

Layout Budgets

Columns
● **Month**
○ **Q**uarter
○ **Y**ear

✔ O
✖ Can
? He

Rows
☐ Show **S**upercategories
☐ Show **T**ransfers
☐ **H**ide Zero Budget Categorie

Enter a category.
Categories let you create reports, graphs, and budgets sorted by category.
Either:
➡ Type the category by hand, OR
➡ Click the drop-down list
Then click the Next button below to conti ▷ Next ? Help

Chapter 19

Creating and Printing Reports

When you collect information about your finances in a Quicken file, you essentially construct a database. You can use the information in a financial database to determine cash flow, net income or loss, tax deductions, and net worth. But first you must arrange, retrieve, and summarize the data. To do so, Quicken provides a variety of reports. This chapter describes how to create and print the reports you need to analyze your finances.

Creating and customizing reports is quick and easy. If you click the Reports button on the Iconbar, you instantly see the report list and a sample report. With the Customize button on the Report button bar, customizing reports is a breeze.

Quicken 4 for Windows includes a new report feature called *Snapshot reports*. Up to six different reports make up the Snapshot Report and are displayed on-screen at the same time. So with just the click of a button, you instantly can see up to six different aspects of your finances.

QuickReports sort through transactions and lists and instantly display reports relative to the current window or list. If you want to see a listing of all checks for contributions to your church, for example, highlight one transaction in the Register that contains your church as payee and choose the QuickReport button. Quicken displays a list of all transactions in the current year payable to the church.

In this chapter, you learn how to do the following:

- Set up Quicken to print reports

- Create Snapshot reports and QuickReports

- Create a report

- Print reports

- Customize reports

- Sort transactions in reports

- Examine report details with QuickZoom

- Memorize reports

- Set report options

An explanation of each report type is included at the end of this chapter.

Displaying Snapshots

Snapshots are reports displayed on-screen that reflect different aspects of your finances. Snapshot reports are displayed in the Snapshot window and can contain up to six different types of financial reports, like net worth, monthly income and expense, actual versus budget net income, and so forth. The beauty of the new Snapshots feature is that with the click of a button, you instantly have reports revealing your financial condition.

To display Snapshots, click the SnpShts button from the Iconbar or select **S**napshots from the **R**eports menu. Refer to figure 19.1 to see how Quicken displays Snapshots.

You can select the **C**ustomize button if you want to choose the number of reports that Quicken displays in the Snapshot window (up to six), select different reports to include, or change the reports in the Snapshot window from graph to text, or vice versa. If you select the **C**ustomize Snapshot button, Quicken lets you change the date range covered in reports, select whether to include subcategories, and select the accounts and categories to use in reports.

Select page

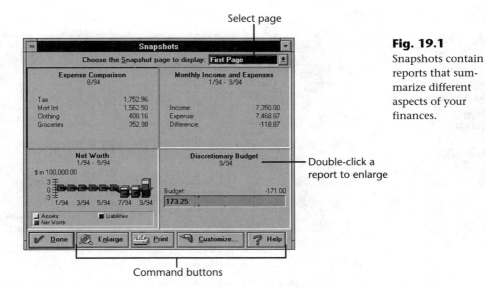

Fig. 19.1
Snapshots contain
reports that sum-
marize different
aspects of your
finances.

Double-click a
report to enlarge

Command buttons

Creating QuickReports

QuickReport enables you to get instant transaction listings relating to the
current window. QuickReports are available when you see the QuickReport
button, as shown in the Register in figure 19.2. (Although the button that
you see in the Register button bar is labeled Report, it is referred to as the
QuickReport button.)

You can create a QuickReport from the following lists or windows:

■ *Category & Transfer List*. Displays a list of transactions assigned to the
  selected category, subcategory, or transfer account. Refer to Chapter 4,
  "Organizing Your Finances," to learn how to create a QuickReport from
  the Category & Transfer List.

■ *Class List*. Displays a list of transactions assigned to the selected class.
  Refer to Chapter 4, "Organizing Your Finances," to learn how to create
  a QuickReport from the Class List.

■ *Memorized Transaction List*. Displays a list of all transactions that contain the selected memorized payee.

■ *Register window*. Displays a list of all transactions that contain the same
  payee as the selected transaction. Chapter 6, "Using the Register," explains how to create a QuickReport from the Register.

QuickReport button

Fig. 19.2
Choose the
QuickReport
button in the
Register button
bar to create an
instant report of all
transactions that
contain the same
payee as the selec-
ted transaction.

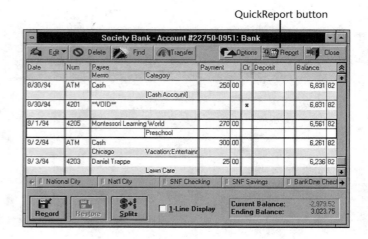

- *Portfolio View window.* For investment accounts, displays a list of all transactions for the selected security. See Chapter 16, "Monitoring Your Investments," to learn how to create a QuickReport from the Portfolio View of an investment account.

When you choose the QuickReport button, Quicken filters transactions in all accounts and displays a listing of transactions that match the list item (for QuickReports from the Category & Transfer List, the Class List, and the Memorized Transaction List), payee (for QuickReports from the Register), or security (for QuickReports from the Portfolio View of an investment account).

Figure 19.3 shows the transaction listing displayed when QuickReport is se-lected for a transaction in the Register that contains the payee *Montessori Learning World*.

Fig. 19.3
Select a transaction
in the Register
and choose the
QuickReport
button to display
a listing of all
transactions with
the same payee
as the selected
transaction.

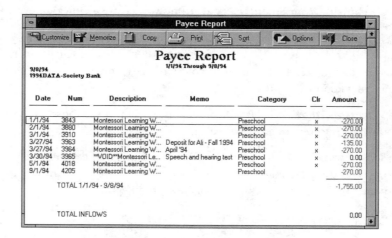

Creating and Reviewing Reports

In this section, you learn how to create any of the 23 preset reports that Quicken provides, such as the Cash Flow Report, Monthly Budget Report, and Net Worth Report. Quicken defines the format of preset reports, but you can customize any preset report to include the information you need. Quicken's preset reports are listed in the **R**eports menu as **H**ome, **I**nvestment, and **B**usiness.

Quicken also enables you to create custom reports from scratch that do the following:

- List specific transactions

- Summarize transaction data by category, class, payee, or account

- Compare data from one period to another

- Compare actual data to budget data

- List the balances in accounts

Custom reports are listed in the **R**eports menu as **O**ther.

In the following sections, you learn how to create a basic report, review the report on-screen, and use the Report button bar to perform actions on the report that you create.

Creating a Report

The following steps show you how to create a Quicken report. Although the reports may differ, the steps for creating reports are the same. If you want to learn about an individual report and what it contains, refer to the sections at the end of this chapter that describe each report.

You can create a report by clicking the Reports button on the Iconbar or by choosing a report from the **R**eports menu, as discussed in the next two sections.

Using the Reports Button on the Iconbar

To create a report using the Reports button on the Iconbar, follow these steps:

1. Click the Reports button on the Iconbar to display the Create Report dialog box, shown in figure 19.4. The Create Report dialog box includes the date range that Quicken uses to create the report and a listing of each report by family: **H**ome, **I**nvestment, **B**usiness, Oth**e**r, and **M**emorized. (You learn about memorized reports later in this chapter.)

Fig. 19.4
Click the Reports button on the Iconbar to display the Create Report dialog box.

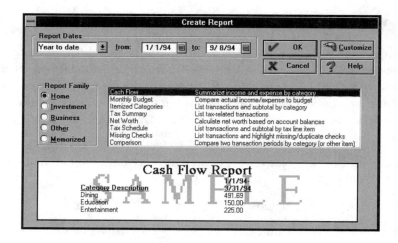

Tip
Use + and – to change the **F**rom, **T**o, and **A**s Of dates one day at a time. Or click the Calendar button in the date boxes to use the mini-calendar.

2. By default, Quicken creates a report from the first day of the current year to today. Or, if reporting on account balances as of a specific day (in net worth reports, for example), Quicken uses today as the default "as of" day. The default dates that Quicken uses to create the report appear in the Report Dates section.

   If necessary, change the dates in the **F**rom and **T**o drop-down list boxes to the date range you want the report to cover. If you are creating a report that shows account balances as of a specific date (like the Net Worth Report), change the **A**s Of date. You can also select a preset date range in the drop-down list box (such as Month to Date, Quarter to Date, Year to Date, and so forth).

3. From the Report Family options, select the report family to display the available reports.

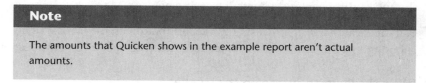

Note

The amounts that Quicken shows in the example report aren't actual amounts.

4. To create the report, double-click a report name, or highlight a report name and then choose OK or press Enter. Quicken creates and displays the selected report in a report window. Figure 19.5 shows the report window for the Cash Flow Report.

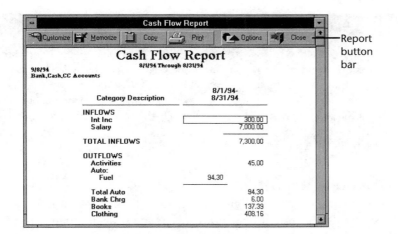

Fig. 19.5

The report appears in a report window.

——Report button bar

> **Note**
>
> You can customize your reports in many different ways, including choosing to include only certain transactions (filtering), changing other options such as the date range, and sorting transaction in different orders. See the sections "Filtering Transactions in Reports," "Customizing Reports," and "Sorting Report Data," respectively, to learn how to manipulate your reports in different ways.

5. To remove the report from your screen, choose the Close button from the Report button bar.

Using the Reports Menu

You also can create a report using the **R**eports menu, which includes a submenu with each report. Follow these steps to create a report from the Reports menu:

1. From the **R**eports menu, choose the report family for the report you want to create. Quicken displays a submenu for the report family that lists each report in that family. If you choose **H**ome from the **R**eports menu, for example, Quicken displays a submenu that lists each Home report that you can create.

2. From the submenu, choose the report you want to create—for example, Cash **F**low to create the Cash Flow Report.

Quicken creates the report for the period from the beginning of the year to the current date.

> **Note**
>
> If you want Quicken to display the Create Report dialog box (see fig. 19.4) when you choose a report from the Reports menu, you can set a report option that tells Quicken whether to skip the Create Report dialog box. When this option is on, Quicken creates the report using the default date range and does not display the Create Report dialog box (fig. 19.4). Refer to the section "Setting Report Options" later in this chapter.

Viewing a Report

You learned how to create Quicken reports so that they appear on-screen. Most reports that you display, however, are too wide or too long to fit entirely in the boundaries of your screen.

To view the entire length of a report on-screen, drag the scroll box in the scroll bar on the right side of the report window up or down. To view the entire width of a report, drag the scroll box in the scroll bar at the bottom of the report window left or right. You also can enlarge the report window as you can any window.

You also can use the keyboard to view reports on-screen, as follows:

Press	To View
→	One column to the right
←	One column to the left
PgUp	Up one screen
PgDn	Down one screen

Using the Report Button Bar

At the top of all report windows is a Report button bar you can use to perform activities after a report is created. The Report button bar has the following buttons:

Customize   Displays the Customize Report dialog box, which you can use to change report criteria. Refer to the "Customizing Reports" section later in this chapter to learn how to change reports.

Memorize | Memorizes the displayed report and its report settings so that you can recall the report the next time you need it. Refer to the "Using Memorized Reports" section later in this chapter to learn how to memorize and recall a report.

Copy | Copies the contents of the displayed report to the Windows Clipboard. Then you can paste the report to another Windows application.

Print | Prints the displayed report. Refer to the "Printing Reports" section later to learn how to print a report.

Sort | Changes the order of transactions in the displayed report by account, date, check number, amount, payee, or category. Note that this button is available only for transaction reports (reports that list transactions). Refer to the "Sorting Report Data" section later in this chapter to learn how to sort transactions.

Options | Displays the Report Options dialog box so that you can change report options. Refer to the section, "Setting Report Options," later in this chapter to learn how to use this button.

Close | Removes the report from your screen.

Tracking Personal Finances with Home Reports

You can select from eight reports in the Home reports family. To see a sample of each report, follow these steps:

1. Click the Reports button on the Iconbar to display the Create Report dialog box (refer to fig. 19.4).

2. Select the **H**ome option in the Report Family box. Quicken lists the following home reports by title and description:

- Cash Flow

- Monthly Budget

- Itemized Categories

- Tax Summary

- Net Worth

- Tax Schedule

- Missing Checks

- Comparison

3. Choose the report for which you want to see a sample. Quicken shows a sample report at the bottom of the Create Report dialog box.

The Cash Flow Report

The Cash Flow Report shows the total cash inflows and outflows by category. The home Cash Flow Report shows transfers to and from other accounts and includes transactions from all bank, cash, and credit card accounts in the current Quicken file. The Cash Flow Report can be extremely valuable. This report shows the various categories of cash flowing into and out of your personal bank accounts, cash accounts, and credit card accounts.

The Monthly Budget Report

The Monthly Budget Report shows actual income and expenses and budgeted income and expenses over a specified period. The Monthly Budget Report also shows the comparison between the actual and budgeted amounts and calculates the differences. This report includes transactions from all the bank, cash, and credit card accounts in the current Quicken file.

To produce a Monthly Budget Report, you must first set up your budget. Refer to Chapter 17, "Budgeting with Quicken," if you need information on setting up a budget. Chapter 17 also shows you an example of a Monthly Budget Report.

The Itemized Category Report

The Itemized Category Report shows each transaction in the current Quicken file sorted and subtotaled by category. This type of report provides a convenient way to see the detailed transactions that add up to a category total.

The Itemized Category Report resembles the cash flow report in purpose and information, except that the Itemized Category Report doesn't include account transfers. If you want to see your cash inflows and outflows grouped and summarized by category, this is the report you choose.

> **Note**
>
> You can replace the default report title, Itemized Category Report, with a more specific title (such as Personal Itemized Category Report) by typing a new Title in the Report Layout section of the Customize Report dialog box. (The Report Layout section appears when you select the Report Layout customize option in the Customize Report dialog box.) You also can specify a range of months in the report.

The Tax Summary Report

The Tax Summary Report—a handy tax-preparation tool to use at the end of the year—summarizes the taxable income items and the tax deductions you need to report on your federal and state income tax returns. The Tax Summary Report shows all the transactions assigned to categories you marked as tax-related. Transactions are sorted and subtotaled by category.

> **Note**
>
> The Tax Summary Report summarizes tax deductions paid with only the bank accounts, cash accounts, and credit card accounts you choose to track with Quicken. If you write tax-deductible checks from two checking accounts but track only one of the accounts with Quicken, for example, you miss some deductions. Refer to Chapter 12, "Estimating and Preparing for Income Taxes," to learn more about the Tax Summary Report.

The Net Worth Report

The Net Worth Report shows the balance on a particular date for each account in your Quicken file. If the file includes all your assets and liabilities, the resulting report is a balance sheet that provides an estimate of your financial net worth. (Balance sheets are described in Chapter 11, "Managing Your Assets and Other Liabilities.")

Net worth is the difference between your total assets and total liabilities. If you own more assets than liabilities, you have a positive net worth. If you own fewer assets than liabilities, you have a negative net worth.

When creating a Net Worth Report, you enter only one date instead of a range of dates. The Net Worth Report doesn't report on activity for a period of time. Instead, it provides a snapshot of the account balances in your Quicken file at one point in time.

The Tax Schedule Report

The Tax Schedule Report summarizes tax-related categories in a way that makes preparing every common income tax schedule easy. By using category information, Quicken adds the transactions that go on each line of each tax schedule. Chapter 12, "Estimating and Preparing for Income Taxes," describes this handy report.

The Missing Checks Report

The Missing Checks Report displays a list of all checking account transactions in check number order with any gaps in the check number sequence identified. The gaps represent a missing check or checks you may need to investigate.

The Comparison Report

The Comparison Report compares income and expenses by category (or other items you select) for two time periods. You can compare, for example, your utility bills for December of last year and this year.

Tracking Investments with Investment Reports

You can select from five reports in the Investment reports family. To see a sample of each report, follow these steps:

1. Click the Reports button on the Iconbar to display the Create Report dialog box (refer to fig. 19.4).

2. Select the **I**nvestment option in the Report Family box. Quicken lists the following reports by title and description:

   - Portfolio Value

   - Investment Performance

   - Capital Gains

   - Investment Income

   - Investment Transactions

3. Choose the report for which you want to see a sample. Quicken shows a sample report at the bottom of the Create Report dialog box. Refer to

Chapter 16, "Monitoring Your Investments," to learn more about the information provided in investment reports.

The Portfolio Value Report

A Portfolio Value Report shows the estimated market value on a specific date of each security in your Quicken investment accounts. To estimate the market values, Quicken uses each security's individual *price history* (a list of prices on certain dates).

Quicken determines which price to use by comparing the date in the report to the dates that have prices in the price history. Ideally, Quicken uses a price for the same date as the date you specify. When the price history doesn't contain a price for the specified date, Quicken uses the price for the date closest to that date.

The Investment Performance Report

Investment Performance Reports help you measure how well or how poorly your investments are doing. These reports look at all the transactions for a security and then calculate an annual rate of return—in effect, the interest rate an investment has paid you.

The date range you use in the investment performance report tells Quicken which time frame you want to use to calculate investment returns. Quicken notifies you if one or more of the total return calculations can't be completed and displays the value as NA.

The Capital Gains Report

The Capital Gains Report attempts to print all the information you need to complete the Schedule D federal income tax form. Taxpayers use Schedule D to report capital gains and losses.

The Investment Income Report

The Investment Income Report summarizes all the income transactions you recorded in one or more of the investment accounts.

Realized gains and losses result when the investment is sold and cash is received. Quicken calculates a realized gain or loss by comparing the cash received on sale with the original cost of the investment. Unrealized gains and losses result when the cost of the investment is compared with the market value to determine what the gain or loss would have been if the investment had been sold.

The Investment Transactions Report

The Investment Transactions Report lists each investment transaction in the Register. Use this report to review your transactions to make sure that you've accurately reflected all security transactions in your investment accounts.

Tracking Business Finances with Business Reports

You can select from nine reports in the Business reports family. To see a sample of each report, follow these steps:

1. Click the Reports button on the Iconbar to display the Create Report dialog box (refer to fig. 19.4).

2. Select the **B**usiness option in the Report Family box. Quicken lists the following business reports by title and description:

    - P&L Statement
    - P&L Comparison
    - Cash Flow
    - A/P by Vendor
    - A/R by Customer
    - Job/Project
    - Payroll
    - Balance Sheet
    - Missing Checks
    - Comparison

3. Choose the report for which you want to see a sample. Quicken shows a sample report at the bottom of the Create Report dialog box.

The P&L Statement

The P&L (profit and loss) statement, also known as an *income statement*, shows the total monthly income and expenses by category for all accounts. Data from transactions from any account in the current Quicken file are included, but transfers between accounts aren't.

CPA Tip: Using a P&L Statement

The profit and loss statement is one of your business's most used and important financial reports. It reports your net income or net loss for a specific time period (month, quarter, year, and so on). Remember that the sales revenue and expenses on the profit and loss statement aren't the same as the cash inflows from sales and cash outflows for expenses for the period. Create a Cash Flow Report to show the cash position of your business.

The P&L Comparison Report

This new report shows a comparison of profit and loss for the current month (or any other month you want to select) and the profit for the entire year.

The Cash Flow Report

A Cash Flow Report resembles a profit and loss statement. This report includes all bank, cash, and credit card accounts and shows the money received (inflows) and the money spent (outflows) by category for each month. The cash flow report also shows transfers between accounts.

The differences between the Cash Flow Report and the P&L Statement are that the Cash Flow Report shows transfers to other accounts and groups cash inflows together and cash outflows together. The difference between cash inflows and outflows is the overall total, which may be positive or negative.

CPA Tip: Monitoring Cash Flow

Cash flow is just as important as profits, particularly over shorter time periods. Besides making money, businesses need to have cash to buy inventory or equipment, to have as working capital while they wait for customers to pay their bills, and to pay back loans from banks and vendors. The Cash Flow Report, which summarizes your cash inflows and outflows by category and account, provides a method for monitoring your cash flow and pinpointing problems.

The A/P by Vendor Report

Because Quicken uses what is called *cash-basis accounting*, expenses are recorded only when you pay your bill. By not paying bills or by paying bills late, your net income or profit and your net cash flow may look better. The problem, however, is that this concept is illogical. Just because you haven't paid a bill by the end of the month doesn't mean the bill shouldn't be considered in assessing the month's financial performance.

Tip
A/P is an abbreviation for *accounts payable*—the unpaid bills of a business.

To address this shortcoming partially, Quicken provides the A/P by Vendor Report, which enables you to see which bills haven't been paid. The A/P by Vendor Report lists all the unprinted checks, sorted and subtotaled by payee.

The A/R by Customer Report

The A/R by Customer Report shows the transactions sorted and subtotaled by payee in all asset accounts. The report doesn't include transactions marked as cleared—that is, transactions marked with an asterisk (*) or x in the Clr field of the Register.

CPA Tip: Using Aging Reports

Good collection procedures usually improve cash flows dramatically, so consider using the customer-aging report as a collection guide. You may want to telephone any customer with an invoice 30 days past due, stop granting additional credit to any customer with invoices more than 60 days past due, and initiate collection procedures for any customer with invoices more than 90 days past due (in the absence of special circumstances).

The Job/Project Report

The Job/Project Report shows category totals by month for each month in the specified date range. The report also shows account balances at the end of the last month. If you are using classes, the report shows category totals by class in separate columns across the report page. The Job/Project Report helps business owners track income and expenses by job, project, customer, or client. This is called *job costing*.

The Payroll Report

The Payroll Report shows the total amounts paid to individual payees when the transaction category begins with the word *payroll*. The Payroll Report includes transactions from all accounts.

CPA Tip: Creating a Payroll Report for W-2 Forms

At the end of the calendar year, create a Payroll Report to help you complete your W-2 forms. Make sure that the time period covered by the report is for the full calendar year (1/1/94 to 12/31/94, for example). The Payroll Report shows the total gross wages paid to each employee and his or her total withholdings (federal, Social Security, state, local, and so on).

You must send a W-2 form by January 31 of the following calendar year to each person you employed at any time during the previous calendar year.

The Balance Sheet

The balance sheet shows the account balances for all accounts in the current Quicken file at a specific time. If the file includes accounts for all your assets and liabilities, the resulting report is a balance sheet that shows the net worth of your business. (Chapter 11, "Managing Your Assets and Other Liabilities," describes balance sheets in more detail.)

Note

Even for small businesses, balance sheets are important reports. Because a balance sheet shows what a business owns and owes, balance sheets give an indication of the financial strength or weakness of a business. The smaller the total liabilities amount in relation to the total assets amount, the stronger the business. And the larger the total liabilities in relation to the total assets, the weaker the business. As a result of these and similar financial insights, banks usually require a balance sheet to evaluate loan applications from businesses.

CPA Tip: Using a Balance Sheet

The balance sheet measures the value of your business at one moment in time. Asset amounts represent values based on original cost rather than replacement costs or earning power (unless you entered any amount other than original costs for assets in Quicken). Liabilities represent the legal claims of creditors who have loaned you money or the unpaid goods or services provided to you. Owner's equity, or net worth, represents a claim resulting from the capital invested by the owners of the business and past profits retained in the business.

The Missing Checks Report

The Missing Checks Report displays a list of all checking account transactions in check number order with any gaps in the check number sequence identified. The gaps represent a missing check or checks you may need to investigate.

The Comparison Report

The Comparison Report compares income and expenses by category (or by another item you select) for two time periods. You can compare, for example, revenues for the first quarter of this year to revenues for the first quarter of last year.

Examining Other Reports

You can select from five reports in the Other reports family. To see a sample of each report, follow these steps:

1. Click the Reports button on the Iconbar to display the Create Report dialog box (refer to fig. 19.4).

2. Select the Other option in the Report Family box. Quicken lists the other reports by title and description as follows:

   - Transactions

   - Summary

   - Comparison

   - Budget

   - Account Balances

3. Select the report for which you want to see a sample. Quicken shows a sample report at the bottom of the Create Report dialog box.

The Other reports family consists of transaction, summary, comparison, budget, and account balance reports. You can use any report option as a template to create a specific report to meet your needs. You may want to list your Register transactions in an order other than chronologically, for example. You may find value in sorting and summarizing transactions by payee or by time periods such as a week or a month, for example. The transaction report enables you to see your account transactions in any of these ways.

Summary Reports extract information from the financial database you create in Quicken's Register. A Summary Report gives you totals by category, class, payee, or account, in addition to any other subtotals you request.

The Comparison Report compares income and expenses by category, class, payee, or account. Comparisons are made between two periods that you specify and the difference is shown in dollars or as a percentage.

Budgeting is a fundamental tool that businesses and individuals use to better manage their finances. One of the ongoing steps in using a budget as a tool is to compare the amount you received as income with the amount you planned to receive and to compare the amount you spent with the amount you planned to spend, or budgeted. The Budget Report enables you to create budget reports tailored to your business or personal needs.

The Account Balances Report shows the balance in your accounts for a specific date. If you have extensive investments with several brokers, for example, and want a report that specifies only those accounts, you can create an Account Balances Report (or a specialized version of this report).

Printing Reports

After you create a report, you can print it or save it to a disk file to be used in another application. Printing reports provides you with a hard copy of your data for the specified period. Reports that you create in Quicken can be useful in providing your bank, creditors, and even the IRS with important financial information.

Setting Up Quicken to Print a Report

Before you can print reports in Quicken, you must set up the program to print to your printer. Quicken includes different printer settings for reports (**R**eport/Graph Printer Setup) and for checks (**C**heck Printer Setup). This section shows you how to set up Quicken to print reports.

To set up Quicken to print reports, follow these steps:

1. From the **F**ile menu, choose Printer **S**etup. Quicken displays the Printer Setup submenu.

2. Choose **R**eport/Graph Printer Setup. Quicken displays the Report Printer Setup dialog box, shown in figure 19.6.

3. Select your installed printer from the **P**rinter drop-down list.

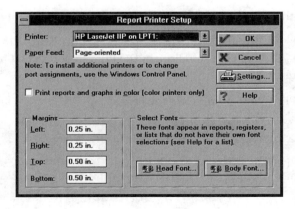

Fig. 19.6

The Report Printer Setup dialog box tells Quicken the printer, type of paper, report margins, and font you are using.

4. Quicken uses Auto-detect to determine whether your printer is continuous-feed or page-oriented. If the paper feed isn't correct, select the appropriate paper feed for your installed printer from the Paper Feed drop-down list.

5. If you are using a color printer and want to print reports in color, select the Print Reports and Graphs in Color check box.

6. Check the Left, Right, Top, and Bottom margins. If necessary, enter larger or smaller values than the preset values that Quicken uses.

7. (Optional) If you want to change the font for the heading or body of the report, choose Head Font or Body Font. Quicken displays the Report Default Headline Font dialog box or the Report Default Font dialog box, from which you can change the font type, font style, and font size. When the heading and body fonts are the way you want them, choose OK to return to the Report Printer Setup dialog box.

8. (Optional) You also can change other print settings, such as the paper tray, paper size, orientation, and number of copies. To change these settings, choose the Settings button. Quicken displays a dialog box for your installed printer. Make the necessary changes and choose OK to return to the Report Printer Setup dialog box.

9. Choose OK to save the printer settings.

Printing a Report

No matter which Quicken report you want to print, you must take the same basic steps, as follows:

1. Create the report you want to print, as explained earlier in this chapter.

2. With the report on-screen, choose the Print button from the button bar (or press Ctrl+P). Quicken displays the Print Report dialog box, shown in figure 19.7.

3. In the Print To section, select the Printer option.

> **Note**
>
> If you want to see a preview of the report on-screen before you print, select the Preview button. Quicken shows the report in the Print Preview window as it appears when printed (using the selected fonts and type size).

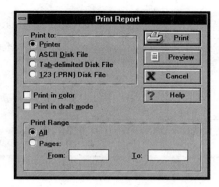

Fig. 19.7
Choose Print from
the Report button
bar to display the
Print Report dialog
box.

4. If you have a color printer and want to print the report in color, select
the Print in **C**olor check box.

5. Select the Print in Draft **M**ode check box, if desired, and if your installed printer supports draft mode printing.

6. Choose the print range. Select the **A**ll option to print all pages of the
report. Otherwise, select the Pa**g**es option and specify the pages you
want to print.

7. Choose the **P**rint button to begin printing the report.

Saving a Report to a Disk File

If you want to use report data in a Windows program, you can save the
report to an ASCII disk file, a tab-delimited disk file, or a Lotus 1-2-3 (.PRN)
disk file.

> **Note**
>
> If you want to use report data in another Windows-compatible program, such as
> Word for Windows or Excel for Windows, use the Cop**y** button from the Report
> button bar to copy the report to the Windows Clipboard.

Complete the following steps to save a report to a disk file:

1. With the report on-screen, choose the Pri**n**t button from the Report
button bar (or press Ctrl+P). Quicken displays the Print Report dialog
box (refer to fig. 19.7).

2. In the Print To section, choose one of the following file formats to save
the report:

ASCII **D**isk File	Saves the report in standardized text format to be used in a word processing program, such as Microsoft Word or WordPerfect.
Ta**b**-delimited Disk File	Saves the report in tab-delimited text format (data items are separated by tab keystrokes to simulate ASCII file format), also to be used in a word-processing program.
123 (.PRN) Disk File	Saves the report to a disk file that can be used in Lotus 1-2-3 or a Lotus-compatible spreadsheet.

3. Choose the **P**rint button. Quicken displays the Create Disk File dialog box.

4. In the File **N**ame text box, type the name of the file to which you want to export the report.

5. If necessary, change the directory and drive where you are sending the report in the **D**irectory list box and the Dri**v**es drop-down list.

6. Choose OK to save the report to a disk file with the name you specified.

Customizing Reports

You already learned how to create a report in Quicken. But what if you want to restrict transactions to those with a particular payee or assigned to certain categories, or what if you want to exclude certain accounts from the report? You can customize each Quicken report so that the report includes the information that is most useful to you. The C**u**stomize button on the Report button bar enables you to modify reports so that Quicken provides the information you want in the format you want.

You can perform the following actions when customizing a report:

■ Change the report layout to rename the report, rearrange the report with different row and column headings, change the accounting organization (income and expense, cash flow basis, net worth format, or balance sheet format), or choose the way Quicken displays the report data (amounts in dollars or amounts in dollars and cents, for example).

■ Choose the account to include in the report.

■ Choose the transactions to include in the report. You can exclude transactions whose amounts are below a specified level, for example, or you can include only payments, deposits, or unprinted checks.

■ Choose the information shown in rows in the report. You can exclude all transfers, hide all subcategories, or include only budgeted categories in reports, for example.

■ Choose the categories and classes to include in the report.

■ Filter or limit transactions in the report to include only the transactions that meet your criteria.

To customize a report, follow these steps:

1. Create a report, as explained earlier in this chapter, to display the Report window.

2. Choose the Customize command button to display the Customize Report dialog box. Note that Quicken inserts the name of the report that you created in step 1 in the title bar. Thus, when you select the Customize button from the Cash Flow Report window, for example, Quicken displays the Customize Cash Flow Report dialog box. You can also select to customize a report by choosing the Customize button from the Create Report dialog box (refer to fig. 19.4).

3. The default report dates are entered in the Report Dates section. Change the date range, if necessary, as explained earlier in the section "Creating a Report."

4. The left side of the Customize Report dialog box lists the customize options available for the selected report. Select the appropriate option from the Customize section.

On the right side of the dialog box, Quicken displays the settings you can change for the selected customize option. As figure 19.8 shows, if you select the Report Layout option from the Customize section, Quicken shows the report layout settings you can change.

5. Change the report settings as desired. The following sections explain how to change report settings for each customize option in the Customize Report dialog box.

6. Choose OK to redisplay the report using the report settings you entered.

Tip

When you select an option, a message appears at the bottom of the dialog telling you what the option does.

Fig. 19.8
When you select
Report Layout,
Quicken displays
the report settings
you can change.

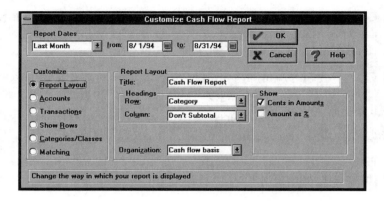

Changing the Report Layout

As mentioned, when you select the Report Layout customize option, the
right side of the Customize dialog box displays the Report Layout box with
the report settings you can change (refer to fig. 19.8).

Depending on the type of report you are customizing, Quicken enables you
to change the settings shown in table 19.1.

Table 19.1   Report Layout Settings

Report Setting	Options
Title	You can enter the title that you want to appear at the top of the report. The title can include numbers, letters, and other characters (up to 39 characters). If you don't enter a title, Quicken uses the report type title, such as Cash Flow Report or Net Worth Report.
Row Headings (for summary reports only)	Category Class Payee Account
Column Headings (for summary, budget, and account balance reports)	Don't Subtotal Week (Sunday through Saturday) Two Weeks (starts on Sunday) Half Month (the first through the fifteenth) Month Quarter (includes three consecutive months) Half Year (starts on the starting date and ends on the last day of the month five months later) Year (starts on the starting date for 365 days or 366 days in a leap year) Category Class Payee Account

Report Setting	Options
Subtotal By (for transaction reports only)	Don't Subtotal Week (Sunday through Saturday) Two Weeks (starts on Sunday) Half Month (the first through the fifteenth) Month Quarter (includes three consecutive months) Half Year (starts on the starting date and ends on the last day of the month five months later) Year (starts on the starting date for 365 days or 366 days in a leap year) Category Class Payee Account Tax schedule
Interval (for account balances reports)	None Week (Sunday through Saturday) Two Weeks (starts on Sunday) Half Month (the first through the fifteenth) Month Quarter (includes three consecutive months) Half Year (starts on the starting date and ends on the last day of the month five months later) Year (starts on the starting date for 365 days or 366 days in a leap year)
Sort By (for transaction reports only)	None Date/Acct Acct/Chk # Amount Payee Category
Organization	Income and expense Cash flow basis Net worth Balance sheet
Show Cents in Amounts	Select to show amounts in dollars and cents
Show Amount as % (for summary reports only)	Select to show amounts in relative terms, as percentages of the total
Show Difference as a % (for comparison reports only)	Select to show the difference as a percentage from the first category comparison to the second
Show Difference in $ (for comparison reports only)	Select to show the difference as dollars from the first category to the second

(continues)

Analyzing Your Finances

IV

Table 19.1	Continued	
Report Setting	**Options**
Show Totals Only (for transaction reports only)	Select to display only the total dollar amount of transactions that meet the criteria you specify
Show **M**emo (for transaction reports only)	Select to include a column for memos
Show Cat**e**gory (for transaction reports only)	Select to include a column for categories
Show S**p**lit Transaction (for transaction reports only)	Select to include the detail from the Splits Detail window

Selecting Accounts to Include in Reports

Although Quicken preselects the accounts used in reports, you can customize the report and select the accounts you want to use.

To select the accounts to include in reports, follow these steps:

1. From the Customize Report dialog box (refer to fig. 19.8), select the **A**ccounts customize option. Quicken displays the Accounts Used section with the list of accounts, as shown in figure 19.9.

Fig. 19.9
When you select **A**ccounts, Quicken displays the list of accounts you can include in the report.

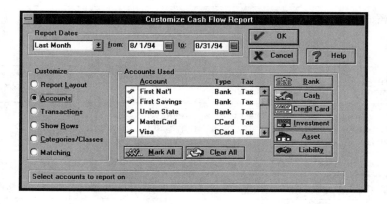

2. Quicken preselects accounts based on the report you create. For a Cash Flow Report, for example, Quicken selects all bank, cash, and credit card accounts. Accounts selected are marked with a check mark to the left of the account name.

To select an account, click it, or highlight the account and press the spacebar. To select all accounts, choose the **M**ark All button.

3. Choose OK to redisplay the report using the selected accounts.

Selecting Transactions to Include in Reports

Normally, Quicken searches all transactions in the selected accounts to create a report. You can customize the report, however, so that Quicken uses only transactions you specify.

To select transactions to include in reports, follow these steps:

1. From the Customize Report dialog box (refer to fig. 19.8), select the Transacti**o**ns customize option. Quicken displays the Select Transactions section with the report settings you can change, as shown in figure 19.10.

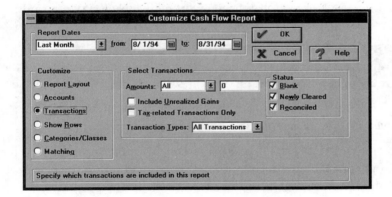

2. To include transactions in a report based on the transaction amount, select All, Less Than, Equal To, or Greater Than from the A**m**ounts drop-down list box. Then enter the amount you want transaction amounts compared to. If you want to include only transactions over $25, for example, select Greater Than and type **25**.

3. If you have investment accounts, select the Include **U**nrealized Gains check box if you want Quicken to include the impact of price increases and decreases for securities in a report.

Tip
To select all accounts in an account type (such as all bank accounts), choose the account type button to the right of the Accounts Used section.

Fig. 19.10
Choose the transaction criteria for a report in the Select Transactions section.

IV

Analyzing Your Finances

4. To include only transactions that are assigned to a tax-related category or subcategory, select the Include Tax-Related Transactions Only check box.

5. Select the transaction types you want to include in the report in the Transactions **T**ypes drop-down list box: Payments, Deposits, Unprinted Checks, or All Transactions.

6. In the Status section, select **B**lank to include transactions without an entry in the Clr field, Ne**w**ly Cleared to include transactions with an asterisk (*) in the Clr field, or R**e**conciled to include transactions with an x in the Clr field.

> **Note**
>
> Quicken includes all transactions in reports, regardless of their cleared status. You shouldn't change the status settings for a report unless you are specifically creating a report to show the cleared status of transactions.

7. Choose OK to redisplay the report using the selected transactions.

Changing Row Information in Reports

You can change the items included as rows in a report by customizing the report. If you select to report on categories, for example, Quicken includes all the category names as row headings in the report.

To change row information in reports, follow these steps:

1. From the Customize Report dialog box, select the Show **R**ows customize option. Quicken displays the Show Rows section with the report settings you can change, as shown in figure 19.11.

Fig. 19.11
Select the information you want to appear as row headings in the Show Rows section.

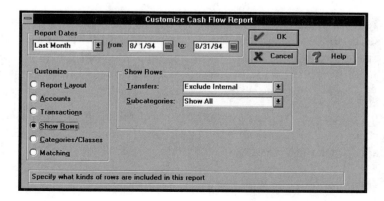

2. From the **T**ransfers drop-down list, select Include All, Exclude All, or Exclude Internal (excludes transfers between accounts included in the report).

3. From the **S**ubcategories drop-down list, select Show All, Hide All, or Show Reversed (displays subcategories with the main categories grouped under them).

4. Choose OK to redisplay the report using the selected rows.

Selecting Categories and Classes to Include in Reports

To select the categories and classes included in a report, follow these steps:

1. From the Customize Report dialog box, select the **C**ategories/Classes customize option. Quicken displays the Select to Include section, which lists the categories and classes (see fig. 19.12).

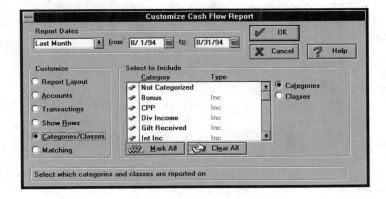

Fig. 19.12
Select the categories and classes you want to include in a report in the Select to Include list box.

2. Select the Cat**e**gories option to show categories in the list. Select the Cla**s**ses option to show classes in the list.

3. Select a category or class from the list. To choose all categories or classes, choose the **M**ark All button. To select a single category or class, click the item or highlight the item and press the spacebar. To deselect a category or class, repeat the select procedure.

Tip
Select only the Not Categorized item from the category list to include only transactions without a category assigned.

Note

When choosing categories, you also can move to the bottom of the category list and select or deselect accounts so that transfers between specific accounts and the accounts included in the report are included or excluded.

4. Choose OK to redisplay the report using the selected categories and/or classes.

Filtering Transactions in Reports

Quicken enables you to specify which transactions to include in a report by specifying criteria that transactions must meet before being included in a report. You can tell Quicken to include only transactions that contain a certain payee, category, class, or memo.

To filter transactions in reports, follow these steps:

1. From the Customize Report dialog box, select the Matching customize option. Quicken displays the Include Transactions If section with the settings you can specify when filtering transactions (see fig. 19.13).

Fig. 19.13
In the Include Transactions If section, define or limit transactions in reports by setting the criteria a transaction must meet to be included.

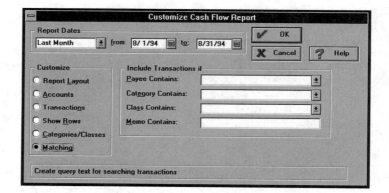

2. In the **P**ayee Contains, Cat**e**gory Contains, or Cla**s**s Contains drop-down list box, enter or select the name of the payee, category, or class you want to limit transactions to. If you want to report on transactions with the payee Carmel Day School, for example, select or enter this exact name in the **P**ayee Contains drop-down list box. If you want to report on transactions assigned to the Utilities category, type or select Utilities in the Cat**e**gory Contains drop-down list box.

You can include more than one item to limit transactions to. For example, you can enter criteria in both the **P**ayee Contains and the Cat**e**gory Contains boxes so that Quicken includes only transactions that contain the specified payee and are assigned to the category you entered.

Note

For categories and classes, Quicken searches entries in the Splits window for split transactions assigned to the specified category or class.

3. In the **M**emo Contains text box, enter the memo you want to limit transactions to. If you want to report on transactions that contain the memo *Gymnastics lessons*, for example, type this entry in the **M**emo Contains text box to limit the report to transactions with the same memo entered in the Memo field.

4. Choose OK to redisplay the specified report filters.

You can use the following match characters to limit a report to transactions that match the criteria you specify:

= (equal sign)	Includes only transactions that exactly match the text you enter (**=Carmel Utilities** finds *Carmel Utilities* only).
.. (two periods)	Includes transactions with unspecified characters where you type **..** (at the beginning, middle, or end of the text) (**..Jones** finds *Nancy Jones*, *David Jones*, and *Scott Jones*).
? (question mark)	Includes transactions with one unspecified character where you type **?** (**?ax** finds *tax* and *fax*).
~ (tilde)	Excludes all matches for the text that you type after the ~ character (**~tax** excludes *state tax*, *federal tax*, and *local tax*).

Note

If you type a tilde followed by two periods, Quicken excludes all transactions except those that are empty in the specified field. If you type **~..** in the **M**emo Contains text box, for example, Quicken includes only the transactions without a memo entry in the Memo field.

Sorting Report Data

For noninvestment transaction reports, you can change how transactions are ordered in the report. You can sort transactions by amount, by payee, by account and then by date, or by account and then by check number.

To sort transactions in a report, follow these steps:

1. Create the report, as explained earlier in this chapter.

2. Choose the Sort button from the button bar. Quicken displays the Select Sort Criteria dialog box.

3. In the Sort Transactions By drop-down list, choose how you want to sort transactions; by date, amount, payee, and so forth.

4. Choose OK. Quicken searches transactions and redisplays the report in the selected sort order.

Using QuickZoom to Examine Report Detail

QuickZoom enables you to examine the transaction detail behind an amount in a report while the report is on-screen. If, for example, you create a cash flow report and want to see the transaction detail behind the amount shown for the category Charity (for charitable donations), you can use QuickZoom to search the Register for all transactions that make up the total amount shown in the report. Quicken displays a QuickZoom Report that shows a list of those transactions. If you want to examine a transaction further or edit a transaction in the QuickZoom Report, you can go to the Register where the transaction was entered.

> **Note**
>
> You can use QuickZoom only in summary, transaction, budget, comparison, investment income, and investment transaction reports. You can't use QuickZoom in account balance type reports, such as the net worth report or the balance sheet.

To use QuickZoom to examine the transaction detail in a report, follow these steps:

1. With the report on-screen, put the mouse pointer on the report item you want to examine. The mouse pointer changes to a magnifying glass icon to show that you can examine the report item (see fig. 19.14).

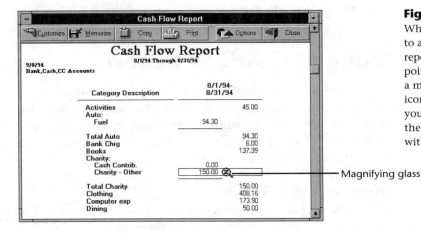

— Magnifying glass

Fig. 19.14
When you point to an item in a report, the mouse pointer changes to a magnifying glass icon to show that you can examine the report item with QuickZoom.

2. Double-click the report item. Quicken displays a QuickZoom Report window listing the transactions that make up the report item you selected (see fig. 19.15).

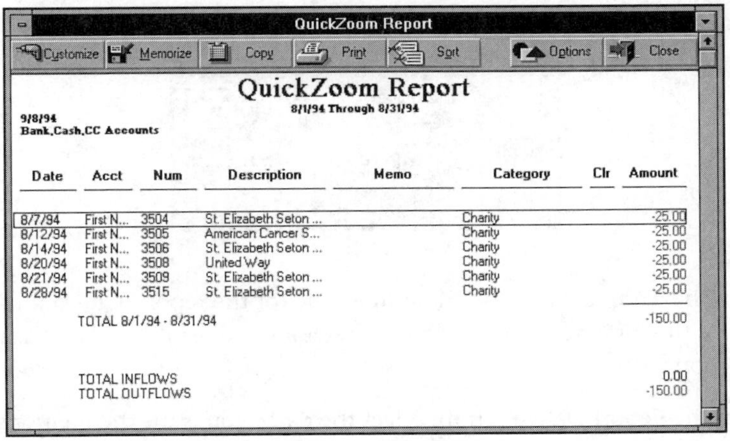

Fig. 19.15
When you examine a report item, Quicken shows the list of transactions that make up the report item in the QuickZoom Report window.

Tip
If you double-click a report item in a transaction report, Quicken goes to the Register where the transaction was entered and highlights the transaction.

3. If you want to see the Register entry for a transaction listed in the QuickZoom Report window, double-click the transaction. Quicken goes to the Register and highlights that transaction. From here, you can make any necessary changes to the transaction.

To return to the QuickZoom Report window from the Register, choose **C**lose from the Register button bar or press Esc.

4. To return to the original report from the QuickZoom Report window, choose the Close button.

Using Memorized Reports

If you have spent considerable time customizing a report to include specific information in a particular format, you will want to save the report settings so that you don't have to customize the report again. Quicken enables you to have a customized report *memorized* so that you simply can select it from a list the next time you want to use it.

Memorizing a Report

You can have Quicken memorize a report after you customize the report and the report is on-screen. To do so, follow these steps:

1. Create and customize the report you want Quicken to memorize.

2. Choose the **M**emorize button from the Report button bar (or press Ctrl+M). Quicken displays the Memorize Report dialog box, shown in figure 19.16.

Fig. 19.16
Enter the report dates and a unique title for the report in the Memorize Report dialog box.

3. In the **T**itle text box, type a unique title for the report. Quicken uses this title only to identify the report; Quicken doesn't display it as the report's title.

4. In the Report Dates section, select the dates you want the memorized report to cover. Select the N**a**med Range option if you selected a preset date range in the Create Report dialog box. To memorize the dates used in the report, select the **C**ustom option. To use the preset starting and ending dates that Quicken enters in the Create Report dialog box when you recall the report, select the **N**one option.

5. Choose OK to have Quicken memorize the report.

Recalling a Memorized Report

Recalling a memorized report with the exact report settings you specified is easy. To recall a memorized report, follow these steps:

1. Select **M**emorized Reports from the **R**eports menu. Quicken displays the Memorized Reports window (see figure 19.17) which lists memorized reports, by title.

Fig. 19.17
Choose **M**emorized Reports from the Reports menu to display the Memorized Reports window.

2. Double-click the memorized report you want to recall, or highlight the report and select **U**se. Quicken displays the report.

Setting Report Options

You can set options to change the report defaults that Quicken uses to create reports. For example, Quicken creates reports using the Year to Date report date range by default. Although you can change the date of any report as you create it, you may want to change the default setting, or the report option, to the date range you use most often. So, if you usually create monthly reports and use Month to Date as the date range, you can change the default to Month to Date so that Quicken automatically creates reports using this date range.

To set report options in Quicken, follow these steps:

1. From the **E**dit menu, choose **O**ptions, or click the Options button on the Iconbar. Quicken displays the Options dialog box.

2. Select the Repor**t**s option to display the Report Options dialog box, shown in figure 19.18. Note that you can also display the Report

Options dialog box by selecting the O**p**tions button in the Report button bar when a report is displayed on-screen.

Fig. 19.18
You can change option settings for reports in the Report Options dialog box.

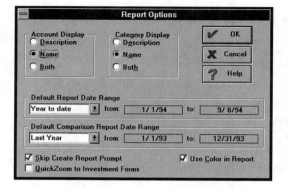

3. Move to the report option that you want to change and turn it on or off. Turn an option on by selecting the blank option or check box for that option. Turn an option off by selecting it again.

4. When you're finished setting report options, choose OK to save the option settings.

> **Note**
>
> If the date range that you most often use isn't included in Quicken's list, you can create a default date range. To do so, select Custom Date from the Report Date Range drop-down list. Then select the start and end dates in the **F**rom and **T**o drop-down list boxes.

From Here...

Now that you know how to create and print reports in Quicken, you may want to review the following:

■ Chapter 12, "Estimating and Preparing for Income Taxes," shows you how to create the Tax Summary and the Tax Schedule reports.

■ Chapter 17, "Budgeting with Quicken," contains examples of the preset budget reports.

■ Chapter 20, "Using Graphs to Analyze Your Finances," describes how to show your Quicken data in graphs.

Chapter 20

Using Graphs to Analyze Your Finances

In previous chapters, you learned how to enter transactions and write checks, track your assets and liabilities, create budgets, and monitor your investments. In Chapter 19, "Creating and Printing Reports," you learned how to produce reports so that you could analyze the information and data that you enter in Quicken. Creating reports is an excellent way to summarize your financial information, but not the only way.

You can create on-screen graphs to show relationships between your income and expenses, assets and liabilities, actual and budget amounts, and individual investments and total portfolio. If you have an installed graphics card, you can create graphs in Quicken. You can create graphs in just seconds based on the transactions that you enter and categorize, the account balances, budgeted data, and investment transactions entered.

Quicken has always let you memorize transactions and reports, and now you can memorize graphs so that you can store graph settings the way you want them. When you're ready to view a memorized graph, just select it from the Memorized Graphs window; the graph is displayed instantly.

In the case of your finances, assessing your financial situation is sometimes easier when you can see a graph that shows an overview or summary of your finances. Graphs show you, for example, the relationship of individual expense categories to your total expenditures. Therefore, you quickly can see what percentage each individual expense category is to your total expenses. Although reports show you information in a format useful in financial analysis, graphs are a visual means for analysis that sometimes have more effect than a list of categories or accounts in a report.

In this chapter, you learn how to do the following:

- Identify each graph format that Quicken creates (bar graphs, pie charts, stacked bar graphs, and line graphs)

- Create graphs

- Use QuickZoom to examine graph detail

- Hide graph data

- Filter graph transactions

- Memorize graphs

- Set graph options

- Print graphs

Understanding Quicken Graphs

Depending on the type of graph you create, Quicken displays the following graph formats:

- *Bar graphs.* Quicken can create bar graphs to compare data within a specified period. The items the graphs compare appear as bars and are shown on the horizontal axis, side by side. The dollar amounts or values of the items being compared are shown on the vertical axis.

- *Pie charts.* Pie charts show the composition of each individual item to the whole. If you graph your income composition, for example, you see the percentage that your salary contributes to your total income from all sources. You also can use a pie chart to help you determine whether you are spending too much in a particular expense category or earning too little as compared to your total income.

- *Stacked bar graphs.* A stacked bar graph shows two trends simultaneously. First, the graphs show the composition of items in the stacked bar, such as the composition of total investments. Stacked bar graphs stack the items that comprise the whole in a single bar. Stacked bar graphs also show how items are comprised to the whole over time.

- *Line graphs.* A line graph shows net values over time or trends. Line graphs in Quicken are superimposed over bar graphs to show how net values change over time.

> **Note**
>
> You can't choose the graph format that Quicken uses to compare data. If you want to use a different format than Quicken uses, you must export the data to another program with graphing capabilities.

Each graph format compares financial information or shows information in a different way. In the following sections, you learn about the different graph formats and what they represent. Each graph that you create includes a *legend* that tells you what each bar or piece of pie represents.

Creating Graphs

This section explains how to create and display graphs, in general. You learn how to select a graph type, display the graph, and remove the graph from your screen.

To create a graph, follow these steps:

1. Choose **G**raphs on the **R**eports menu or click Graphs on the Iconbar to display the Create Graph dialog box, shown in figure 20.1.

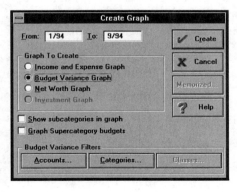

Fig. 20.1
Select the graph that you want to create in the Create Graph dialog box.

2. Enter the dates that you want to limit transactions to in the **F**rom and **T**o date boxes. If you want to see your income and expenses for the first six months of the year, for example, enter **1/94** in the **F**rom date box and **6/94** in the **T**o date box.

3. In the Graph To Create section, select the graph that you want to create by selecting the appropriate option. You can choose from the following graphs:

Tip
You can use the + (plus) and – (minus) keys to change the day or month by increments of one.

Income and Expense. Analyzes the items that make up your total income, items that make up your total expenses, and your spending and earning trends.

You also can use these graphs to compare your total income to expenses. Common questions you can answer with income and expense graphs include:

- Has my income increased over time?

- By what margin is my income more than my expenses?

- Am I overspending?

- What sources make up my total income?

- What expenses make up my total expenses?

- Have my expenses increased or decreased over time?

Budget Variance. Compares your actual income and expenses to your budgeted income and expenses.

The budget reports that you learned how to create in Chapter 17, "Budgeting with Quicken," also tell you how your budget compares to your actual income and expense. The budget and actual graphs provide a visual comparison that enables you to assess quickly how successful (or unsuccessful) you are in sticking to your budget.

You can use the budget variance graph to compare actual amounts to budgeted amounts, and identify areas where you are over or under budget.

Common questions you can answer with a budget variance graph include:

- Am I sticking to my budget?

- How much more can I spend and still stay within my budget?

- In which areas am I over or under budget?

> **Note**
>
> You can't display budget and actual graphs without creating your budget first. Refer to Chapter 17, "Budgeting with Quicken," to learn how to create a budget. Budget variance graphs are created from the categories that you assign to transactions and the categories that you establish budget amounts for.

Net Worth. Analyzes the assets that make up your total assets, the liabilities that make up your total liabilities, and how your assets and liabilities have changed over time; also compares your total assets to your total liabilities.

Common questions you can answer with net worth graphs include:

- Do I have more assets than liabilities?

- How has my *net worth* (assets minus liabilities) changed over time?

- What assets make up my total assets?

- Have my assets increased over time?

- What liabilities make up my total liabilities?

- Have my liabilities increased or decreased over time?

Investment. Shows how your portfolio is distributed (stocks, bonds, options, Treasury bills, and so on) and the changes in your portfolio value over time.

Note

You also can create graphs from the Portfolio View of an investment account. You can create a graph that shows, for example, the price trends of your security holdings within an account. Refer to Chapter 16 to learn how to create graphs from an investment account.

Common questions you can answer with investment graphs include:

- Is my investment portfolio value increasing?

- How diversified is my investment portfolio?

- Are the prices of my individual holdings increasing?

Note

If you don't track your investments by using Quicken's investment accounts, you can't create investment graphs. Refer to Chapter 16 to learn how to use Quicken's investment accounts.

4. To include subcategories in the graph that you are creating, select the **S**how Subcategories in Graph check box.

> **Note**
>
> The filter buttons shown at the bottom of the Create Graph dialog box are used to limit the data that Quicken uses to generate a graph to specific **Ac**counts, **C**ategories, and **Cl**asses. Selecting options to include in a graph is explained later in the section "Filtering Graph Transactions."

5. Choose C**r**eate to display the selected graph. Quicken always displays two graphs in the graph window for each graph that you select in the Create Graph dialog box. (If you want graphs displayed in two separate windows, select the **C**reate All Graphs in Separate Windows option, as explained in a later section "Setting Graph Options.")

6. When you are finished reviewing the graph, select Close or press Esc to remove the graph from your screen.

Using QuickZoom to Examine Graph Detail

Quicken's QuickZoom feature enables you to see the detail behind an item in a graph. QuickZoom works the same way in graphs as in reports (see Chapter 19). When the mouse pointer changes to the magnifying glass icon, you can use QuickZoom to get more information about a particular element in a graph. Just double-click the graph element to display the QuickZoom Graph.

When you use QuickZoom to see the detail of a bar in a bar graph, Quicken creates a pie chart showing the composition of the bar. Figure 20.2 shows the QuickZoom Graph window displayed with a pie chart that shows the composition of a bar in a bar graph.

Tip
To move the QuickZoom Graph window so that you can see the details in the original graph, drag the window's title bar toward one edge of the screen.

You also can use QuickZoom to investigate a pie slice or legend item. Just double-click the pie slice or legend item to display a bar graph showing the dollars (by month) of the pie slice or the legend item. Figure 20.3 shows the bar chart displayed when you use QuickZoom to investigate a legend item or pie slice.

If you need to see transaction detail for an item in a QuickZoom graph, double-click the item to display a list of transactions, as shown in figure 20.4. From the transaction listing, you can go to the Register for a specific transaction by double-clicking the transaction.

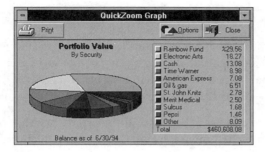

Fig. 20.2
When you use QuickZoom to examine the detail of a bar in a bar graph, Quicken creates a pie chart in the QuickZoom Graph window that shows the composition of the bar.

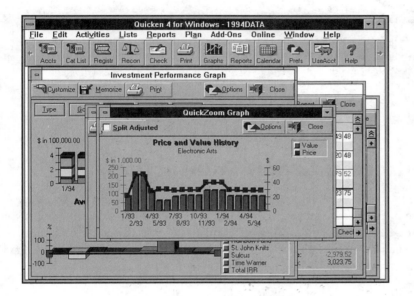

Fig. 20.3
When you use QuickZoom to investigate a pie slice or legend item, Quicken displays a bar graph that shows the dollars (by month) associated with the pie slice or legend item.

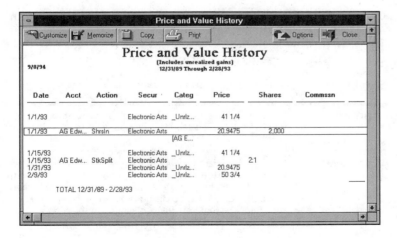

Fig. 20.4
Double-click an item in a QuickZoom graph to display the transactions that make up the item.

IV

Analyzing Your Finances

Hiding Graph Data

You can hide a pie slice or bar in a graph so that the remaining graph items appear bigger. If a category makes up a very large piece in a pie chart, for example, you may have difficulty seeing the other pieces. By hiding the largest piece, you free up space for Quicken to display the remaining pieces.

To hide a pie slice or a bar in a graph, Shift+click the pie slice or bar (press Shift as you click the left mouse button). To reveal the item, recreate the graph.

> **Note**
>
> Hiding a graph category isn't the same as selecting not to include a category in the graph when it's created. When you filter categories (see the next section) by deselecting a category from the graph, Quicken doesn't include the category in its analysis as it creates the graph. When you hide a graph category, Quicken still calculates the category value but doesn't display the value.

Filtering Graph Transactions

You can choose which transactions Quicken includes in graphs by *filtering* them. For income and expense, budget variance, and net worth graphs, you can select the accounts, categories, and classes that Quicken uses to display the graph. For investment performance graphs, you can select the accounts and securities that Quicken uses to display the graph.

To filter graph transactions, follow these steps:

1. Click Graphs on the Iconbar to display the Create Graph dialog box (refer to fig. 20.1).

2. Enter the date range and select the graph type that you want to create.

3. Select the following buttons to filter transactions:

Accounts	Displays the Select Accounts to Include dialog box, where you can select the accounts that you want to include in the graph.
Categories	Displays the Select Categories to Include dialog box, where you can select the categories that you want to include in the graph. If you select the Show Subcategories in Graph check box in the Create Graph dialog box, you also can select the subcategories that you want to include in the graph.

Classes	Displays the Select Classes to Include dialog box, where you can select the classes that you want to include in the graph.
Securities	Displays the Select Securities to Include dialog box, where you can select the securities that you want to include in the graph (only for investment performance graphs).

4. In the appropriate dialog box, select the items from the list that you want to include in the report by double-clicking the item. When you include an item, Quicken enters a check mark next to the item. To include all items, choose **M**ark All. Choose C**l**ear All to exclude all of the items.

5. When you are finished making your selections, choose OK to return to the Create Graph dialog box.

> **Note**
>
> If you filter graph transactions by selecting accounts, categories, classes, or securities, Quicken places a check mark on the appropriate button in the Create Graph dialog box. If, for example, you select accounts to include in a graph, Quicken places a check mark on the Accounts button in the Create Graph dialog box. The check mark shows you that the transactions in a graph have been filtered.

6. Choose C**r**eate to display the graph using the selected accounts, categories, subcategories, classes, or securities (for investment performance graphs).

Using Memorized Graphs

If you have spent considerable time customizing a graph to include specific categories, accounts, classes, or securities (for investment graphs), you will want to save the graph settings so that you don't have to customize the graph each time you want to view it. Quicken enables you to have a customized graph *memorized* so that you simply can select it from a list the next time you want to use it.

Memorizing a Graph

You can have Quicken memorize a graph after you customize the graph and the graph is on-screen. To do so, follow these steps:

1. Create and customize the graph you want Quicken to memorize.

2. Choose the **M**emorize button from the Graph button bar (or press Ctrl+M). Quicken displays the Memorize Graph dialog box, shown in figure 20.5.

Fig. 20.5
Enter a unique title for the graph in the Memorize Graph dialog box.

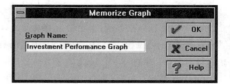

3. In the **G**raph Name text box, type a unique title for the graph. Quicken uses this title only to identify the graph, but doesn't display it as the graph's title.

4. Choose OK to have Quicken memorize the graph.

Displaying a Memorized Graph

Displaying a memorized graph with the exact graph settings you specified is easy. To recall a memorized graph, follow these steps:

1. Click the Graphs button on the Iconbar to display the Create Graph dialog box (see fig. 20.1).

2. Select the Memorized button. Quicken displays the Memorized Graphs window, shown in figure 20.6, with a list, by title, of all memorized graphs. Note that you can also display the Memorized Graphs window by selecting Memori**z**ed Graphs from the **R**eports menu.

Fig. 20.6
The Memorized Graphs window lists all memorized graphs by title.

3. Double-click the memorized graph you want to display, or highlight the graph and select **U**se. Quicken displays the Recall Memorized Graph dialog box, where you can change the dates for transactions included in the graph and other graph criteria.

4. Choose OK to display the graph.

Setting Graph Options

You can set graph options so that graphs appear the way you want them. To set graph options, follow these steps:

1. Create a graph as explained previously in this chapter.

2. In the graph window, choose the **O**ptions button from the Graph button bar. Quicken displays the Graph Options dialog box, shown in figure 20.7.

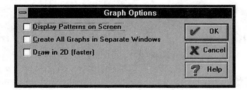

Fig. 20.7
The Graph Options dialog box provides settings that establish the way graphs appear on-screen.

3. By default, Quicken uses solid colors to represent data in graphs. If you prefer black-and-white patterns, select **D**isplay Patterns on Screen.

> **Note**
>
> If you use a monochrome monitor, select **D**isplay Patterns on Screen. Otherwise, you may have difficulty differentiating the bars on-screen. You also should select **D**isplay Patterns on Screen if you are printing to a black-and-white printer so that you can see what the output will resemble.

4. Each Quicken graph that you create actually consists of two parts. The contents of the two parts vary, depending on the graph that you create. By default, Quicken displays both parts of the graph in one window. To display both parts of a graph in separate windows, select **C**reate All Graphs in Separate Windows.

5. By default, Quicken displays all graphs in three dimensions. You can change the appearance to show two dimensions by selecting D**r**aw in 2D. Use this option if you find that your computer takes a long time to draw graphs in three dimensions. Be aware, however, that graphs that Quicken draws in two dimensions also print in two dimensions.

> **Note**
>
> Graphs that you create in 3D in Quicken don't include a third axis; as a result, they aren't truly three-dimensional. 3D graphs are actually 2D graphs with shadows added to show depth within the graph.

6. Choose OK to save the graph options and return to the Quicken for Windows Options dialog box.

7. Choose **D**one to close the Quicken for Windows Options dialog box.

Printing Graphs

After you select and display a graph and (if necessary) filter the transactions included in the graph, you're ready to print the graph.

Before you can print graphs in Quicken, you must set up the program to print to your printer. Quicken includes different printer settings for reports and graphs (Report/Graph Printer Setup) and checks (Check Printer Setup). Chapter 19, "Creating and Printing Reports," shows you how to set up Quicken to print reports and graphs.

After the printer is set up, you can print graphs from Quicken. To print graphs, follow these steps:

1. Turn on your printer and make sure that it's online.

2. Display the graph that you want to print.

3. From the graph window, select the Pri**n**t button or choose **P**rint Graph from the **F**ile menu (or press Ctrl+P). Quicken begins printing the graph.

From Here...

You may want to review the following now that you know how to create graphs in Quicken:

- Chapter 16, "Monitoring Your Investments," is where you learn how to set up investment accounts and enter transactions to manage your portfolio. Quicken provides several graphs that you can use to evaluate the performance of your investments.

- Chapter 17, "Budgeting with Quicken," shows you how to set up a budget in Quicken. Various budget graphs are available to help monitor your actual versus budget activity.

- Chapter 19, "Creating and Printing Reports," explains how to enter printer settings so that you can print reports and graphs in Quicken. These printer settings must be entered before you can print the graphs that you learned how to create in this chapter.

Part V

Managing Quicken for Windows

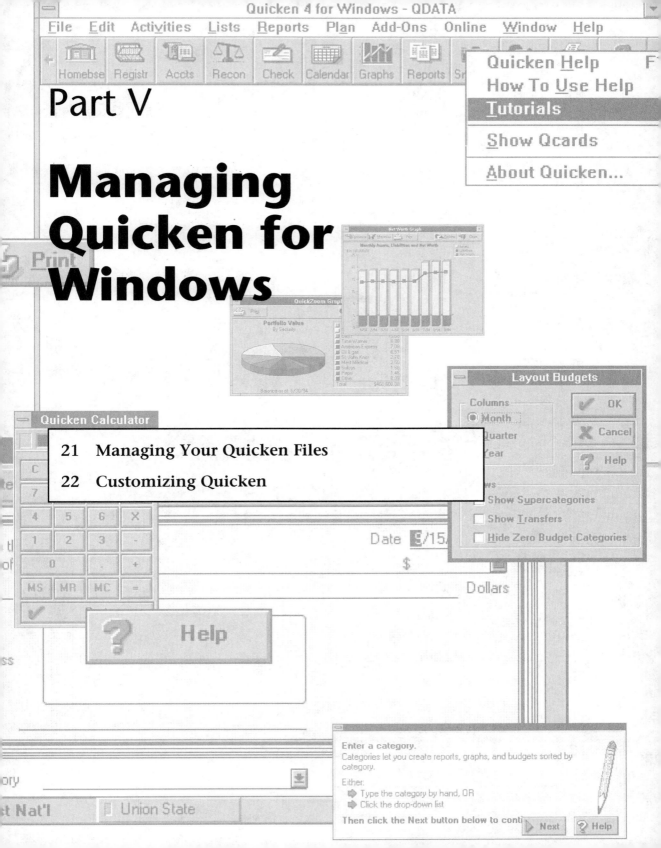

Quicken 4 for Windows - QDATA

File　Edit　Activities　Lists　Reports　Plan　Add-Ons　Online　Window　Help

Homebse　Registr　Accts　Recon　Check　Calendar　Graphs　Reports　Sr

Quicken **Help**
How To **Use** He
Tutorials
Show Qcards
About Quicken.

Print

Net Worth Graph
Monthly Assets, Liabilities and Net Worth

QuickZoom Graph

Print

Portfolio Value
By Security

Cash
Time Warner
American Express
OEG gas
St. John Knits
Med Medical
Sukus
Pepsi
Other
Total

Balance as of 9/30/94

Layout Budgets

Columns
- ● **Month**
- ○ **Quarter**
- ○ **Year**

✓ O

✗ Car

? He

Rows
- ☐ Show **Supercategories**
- ☐ Show **Transfers**
- ☐ **Hide Zero Budget Categori**

Quicken Calculator

			0
C	CE	<-	%
7	8	9	/
4	5	6	X
1	2	3	-
0		.	+
MS	MR	MC	=
✓			

rite Checks: First Nat'l

Options　**Rep**

Delete

Pay to t
Order of

Date **9**/15

$

Dollars

? **Help**

Address

Memo

Category　⬇

■ **First Nat'l**　■ Union State

Enter a category.
Categories let you create reports, graphs, and budgets sorted by
category.
Either:
➡ Type the category by hand, OR
➡ Click the drop-down list
Then click the Next button below to conti　▷ **Next**　? **Help**

Chapter 21

Managing Your Quicken Files

Until now, you have worked with only one Quicken file in this book. Quicken enables you to add more files so that you can maintain separate files for more than one household or business. With multiple files in your Quicken system, you easily can work with several different files by switching from one to another. Although you can create multiple Quicken files, you can only work in one at any given time (unlike word processing programs that let you have several different document files open at the same time).

In this chapter, you learn how to perform the following tasks:

- Create a new Quicken file
- Open and close a file
- Copy and rename Quicken files
- Delete a Quicken file
- Reindex a file
- Back up and restore your Quicken data
- Archive, export, and import file data
- Assign, change, and remove passwords

Working with Quicken Files

Quicken assigns a filename to each file. As you learned in Chapter 1, the name for the first file added to the Quicken system is QDATA. Each Quicken file consists of five data files with the same filename, but with different extensions—QDI, QDT, QMT, QNX, and QST. You can find these data files in the directory where you store Quicken for Windows data (such as C:\QUICKENW). Quicken stores in these data files the financial information you enter in the Register.

Quicken stores accounts you define in files and enables you to have more than one file. The obvious question when you begin defining new accounts, then, is to which file an account should be added. You usually find these decisions fairly easy to make.

The general rule is that you store related accounts together in a separate file. Accounts are related when they pertain to the same business or the same household. If you use Quicken for home accounting and for a commercial printing business, for example, you use two files: one for home and one for business. If you use Quicken for three businesses—a consulting practice, a small publishing business, and a restaurant—you use three files, one for each business.

Creating a New File

When you installed Quicken, you created at least one file, named QDATA by default (the QDATA file has five data files, as explained in the previous section). Until you create a second file, any accounts you set up are added to QDATA. To add a new file to your Quicken system, follow these steps:

1. Choose **N**ew from the **F**ile menu to display the Creating New File dialog box, shown in figure 21.1.

Fig. 21.1
The Creating New File dialog box confirms that you want to create a new Quicken file, not a Quicken account.

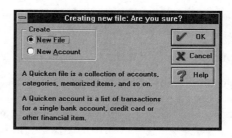

2. Choose the **N**ew File option to create a new file.

3. Choose OK. Quicken displays the Create Quicken File dialog box, shown in figure 21.2.

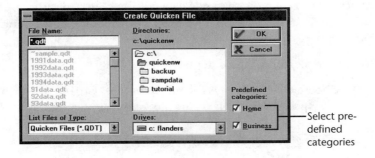

Fig. 21.2
Name your new
Quicken file in the
Create Quicken
File dialog box.

Select pre-
defined
categories

4. In the File **N**ame text box, type the name for the new file.

The name you enter must be a valid DOS filename, which means any combination of up to eight characters, but no spaces. Refer to the DOS user's manual if you have questions about DOS file-naming conventions.

5. (Optional) From the **D**irectories list box, select the directory where you want your new Quicken file located. By default, Quicken stores data files in the Quicken for Windows program directory (such as C:\QUICKENW).

You really don't need to change the default directory name unless you have a personal preference where the new Quicken file is located. Quicken, however, does enable you to change the default directory.

6. In the Predefined Categories section, select the categories that you want to use in the new Quicken file. To use predefined home or personal categories, select the H**o**me check box. To use predefined business categories, select the **B**usiness check box. To use home and business categories, select both check boxes. (By default, Quicken assumes that you want to use both predefined home and business categories.) Refer to Chapter 4, "Organizing Your Finances," for more on using predefined categories.

7. When the Create Quicken File dialog box is complete, choose OK to create the new file. The new file opens automatically, and Quicken displays the Create New Account dialog box so that you can set up your first account in your new Quicken file. Refer to Chapter 3, "Defining Your Accounts," to learn how to set up your first account.

Opening a File

When you create more than one data file, Quicken opens the last file that you used upon startup. You must open a different file if you want to view a different one.

To open a file, follow these steps:

1. Choose **O**pen from the **F**ile menu (or press Ctrl+O). Quicken displays the Open Quicken File dialog box, shown in figure 21.3.

Fig. 21.3
Select the file that you want to open here.

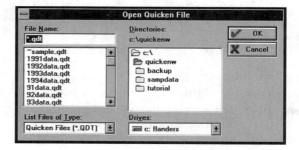

2. By default, Quicken lists the data files in the Quicken program directory (such as C:\QUICKENW). If necessary, change the directory in the **D**irectories list box if the file that you want to open is located in a different directory.

3. Select the Quicken file that you want to open by typing the filename in the File **N**ame text box or by clicking the filename in the list box. Just make sure that the filename for the file that you want to open appears in the File **N**ame text box.

4. Choose OK to open the file. Quicken saves and closes the file you were working on, and then opens the selected file.

Closing a File

To close a Quicken file, just exit the program or open another Quicken file. When you exit Quicken, your work in the current session is saved automatically. When you decide to open another file, Quicken automatically saves and closes the file you were working on before opening the new file.

Copying Files

You can make a copy of your Quicken file, perhaps to give to your accountant to use with her or his Quicken program. You can copy all transactions from a file or select a date range of transactions to copy. You must open the file that you want to copy before you to copy the file. Refer to the earlier section "Opening a File" to learn how to open a file.

To copy the current Quicken file, follow these steps:

1. Choose **F**ile Operations from the **F**ile menu.

2. From the **F**ile Operations submenu, choose the **C**opy command. Quicken displays the Copy File dialog box, shown in figure 21.4.

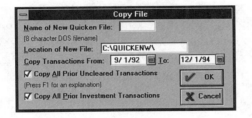

Fig. 21.4
Enter the name and location of the file to which you want the current file copied.

3. In the **N**ame of New Quicken File text box, type the DOS filename for the new Quicken file.

4. In the **L**ocation of New File text box, type the path (drive and/or directory) to which you want to copy the file.

5. In the **C**opy Transactions From and **T**o drop-down list boxes, select the beginning and ending dates for transactions to be copied.

6. Select the Copy **A**ll Prior Uncleared Transactions check box if you want to copy transactions dated before the dates in step 5 that haven't yet cleared the bank (as indicated in the Clr column in the Register). If you don't want to copy these transactions, leave this check box unselected.

7. Choose OK to copy the current file to the filename that you typed in step 3.

8. After the file is copied, Quicken displays the File Copied Successfully dialog box (see fig. 21.5). Select the **R**eload Original File option to re-open the file that you just copied. To open the new file that you just created, select the **L**oad New Copy option.

Fig. 21.5
The File Copied Successfully dialog box appears after you copy a Quicken file.

9. Choose OK to open the appropriate file.

> **Note**
>
> If you choose to open the new copy of a file, your original file is saved and closed.

Renaming a File

You can edit the names of existing files, if necessary. You may want to edit a filename, for example, if you named the file incorrectly. Suppose that the filename for the business Acme Manufacturing is ACME_MFG. If the business name changes to Acme Incorporated, you can change the filename to ACME_INC. To rename a filename, follow these steps:

1. Choose **F**ile Operations from the **F**ile menu.

2. From the File Operations submenu, choose Re**n**ame. Quicken displays the Rename Quicken File dialog box.

3. (Optional) To edit a file in some directory other than the default (such as C:/QUICKENW), select the directory in the **D**irectories list box.

4. In the list box under the File **N**ame text box, select the file that you want to rename.

5. Type the new filename in the New name for Quicken **F**ile text box. Make sure that you use a valid DOS filename.

6. Choose OK to rename the file. Quicken returns to the file in which you now are working.

Reindexing a File

The most essential of the five files that Quicken creates when you create a new file is the .QNX file. The .QNX file is the index file that improves access to your financial data. This file is vital to your Quicken data file. If you turn off your computer before exiting Quicken, you might damage this file. Quicken, however, includes a safeguard within the program to protect this file. If the index file is erased or becomes unsynchronized with its data file, Quicken automatically regenerates the index file, or reindexes the file.

Now, with Quicken 4 for Windows, you can perform the reindexing procedure yourself if you need to rebuild the index file to recover a damaged data file.

> **Caution**
>
> Be sure to make a back up copy of your file before reindexing the file to safeguard the data in your file from mishap.

To reindex a file, select **F**ile Operations from the **F**ile menu and then choose Re**i**ndex. Quicken performs the reindexing procedures and displays a message when reconstruction is complete.

Deleting a File

Quicken enables you to delete files that you inadvertently added or that you no longer use. Deleting a file is almost always a bad idea because when you do, you essentially are deleting all the accounts in the file. After a file is deleted from your Quicken system, you may not be able to restore it.

If you no longer are tracking any of the accounts in the file, you can delete the entire file. This may be the case if you set up a special file for learning to use Quicken and no longer use the file. To delete a file, follow these steps:

1. Choose **F**ile Operations from the **F**ile menu.

2. From the File Operations submenu, choose **D**elete. Quicken displays the Delete Quicken File dialog box.

3. (Optional) To delete a file from a directory other than the Quicken default directory (such as C:\QUICKENW), in the **D**irectories list box, select the directory where the file is located.

4. In the list box under the File **N**ame text box, select the file that you want to delete and then choose OK.

Tip

Make a backup copy of all files before you delete them to protect from losing data that you may need later.

V

Managing Quicken

5. Quicken displays the Deleting File message box to confirm that you want to delete the selected file. Type **yes** if you are sure that you want to delete the file. Then choose OK to delete it.

Backing Up and Restoring Files

Although you may be a careful computer user, everyone loses data (this author once lost a whole three months' worth!) at one time or another. To avoid losing important financial data, you need to back up your files regularly.

Backing up means that you make a second copy of all Quicken data files (including Q3.DIR, QDATA.QDT, QDATA,QNX, QDATA.QMT, QDATA.QST, and QDATA.QDI). Back up these files so that if your original Quicken data files are damaged, you can use the backup copies to restore the damaged files to original condition.

You can back up and restore by using DOS file commands or one of the popular hard disk management programs. For convenience, you may find the Quicken backup and restore options easier to use. The following sections discuss these backup and restore options.

Backing Up a File

You need to make two important decisions about backing up files. First, you must decide how often you need to perform a backup. Although opinions on the subject vary, a good habit to form is to back up data files after you complete a session in which you enter or change financial data. When you finish entering the first set of account transactions, for example, back up all the data files.

Most people back up financial records daily, weekly, or monthly. After you spend time working with Quicken and become familiar with data file restoration procedures, you can estimate more accurately how often you need to back up files.

Second, decide how many old backup copies to keep. Usually, two or three copies are adequate. Suppose that you back up the data files every day. On Thursday, a co-worker accidentally deletes the data file. If you keep two old backup copies in addition to the most recent backup copy, you have backups from Wednesday, Tuesday, and Monday. If the Wednesday copy is damaged (an unlikely but possible situation), you still have the Tuesday and Monday copies.

Caution

Store these data file backup copies in a safe place. Don't keep all backup copies in the same location. If you experience a fire or if someone burglarizes your business or house, you may lose all the copies—no matter how many backups you keep. Store at least one copy at an off-site location.

Note

Without regular backups, you may lose financial records. Obviously, backing up files is important. Because backing up is so important, Quicken provides a backup message that periodically reminds you to back up the current file.

Tip
You can customize the Iconbar to include a Backup icon (see Chapter 22). Then, just choose the icon to back up the current Quicken file.

To back up your Quicken files, follow these steps:

1. From the **F**ile menu, choose **B**ackup (or press Ctrl+B). Quicken displays the Select Backup Drive dialog box, shown in figure 21.6.

2. Select the **C**urrent File option if you want to back up the file that is now open. If the file that you want to back up isn't open, select the **S**elect From List option.

3. From the **B**ackup Drive drop-down list box, select the drive to which you want to back up the selected file. Then choose OK.

Fig. 21.6
You can back up the current file or select the file that you want to back up from a list of all your Quicken files.

Caution

Although you can choose to back up to your hard disk drive, you should back up to a floppy drive. If your hard disk fails, you risk losing the backup of your work, as well as the original.

4. If you selected to back up the file that you are now working in, Quicken begins the backup process.

   If you chose to back up another file, Quicken displays the Back Up Quicken File dialog box. If necessary, select the directory of the file that you want to back up from the **D**irectories list box and the drive containing the file from the Dri**v**es drop-down list box. In the list box under the File **N**ame text box, select the file that you want to back up, or type the name of the file and path in the File **N**ame text box. Then choose OK to begin the backup process.

5. When the backup process is complete, Quicken displays a message box to confirm that the file was backed up successfully. Choose OK to return to the current file.

   If the file you are trying to back up can't fit on the disk, an error message alerts you that the disk is full, and Quicken enables you to insert another disk.

6. Remove the backup disk(s) from the disk drive and store the disk(s) in a safe place.

> **Note**
>
> If you have trouble remembering to back up your file, Quicken helps remind you. When you exit the program, Quicken checks to see whether you've backed up the file recently. If not, Quicken displays a prompt advising you to back up before you exit. Just follow the on-screen prompts.

Restoring Backed-Up Files

Eventually, someone or something may accidentally delete or destroy a data file. A computer can malfunction, or a coworker may spill the contents of the pencil sharpener or a cup of coffee on the floppy disk that contains the Quicken data files. If you recently backed up these files and were diligent about printing copies of the Register, you should experience no serious setbacks. You can restore the Quicken files by using the backup copies.

To retrieve Quicken data from a backup copy, follow these steps:

1. Make sure that the Quicken file to which you want to restore data is open. If your QDATA file is damaged and you want to restore the backup copy data, for example, open the QDATA file.

2. Choose **R**estore from the **F**ile menu. Quicken displays the Restore Quicken File dialog box.

3. From the Dri**v**es drop-down list box, select the drive where your backup file is located. If your backup file is on a floppy disk located in drive A, for example, select a:.

4. In the **D**irectories list box, select the directory where the backup file is stored. If you backed up your data file to a floppy disk and the disk is in drive A, for example, select a: from the **D**irectories list box.

5. Select (or type) the backup filename that you want to restore.

6. Choose OK. Quicken alerts you that if you proceed with restoring, you will overwrite the existing (or current) file. To proceed, choose OK. Choose Cancel to discontinue restoring the backup file.

7. After the restoration is complete, Quicken displays the File Restored Successfully dialog box. Choose OK to return to the current file.

8. Using the most recent printed copy of the Register, reenter each transaction that you entered for each account between the time you backed up and the time you lost the data.

9. Back up these files, as you learned earlier in this chapter, in case another accident causes you to lose the Quicken files again.

> **Note**
>
> If disaster befalls your Quicken data files that you didn't back up, you must reenter each Register transaction. The up-to-date printed copies of each Register show the data that needs to be reentered. If you don't have up-to-date copies of each the Register, you need to reenter each transaction from the original source documents— checks, deposit slips, receipts, and so on. Regularly back up your Quicken data files to prevent disasters from causing you to spend painful hours recreating data.

Copying Files at Year's End

Theoretically, Quicken enables you to store up to 65,534 transactions in a file's Registers. Practically, these limitations are much lower. You may not be limited by space on your hard disk, but you probably don't want to work with thousands or tens of thousands of transactions in Registers.

Quicken provides a two-fold solution for dealing with the problem of ever-growing data files: Quicken enables you to archive the previous year's transactions to a separate file or create a new file that contains only the new year's data. When you archive data in the current file, the archive file contains data from the previous year and the current file is left untouched (contains both previous and current year data.) When you create a file for the new year, Quicken saves a copy of your current file and then deletes any transactions from the prior year (before January 1st of this year) from the current file. This two-fold solution means that you can break down large files into smaller, more manageable files.

For most users, the most convenient time to archive or start a new year file is after completing the annual income tax return and after any year-end reporting. At this time, all transactions from the prior year should have cleared the bank, and you have printed all necessary Quicken reports. Now, an archive copy of the files can provide a permanent copy of the data you used to prepare the year's financial reports. A new copy of the file also enables you to start a new year without a load of old, unnecessary data.

Archiving File Data

When you archive file data, Quicken copies the previous year's transactions to a separate file that is saved and can be used at any time. The transactions in the current file remain intact, for the previous year and current year.

To archive file data, follow these steps:

1. Because you can archive data from the current file only, you first must open the file with the data you want to archive.

2. Choose **Y**ear-End Copy from the **F**ile menu. Quicken displays the Year-End Copy dialog box, shown in figure 21.7.

Fig. 21.7
Select an option to archive file data or start a new year file here.

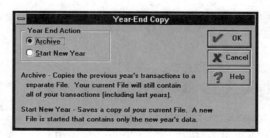

3. Select the **A**rchive option.

4. Choose OK. Quicken displays the Archive File dialog box, shown in figure 21.8.

Fig. 21.8
Quicken enters default settings for the archive file here.

5. If necessary, change any of the default settings in the Archive File dialog box. Choose OK to begin archiving data.

> **Note**
>
> By default, Quicken names the archive file using the current filename and the preceding year, locates the file in the Quicken program directory, and includes transactions only through the end of the preceding year.

6. When the archive process is complete, Quicken displays the File Copied Successfully dialog box. Here, select the **U**se Current File option to continue using the current file, or the U**s**e Archive File to close the current file and open the archive file.

7. Choose OK to use the selected file.

Starting a New File at Year's End

When you start a new file at year's end, Quicken saves a copy of the current file first. This copy becomes the "old" file, and its data isn't disturbed. Your current file then becomes the "new" file. Quicken then deletes any transaction data from the previous year (transactions dated before January 1st of the current year) from the new file. Therefore, your new file contains only current year data.

> **Note**
>
> If you start a new file, Quicken may include some transactions from previous years, such as investment transactions and any uncleared transactions. You need to keep these transactions in a working copy of a file because the investment transactions are needed for investment record-keeping and the uncleared transactions are needed for bank reconciliations.

To start a new year file, follow these steps:

1. Open the file from which you want to start a new year file.

2. Choose **Y**ear-End Copy from the **F**ile menu. Quicken displays the Year-End Copy dialog box (refer to fig. 21.7).

3. Select the **S**tart New Year option.

4. Choose OK. Quicken displays the Start New Year dialog box, shown in figure 21.9.

Fig. 21.9

With the Start New Year dialog box, you can move transactions before a specified date to a separate file.

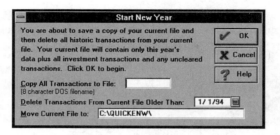

5. In the **C**opy All Transactions to File text box, type the filename you want Quicken to use for the new file.

> **Note**
>
> If you create a separate set of Quicken data files for each year, consider including the year number in the filename. You can name the data files from 1994 as QDATA94, the data files from 1995 as QDATA95, and so on. Including the year number in date filenames enables you to determine easily which year's records are contained in a particular data file.

6. In the **D**elete Transactions From Current File Older Than drop-down list box, select the date before which Quicken should delete transactions. If you want the file to contain only transactions dated from 1/1/95 to 12/31/95, for example, enter **1/1/95** in this field.

7. Specify the location, if other than the Quicken program directory, for the new file in the **M**ove Current File To text box.

8. When the Start New Year dialog box is complete, choose OK.

9. Quicken displays the File Copied Successfully dialog box. Here, you can select the **U**se Old File option to use the file with the older transactions,

or the Use File for New Year to use the new year's file. Select OK to use the file.

Exporting and Importing Files

Exporting is the process by which a software program makes a copy of a file in a format that another program can read. You may want to export the information stored in the Quicken Register so that you can retrieve and use the information in a database program, such as dBASE, or in a spreadsheet program, such as 1-2-3.

Importing is the process in which information created by one software program is retrieved by a second software program. You may want to import into Quicken the information created by an accounting program, such as DacEasy, so that you can use Quicken's reports to summarize the information.

> **Note**
>
> If you want to copy the Accounts, Category & Transfer, or Memorized Transaction list from one Quicken file to another, you can export the list to a .QIF file and then import the .QIF file to the other Quicken file. From the **F**ile menu, use the **I**mport and **E**xport commands to copy lists to other Quicken files.

When you export file data, Quicken creates an ASCII text file from the current account's Register transactions. You then can use this ASCII file in another software program. To export file data, choose **E**xport from the **F**ile menu. Then enter the path and filename of the Quicken file that you want to export, the Quicken account to export, and the date range in which to limit exported transactions. You can also select whether to export transactions, the Account List, Category & Transfer List, and memorized transactions.

You can also import file data that has been stored in the Quicken .QIF format. This format is the same one Quicken uses when exporting data. The steps for importing parallel those for exporting data.

Using Passwords

Anytime you deal with financial information, you must maintain the information's integrity and safeguard the system that stores the information from unauthorized entry. Using passwords in Quicken enables you to control the access or restrict transactions from being modified in your Quicken files.

Tip
To move transactions from one account to another, you can copy or export the data from the account and import it into the other account using the **F**ile menu's **E**xport and **I**mport commands.

V

Managing Quicken

Passwords represent an internal control mechanism. With Quicken, you can use passwords to limit access to the data files in which you store financial records.

You can use two kinds of passwords in Quicken: *file* and *transaction* passwords. The file password that you assign to the current file provides access to the accounts in the file. If you want each file in your Quicken system to use a password, you need to set up a file password for each file. The transaction password restricts anyone without access to the password from adding, changing, or deleting transactions before the date you specify.

Note

When using passwords, consider the following precautions:

- Make sure that you don't lose or forget the password. If you lose the password, you lose your data. Record the password in a safe place.

- Don't share your password with anyone who doesn't need to know it.

- Someone may discover your password and you may be unaware that they have access. As a precaution, periodically change your password.

- Use nonsensical passwords of at least six characters. The passwords you create with this procedure are extremely difficult to guess.

- Make sure that you don't use a seemingly clever password scheme, such as month names or colors, as passwords. If you set the transaction password to *blue*, a curious user may not take long to figure out that the main password is *red*.

Assigning a Password

File passwords prevent unauthorized users from accessing any of the accounts in a Quicken file. Transaction passwords prevent unauthorized users from adding, changing, or deleting transactions dated before a date that you specify when you assign the password.

To assign a file or transaction password to the current file, follow these steps:

1. Choose Passwords from the File menu. Quicken displays the Passwords submenu.

2. Choose File or Transaction. Quicken displays the Set Up Password dialog box, shown in figure 21.10, or the Password to Modify Existing Transactions dialog box, shown in figure 21.11.

Fig. 21.10
Assign a file
password in the
Set Up Password
dialog box.

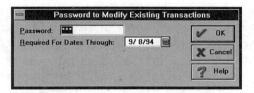

Fig. 21.11
Assign a transac-
tion password in
the Password to
Modify Existing
Transactions
dialog box.

3. To define either password, type the combination of letters and numbers you want to use as a password in the **P**assword text box. You can use up to 16 characters, including spaces. Quicken doesn't display the characters as you type them; instead, it displays asterisks (*).

> **Note**
>
> Quicken doesn't distinguish between the use of upper- and lowercase letters in establishing or using passwords.

4. For transaction passwords (see fig. 21.11), select the date through which the transaction password is required in the **R**equired For Dates Through box.

5. Choose OK. Quicken displays the Confirm Password dialog box and asks you to retype the password to confirm that you know exactly what you entered. Type the password, exactly as you entered it in step 3, and choose OK.

> **Note**
>
> When you assign a file password, Quicken doesn't activate the password until you close the file or exit the program. When you try to open the file the next time, Quicken requires that you enter the file password.

When a file password is assigned, Quicken asks you for the password before opening the file. Figure 21.12 shows the Quicken Password dialog box

V

Managing Quicken

displayed when attempting to open a file. Type the password and then choose OK to open the file. (As an additional precaution, Quicken doesn't display the password as you type.) If the password was entered incorrectly, Quicken displays a message that you entered an incorrect password and access the selected file is denied. You must select the file to open again and type the password correctly before Quicken opens the file.

If you want to record a transaction dated earlier than the date specified when you assigned the transaction password, Quicken requires that you enter the transaction password in the Quicken Password dialog box. As with file passwords, Quicken doesn't display the transaction password as you type.

Fig. 21.12
Type the file password in the Quicken Password dialog box to open a file.

> **Note**
>
> If you assign a transaction password to a file, Quicken activates the transaction password immediately during the current work session. Unlike the file password, you don't have to exit the program or change to a different file and then reopen the file with the transaction password to activate the password.

Changing or Eliminating a Password

You can change the assigned password. You must enter the existing password, however, before Quicken enables you to change it. This precaution prevents unauthorized users from entering the Quicken system, changing the password, and then accessing your data file. You also can remove passwords to eliminate password protection from your file and transaction data.

To change or eliminate a password, follow these steps:

1. Choose Passwords from the File menu. Quicken displays the Passwords submenu.

2. Choose File to change or delete a file password; choose Transaction to change or delete a transaction password.

   Depending on the password type you choose, Quicken displays the Change Password dialog box (see fig. 21.13) or the Change Transaction Password dialog box.

Fig. 21.13
You change or
eliminate a file
password in the
Change Password
dialog box.

3. To change the file password, type the old and new passwords in the Change Password dialog box and choose OK. You now can use the new password.

To delete the file password, type the old password in the **O**ld Password text box and leave the **N**ew Password text box blank. Choose OK to eliminate the file password.

You change or eliminate a transaction password in exactly the same ways. You also can change the date through which the transaction password is required in the appropriate check box.

From Here...

Knowing how to work with data files is important to mastering Quicken. From here, however, may want to review the following:

- Chapter 3, "Defining Your Accounts," shows you how to create the accounts that you need when you set up a new Quicken data file.

- Chapter 4, "Organizing Your Finances," explains categories and their use in Quicken. You learn how to set up categories to use in a data file.

V

Managing Quicken

Chapter 22

Customizing Quicken

When you install Quicken, the program makes some assumptions about how the program ought to work and how elements within the program should appear. These assumptions are called *options*. Options control how you enter transactions and checks, how the Register appears, how QuickFill works, how Quicken lists items in reports, and how the program works.

You can change these options so that Quicken works to suit your needs. If you don't want Quicken to display a confirmation message each time you edit a transaction, for example, you can turn off the **R**equest Confirmation Before Changes option. If you want to change the fonts and colors displayed in the Register, you can set the font type and style options and change the color of the Register for each account type.

Many options in Quicken are explained elsewhere in this book. This chapter explains how to set options that aren't covered elsewhere. This chapter also shows you where to go to learn about options explained in other chapters.

In this chapter, you learn how to perform the following tasks:

■ Access Quicken for Windows Options

■ Set general Quicken options

■ Customize the Iconbar

Accessing Quicken for Windows Options

Quicken for Windows Options refer to the six groups of options that you can set; **G**eneral, **C**hecks, **R**egister, R**e**ports, R**e**minder, and **I**conbar. When you install Quicken, the program presets all options within these groups to their default settings and values. You can change option settings any time you want the program to work differently. The options you set in the current Quicken file are valid only for that file. If you use more than one Quicken file, you also must set options in the other files.

> **Note**
>
> When you change a Quicken option, the change is in effect for the current session and all future sessions. You can change an option setting at any time, however.

To access Quicken for Windows Options, choose **O**ptions from the **E**dit menu or click the Options button on the Iconbar. Quicken displays the Options dialog box, shown in figure 22.1.

Fig. 22.1
The Options dialog box includes options that represent areas of the program that you can change.

Select the button for the options you want to set or change (table 22.1 describes these buttons). Quicken displays the appropriate dialog box. Then, in the dialog box, make your option settings and then choose OK. Quicken saves your option settings and returns to the Options dialog box. Choose Close to remove the Options dialog box.

Table 22.1 Options in the Options Dialog Box	
Button	**Options Included**
General	Controls a variety of options for using Quicken, such as the colors used in screens, which month the working calendar starts with, whether tax schedules are used, and so forth. You learn how to set general options later in this chapter.
Checks	Controls options on how you enter information in the Write Checks window, how Quicken prints checks, and how QuickFill works when writing checks. Refer to Chapter 5, "Writing and Printing Checks," to learn how to set **C**heck options.
Register	Controls options on how you enter information in Registers, how Registers are displayed, and how QuickFill works when entering transactions in Register. Refer to Chapter 6, "Using the Register," to learn how to set **R**egister options.

Button	Options Included
Reports	Controls options on how Quicken creates reports. Refer to Chapter 19, "Creating and Printing Reports," to learn how to set Report options.
Reminders	Enables you to activate and schedule Billminder and Quicken Reminder messages and indicate whether calendar notes are shown in reminder messages. Refer to Chapter 14, "Scheduling Future Transactions," to learn how to set Reminder options.
Iconbar	Enables you to customize the Iconbar displayed at the top of the Quicken application window. Later in this chapter, you learn how to set Iconbar options to add, edit, or delete an Iconbar icon.

Setting General Options

General options control the way Quicken performs, the colors used in Quicken screens, and which month starts your financial year. To set general options, follow these steps:

1. Choose **O**ptions from the **E**dit menu or click the Options button on the Iconbar to display the Options dialog box (see fig. 22.1).

2. Choose the **G**eneral option. Quicken displays the General Options dialog box, shown in figure 22.2.

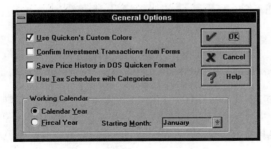

Fig. 22.2
You can change the default settings in the General Options dialog box.

3. Change any of the General Options settings, which are described in table 22.2.

4. When you finish changing option settings in the General Options dialog box, choose OK.

5. Choose Close to remove the Options dialog box.

V

Managing Quicken

Table 22.2 Options in the General Options Dialog Box	
Option	**Action**
Use Quicken's Custom Colors	Overrides the colors set in the Windows Control Panel and displays a gray background with a 3-D effect.
Confirm Investment Transactions from Forms	Displays a confirmation message each time you enter a transaction in an investment form before entering it in the investment Register.
Save Price History in DOS Quicken Format	Saves the price history in investment accounts to Quicken DOS format (select this option if you plan to begin using Quicken for DOS).
Use **T**ax Schedules with Categories	Adds a **F**orm text box in the Set Up Category dialog box so that you can assign a tax form or schedule to a category.
Working Calendar	Refer to Chapter 1, "Preparing to Use Quicken for Windows," to learn about this new option.

Customizing the Iconbar

The Quicken Iconbar enables you to select preset icons to perform frequently used functions. Such functions include displaying the Account List, the Category & Transfer List, the Register, the Write Checks window, and so forth.

You can change the icons displayed in the Iconbar by adding a new icon or by editing or deleting an existing icon. You can set up icons to open an account that you use frequently. You also can rearrange the icons on the Iconbar.

Changing the Iconbar Display

If you want to change the way icons appear in the Iconbar, you can change the Iconbar display. By default, Quicken shows the graphic along with the label. You can set Quicken to show only the icon graphics or the icon label, or not show the Iconbar at all.

To change the Iconbar display, follow these steps:

1. Choose Options from the **E**dit menu or click the Options button on the Iconbar to display the Options dialog box.

2. Select the **I**conbar option. Quicken displays the Customize Iconbar dialog box, shown in figure 22.3. This figure shows the default settings.

Fig. 22.3
The Customize Iconbar dialog box contains options that control how Quicken displays the Iconbar.

3. By default, the Show **I**cons and Show **T**ext check boxes are selected in the Iconbar Display section so that both icons and text are displayed in the Iconbar. To show icons only, select the Show **T**ext check box to remove the check mark. To show text only, select the Show **I**cons check box to remove the check mark. To hide the Iconbar completely, remove the check marks from both check boxes.

4. Choose OK to save the Iconbar settings; then choose Close.

You easily can change the order of the icons displayed in the Iconbar by dragging the icon (with your mouse) in the Iconbar to a new position. Quicken also provides several icons that you can add to the Iconbar. Each icon represents a specific action of its own. Add an icon by selecting **N**ew from the Customize Iconbar dialog box (see figure 22.3). Select **E**dit or **D**elete to change or remove an icon in the Iconbar.

Setting Up an Icon to Open an Account

If you use a particular account frequently, you can set up an icon to open the account and display a window that you specify. If you have several credit card accounts set up but use your VISA account most often, for example, you can set up the UseAcct icon to open the VISA account Register.

To set up an icon to open an account, follow these steps:

1. From the Customize Iconbar dialog box (see figure 22.3), select **N**ew. Quicken displays the Add Action to Iconbar dialog box.

Tip
You can return the Iconbar display to its default setting by choosing the **R**eset button in the Customize Iconbar dialog box.

Tip
To set up additional icons to open other accounts, add a new icon to the Iconbar, and select the Use a Specific Account action from the Icon **A**ction list in the Add Action to Iconbar dialog box.

V

Managing Quicken

2. Scroll the Icon **A**ction list to highlight the Use a Specific Account action.

3. Select OK. Quicken displays the Assign Account to Icon dialog box, shown in figure 22.4.

Fig. 22.4
Set up an icon to
open an account
in the Assign
Account to Icon
dialog box.

4. From the **A**ccount to Load drop-down list box, select the account that you want to open with the UseAcct icon.

5. From the options in the Load As section, select the type of window you want Quicken to load for the selected account.

6. Choose OK. When you select the UseAcct button on the Iconbar, Quicken displays the window that you specified for the account.

From Here...

This chapter showed you how to customize general features in Quicken. Review the following chapters to learn how to customize specific features:

- Chapter 1, "Preparing to Use Quicken for Windows," shows you how to set the General option that sets up your working calendar and your financial year.

- Chapter 5, "Writing and Printing Checks," explains how to set check options.

- Chapter 6, "Using the Register," shows you how to set Register options not only to change the way transactions are entered, but also to change how the Register appears on-screen.

- Chapter 14, "Scheduling Future Transactions," explains how to set reminder options.

- Chapter 19, "Creating and Printing Reports," describes the report options that you can set to control the way Quicken creates reports.

Installing Quicken 4 for Windows

Before you can use Quicken 4 for Windows, you must install the program on your hard disk. This appendix explains the software and hardware requirements for Quicken and provides the steps you need to install the program.

> **Note**
>
> If you have a previous version of Quicken for Windows or Quicken for DOS 5, 6, or 7 on your hard disk, installing Quicken for Windows will have no effect on these programs. To safeguard your data, however, you should back up your existing Quicken data files before you install Quicken 4 for Windows.

Reviewing the Program Requirements

The following sections review the software and hardware requirements to install and run Quicken 4 for Windows.

Hardware Requirements

You need the following hardware to work with Quicken 4 for Windows:

- IBM 386SX (or higher) or 100 percent compatible computer

- At least 2M of RAM

- One floppy disk drive, either 5 1/4-inch or 3 1/2-inch

- Hard disk drive with at least 7M of free disk space

- VGA or SVGA monitor, or better

- Microsoft mouse or compatible pointing device (optional but recommended)

- Microsoft Windows-compatible printer (if you plan to use Quicken to print checks, reports, or graphs)

- A modem that works at 300, 1200, or 2400 baud (if you plan to use Intuit's online services)

Software Requirements

You need the following software to work with Quicken 4 for Windows:

- MS-DOS or PC DOS, Version 3.1 or later

- Microsoft Windows 3.1 running in Standard or Enhanced mode

- Quicken 4 for Windows program disks

Installing Quicken 4 for Windows

Although not essential, knowing a thing or two about working with Windows helps before you step through the installation. You should know how to select menu options, click the mouse, enter data into text boxes, select command buttons, and work with scrollable list boxes. If you previously worked with Windows, you probably know how to do all these things. If you are new to Windows, however, learn the basics before you continue with this installation. You can use Quicken's Introduction to Windows Tutorial from the Help menu, after installing Quicken.

Installing Quicken 4 for Windows is easy and takes just a few minutes. You can install Quicken using Express Installation and have Quicken create the subdirectory and program group in which the program is installed. You also can customize the installation so that Quicken is installed in a different directory or a different program group.

Using Express Installation

To use Express Installation to install Quicken 4 for Windows, follow these steps:

1. Type **win** at the DOS prompt and then press Enter to start the Windows program.

2. Make sure that the Program Manager window is active. If it isn't, double-click the Program Manager icon or press Ctrl+Esc to display the Windows Task List. From the Windows Task List, click Program Manager or use the arrow keys to highlight Program Manager and then press Enter.

3. Insert the Quicken 4 for Windows program Disk #1 in drive A or B.

4. With the Program Manager on-screen, choose **F**ile **R**un. The Run dialog box appears.

5. Type **a:install** (or **b:install**) in the **C**ommand Line text box.

6. Choose OK or press Enter. If you're upgrading a previous version of Quicken, a dialog box is displayed that asks if you want to move your existing Quicken data files to the version that you are installing. Select **Y**es to upgrade your existing data files or select **N**o to continue to use your data files in an old version of Quicken. Next, Quicken displays the Quicken Install window (see fig. A.1).

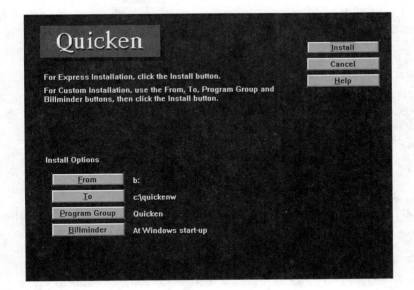

Fig. A.1
If you don't want to change any of the default installation settings, choose the Install button in the Quicken Install window for Express Installation.

7. To choose Express Installation, choose **I**nstall. Quicken for Windows displays a gauge to show you how installation of the program is progressing.

8. When prompted, remove the program disk from drive A or B and insert the next disk. Choose OK after you insert the next disk.

9. When installation is complete, Quicken for Windows displays the
   `Quicken is installed...` message shown in figure A.2. Choose OK to
   return to Windows.

Fig. A.2
Quicken for
Windows displays
a confirmation
message that the
program has been
installed.

The Quicken for Windows icon is placed in the Quicken program group, as
shown in figure A.3. Double-click the icon to start Quicken 4 for Windows.

Fig. A.3
The Quicken for 4
Windows icon in
the Quicken
program group.

Using Custom Installation

To customize the installation of Quicken 4 for Windows so that you can
change the directory, drive, or program group in which the program is installed, follow these steps:

1. Follow steps 1 through 7 in the preceding section to display the
   Quicken Install window.

2. To install Quicken 4 for Windows in a different directory or on a different drive, click the **T**o button to display the Destination dialog box
   shown in figure A.4. By default, Quicken creates a subdirectory named
   QUICKENW in the root directory of your hard disk (usually drive C).
   The Quicken program and data files are stored in this directory.

3. To change the directory, select the desired directory from the **D**irectories list box. (Click the up or down arrow at the right of the **D**irectories
   box to scroll through the list of directories.)

   To create a new subdirectory other than QUICKENW, type the desired
   subdirectory name in the **C**reate New Subdirectory text box.

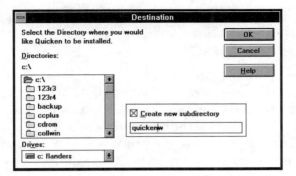

Fig. A.4
The Destination dialog box enables you to change the directory and subdirectory in which Quicken is installed.

To change the current drive, click the down arrow in the Dri**v**es drop-down list to display other drives. Then click the desired drive.

4. When your changes are complete in the Destination dialog box, click OK or press Enter to return to the Install Quicken window (refer to fig. A.1).

> ### Note
>
> For most people, the default Quicken directory (QUICKENW) works fine. The one group of users who may want to specify a different directory are users who previously used Quicken for DOS. If you used Quicken 3, 4, or 5, for example, you probably want Quicken for Windows to use the same data files. To arrange this setup, install Quicken 4 for Windows in the existing Quicken directory, probably QUICKEN3, QUICKEN4, or QUICKEN5. Thankfully, Quicken for Windows' capability to use existing Quicken files means that you don't have to worry about importing old data files.

5. To install Quicken 4 for Windows in a different program group, from the Install Quicken window click the **P**rogram Group button to display the Which Program Group Should Quicken Be Added To? dialog box (see fig. A.5).

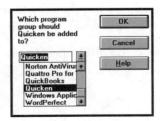

Fig. A.5
Change the Windows program group into which Quicken places the Quicken icon to start the program.

6. From the drop-down list box, select the program group into which you want to install Quicken 4 for Windows. Then choose OK or press Enter to return to the Quicken Install window.

7. If you want to change the way Billminder (Quicken's on-screen reminder system) runs, choose the **B**illminder button. Quicken displays the dialog box shown in figure A.6, which asks when you want the Billminder program run. The three choices offered are never, when you start the computer, or when you start Windows. Indicate when you want the Billminder program run by clicking the appropriate option.

Choose OK to accept the Billminder setting and return to the Quicken Install window.

Fig. A.6
When you install Quicken, you can select when the Billminder program runs. You must reinstall Quicken to change your selection later.

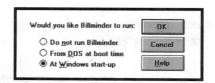

Note

When you turn on your computer or start Windows, Quicken's Billminder program reminds you of bills to pay, checks to write, and notes that you've made in the Financial Calendar. This handy feature can save the price of Quicken and this book many times over by eliminating or minimizing late payment fees. To run the Billminder program when you boot your computer, Quicken adds a line to the AUTOEXEC.BAT file. To run the Billminder program when you start Windows, Quicken adds a line to the WIN.INI file.

8. At the Quicken Install window, choose **I**nstall. Quicken for Windows displays a gauge to show you how installation of the program is progressing.

9. When prompted, remove the program disk from drive A or B and insert the next disk. Choose OK when you have inserted the next disk.

10. When the installation is complete, Quicken for Windows displays the Quicken is installed… message (refer to fig. A.2). Choose OK to return to Windows.

Index

Symbols

$ (Amount) field, 95
… (ellipses), 39

A

A/R by Customer Reports, 396
accessing
menus, 38-39
Quicken Homebase system, 45
Account Balances Reports, 399
Account command (Lists menu), 62, 127, 324
Account Graph (Financial Calendar), 301-302
Account List, 57-66
Account Selector Bar, 66, 92, 130
accounts
adding, 56-66
asset accounts, 54
Setup, 230-232
tax-deferred, 232
updating balances, 237
balances
adjusting, 185-186
dating, 231
detailing, 231
recording, 59-62, 231
balancing, 175-181
cash accounts, 55, 236-237
categories, 68-77
checking accounts, 21-24, 54
college savings accounts, 373-375
credit card accounts, 54
creating, 22

detailing, 192
naming, 191
paying bills, 197-201
reconciling, 194-197
recording credit limits, 192
Setup, 190-192
tax schedules, 192
tracking activity, 193-194
data entry, 61
defining, 55-66
deleting, 64
displaying, 62
editing, 62-63
electronic payment Setup, 264-265
increasing file capacity, 57
IntelliCharge account Setup, 199-200
interest, 177
investment accounts, 55, 318-319
liability accounts, 55
Setup, 230-232
tax schedules, 232
updating balances, 237
money market accounts, 54
naming, 22, 59, 231
open icons, 457-458
opening balance adjustment, 183-184
Reconciliation Reports, 178
reconciliation errors, 186
reconciling, 175-181
Register, 23
retirement accounts, 375-378
savings accounts, 22, 27, 54

Savings Goal accounts, 366-367
selecting, 58, 65-66
for Forecast Graphs, 311-312
for reports, 406-407
service charges, 177
tax deferred accounts, 61
transactions
assigning categories, 70
transferring, 235-241
transfers, 141-143
Accounts Used section (Custom Report dialog box), 406
accrued interest on securities (investment transactions), 334
activating Register, 65
activities (Quicken Homebase system), 45
Activities menu commands
CheckFree, 264
Create New Account, 58
E-Mail, 278
Financial Calendar, 295
Homebase, 45
Loans, 205
Pay Credit Card Bill, 194
Portfolio View, 344
Recategorize, 82
Reconcile, 176
Update Balances, 327
Use Calculator, 155
Write Checks, 90
Add Action to Iconbar dialog box, 457
Add Shares to Account dialog box, 324